The Fear of Being Challenged

Democratically Independent; I Am the Realacrat

Bryian Revoner

iUniverse, Inc.
Bloomington

The Fear of Being Challenged
Democratically Independent; I Am the Realacrat

iUniverse books may be ordered through booksellers or by contacting:

iUniverse
1663 Liberty Drive
Bloomington, IN 47403
www.iuniverse.com
1-800-Authors (1-800-288-4677)

ISBN: 978-1-4502-7655-9 (sc)
ISBN: 978-1-4502-7657-3 (dj)
ISBN: 978-1-4502-7656-6 (ebk)

Printed in the United States of America

iUniverse rev. date: 1/27/2011

DEDICATION:

I dedicate this to Bryian "The Revoner" R. You've heard of "Joe the Plumber." Well, I'm "Bryian the Box Mover." All I do is move boxes for a living, and my income is nowhere near a plumber's net worth.

I dedicate this to S.H. for showing me that it was time for me to sit my old, tired ass down somewhere.

I dedicate this to the Dumpster, for showing me personally what the view of the bottom of the barrel looks like from underneath it.

I dedicate this to the family members who made me go to church, where I had to listen to big wigs get up and say prayers for everyone in there except me.

I dedicate this to the professor who said to me: "You're the worst journalism student I've ever seen! Your writing ability is mediocre at best. You have no business here!"

I dedicate this to Mrs. Falls; my sixth grade, reading teacher who replaced Mrs. Bonady, as she embarrassed me in front of the entire class by saying: "What a horrible student you are! Are you blushing? Oh, I forgot! You can't blush, because your Black, ugly, dog face can't blush. Your friend Joel can blush, but you are just too ugly and too Black!"

I dedicate this to my sixth grade, music teacher Ms. Persons, for standing me up in front of the entire class; taking a report that I had written and throwing it in the floor, as she said: "You're the sorriest student I've ever had. Get down on the floor where you belong, and pick up that garbage you wrote!"

Lastly, I dedicate this to my genetic advisors for helping to convince me to pass on opportunistic buses that were right there waiting for me, because there was always a better one still to come. Well, after almost 30 years, I'm still waiting! I guess that joke is on me!

Be conservative with the money in your wallet, ~Eugene Revoner
But be liberal with possibilities in your mind. ~Bryian Revoner

The White establishment doesn't have a real plight, so they've manufactured one through fear mongering. ~Julie Kindle Driscoll

CONTENTS

Introduction

Preface

Realacrat—one who governs or manages through realistic goals and realistic limitations. One who is just as ready to lead the barren as they are to lead the herd. You can always paint a picture, but you can't always make the people see it or understand it. We will not pass legislation to kill the puppet, but we will construct the ideologies needed to challenge the puppet master. We redefine the impossible without allowing the impossible to limitedly define us, because a Realacrat is an ideology first and a political party second. While Democrats and Republicans examine the politics, Realacrats examine the views that create and embellish politics! If you can define the view, then you can define the person. If you can define the person, then you can anticipate their voting preference! If you can find commonality within the voting preferences, then you have just pinpointed your potential base! Realacrats will always lean towards the continuation, the enhancement, and the preservation of their species before committing to the theoretical views of our religious ideologies.

Welcome to the ideology of the Realacrats, where the anticipation of the future defeats the reminiscence of the past, where the dreams of one can change the lives of all, where understanding is a gift that can only be understood when it is applied, where we realistically search for what we will realistically find, and where the narrative you write will be penned in the ink of your own individuality. We will not ask that you believe in God, but we will ask that you believe in yourself, because many of the treasures we seek lie hidden in plain sight, but blinded eyes led by filtered ears will prevent many from finding them. Realacrats will ensure that it does not prevent all, for the fear of being challenged will not go unchallenged by what will come to be known as the Realacrat ideology! I am Independently Democratic, and I am Democratically Independent. I am the Realacrat, and this is the Realacratic mission statement!

The fear of being challenged is a fear that few people ever learn to control, and in most cases; the fear controls the host instead of the host controlling the fear, which only helps to create and sustain bigotry, racism, paranoia, sexism, corruption, abuse of power, social and political recession, unwarranted violence, unfounded religious-based tirades, monumental hypocrisy, lies of historic proportion, dishonest propaganda and unjustifiable witch-hunts similar to the ones orchestrated during the Puritan era. The election of President Obama has culminated with all the above, with even more to come within this alleged post-racial society. So when this highly secretive band of radicals approached and recruited me about a possible, new, ideological platform, I decided to accept the challenge instead of living in some erroneously manufactured fear of it. If they had tried to coax me into this position two years ago, I would have dismissed it as not Black enough, but I am no longer afraid to expand the imaginary, shackled boundaries of a narrowly perceived Blackness. All of this reminds me of the old narratives about the world being flat and how people would fall off it if they went too far. That sentiment reminds me of the present-day health care protest antics, because fear breeds paranoia and paranoia is the antithesis of logic, which is the DNA blueprint of a cognitive collapse.

I don't want to be in a party that is ruled by fear, and I refuse to be in a party that uses fear to rule, because fear is the fertilizer that nourishes incompetence. We need a new ideology on life and politics; one that challenges the fear as much as the fear challenges it, an ideology not afraid to see what's behind the green door, the liberal door, or the minority door! We don't need a fearful ideology similar to the propaganda that killed Julius Caesar, which was ill-fatedly based on what some misinformed fear mongers thought he might become. After all, this ideology failed miserably when you consider what killing

Caesar had caused them to become. The foundation of this ideological platform will be solely based in reality and not the fear of it. This will be a platform where anyone can opine their minds without having to suffer any egomaniacal consequences or bootlick some jealous, overbearing, office, water-cooler God, who hides behind a microphone in a radio booth and constantly positions himself or herself as a demagogue of extremely exaggerated and self-appointed political importance! Our ideology is no more afraid to tackle a 500-lb. gorilla than we are to tackle a 1,000-lb. elephant with a noose in its pocket! There will be no scared donkeys in this party!

As a Realacrat, there are no longer any exclusively signed contracts with the Democrats, and there definitely won't be any exclusively signed contracts with the Republicans. I still agree with the liberal, progressive ideology. I just refuse to be pigeon-holed by the politics of politics. My only real beefs with some of the Democrats are certain leadership maneuvers in regard to their political agendas, their will to push those agendas, and their unwillingness to declare a counter-war on the conservative movement, which I despise even more than I despise the Republican Party! If Republicans could limit their conservatisms strictly to a financial basis, I think true ideological brainstorming could be utilized to govern more effectively, but I will not align myself ideologically with conservative, social aspects, because I don't believe conservatism has a legitimate place in the democracy of the people or the democracy of the individual! I just find it incomprehensible to somehow conservatively personify a declaration of independence! You're either free, or you're a slave! This is why I feel like political and social war must be unleashed on the conservative canon, and since I don't know if Democrats are up for the challenge of embarking on this challenge, I have decided to reinvent myself and my ideology from a straight-ticket Democrat to a far more individualistic Realacrat, in hopes of becoming the catalyst that spurs on a social and political assault on conservative fear. Yes, I still lean left, because the lean of my lean still leans the same! In my description, a Realacrat is the definitive version of a political free agent, who can side or vote with any idealistic sweetener offered up as an extension of potential and cooperation. As an independent, democratic Realacrat, I will no longer vote the Democratic line or any other political line! I will now only vote my line!

There are some who have questioned my credentials regarding my aspirations to speak on such issues. Some have been quick to point out the fact that I am not a doctor, a lawyer, a journalist, a politician or a government official, but this is exactly the way I planned it. There needs to be a political party in which high social and high economic status is not always the main prerequisite for validity. All of the political parties and government agencies always claim to be in complete touch with the people, despite spending the bulk of their time with a select, well-to-do few whose credentials are usually based more on the size of their bank account than the substance of their ideas. The Realacrat Party will be one that actually engages the truck driver, the assembly-line worker, and the real Joe the Plumber, because you don't have to be a rocket scientist to understand the plight of individuals who clearly are not rocket scientists. I will have more to say about my lack of credentials later on!

Basically, the Realacrat ideology of this book can be personified in this way. Imagine the famous image of the last supper. There is one extremely long table filled to capacity with food, drinks, and all-around prosperities. For as long as anyone can remember, this table has been completely dominated by one group of powerbrokers. As you look at the faces along this table, you quickly begin to realize that every individual seated there appears to be a White male. Well, the Realacrat ideology has plans to change the line-up of this picture once and for all. So please allow me to make this statement loudly, clearly, and unambiguously. The Realacrat Party IS NOT HERE TO TOTALLY REMOVE THE WHITE MALE FROM THE LAST SUPPER TABLE, but what the Realacrat Party is here for is the addition of more seats to the table, so that others will have just as many opportunities to indulge as the traditional, select few have consistently been afforded in the past. I think there is enough political and economic fried chicken for everyone to get a piece! Unfortunately, the inclusion of others has often caused great fear and has often been met with great resistance. In Realacrat ideology, I would have to hypothesize that any fear of opulent inclusion is obviously marred in severe egocentrism, corporate and societal greed, self-inflicted insecurities, hedonistic jealousy, and the fear of being challenged based on some narrow-minded, manufactured, fear mongered plight of a minority taking away an upper-class job, taking away an upper-class woman, or financially being able to infiltrate an upper-class neighborhood!

Now, some will call this "Last Supper Proposal" socialism, but I call it an equal opportunity. If the government unjustly takes a seat away from someone who has legitimately earned it, just to redistribute it to someone else whose only talent is to extend an empty hand that longs to be filled, I would then agree to call it socialism, but Realacrats want the opportunity to have the seat, not a bailout! This is not an idea to help redistribute the wealth. This is economic, self-motivating capitalism! The government's job is to enforce the rules to try and help ensure an equal playing field, so let the competitions begin, as we work to eliminate what I refer to as "Scripted-Capitalism."

This book and this political ideology is where I have decided to make my stand, and it will be an unwavering stand of my convictions and my moral core. Here, I will vividly elaborate my points of view, which will be the ideological building blocks of the Realacrat Party, as I am the only acknowledged Realacrat at this moment. For the time being, this party only exists in my mind, but for the time that is yet to come; it will hopefully exist within the minds of many others. This book will be my best recruitment tool, because there are Realacrats out there, they just don't know it yet! Inclusiveness, freedom, and recruiting will be three of the main staples of the Realacrat ideology, along with the willingness to throw political and societal caution to the wind for one's own ideological platform. My unwillingness to water down this book, my convictions, and my ethnicity are all vintage Realacrat virtues! I will not allow myself to become an ideological slave to outside containment, and I would expect no less from any would-be Realacrat. Shooting for the stars is not a crime, so don't allow yourself to be unjustly prosecuted as if it was. This is the reason why I decided to go through with my plans for this book. This is the reason why I will not cut or cover my dreadlocks in an attempt to water it down commercially. This is the reason why I will not re-route my beliefs just to arrive at an artificial destination of commonality with those who demand that I do so, because a revolution does not tip-toe, it stands firm with its head held high, ready to face the elements, even if it means the expiration of all loose associations and paper-thin relationships, because the fear of lost relationships and false admiration is no different than any other fear.

You can't be true to yourself, when you are consumed by the fear of not being true to others. I fully understand how this literary venture could end up costing me in every aspect of my life. The strong majority of my White cohorts may decide to abandon me, because of this book and the ideology it represents, which is not Republican, not conservative, and not ethnically subservient, while the bulk of my African-American cohorts will, in all likelihood, dismiss all of this as further confirmation of my misguided quest to be White, but in reality this is just my sovereign quest to be me, even if it means ideological exile. I'd rather be true to myself and be alone than to be true to the strings of the puppet master while performing a soulless ditty in front of an empty audience filled with empty people. I rather walk alone with the truth as oppose to leading the crowds with a lie! If this book in any way compromises the substance and integrity of those who choose to affiliate with me, then it is their problem and not mine, because if the status of my acceptance depends on my willingness to muffle my voice, derail my train of thought, handicap my intellectual independence, or enslave myself to passiveness, then it is time to turn out the lights, because this party of subservience ends now! Although some have suggested that I abandon my core for the opportunity to gain more, I strongly disagree, and I now ask them this question. How can you truly give up on something you truly believe in? The substantive points made in this book have my absolute support, and whoever agrees with my assessments or agrees with my ability to independently choose a path is always welcome.

Hopefully, this book will inspire people to think about life and all the possibilities within it. The true chore of a real writer should not be to linguistically steer the reader through a judgmental and self-righteous litany of dictating ultimatums over to the author's position, but instead to subconsciously coax, interest, and motivate the reader to the point where that individual cares enough about something to form or re-evaluate their own opinions or belief systems. This book will optimistically be the catalyst for such cerebral behavior, because you cannot swim deeply in shallow water, and you cannot think deeply within shallow thoughts. Maybe the ideology of this book can induce more of an interest within the deeper end of the political pool. If I, as an author, fail to evoke emotion and thought stimulation, then I have failed in my mission to help sabotage any reluctance based on fear that could ultimately destroy the will to get involved. Regardless of every ambition within this project, the two main goals above all else are the expansion of Realacratic viewpoints and recruiting of independent, ideological, cognitive development.

The Uno Story

Now I will share a story about a childhood hustle I used to run that I am convinced can and will shed some much needed light on the stench of racism, favoritism, and the fear of being challenged on a basic level. I used to play a very popular card game called Uno. I was a fairly good player, and I usually won more than I lost. Originally, it was all about competition and sportsmanship, but eventually, my ambitions to be on top consumed me, and at that point; the competition and the sportsmanship was replaced by corruption and greed! Even though I won most of the time, that eventually wasn't good enough to sustain my feeding, frenzied ego; so I developed a plan that would ensure and almost guarantee that I would win 99.9% of the time. Since I was the only kid on the block who owned a legitimate, full deck of brand, new Uno cards, it gave me a home court advantage that I took full advantage of, by placing small markings on the backs of all of the big, important cards that were game changers. This allowed to me read my opponents cards without actually seeing them. I then knew how to defend them, but they had no idea how to defend me, because they were unaware of the markings, and they were just as unaware of the meanings of the markings.

This was as unfair as it gets. Needless to say, I ruled the game with an absolute fist of dominance draped in invincibility. No matter how crafty, how hard, or how determined my opposition was; they were no match against my unfair, unknown advantage. I took the winner's pot almost flawlessly. I took candy, money, toys, gadgets, and so on. People began to refer to me as the "Unbeatable One," and I began to believe it. Guys and gals of all ages came from all around the neighborhood to challenge me, but they all left empty handed, not because I was really that good, but because I had a built-in, systematic, institutionalized advantage very similar to the advantageous odds of the casinos. An occasional upset was always possible, but the more you played me in Uno; the more likely you were to lose. It got to the point where it was almost like winning by default. This toll of defeat devastated my competition and shredded their competitive confidence. When they played me, they expected to lose, and they did unmercifully, while I, on the other hand, expected to win, which I did unmercifully!

Life was good, and I was the undisputed ruler of all that I surveyed in my card playing world, until a true wild card appeared that would lift the shroud on my con forever. A new, unknown challenger shows up one day and challenges me to a duel. I quickly make short work of him like I'd done to so many others on my magnificent run of excellence, but then it happened! The new challenger pulls out an unopened deck of sparkling, new Uno cards and says to me, "Okay, now let's play a few rounds with this new deck of Uno cards Mr. Big Shot," and just like that, my run was done! Once this new challenger introduced the aspect of change to my self-preserving, rigged, status quo system, by bringing in a new unadulterated deck of Uno cards, which forced the event to become an equal playing field, my dynasty came to an abrupt end. I still won games, but I was never a dominant force again. Anybody could win now—girls, boys, the young and even the old. As I watched helplessly as all of my admiration and legendary status went down in flames, I lashed out in anger at this new comer calling him a Socialist, a Muslim, a Muslim extremist, a Communist, a Marxist, an atheist, a fraud, a cheater, Hitler, a terrorist, and an African imposter, even though it was abundantly clear that the only fraudulent cheater in the area was me! The fear of being challenged was really the fear of someone else's success, the fear of my own possible defeat, and the fear of losing my influential grip. As long as I had the entire Uno world playing from my rigged deck of cards, I was always in complete control of who won and who lost, which is actually a fear of the freedoms of democracy and the fear of being challenged! Scripted-Capitalism is a very lucrative venture for the person who writes the script, but it crumbles like the Berlin Wall when a new script is introduced, because someone dared to seek change!

Why I Did Not Want To Write This

As many of you well know by now, the odds of anyone actually reading this book are slim to non-existent. Writing a book was never my intention anyway. I never aspired to be an author. To me, being an author of a book or any other literary work was much too White for me. As far as I was concerned, writing a book was White culture and reading a book was White culture. Hell, I even believed that picking up a book was White culture. To be quite honest, I felt like a Carlton Banks, from the television show "The Fresh Prince of Bel-Air," Oreo Cookie for even entertaining the thought of a book, but now that I've written it, I don't quite know how to feel about it. I forced myself to think outside of the box for a change. I reluctantly stepped away from my comfort zone of self-victimization and apathy. I had always relied heavily on the "I can't" crutch as I hobbled alongside mediocrity and sometimes sub-par mediocrity. My only goal in life was to be a drug dealer/gang member/criminal/thug/pimp/weed smoking/gangsta rapper with a semi-automatic assault weapon. This was my only dream. Things such as education and politics were meaningless to me. I only went to school because my parents made me go. I only made decent grades because I learn efficiently, rapidly and with little effort. It was never due to my enthusiastic love for higher learning, because I never actually read the material in school. I just did enough to get by. All of my friends dabbled in street credibility while I had none. The quest to acquire this street credibility began to consume my life. Even when I was in college at East Arkansas Community College in Forrest City, Arkansas and at Arkansas State University in Jonesboro, Arkansas, I spent the vastness of my time in the streets. I often slept in class during the day and roamed the streets in search of crime and passion during the night. If I could do it all over again today, I would have dropped out of school and became a drug dealer, so I can have some gangsta rims, some gangsta apparel, some gangsta mentality, some gangsta success, some gangsta groupies, and the overall gangsta lifestyle. I was more than content to live the African-American dream of being ghetto fabulous in a box, and that box was the hood—my hood! I wanted very badly to be accepted by my peers, but their area of expertise was street knowledge, not academics. Nevertheless, while I was in what I perceived to be the White man's college in a predominately, sometimes totally, White classroom; my homies were out running the streets and picking up bitches. So, I began to bail on college and focused more of my time on the streets. There's an old rap song called "Ain't No Future in Your Fronting"[1] by the late,

1 MC Breed, "Ain't No Future In Your Fronting," *The Best of Mc Breed*, 2003

great MC Breed that talked at length about how there is no future in constantly showing off what you have, because you are never guaranteed to hold on to it, especially on the mean streets of the African-American ghettoes. Basically, the song was saying that our ghetto mechanisms were short-lived at best. Shiny rims are top-of-the-line today, but they will be out of style next month, as some newer rims debut and everyone rushes to retrieve them. There is far too much emphasis placed on things with temporary value in the African-American community, and I was the prime example of it. Despite college being a long-term investment that could potentially make me very successful throughout my entire life, I was willing to throw it all away for an evanescent one-hit wonder of rims and bitches. Writing a book is based on a premise very similar to the college premise, because there is nothing quick, fast, or shiny about it. It takes a long-term vision to be an author, and it will also take a long-term vision to be a Realacrat! So whether or not this book becomes successful is secondary to me, because I, even at this very moment, still regret and rue the day that I ever became affiliated with this current environment. If I had it to do all over again, I would have never stepped foot in Arkansas. My immediate family would not exist to me, and I would be standing on a corner in North Memphis with a nine-millimeter Glock in my hand just like any other young, Black male from the hood, but instead; I have to settle on being a measly author, but it is what it is, which means that I can write better than I can commit homicides. I guess I might as well accept it.

Fortunately or unfortunately, depending on how you look at it, my quest to be a gangsta rapper/drug dealer failed miserably, and my academic aspirations failed almost as badly, as I graduated college near the bottom. Hell, it almost didn't even happen. Now many of you maybe puzzled at what any of this has to do with Realacrats. The moral of my story should not be overlooked. Its allegorical importance can be applied to all walks of humanity. My advice to each and every one of you is to never ever try to be a triangle in a square; meaning, you can't successfully perform some sort of genetic metamorphosis into the person you think the world would like you to be. As the old sentiment goes, the best thing any of us can do is to just be ourselves, even if it means we walk alone for stretches at a time. You can't allow your fear of populous abandonment to cause you to make bad, self-destructive decisions in your personal life or in your political views. There will be times in your life when the only one who gets you will be you. You can either stick to your guns, or you can create, promote, and become a new persona as you try desperately to merge that proverbial triangle into society's square. If you are lucky enough to coax it in, it won't take much to knock it right back out again, because it does not belong there. No matter how unpopular it may be, the ability and discipline needed to stay true to you is the best thing any of us can ever hope to achieve. One should never be ashamed to be their own person, follow their own lead, think their own thoughts, and act on their own actions, even if it means the applause is delayed. This is why I am here today. I'm finally here to acknowledge what I am. Despite all of my fanatical street detours, I'm right back where I originally started. I'm as unpopular as I've ever been, and I don't have an ounce of street credibility, with my only option being the same option I had many years ago, which is the same academically-based option I abandoned those many years ago. This time, instead of investing in the gangsta rapper vision or the drug dealer dream, I have decided to embrace my ability to conjure up ideas and concepts and possibly even start a new political party with a new political way of thinking. Yes, it's a long shot, but it's no more of a long shot than my previous aspirations of becoming a gang member/ gangsta rapper. So bigots beware, because the pen reaches farther than the sword, and it recruits more than it kills!

My Freedom Moment

I had no plans to pursue any of my literary aspirations. I was more than happy to continue on with my menial, lethargic life of laboring for others and allowing others to be the decision makers, as I continued to be cognitively cozened into believing that I was unqualified to make such decisions for myself. It was much easier to sit back as a spectator than it would ever be to take a stand and challenge the status quo, especially when these geniuses had totally convinced me of their intellectual dominance and my intellectual bare cupboards. I actually believed that I was genetically disadvantaged, while others opposite to me were genetically entitled, and I used this principle for years to justify my failures. In my mind, I was cognitively limited and personally underprivileged. My fears of being challenged by others in society and my own lack of self-esteem were things I ducked whenever possible. Society handed me the shackles, and I had willingly and literally placed them around my mind and thrown away the key. Even though I knew I had the ability to free myself, I had no confidence in my abilities to survive without the shackles. They had become my "Linus" blanket!

As I continued to hide from my challenges, a funny thing happened on the way to my flipside utopia. A guy named "Shopping Cart Bart," who once worked with me at a local grocery store in Wynne, Arkansas; came face to face with me at the local Wal-Mart and made a statement to me that will resonate within me for the rest of my life. He and I used to work together gathering shopping carts, and he never grew tired of preaching to me about how God was White, and White people were meant to rule the world. This time he and I were discussing young, African-American athletes who receive far too much money to play a sport. My feelings were ambiguous at best about the entire situation, but I did state my support for young, African-American athletes. The way I see it, I'd rather see them locked into contracts instead of locked in a penitentiary. But Bart, who just happened to be a staunch Republican, had made up his mind to use this opportunity to take a swipe at my status, as he looked at me and said, "You and the rest of those monkeys have an extra muscle in y'all's legs that makes y'all run faster anyway. That's why y'all made such good slaves, but one thing is for damn sure, you won't have to worry about making any money with your dead-end job, if you even have a job! You're just a flunky and that's all you ever will be. I'll bet you are the only one in your family that works. The rest are probably on welfare and food stamps; living off of the White man's money!" He then said, "White men, like me, hold up jobs and families! Niggers, like you, only hold up banks and people," but what this pompous asshole failed to mention was that he had been in jail for theft, selling drugs, domestic abuse, and the distribution of hot checks! His criminal record was as long as any other common criminal, but he felt that he still had a trump card over me, which is the White-is-right argument, where the guy who is White will quite often be given the believability factor of possessing the right answer, while others, including women; will usually be given that same believability factor, but only this time; it will be used to indicate that these particular groups are devoid of any answers, which is nothing more than a glorified smokescreen!

Next, he began slamming Hillary Clinton for being too friendly with Barack Obama. He then went on to brag about how the Republican Party would never allow a Black man and White woman to be together in any capacity! He said Sarah Palin was better than Hillary, because she knew to stay in her place with her own race. After that, he looked me dead in the eye and said, "Only a White man can be president, because White men don't make mistakes. You and your ape buddy, Obama, are just a couple of thugs, and that's all you two ever will be in this country!" By this time, I'd heard enough from this Tea Bagger wanna-be! I was finally able to see through the hologram of supremacy and propaganda that had been passed off as truth to people like me who were gullible enough to believe it. I had spent years hiding from the challenges of truth only to meet it face to face when I least expected it. I told this crap-shoveling, bathroom-bigoted, meet the Waltons on crack, five-star fool, who might as well be the poster boy for inbreeding, that the only thing he could ever hope to be the president of was the "I just got through humping my sister, and I liked it!" fan club! I told Bart that it no longer mattered to me if Obama won the election, because my gloves were now off, my shackles were now broken, and his reign was over!

I'm reminded of when the superhero character called Batman saw his parents killed in front of him, it became his greatest motivation, as he dedicated his life to fighting crime, and he also confronted his greatest fear, which was the fear of the bat! In a similar fashion, once I destroyed the power of bigoted Bart by breaking free from the shackles he'd helped to convince me that I was bound by, it became my motivation to do whatever I could possibly do to free as many as I could possibly free, and the Realacrat ideology and my conquering of my authorial fears is only the beginning! Freedom is a beautiful thing, and I believe everyone should experience it.

If every gascon rocket scientist at the political water-cooler can embellish their points of view, then I might as well pitch a tent at this circus to embellish mine, and just because my views challenge the water-cooler Gods, it does not mean that my ideologies are unworthy, and it does not mean they shouldn't be given a chance to compete based on some mythological, unsubstantiated pecking order like genetic entitlement. Realacrats will definitely take the stand against genetic entitlement! It's this kind of mentality that has pummeled America from the very beginning. No matter how drunk, how high, how arrogant, how shortsighted, how narrow-minded, how egotistical, or how ethnically offensive these Einstein's were, they always had better solutions than you or me because the reflection they saw in the mirror gave them a genetic advantage. This is the main reason why I decided to write the book. The Democrats dance around this issue while the Republicans seem to be happy to reinforce it. It's time for somebody to take out the propaganda trash. The fight against genetic entitlement will be a mainstay of the Realacrat ideology. It's time for a new party, a party that will deliver an unequivocal no to Jim Crow, and restore the dignity of humanity to all people. None of us can ever make any undisputed, legitimate claim of possession in regards to a universal righteousness, because none of us will ever achieve such a thing!

10 Things a Realacrat Should Know

I have always had a lot to say about politics and philosophy in private, and I loved to voice my opinions at the television where no one else could hear me. Realacrat lesson number 1: never give away for free what you can sell. Realacrat lesson number 2: learn to recognize talent and potential talent when you see it. Realacrat lesson number 3: if a tree falls in the middle of a deserted forest, does it actually make a sound? If your ideologies remain in your deserted forests, can they ever be realized? Realacrat lesson number 4: be who you were born to be, accept who you truly are, and walk the path to your destiny sooner rather than later, because one way or another you will be forced to face who you are. Realacrat lesson number 5: never be afraid to cut your losses because nothing last forever, so why expect eternity. Realacrat lesson number 6: people are people and race is a distraction used as a tool for the destruction of civility, progress, and humanitarianism. Realacrat lesson number 7: pay attention and observe your surroundings, because sleepwalkers end up on the menu of corruption with the fork of exploitation stuck up their asses. Realacrat lesson number 8: complacency is the shortcut to defeat. Realacrat lesson number 9: all knowledge is not created equal, but all knowledge should be learned from and distributed equally, because wrongfulness can enlighten just as much, if not more, than righteousness. Realacrat lesson number 10: great leaders don't wear sunglasses, because a blurred vision is the equivalent of not having a vision. To be a true leader, you have to embrace the roars of the crowds and the silence of their departures. No matter what any of us do, we can't please everyone, nor should we try.

I now introduce to all of you my dream for a new and innovative political ideology called the Realacrat Party, where differences are not always marred in fear, but instead are always given the opportunity to prove they can work in a place where one's origin will not a be a measuring stick for one's current location. The Realacrat Party will also be a place where pre-conditions will never be the only conditions. A person once asked me: "If you were in charge of both of the major political parties, what would you do? If you could start your own political party, what would you do? What is the worldly view of Bryian R.?" Well, I'm about to respond to those questions all throughout this book.

The Realacrats

The Realacrat Platform

The questions I hear more than any others are; "Why did you decide to try and start you own party/political ideology? Weren't you happy with the Democrats? If not, what was the problem? You have your Black president, so shouldn't that be enough?" Well, my answer to these questions is a resounding no, because it's not enough! I'm sitting at home watching the release of the two Asian-American journalists who were held captive in North Korea and were being brought back to the United States with the patriotic help of former president Bill Clinton, who went to North Korea and met with Kim Jong-il to help secure their release. I was very proud of Bill Clinton's actions in North Korea. I thought he showed exactly why he was so well-liked by so many during his presidency. Clinton's personality encourages unification prospects, not divisive prospects. The Realacrat Party could definitely use a Bill Clinton in some form of a leadership role. The post-presidential actions, behaviors, and politics of both him and George H. Bush leave much to be desired by Realacrats. As a party, we would immediately make plans to work with both of these great humanitarians. This is why I want a new party. I want to further enforce and endorse the humanitarian side of politics, which is the side that usually ends up misplaced and forgotten. I want a party that will fight and stand up against corruption, especially social and ethnic corruption, not reinforce it based upon some family upbringing cop-out. I want a party that will value solutions over shots fired, and one that will talk more and fight less. This will not be a party that preaches family values on one hand while establishing a genetic pecking order on the other. We need a party willing to learn from that which is not understood and not destroy it out of unbridled and unwarranted fear. We need a party that understands completely that it does not own the exclusive rights to God or the rights to refute someone else's belief in God. Realacrats will follow the teachings of Jesus Christ instead of trying to re-route the teachings of Jesus Christ. For example, Realacrats will go out into the community and recruit potential Realacrats the same way Jesus Christ went out and recruited potential Christians, by displaying a vision welcome to all who want to participate, not to indoctrinate a particular religion, but to indoctrinate the true concept of equality for the people, because a religion devoid of equality and filled with intolerance is not very theological; but it is pure totalitarianism. The Realacrat temple will not be a temple where only the rich and the uppity are able to gain entry. It will be a party for anyone interested in reinstituting the humanitarianism back into politics, because Realacrats will be the ultimate community organizers, very similar to the brave, unselfish work of someone like a Barack Obama, even though Republicans mocked and laughed at him for it. Realacrats look at it this way. They mocked and laughed at Jesus Christ for trying to develop something positive out of the so-called undesirables of the time and also for trying to establish equal access to the temple for these sinful, downtrodden, poor people. Realacrats understand that Christianity is not a perch you sit upon so you can look down, and laugh at those less fortunate than you. Nevertheless, this is not a party exclusive to the teachings of Jesus Christ or any other prophet, but this is a party exclusive to teachings in general, from all corners of the globe, because Realacrats figured out a long time ago that you don't have to be a Christian to be a humanitarian, but you do have to be a humanitarian to be a Christian; anything less would be nothing more than a charlatan, masquerading ball for the dancing hypocrites who only move to impress man.

Realacrats will be intellectually free, and they will not bow to unions or websites. We don't cross over to you; we make you cross over to us. I want a party that is not a party of cowards. Realacrats will not behave like timid chickens only focused on the economic aspects of cutting and spending. Forrest Gump can cut a program, and Forrest Gump can spend a lot of money, but it takes true character to go out and invest in people's character, especially those people who do not look like you. That, however, is exactly what the Realacrat Party will do first and foremost; starting with people like Laura Ling and Euna Lee. In the eyes of a Realacrat, both of these women are just as important and just as special as Sarah Palin or Bristol Palin. The Realacrats will not be afraid to fight, and they will not be afraid to challenge, even if it means staring down Rush Limbaugh and his Limbaugh legion, along with every bigoted thought they can think of. The Realacrat Party will always be there to give a voice to the voiceless and to give a platform to the disenfranchised. Realacrats believe it is dead wrong for the government to be so tax-happy, as it recoups from the invisible Americans who only become more invisible when it's time to designate seats in the governing process or a helping hand in the loaning process. If we are good enough for you to take our money, then we are good enough to be governmentally represented. The Realacrats will not be a party dominated and dictated by rich, old, White, men or any other special interest assemblage. The genetic and economic pecking order pecks its very last in the Realacrat Party. It will be a place where the best people are put in the best positions to find success for the movement and for themselves.

Like the vision of the founding fathers, the Realacrat Party will be a party for the people and of the people. It will be a party of feasibility, a party of genuine choices, a party of the common sense approach, a party of economic liability, a party of problem solving, a party of the impoverished poor, a party of the middle-class, a party of the rich, a party for the poor working class, a party for small-and large-business owners, a party for Asian-Americans, a party for African-Americans, a party for Hispanic-Americans, a party for gay Americans, a party for bi-racial Americans, a party for overlooked Americans, a party for Native Americans, a party for White Americans, a party for celebrity Americans, a party of better education, a party of new agricultural standards, a party for cleaner more futuristic energy, a party that returns surpluses to the taxpayers, and most of all; a party of individual freedom! In other words, anyone can join, but no one has to stay.

We want solution finders, not problem designers, and it does not matter what religious background one has, because Realacrats don't care where you plan to go when you die, they only care where you plan to go while you are alive, because life is the greatest mechanism one can use to experience achievement. Death is merely the conclusion of such accomplishments. No matter how any of us choose to view it. There is only one race; the human race! It's a race we all must prepare to run, hope to endure, and utilize our chances to lead. We all start at the same origin, follow the course in the same direction, and finish up at the same destination! Some of us may see different sights along the way, but we must all run that same gauntlet of choices based on our own perceptions of what is wrong and what is right! Our politics represents the constant struggle to control the journey.

The Realacrat Philosophy

The Realacrat philosophy is simple, effective, and efficient when it comes to the federal government. The federal government's objective should be to help the American people when needed. I don't think there are many people in this country that would be opposed to such a notion. During this current economic era of colossal businesses with colossal failures, the taxpayer has faced a serious financial crisis. While the government bails out failing companies on Wall St., traditional mom-and-pop shops, and other manufacturing jobs on Main Street have definitely bitten the bullet, and the American people are definitely feeling shunned by it all. The government has promised to keep the little taxpayer in mind, but the little guy has heard that one before. It's this kind of sentiment that has helped to create an environment of distrust, leeriness, and blatant dislike for the government, most recently seen in the Tea Party. Some are so angry now that they would like to see the government completely out of their lives for good. I personally don't agree with this policy, because I believe the government is needed, no matter how inefficient it has become. The government has to do a much better job working with and not against the American people, and this is not at all difficult to accomplish.

The government should do everything in its power to create jobs in the United States. If the people can't work, then the tax revenue takes a hit. If it means passing legislation to regulate a new tax code for American manufacturing companies or other manufacturing companies that are willing to do business with the United States and in the United States, then pass it as a federal law. Conservatives will be livid at the show of federal force, but I call it leadership, and leadership sometimes demands stepping on someone's feelings to get a more prolific production. Any companies found to be shipping jobs overseas should be taxed for it on every level, maybe not vindictively--but honestly. Conservatives will sit around, and bark about the inadequacy of the federal government to act, but when the feds do act, the first thing they accuse them of is trampling on state's rights by doing too much. With the economic shape of Michigan and California in 2009, government prodding should be the least of their worries. They've already financially trampled themselves. Realacrats would suggest sending both states new industry, whether it's green jobs, wind turbines, hybrid factories, clean coal, newly-formed American companies like American I.N.C., or technologically revamped state-of-the-art off shore oil drilling programs, because these systems have to be updated to the highest safety standards possible based on the colossal, British Petroleum (BP), oil spilling debacle of 2010 in the Gulf of Mexico. What BP.....(Big Problems!) has done to the environment is the ecological equivalent to what Goldman Sacs, Enron, the Bernie Madoff's, and the Wall St. Crooks have done financially to the economic environment! In BP's case, they're too big to fail and too irresponsible to succeed!

If the federal government can find a way bring in the employment base, it will then be up to each state to make it function. The feds cannot actually install, and run the assembly lines for you. As for all of the dissent over green jobs, a job is a job is a job, as long as it has decent pay, and it keeps you out of the unemployment line. Now that's a people's bailout that would provide revenue in return. They can either go to work or to the soup lines—the choice would be theirs.

The government bears the sole responsibility of protecting the American people from all attacks. The military must be strong, and it must be intelligent. Every effort must be made to ensure the safety of the United States, even if it means putting the fear of God into someone; but only as a last resort. The removal of military options from the arsenal is not a wise move. All avenues should be left open at all times. You never know who or what you might encounter around the next corner. It could be some aspiring bully in North Korea, or it could be Somali crumb-snatchers in the Indian Ocean; anything can happen! Intelligence agencies must be given a full range of access to all potential trouble scenarios. The allowance of all top law enforcement and other government-based agencies to continue on living behind great walls of incompetence, separation, cooperative dysfunctionalism, and nonchalant confusion is the zenith of the "Keystone Kops" scenario and must be remedied at once, because poor communication will not produce an exceptional result of any kind! The United States cannot allow itself to be caught with its pants down again, because there are many rogues just waiting for this country to drop the soap. The United States cannot afford to be cognitively out-dueled or unknowingly duped into submission by its own arrogance or its own gullibility. Military sub-committees and intelligence agencies must be operated by qualified members willing to make tough decisions in the interest of the United States. Wild-eyed, religious zealots and Internet tough guys need not apply.

Now, there are many people who are going to be upset with me for saying and suggesting all of this, but I don't really care at this point! As a Realacrat, I'd rather see your ego collapse, as opposed to our financial structures, because there are too many dunderheaded cretins in this country who would rather watch the entire nation sink into a deep depression, so we could all be on the street corners selling apples again, before they would ever relinquish their phony, megalomaniacal, religious doctrines of control. I remember having a discussion with this counterfeit Christian about how some conservative policies were limiting the economic gains of the country, while other countries around the world were laughing all the way to the bank. He said he'd rather the country be morally profitable than economically profitable, and that is where I draw the line as a Realacrat. You can take your Monopoly money morality, and stick it where the sun fails to shine; and the soap fails to reach! The government's job is the economic progression of the country, not the religious progression of your agenda. To be a Realacrat, you don't have to be religious. You don't even have to be a Christian, but you have to be realistic! Realacrats walk forward not backwards, which translates into independently democratic and liberally solutionary, which is the contrary of conservatively cowering as some rank and file Republican with marching orders.

Hell, I'm just like you. I sit around and wish for my good old days too—but unlike many conservatives, I realize that wishing and receiving are two different things that rarely ever correlate. What most people are left with is the never-ending, goose chase of the dragon; a mythical, unattainable dream that cannot be realistically realized. For example, I have spent years of my life chasing the remnants of a past relationship that was once very good to me. There is not a day that goes by that I do not think about what I once had. In the years since our relationship ended, I have governed all of my relationships in a manner similar to my previous, emotional Camelot. I've hunted high, and I've hunted low. I've returned to past stomping grounds, and I've even gone so far as to associate myself with individuals who are as close as I could possibly get to my past damsel in distress. But despite all of my best efforts, despite all my best prayers, despite all my best hopes, and despite all my best actions; I, like all the king's horses and all the king's men, could not put my "Humpty Dumpty" back together again. It didn't matter whether I prayed to Jesus Christ, Allah, or Buddha, and it didn't matter whether I voted Democrat or Republican. I could not return to my Camelot and neither can you! Conservatives should take a page out of my book, and realize that the world they loved and cherished is no more, and there isn't much they can do about it. There are some conservative beliefs that may have to go into File 13, and there could be some liberal beliefs that may have to go into File 13 as well, but the point is this. It takes a realistic, Realacratic rationale to shed one's political, emotional, comfort-zoned skin in order to move into the future. No one said it was going to be easy. The best Realacrat advice that I can give is simple. To liberals, you don't have to overdo the change; sometimes small changes can have huge results. To conservatives, not all change is bad. Some changes are necessary. It almost makes more sense to consider appointing the Democrats to be in charge of developing new proposals, and then appointing the Republicans to be responsible for finding the cheapest, most cost efficient way of implementing them. Realacrats would suggest getting the President of the United States, the leader of the Republicans in Congress, the leader of the Democrats in Congress, and one Independent/Realacrat to brainstorm opportunities, because there are times when there are simply too many heads and not enough hats to create a viable production.

WHAT MAKES A GOOD REALACRAT?

So, what kind of people would make great Realacrats? In my opinion, it would have to be the kind of people who think objectively, and the kind of people who conjuror up their own visions. It would have to be the kind of people who live outside of the box, and the kind of people who are true mavericks. Realacrats represent people who strive to be innovative and often fly largely under the radar. They are the kind of people who are often misunderstood and underestimated; the kind of people who are repeatedly laughed at and scoffed at for their unorthodox ideologies. They would also represent the kind of people once referred to as bookish or nerdy, but Realacrats would also include individuals known as "people people," like a Bill Clinton, who can draw different walks of life with a unifying message of inclusion. We need people who are not just the latest version of the same record we've been hearing for years now. For example, U.S. Texas Rep. Ron Paul is a very creative candidate who receives minimal coverage from the press. He's known more for being weird and quirky than he is for having fresh new ideas—of which he has an abundance of. The American people simply pass him off as insignificant or humorous in the same way that they ignore former California Governor Jerry Brown, former presidential candidate Ralph Nader, Vermont Senator Bernie Sanders, and Ohio Rep. Dennis Kucinich. Hell, you explain to me why California Governor Arnold Schwarzenegger is viewed as a legitimate candidate, and Ron Paul and Dennis Kucinich are largely looked upon as secondary, sixth-man bench riders, when it is unmistakably clear that both of these men could run rings around Governor Schwarzenegger in the political dogma department. But then again, the Terminator runs rings around the both of them combined in popularity contests. It's too bad that popularity doesn't translate into visionary leadership for the future. The Realacrats have to break this monotony and uniformity in political choice, and the way we will accomplish that goal is with a curve ball I call the "Kurt Cobain Maneuvers."

In short, we would think outside of the zip code, outside of our comfort zones, outside of our own backyards, outside of our country clubs, outside of our own churches, and most importantly, outside of our mentalities. One of the great things about Kurt Cobain and the grunge movement of the 90s was its distinct difference from the well-established status quo, because Seattle was far; far away from the overplayed clichés of New York and Los Angeles. The record company, I think it was Geffen, took a major gamble on going outside of the loop with something completely different and foreign to the then-current establishment, but it proved to be the right move to make, and it worked very well. If you want new ideas, then maybe you should look in new areas. In other words, why don't we see what the person from Timbuktu can do? Let's apply that strategy to politics! Not only will we look outside of the loop geographically, but also outside the ideological loop. Sarah Palin was geographically outside of the loop, as she was from Alaska, and I thought the choice was a gutsy move by John McCain, but her policies were the same, old, generic, conservative, religious-based, mainstream ideas of the typical Republican brand. Maybe this is why they like her so much. Nevertheless, we as Realacrats will recruit a Ron Paul, a Dennis Kucinich, or a Bernie Sanders. We will not continue to draft the same players over and over again when they routinely show tendencies of counter-productivity. The Realacrats will take a much harder look at those candidates and players that are usually passed over; because it is there that you are more likely to find a diamond in the rough. Fools always tend to rally around and throw all of their support behind other fools, while practical guys with common sense finish just ahead of the nice guys. They end up in the friend zone, and the common sense guys end up in the out of office zone. Realacrats will also take the time to discuss political issues with political personalities such as: Glenn Beck, Lou Dobbs, Bill O'Reilly, Sean Hannity, Anderson Cooper, Campbell Brown, Juan Williams, Jessie Jackson Sr., Steve Harvey, Roland Martin, and other media moguls to gain a better and wider perspective on different viewpoints and concerns. In the Realacrat Party, there will be no followers, only allies and associates, because Realacrats won't ignore someone's ingenuity under the sun and then recruit their ideologies under the moon! A good Realacrat's job is not to tell you what to think. It is to create an environment that supports and encourages your desire and your ability to think for yourself!

Patriots of Humanity

So, what specifically makes a person a patriot? If I was a betting man, I'd say it was the same virtues that would make an individual a Realacrat! The word patriot gets tossed around quite a bit nowadays, usually by characters who have self-appointed themselves as the sole authority on patriotism, which basically means they have a primary say in who gets to be called a patriot, and who gets snubbed. The general and more traditional imagery of the patriot is the Uncle Sam figure who loves his country almost as much as he loves God. I even heard a minister once hypothesize that God was an American, and the American flag flew high and proud in heaven. I found this one-sided old-wives' tale to be risible and mirthful at best, but you would be surprised at how many have based their entire destiny on this egocentric premise. By all accounts, the description perfectly fits the conservative movement, but that's only if you believe these particular actions are the blueprints and materials that extract patriotism.

The Realacrat answer to that would be a resounding no. Real patriotism is built upon valor and caution. Patriots of humanity align themselves with what they deem to be right, and they are not bound by or to any specific cause at any specific time, because a patriot of humanity will always question a marching order before they decide to step to it! It seems as if some cable news outlets have mistaken patriotism with team play, since it has been long understood that patriotism is usually thought to be the blind, ambitious loyalty that would follow any half-baked lunatic with a flag in his pocket, while boot-licking the 800-pound political gorilla, not challenging the 800-pound political gorilla, falling in line when the fat lady sings or the fat man speaks, following the proper pecking order, believing in lies as long as it helps your cause, and voluntarily extinguishing any visionary flame that collides with party lines! All of these ideologies may seem to be very unrealistic, but they are definitely a reoccurring theme. Whenever someone speaks out against the judgment of power, no matter how corrupt it may be, the consequences can be brutal, because people tend to lean more favorably on the brash rush to a fallacious judgment, than the cautious questioning of perception

During the 2008 presidential election, there were many White people who struggled internally and externally about whether or not to vote for Barack Obama. I knew one guy named Jay who admitted he'd been catching pure hell over this issue. He said his entire family consisted of conservatives and Christians, who all hated Barack Obama. Some were even making monetary bets on how long he would make it if he, by some fluke of the imagination, got elected, while some were drawing pictures of Barack Obama as a monkey eating a banana with an expiration date on it. Jay told me he was a Democrat and had been a Democrat for quite some time now, yet he had never faced such ridicule and stiff opposition about it until now. He said there were even certain members of his family who threatened to discontinue their relationships with him if he voted for some second-string nigger like Obama! In spite of overwhelming criticism and castigation, Jay told me that he cast his ballot for Barack Obama anyway because he felt Obama was the right man for the job at the time. He then admitted that he has been lying to his wife and family ever since; saying that he'd voted for John McCain like they'd told him to do. Jay is a patriot of humanity and a Realacrat for not allowing anyone or anything to dictate or control his choices. And oh by the way, Jay is not his real name! He asked me to conceal it, so I did!

Patriotism does not have to be limited to the United States. True patriotism is the ability and vision to see the good in the entire world, not just your part of it. You can be a patriot in many different ways besides just being a lackey or a yes-man for self-serving, domestic, propaganda. A real patriot must have confidence above all else, and this is one thing I see mysteriously missing from these current, patriot landscape induction ceremonies. Patriotism is the courage to not only to jump on the bandwagon, but more importantly, it is the courage to know when it's time to jump off. These are the kinds of individuals I consider to be patriots of humanity, and they are exactly who the Realacrat Party will strive to engage. Patriots of humanity are extremely individualized. They possess the ability to set in motion the wheels of freedom, because good leaders carry the keys to freedom, but it's the great leaders who carry the ability and courage to use them to enact freedom. Many of these one-dimensional patriots lack the true grit to make tough decisions, especially when it requires independent thinking and analogy. Patriots of humanity voice what they believe in, not always necessarily what their constituents believe in. They are very similar to the maverick character John McCain tried to portray himself as. Patriots of humanity fully understand the consequences and the vast importance of choices. We are all forced to make some tough choices during our lifetime, but then again, that is what life is all about. You can try to steer and manipulate all you want, but in the; end it's up to each individual to choose a path. If you love someone, you have to be willing to set them free, so they can choose that path, whatever that path may turn out to be! There is nothing more unpatriotic than the fearful manipulation used to dictate your own personal doctrines unto others. If you really want to be a true patriot, you should try facing your unsubstantiated fear of freedom, reality, and change. The one thing that Realacrats and patriots of humanity have in common is the fortitudinous valor to confront corruption, even when the arrow of judgment points inward! Our goal should always be the proliferation of a genuine and equally accessible truth constructed to build a better road towards a humanitarian utopia! Never allow the fear of being challenged to become the roadblock that detours the progression of your decisions, and a patriot of humanity; you will be.

The Realacrat Battle Plan

The Realacrat battle plan will greatly depend on our ability to recruit fresh new faces with fresh new ideas. A new party does not need a newer version of more of the same. The Realacrat platform must provide a choice very different than the status quo, and we have outlined much of that here. Our goal will not be to recruit unions or big corporations. We don't intend to join them. Our goal is to have them joins us, because we will be very leery of sharing a financial bed with either of them. The first couple of nights you screw them, and for the rest of your political life; they'll screw you. I guess that he who screws last and continuously--screws best. And now for my most controversial, battle, plan proposal, a plan that will change the game of politics for good. It's time to forget about the presidency and the chase for the White House. We will let some other band of cretins pursue that goose chase. From what I have seen, having a man in the White House is not necessarily a productive venture, especially if you don't have some pull in Congress. This brings me to my new, innovative game plan. The Realacrat Party will not pursue possession of the White House, but it will pursue as many seats in Congress as humanly possible, starting with the House of Representatives. I call this the "Black Caucus Maneuver." Even though the Congressional Black Caucus never had enough votes to have full control over Congress, they did have enough votes to make their presence felt in Congress. Congressional members of both parties, including the president, were forced to consult with the Congressional Black Caucus on all matters because of their significant, voting block numbers, which could come in extremely handy for whichever party required those votes to pass legislation. The Realacrat goal will be to achieve more seats than the Congressional Black Caucus. If that number can grow large enough, the Realacrat Party can use its voting size as leverage to enhance its own political agenda, and a strong influence in Congress is the best way to achieve this. The presidency is often a puppet show of public appearances, well-written speeches, and scripted postcard moments onboard U.S. aircraft carriers, especially if you have a president who is unwilling to take charge of his policies and an often dysfunctional Congress that sometimes resembles an insane asylum more than a branch of government. Therefore, Congress is where we will set our sights. It may not be as glamorous, but it is far more productive, and Realacrats would rather have production over popularity any day. The same plan could be inaugurated into state and local politics, as well as city councils and the general assemblies.

The Realacratic/Democratic/ Independent Steakhouse Proposal

Thanks specifically to the pitfalls of the conservative ideology, I now realize more than ever, just how much I love and understand the socially, liberal ideology! After spending time with both conservatives and liberals, my vote is now in, and it is a resounding two thumbs up for the liberals! The more I learned about the liberal; the more I was able to find common ground, but the more I learned about conservatives; the more I realized that race relations here in America are still paper thin in a large number of interactions! My relationship with conservatives is almost always in a limited capacity, and whatever commonalities we find will almost always be limited as well, and will habitually cut across racial lines! The conservative guy has to constantly watch what he says around me; more so than a liberal, and I find myself constantly scanning his verbal horizon for any inkling of ethnic/class driven disrespect, and it can prove to be very taxing emotionally for both parties!

I'd rather spend my time with liberals, Democrats, Independents, and moderates! Through my personal experiences, I've found that I can usually work with any of these groups. In general, they all seem to be more tolerant and more open to possibilities! For example, If I was designated to develop a science project with Mitt Romney, Sarah Palin, Rush Limbaugh, and Glenn Beck, there is a more than favorable chance that a physical square off would likely occur between Romney and me, Palin and me, and most definitely, Limbaugh and me! Believe it or not, I think Glenn Beck is the only one I could halfway come to an agreement with. On the other hand, If I was designated to develop a science project with Secretary of State Hillary Clinton, President Obama, Speaker of the House Nancy Pelosi, and some unknown Independent, I feel confident that no physical square off would ever take place and an agreement would be forthcoming!

It's no coincidence that 99% of my political supporters on Facebook are Democrats, liberals, and Independents. It's also no coincidence that about 90% of my friends on Facebook are Democrats, liberals, and Independents. The political atmosphere is intoxicatingly unifying, and I'd like it to continue beyond Facebook. In my imaginary world, the same world that houses the Realacrat ideology, I often dream of a place outside of the computer where I could meet up with all of my Democratic, liberal, Independent friends for breakfast, lunch, dinner and so on, and in my dream, it was an actual place called the Realacratic/Democratic/Independent steakhouse, whichever name fits! It would be a place where pictures of past and present great Democrats and up and coming Independents are prominently displayed, with Democratic facts, figures, and propaganda representing the scenery. You could have the Obama Rib eye, a Joe Biden beer, Hillary Clinton ice cream, the liberal, American sushi, Independent fries, a John F. Kennedy super steak, an Abraham Lincoln, log cabin burger, the Bill Clinton barbeque, and a Michelle Obama veggie menu, just to name a few.

There are many of you who probably think that I'm crazy for suggesting such a folly, but I'm serious! A place like this would be great for networking regionally and locally, and it would be a fabulous way to raise money for upcoming campaigns. Whenever a nationally recognized, regionally recognized, or locally not so recognized candidate or politician was in the area, they could stop by to meet and greet with the people, which would be more than likely partisan! This venture would be perfect for registering new voters and rallying the core base during election time, especially on Election Day! This idea could be used to help feed the homeless, to help register undocumented immigrants, establish a place of diversified employment, and provide basic governmental information to those in need! In my opinion, this would be the flip side of the fat cat, Wall St. Bailout! This would be Main St. at its finest, and they could be dispersed all over the nation!

I got the idea from the Red Cross, blood drive tours. The Red Cross, which is arguably the most underrated organization of all time, routinely goes out on blood donation tours to collect blood. Donors get free food and drinks, and the Red Cross gets blood donations! Why not apply that same process to politics? On Election days, free transportation to and from the polls, along with free transportation to the steakhouse for free meals could be provided for by the political party in charge. The goal would be to get the people registered, get the people a ride, get the people to vote, and then get the people fed, not necessarily in that particular order!

This would be the sign that would hang with these words: "We are the Democrats; a party of tolerance, diversity, equality, inclusion, and individual freedoms. We think with our openness, and we live for our possibilities. Our goal is to make the government help you just as much as the government expects you to help it, because we are America, and America is us, and it's time that we start to make our lives reflect that! So join with us in the Democratic ideology as we work to improve our country, our world, and ourselves"! This is our Democratic mission statement!

Realacrats for Everyone

In the Realacrat Party, all of these unjust, minority-based denials will be met with swift opposition. The reality of it all is this: it will take every American to keep the country alive. It will take every American to make the country rebound. It will take every American to keep the country strong. It will take every American to move the country forward. It will take every American to defend this nation. It will take every American to rebuild this nation. It will take every American to produce American goods and services, and it will take every American to ship and transport those goods. It will take every American to make the country better for our children than it is for us right now, so quit it or get with it!

The time has come for every American citizen to become more involved with their own future and their own destiny. Every American deserves a chance to speak out and seek out in a place where character, ability, determination, ambition, intelligence, mature work ethic, and personal responsibility reign supreme over ignorance, arrogance, bigotry, chauvinism, sexism, deception, incompetence, apathy, misinformation, and corruption. In the Realacrat reality, an individual's culture or religious preference will not be insulted, nor will any personal faith be purposely touted over all others. I agree with the concerns of Mr. Ben Jealous of NAACP about the Limbaugh legion's misguided quest for a return to the glory of the olden days of White, male domination, despite the fact that White males continue to dominate most of the country anyway. Apparently, the historic emergences of Barack Obama, Judge Sonia Sotomayor, and others similarly patterned have caused great concern for many—but not for the Realacrat ideology. Contrary to popular belief, diversity is not a dirty word, nor is universal across the board success. Once more, the possibility of wealth raining down on the many, instead of the elitist few, is not socialism. People use the word socialism as a sly replacement for genetic and religious favoritism. Even though the concept of the poor and underprivileged, and usually a minority, pulling themselves up from the depths of oppressive disenfranchisement is supposed to be the American dream, it is instead treated more like a dirty deed, depending on who accomplishes it. There must be a party where the success of all is championed above the insecurities of the few.

I believe a page should be taken out of the WWE's playbook, the NFL's playbook, and the NBA's playbook. I believe in the strategy of the draft and the strategy of recruiting for the Realacrat Party. The spectacular accomplishments of these major and lucrative organizations cannot be denied. For example, whether you like President Obama or not, it's hard to dispel the well-orchestrated game plan undertaken by the Democratic Party in locating, vetting, and supporting their presidential candidate—and I stress the word candidate. Senator Obama was personally selected and heavily recruited by the ranking Democrats in government, in spite of already having a potent presidential frontrunner candidate in Hillary Clinton. It was most definitely a gutsy move by the Democratic Party, but it worked. Instead of believing that minorities were incapable of winning, they promoted and upheld the candidate they thought was best suited to win the White House in 2008, even if it meant picking a minority. Evidently, the political version of the NCAA tournament selection committee[2] was very precise in their scouting reports on Barack Obama's unyielding ability to woo and communicate to all people, and not just his own party! Conservatives would call this an offshoot of Affirmative Action, but I call it progress at its finest. The idea of recruiting the best and most qualified individuals is an excellent battle plan, and the Realacrats will fully embrace that plan. There is a huge difference between a coon quota and a loaded, talented quota. We don't want the good ol' boys network. Realacrats want the old Pete Carol, USC network or the Bill Belichick, New England Patriots network. We want the best intellectual athletes available, and we intend to find them. Much like a college team or a professional team, our roster will be the epitome of diversity and the epitome of the very best humanity has to offer.

AFRICAN-AMERICANS

The Realacrat Party will do everything in its power to offer the African-American community a viable alternative to both the Democrats and the Republicans, despite the huge amount of difficulty it will face to even get the attention of the African-American community, since the Democratic Party has brought forth Barack Obama as the Democratic nominee before he was elected President of the United States of America. Under normal circumstances, I would not be asking African-Americans to weigh their political options regarding the Democratic Party, but the African-American community needs a priority makeover, and the Barack Obama era is the perfect time to undertake it, because just having Obama in the White House is not enough. The African-American community needs to be addressed directly, and not in some

2 Wikipedia, NCAA basketball tournament selection process, http://en.wikipedia.org/wiki/NCAA_basketball_tournament_selection_process

theme-based, symbolic gesture. Bill Cosby attempted to address this very issue a few years ago and came under intense fire for doing so. Even Barack Obama has been accused of talking down to Black people when he chastised the missing fathers all across this nation. The African-American Community has a self-destructive tendency to prioritize against their own progression, and that needs to be re-routed in a more positive direction, and the existence of a President Obama probably will not be enough to make this happen. As President Obama is forced to leave behind his community organizing days, it's time for a new party to pick up where he left off. You can still vote as a Democrat, but you can also began to mobilize as a Realacrat, especially in cases where the Democratic Party's presence is not as visible as it should be. The Realacrat Party will recruit young, African-American scholars the same way scouts recruit young African-American athletes. It's a controversial job, but someone has got to do it. Look at it this way. If Barack Obama and Bill Cosby were unable to directly address the African-American community about its own semi-self-inflicted demise, what could someone like Sarah Palin possibly even dream about doing or saying in response to this growing African-American dilemma? The Republican Party and the conservatives might as well be public enemy number one in signing up for this job. No matter how unfair it is, a Rush Limbaugh, a Sarah Palin, an Ann Coulter, a Bill O'Reilly, or a Sean Hannity would be simply drawing a Ku Klux Klan bull's-eye on their backs if they ever decided to go into the African-American communities like Father Phleger does on a routine basis in Chicago, Illinois. And furthermore, it would probably be a cold day in hell when any of those previously named conservatives ever found themselves ethnically conscious enough to recognize or speak about anything at all in the African-American community, because Republican Party conservatives have absolutely no credibility in the African-American community. African-Americans don't trust the Republicans and the Republicans look extremely timid about engaging African-Americans. This is not how relations are made better, and I don't think either side has any intentions of trying to change it, but that's where Realacrats come in, because we are not afraid to build bridges, and Republicans will have to lose their fear eventually as U.S. demographics continue to shift.

Native Americans

For many years in this country it has been a tradition to overlook entire groups of people based on the "water in a boot" criterion. It's a fickle-minded embodiment where idiots who lack the typical know-how needed to pour water out of a boot are allotted the authority to unfairly appoint themselves into positions of prestige. So my question is: "What in the hell has happened to the Native Americans, formerly known as American Indians?" Don't get me wrong, I know the predictable, White guy prototype is always in abundance, but you can't tell me there aren't qualified Native Americans in this country. I applaud Van Jones for at least bringing this subject to the light! It's no secret that Native Americans haven't been and are not being recruited for much of anything currently. For all intents and purposes, they might as well be on Mars—or locked away in casinos. I had an arrogant, pompous conservative once display his feeling on the plight of the Native Americans in this country. This tobacco spitting, 30-pack-of-Solo-beer-drinking, local yokel had this to say: "It's not our fault that we had to take all of the Indians' land. God told us to do it. He said it was really ours because we were Christians, and they were savage barbarians. I don't understand why they always complain about things like our Runnin' Joe, red sambo, sports mascots either. They should be happy we even allow them to be mascots! We gave them casinos! They should just pull the slot levers and be happy."

Here we go again, because this sounds eerily similar to the corrupt policies of absolute power. As a Realacrat, I urge Native Americans to aspire to be and do more. Compared to the Jews, Asians, and African-Americans, I'd say that the Native Americans have had the least productive rebound against racial oppression. As long as you sit on the sidelines, the sidelines are where you will remain. Undoubtedly, the world couldn't care less, but it's up to you to change that. You don't need the world to care! You just need you to care! Native Americans once displayed one of the fiercest and most ambitious drives of any group of warriors ever assembled. Maybe it's time to relocate and reinstitute that ferocity. It's not always your fault for being defeated, but it is always your fault for staying defeated. There is a voice within you that needs to be asserted into the mainstream. Your stories need to be and deserve to be heard like anyone else's. The West was lost yesterday, but it does not have to be continuously lost today or tomorrow. The one thing John McCain said on the campaign trail in 2008 that struck a chord with me was his "Fight fight; stand up and fight" chant. John McCain was right, even though he probably wasn't talking to you or me, as African-Americans or Native Americans. Whether it's the Realacrat Party or some other party, the Native American input must be restored into relevance with American humanity, not by a red sambo quota, but by motivational possibilities and a keen eye for potential talent. Instead of preaching and fear mongering about all the different groups of nationalities, the Realacrats will engage different entities of people for the good of one nation under God, meaning one of the nations under God, which is a nation of one composed of many, where all are equal in value.

More Federal Holidays

I never quite understood the opposition to the Martin Luther King Jr. holiday by the state of Arizona and its U.S. Senator John McCain, who has since apologized and admitted that he made a mistake in his opposition to the King Holiday, when every other state in the United States was acknowledging it except for Arizona! Well, is it a coincidence that president Obama is arguably the most hated president of all time, and the King Holiday is arguably the most hated holiday of all time! I'm independently democratic, and I am the Realacrat, so it's up to me to tell it like it is, and I'm going to do that right now! In all of my days since the King Holiday became a federal law, I have never ever physically met a White person brave enough to publicly admit that they like it! On the contrary, I have never ever met an African-American brave enough to publicly admit that they didn't like it! White people always throw up the proposal of Robert E. Lee's birthday as a national holiday! They don't understand why King deserves it, but Lee does not! Dr. Martin Luther King is a symbol of freedom for all! Robert E. Lee is a symbol of freedom for his neck of the woods, which was a neck of the woods where my neck would be in danger of finding its way inside of a nigger noose! King gets the holiday—end of story!

After observing so much of the hatred, the disdain, and the reluctance or refusal to celebrate the King Holiday, I'm now ready to take it a step further to really infuriate the minority recognition haters with two new federal holiday proposals, which mark two specific events that took place right here on American soil! My first proposal is to make Juneteenth/Freedom Day/Emancipation Day, which is June 19th, a nationally recognized federal holiday. The fact that there is no federal holiday commemorating the end of slavery is a preposterous outrage, and it needs to be rectified without delay. I couldn't care less about the numerous conservatives, in and out of government, who will be literally fuming at what they will consider to be partial slave reparations. This is something that Realacrats will be more than willing to fight for until the dying end, because you can't sit here with a straight face or a Christian heart and say that African-Americans don't deserve it! I challenge anyone to face the world and make that statement!

My second holiday proposal will only douse the flames of majority insecurity even further, as I am now ready to establish my unyielding support for a nationally recognized federal holiday to honor the plight of the Native Americans in this country. I find it unacceptable that there is no nationally recognized, federal holiday commemorating the struggles of Native Americans in this country, and I, again, couldn't care less about the numerous insecurities that will explode in anger, at what they will consider to be partial Indian reparations. Realacrats will, again, be more than willing to fight until the bitter end to correct this injustice. As I re-ask this question, who can sit here with their so-called righteousness, and say that the Native Americans don't deserve it! If you believe the Native Americans don't deserve a federal holiday based on their monumental contributions and their exorbitant struggles within this country, then I challenge you to step out in front of a worldwide audience, and tell the world that the Native Americans are unworthy!

The Realacrat Party and Women

I am strongly in favor of a new party formation in this country. Speaking as a lifelong Democrat, there are numerous occasions when I am officially fed up with both parties. I've never been much of a fan when it comes to The Republicans, but I lived and died with the Democrats! I still fully support Bill Clinton, and I love the current Secretary of State Hillary Clinton! She is still my favorite candidate of all-time, and she is the only person who could possibly cause me to develop a real conflict of interest between my future Realacrat possibilities and the Democratic Party. I was a staunch Hillary supporter, and I cast my vote for her in the Arkansas Primaries in 2008. I still vehemently support Hillary

Clinton. When Barack Obama decided not to align himself with her for the Vice-Presidency slot, my alliances to The Democratic Party began to wane, as I was forced to ask myself a very tough question. Why wasn't Hillary Clinton chosen to be his running mate? What does Joe Biden have that Hillary does not have? I don't know exactly what it is, but I've got a feeling I have one too. Make no mistake about it. My support of the Democratic Party in 2008 was more of an anti-Republican vote than it was a pro-Obama vote. I wanted Hillary Clinton, and I'm still not happy about her not being on the ticket. I wanted the dream ticket, and I wanted double history to be made, by having the first female vice president to go along with the first African-American president or vice-versa! As a Realacrat, there was no chance in hell that I wouldn't have made that dream a reality! I know the Limbaugh legion was against it, but Realacrats don't give a rat's ass about the advice of the Limbaugh legion. Now I still support President Obama and his cabinet, but I will never support Obama's decision to pass over Hillary Clinton. Joe Biden seems like a good man, and I think he would have made an excellent Secretary of State, but the passing over Clinton for him was one of the most bone-headed moves I've seen in politics! If you get a chance to assemble a dream team/ticket, it's your responsibility to pick it up and run with it! Not giving Hillary Clinton the chance to even play for the position, in my stance, is unacceptable and unforgivable; and I would be very happy if Joe Biden had to step down, possibly in the second term, if President Obama is somehow able to repeat, for some strange unknown reason; allowing Hillary Clinton to move up into her rightful, well-earned, well-deserved, historic position, because I, under no circumstances, want Sarah Palin to claim that glory first! I don't care if she wins the presidency later! I just don't want Palin, or any other conservative candidate, to make that history of the first female president/vice president! And furthermore, I honestly don't want any other Democratic candidate to make that history either! The same ideology that convinced Obama to snub Hillary Clinton is probably the same ideology that convinced Obama to seek out bipartisanship as a viable option!

I was happy to see the history being made with the election of President Obama, but after that; I began to see how some of the current Democratic Party leaders were drifting away from I would like to see politically, and Hillary's non-VP nomination was the beginning of it. In my opinion, Hillary Clinton should have been the presidential nominee with Barack Obama as her running mate. I just felt Obama should have gone in first as a vice-president, and it would have still been historic. Furthering my opinion, I also feel that Obama just being a vice-president would have been far less intimidating to the country, which in return could have yielded a better political production volume in the end. Honestly, I believe Republicans and conservatives hate Obama far worse than they could ever hate Hillary Clinton, and I didn't think that was possible. I wonder why? I'm being sarcastic! I know why! I also know that there are many people who till this very day still haven't publicly admitted they voted for President Obama. So you know there are going to be numerous politicians who will build a fort specifically to work against him. I only hope Barack Obama's victorious election does not turn out to be the crowning achievement of his presidential career, because Democrats have been known to quit on their leaders under the scrutinizing heat of Republican ridicule.

So what about the role of women in the Realacrat Party?

Women are more than welcome in the Realacrat Party. Women will have the same opportunities as men, and they will be paid the same amount of money for doing the same amount of work as men. My ego is not so inflated that I don't realize the superb qualities of women. For all of my current and pre-Realacratic life, I have been bombarded by one-sided suggestions that women were not genetically built to be leaders. I find it mesmerizing how men are the ones who push this ideology, because they are also the ones who stand to benefit, and they are the ones who have benefited the most from this ideology. How ironic is that? I also find it quite ironic that the suppression of women into secondary roles is one thing that Christians and Muslims have in common, despite Christianity being held in a much higher regard than the often vilified Islam. As a Realacrat, I would have to hypothesize that since man interpreted the religious scriptures; man also interpreted the outcome of those religious scriptures; vaingloriously putting himself atop the mortal mountain in a first come first serve basis. So think about that for a minute! Basically, man's early bird status, his advantageous muscular development, and his testosterone based strength have somehow made him cognitively superior, and therefore fit to lead. Well, Realacrats will steadfastly refuse all seating arrangements on that ship of misogynistic, benightedness! Men make just as many poor decisions as anyone else. In the end, you've either prepared yourself, both mentally and physically, for the task at hand, or you haven't! Gender has nothing to do with it.

It wasn't Realacrat philosophy that disqualified women from their right to vote for all of those years. It wasn't Realacrat philosophy that suggested women only have two destinations, which would be the kitchen and the bedroom. It wasn't Realacrat philosophy that struck a blow for the White man based on some perilous, unscrupulous display of manhood in a domestic abuse pattern reminiscent of a scene in the movie *Mississippi Burning*. It wasn't Realacrat philosophy that has suggested and stated publicly that a move to England or Canada would suffice if a woman were elected President of the United States. It wasn't Realacrat philosophy that spurred those old, tired, penis-toting conservative men to try and dictate if a baby can be extracted from a woman's womb. It wasn't Realacrat philosophy that suggested and publicly stated how the worst ranked men's tennis player could beat the women's top ranked tennis player. Honestly people, what was the basis for that comparison? It is the textbook version of the dominant male beating his chauvinistic chest, and it is the exemplification of the fear of being challenged! It wasn't Realacrat philosophy that has consistently stated that women are too emotional to be true leaders. It wasn't Realacrat philosophy that labeled women as being too weak, too timid, too gullible, and too estrogenic to be tough on other world leaders. It wasn't Realacrat philosophy that suggested a woman's menstrual cycle severely limits her ability to call in an air strike. It wasn't Realacrat philosophy that suggested a woman's vagina was enough to cause her to not be taken seriously on anything besides sex. It wasn't Realacrat philosophy demanding women be covered from head to toe and walk behind their men in public. It wasn't Realacrat philosophy that has continually suggested that a man's upper-body strength is what makes him genetically superior and intellectually superior to women. I know! How do pectoral muscles equate into intellectual thought stimulation or cerebral processing? It wasn't Realacrat philosophy that has suggested that women are only experts at fashion, shopping, and shoes. It wasn't Realacrat philosophy that recommended that women on average deploy about a million words a day, in which only five to ten of them have any real substance. It wasn't Realacrat philosophy that stated how women get all of their great ideologies from men's intellectual leftovers; White men in particular! It wasn't Realacrat philosophy that questioned Mary Magdalene, feared Mary Magdalene, discredited Mary Magdalene, and slandered Mary Magdalene all in the name of White male, theocratic chauvinism. And most importantly, it was not the Realacrat ideology that formed a secret, political coup to specifically recruit a male candidate in hope of wrestling away the Democratic nomination from Hillary Clinton in 2008, because they lacked confidence in a female nominee.

I think the record speaks for itself. Realacrats will never be afraid to vote for a woman's leadership, because Realacrats don't walk around with their heads stuck up their pompous asses. Realacrats don't allow themselves to be carried away by the highly accepted belief about God creating man first, in the image of himself. All that means is that man was here first. First does not always translate into the best leadership, but it does usually translate into absolute arrogance and vanity. Realacrats don't get beleaguered by Eve[3] being coaxed into sin by the serpent either. Truthfully, the only reason that Adam didn't get coaxed is because the serpent, in all likelihood, didn't see him first. All the serpent would have had to do is question Adam's manhood, and he would have stripped the entire tree of forbidden fruit. Remember, it was Eve who prodded Adam into eating the forbidden fruit, so who's leading who here? It appears that Adam was the south end of the northbound moose on that one. Let's just cut to the chase! If that same, evil serpent came here today, right here right now, and setup a forbidden, apple booth of a new, Viagra-like substance that guaranteed a Rock of Gibraltar erection that would make any man stretch to no less than nine inches in length, the line of willing, male participants would be long enough to wrap around the equator. All of these misguided, misleading, overly sexist concepts are what other parties use to discredit women from leadership roles, but being an African-American, I don't get duped too easily by conservative, male propaganda, and neither should you. I look forward to some female ingenuity in the political realm.

3 Wikipedia, Forbidden Fruit, http://en.wikipedia.org/wiki/Forbidden_fruit.

Realacrats Attack

Realacratic Disdain at Democrats

Speaking as a Realacrat, I do believe in civility and compassion, if at all possible. I want a party that will be nice; that is, until it's time to not be nice. Unlike the Democrats, the Realacrats will be a unit that will not be afraid to punch the principals of conservatism with the gloves of individuality and progressiveness—repeatedly if necessary! We will not turn the other cheek, unless it's the lower cheek, as we tell you to kiss our integrated ass. I am a former Democrat, so I will more than likely agree with them on many issues, but I vehemently disagree with their passive responses and feeble counter-attack strategies. I absolutely disagree with the way Democrats allow Fox News to bludgeon them at every turn. Glenn Beck, Bill O'Reilly, Monica Crowley, Laura Ingram, Dick Morris and many others routinely kick the Democrats up one side, and then walk all over them on the other side. Now don't get me wrong. I agree with O'Reilly and Beck on some issues, but I will not hesitate to call a fool a fool whenever I hear or see one. Democrats don't seem to grasp the determinations of when to be nice versus when to be nasty, and that is unacceptable to a Realacrat. Basically, what I detect in Democrats in regards to Republicans and conservatives is fear, which is also unacceptable. If it weren't for James Carville, the Democrats would be almost completely spineless. Hillary Clinton is also not afraid of the Republicans, and that is why she should be at the top or near the top of the ticket. I hear more moxie from people like David Letterman,

Jon Stewart and Bill Maher than I do from actual Democrats. When entertainers promote better leadership than your party leaders, it's time to exit stage left.

How long will Democrats walk around in fear of Republicans and conservatives, as they use the old "I've got God on my side argument." Trust me Democrats, if God has something to say to you or me, he won't appoint the idiot with the biggest mouth and the most corruptive interpretations to be his messenger! Democrats cannot allow Republicans to hornswoggle them into believing that Jesus is going to judge their governmental policies. On judgment day, do you really believe Jesus is going to say to you, "Did you pass Barack Hussein Obama's healthcare reform? You did? Well, you disobeyed my rules, and now you must burn eternally in the pits of hell!" First of all, Jesus would already know everything you've ever done anyway, so that entire exchange is unintelligent. Republicans and conservatives DO NOT have the only solutions on being right, nor do they have it on being with God. The United States does not own God's love, nor do the Republicans, because God is not an American—so get over it! The Democrats have to make a choice, and then withstand everything that comes along with that choice. It could mean they are called unpatriotic, Godless, liberal, insane, terrorist sympathizers, poor people sympathizers, gay sympathizers, Native-American sympathizers, Arab-American sympathizers, Hispanic-American sympathizers, humanitarians, or the age, old classic--nigger lovers! Democrats should then turn around and say one simple line to these self-righteous gluttons: "Sticks and stones may break my bones, but gutless, bigoted, erroneous, elitist, monumentally biased, self-authoritative propaganda will never hurt me!" The Democrats need to grow a set! Why even vote for President Obama if you knew you were going to be too afraid to fight for and with him?

This all reminds me of the civil war, where the South had all of the qualified military generals while the North had a who's who cast of questionable incompetence. Today, the Republicans are the South, and the Democrats are the North. Outside of Hillary Clinton and President Obama, the bulk of the Democratic Party, at times, appears to be a vast abyss of no one, while the Republican Party is stacked from top-to-bottom with political, rabblerousing foot soldiers, like Rep. Michelle

Bachmann of Minnesota, Rep. Joe Wilson of South Carolina, Kentucky Senator Mitch McConnell, and Senator Lindsey Graham of South Carolina, who are all more than capable of stepping in immediately as the heads of their party and rallying their bases to victory, while filching a few "Blue Dog" Democrats along the way! Vice-President Joe Biden is not a leader! Rep. Charlie Wrangle of New York is not a leader! Senator Joe Lieberman of Connecticut is not a leader! Rep. Bart Stupak of Michigan is not a leader! I wouldn't follow Stupak to an all-access strip club! Senator Chris Dodd of Connecticut is not a leader! Senator Evan Bayh of Indiana is not a leader! I never did like him, even before he became a quitter! Rep. Marion Berry of Arkansas is not a leader! I can't believe he didn't support the Health Care Bill of 2010! Howard Dean, head of the Democratic National Committee, is not a leader! If Howard Dean were any more invisible in the national media, he would have to be erased from political existence. None of these Democratic heavy hitters do anything to inspire me, but I am definitely not convinced that numerous qualified individuals do not exist within the Democratic Party. Rep. Barney Frank of Massachusetts does more to fire me up than any of them, and I also like the political moxie of Rep. Alan Grayson from Florida. Both he and Frank are intellectually fearless, and they always show up for a fight. I was never impressed with Barney Frank until he went up against Bill O'Reilly more than once and held his own! If a Democrat cannot challenge the likes of a Bill O'Reilly, then I have no political faith in them.

Speaking of Democrats, I was not much of a fan of House Speaker Nancy Pelosi either, but the way she rallied the Democratic troops in 2010 to ensure passage of the great Health Care Bill is admirable and impressive, because I had absolutely no confidence in her abilities! Her stubbornness to stay on the Democratic Party's course and support President Obama in the face of intense conservative and public scrutiny is something the Democratic Party has been sorely lacking for years, and it's also something it needs more of! There is no doubt in my opinion that Nancy Pelosi and Nevada Senator Harry Reid are two of the best legislators of the modern era, but as Democratic candidates who can rally their bases out into the polls on election day; neither of them would be my first choice for that responsibility! The Democratic leadership's main goals should be to rally their base as much as humanly possible, woo as many independents as humanly possible, and develop an effective counter strategy aimed squarely at the GOP. It just seems like there are far too many Democrats similar to a Joe Biden or a Joe Lieberman, who are halfway decent at rallying their base, but not so great at rallying independents, pirating a few moderate Republicans, or enduring 12 rounds in a political death match with the GOP. Republicans have made careers off of pillaging Democratic support! During the 2008 presidential race candidate Barack Obama turned the tables on the Republicans, as he ventured into traditionally Republican strongholds like Virginia, and the strategy paid off, but I'm not convinced that the Democrats will have enough ingenuity to reinvent a political bold move into a political mainstay! The Democratic Party is just as likely to go out and locate another Michael Dukakis as they are to nominate another Barack Obama! This is the kind of political incompetence that has caused me to become a Realacrat—not because the mighty Republicans were able to use the "God is a conservative" approach in a submissive tone to tactically dupe and scare me out of the party, but because the Democrats show too much fear, along with an uncanny ability to stay asleep at the wheel as they continually pass over golden opportunities that eventually end up in the hands of the Republicans, who are not even in legislative power at the moment.

The Democrats always seem to have no answers! Republicans hoodwink, swindle and turn the word liberal into a dirty word, and Democrats have no answers. The Republicans have their own freaking network, which is Fox News, and it is the emergence of this 24-hour media-based bully pulpit that has allowed the Republicans to continue controlling the country even though they failed to win the election in 2008. With President Obama, an African-American, now in the White House, the Fox News megaphone now trumpets louder than ever before, while Democrats still have no answers. Contrary to what Fox News would have you believe, CNN is not the antithesis to Fox News, but is the only network that could possibly give Fox News a run for its money. CNN is, at best, is passively friendly to the Democratic cause, but Fox News is aggressively and staunchly behind the Republican cause, giving Republicans a cable, news, media advantage. Democrats should have begun using CNN as a counter-attack mechanism a long time ago, because the cable news market is the new frontier of the modern media. Where is the leadership?

If a Realacrat was in Command of the Democrats

Now, since Democrats are unable or unwilling to draft a new battle plan to try and attain a new strategy to face off against the Republicans, I will delegate my own Democratic political strategies in my final act as a traditional, straight ticket Democrat. The first move would be to replace Howard Dean as the leader of the party. Dean makes a great foot soldier, but as a leader; he leaves me feeling politically bland. I get more energized from listening to great motivational and analytical speakers, like Bill and Hillary Clinton, Jessie Jackson Jr., and Montana Governor Brian Schweitzer, who is phenomenal. The Democratic Party should unquestionably go after such intellectually savvy people as Bill "The Democratic Yoda" Maher, Gwen Ifill, Steven A. Smith, Michael Moore, Scott Van Pelt, Colin Cowherd, Dr. Michael Eric Dyson, Dr. Cornel West, Condoleezza Rice (because it never hurts to try), Kweisi Mfume, Jessie Ventura, Janeane Garofalo, the outstanding Rachel Maddow, and possibly the great Keith Olbermann—but especially Bill Maher! I feel he is the best available pick in the draft on Mel Kiper Jr.'s big board of politics. If you want someone who can go toe-to-toe with Anne Coulter, Bill O'Reilly, Sean Hannity, and Glenn Beck all at the same time, then Bill Maher is your political equivalent to yoda! Democrats should be recruiting Bill Maher harder than every single team in the NBA tried to recruit LeBron James when he became a free agent. The Realacrat Party is already recruiting Bill Maher!

The next move by the Democrats should be an attempt to broker a deal between HBO and CNN for the airing rights to a show like Bill Maher's "Politically Incorrect." I don't know if CNN would have the backbone to do it, but they should; as they once aired the vaudeville antics of Glenn Beck—which never seemed to make any sense whatsoever to me or anyone else for that matter. Airing Glenn Beck on CNN would be the equivalent of airing the Al Sharpton show on the Ku Klux Klan network. Bill Maher is a primetime player, and CNN and the Democratic Party should have enough sense to know it. As the old saying by Chris Vernon, of "The Chris Vernon Show," goes, "You mess with the bull! You get the horns!" Bill Maher is the perfect candidate for the job of turning back the political horns towards Fox News! I also believe Democrats should consider allocating Roland Martin his own show on CNN. It would be Bill Maher and Roland Martin versus Bill O'Reilly and Glenn Beck! Let the political fireworks begin!

My final suggestion to the Democratic Party is to pick up the NFL/NCAA playbook by locating the best political players and utilizing them on the political field of play. The current Democratic Party lacks leadership, courage, determination, fearlessness, and most importantly, a political killer instinct of attack. Basically, I would reinstate Harold Ford Jr. into a prominent party role with John Edwards as a political ghostwriter and ghost advisor, because the John Edwards' ideological platform was a good one. I actually liked it better than Hillary Clinton's platform. The Democratic Party's underutilization of Harold Ford Jr.'s abilities is a crime. I also liked Harold Ford Jr.'s ideology better than Barack Obama's. Harold Ford Jr. has to get back in the game. The Democratic leadership has to get him back in the game. James Carville should be designated as the official Democratic spokesperson, political assassin, or White House Press Secretary and former President Bill Clinton should be a top Democratic advisor with an official role within the party. If it was up to me, Howard Dean would be demoted and Bill Clinton would head the party. I don't hate the views of such Democratic royalty as a Howard Dean or a Joe Biden, but their leadership tactics in a head-to-head matchup against the Republicans has failed to build election confidence within me. I would also recruit the more-than-worthy talents of Retired General Wesley Clark. I would have vetted him long before I ever vetted Bill Richardson. Jessie Jackson Jr. would be the next Speaker of the House of Representatives after Nancy Pelosi steps down, and I would make every possible attempt to woo the phenomenal Gwen Ifill. I believe she is the most Democratic speaker not officially in the Democratic Party. Gwen Ifill's political articulations are more than enough to go toe-to-toe and heel-to-heel with Sarah and the Palinators on any political issue. If the Democrats don't recruit Gwen Ifill for a top party position, they should have the political taste slapped out of their mouths! Katy Couric couldn't politically ambush Gwen Ifill if she was in a diabetic coma—the same could also be said for the exceptional Janeane Garofalo. Democrats should then attempt to resurrect the spirit of Senator John Kerry of Massachusetts from the watery grave he sunk into after he was so unceremoniously swift boated out of the White House in 2004. Yeah, I said John Kerry! I still like John Kerry, and I've always liked him. He lost the election of 2004, so does that mean he has to sit around with his head down on the sidelines for the rest of his political career? The Democratic Party needs congressional leadership now more than ever, with the loss of the great Ted Kennedy, and former Senator of Massachusetts John Kerry is just as good of a candidate as anyone else in the party. If the Republicans had swift-boated me and called my honor, patriotism, military service and character into question, similar to how they acted regarding John McCain's alleged Black child during the Republican primaries against President Bush, I would be a political vampire waiting in ambush to feast on Republican blood. The Democrats should be ashamed for having pro-bowl, NFL talent, but only engaging minor league replacement players. Who's going to be the one to step up and kick the sleeping donkey in ass? If you can't fend off a comatose donkey, you might as well forget about challenging a greedy, arrogant, self-absorbed, slyly bigoted, colossally selfish elephant. So be assured of one thing Democrats, if you continue to drop the soap, Simba the elephant will most definitely screw you out of the next election. This is why I can no longer wait on the Democrats. **I'll always agree with the traditional, ideological platform of the Democratic Party, even if I don't always agree with the current version of the Democratic Party! From here on out, if a Democrat fails to live up to traditional, Democratic standards I will replace them.**

Realacratic Disdain at Republican Arrogance

Since Democrats won't do it, I guess this now looks like a job for a Realacrat. So let me start by saying that anyone who suggests that it was somehow inappropriate to go into North Korea to rescue the two Asian-American journalists is a worthless piece of paramecium sh*t! Anyone who suggests that the freedom of these two Asian-American journalists was not worth the political cost to the United States is a low-life, puke bucket. Republicans and conservatives have some nerve to go around and question the validity of Bill Clinton's purpose in North Korea. A local Republican made this statement to a group of independents and Democrats regarding the situation, "Bill Clinton, also known as Slick Willie, only went to North Korea so he could get some sideways, chink pussy with his cigar, because he is nothing but a gutless womanizer." He then went on to explain how he'd never heard about this story until the journalists were actually set free, but he did hear about Bristol Palin being viscously mauled by David Letterman. I then asked the holy rolling Republican why a barefaced majority of the leaders called to negotiate with other countries around the world on behalf of those held in captivity were strongly affiliated with the Democratic Party. If such world renowned, worldly respected Democrats like Bill Clinton and Jessie Jackson Sr. are so roguish and shallow, why haven't there been more family values Republicans called upon by other countries to negotiate the freedom of the many unlucky prisoners who've found themselves in an international bind. Jessie Jackson Sr.'s hostage negotiations are the stuff of legends. It's amazing how quickly people forget! With the exception of George H.W. Bush, the Republicans don't have a real humanitarian, and that in itself speaks volumes about the party's character, which is yet another reason why I could never be a Republican.

Others have suggested that the United States should have left the two Asian-American journalists in North Korea to teach Kim Jong-il a lesson and deny him any press opportunities and photo ops with former president Bill Clinton, which is about as dumb as I've heard! Regardless of the reason, Kim Jong-il decided to free the two journalists, while some conservatives, here in this country, have suggested that freeing them was not necessarily a good move. Now I ask you, who's the real asshole? It takes a special kind of foolishness to find fault in the freeing of another human being, but it looks like some in the conservative movement have found a way to acquire it. In the spirit of Hall & Oates, I can't go for that and neither should Democrats, but they do. I'm sick of the Republicans and their idiotic vilifying, and I'm sick of the Democrats for being political patsies.

So let's get one thing straight right out of the gate Republicans! Realacrats do not want to be identified with Republicans any more than Republicans want to be identified with Realacrats. You think you have God on your side, but Realacrats believe you have your customized version of God on your side. You think you own the Christian religion, but Realacrats wonder how the Christian religion could ever own you. You think you have the best policies for the people. Realacrats believe you only have the best policies for your people. It seems that everything has to be about your people or your team's agenda. It's either your way or the highway. Compromising is for the weak, and dropping bombs is for the strong. You're either with the conservative movement or you're a socialist, a communist, or Hitler! The Republican/conservative idea of compromise is agreeing with everything they say, because they have the moral high ground, as Democrats come moping over with their tails between their legs fearing the Republican-based wrath of God. I haven't seen this much horse crap since I watched the droppings collector at the Kentucky Derby.

Again, I go back to the magnificent job done by Bill Clinton in North Korea to help garner the release of those two Asian-American journalists, with a major behind the scenes assist from the Obama administration! There were only a few Republican/conservative top dogs like Bill O'Reilly who had the political gumption to commend Clinton for his patriotic actions. The Republican brand as a whole just could not muster enough humility to embrace Bill Clinton's positive influence around the world. Maybe, Republicans are jealous because they just can't rally such support for themselves around the world or anywhere outside of NASCAR, the NRA, or the conservative Christian movements. There is nothing more pathetic than a party or a person who simply cannot manage to look beyond their wounded ego enough to recognize a good thing when they see one. This is the type of blindness that must be avoided at all costs, because no party is too high and mighty to acknowledge a positive display, not even the Republicans/conservatives. You know; things look and smell much better once you take your "Party of No" head out of your political ass!

Republicans and Their Tactics

I, like most other people in the country, watched the campaign trail in 2008. I watched the Republican National Convention, and I also watched the Democratic National Convention. The one thing I noticed about the Republicans was their constituents. The whole thing reminded me of the empire from the Star Wars series. As the cameras scanned the crowd, all of the faces looked the same. It reminded me of the good-old-days when minorities were not allowed entry into public places; those days when everything and everybody was White. When I hear conservatives yell and scream about conservatism, is this the concept with which they are trying to reunite the country? Conservatives just fail to come across as open people. The more I looked at the Republican convention, the more I felt out of place. There was a vibe that made me feel unwelcome, and I'm sure I was not the only non-White who felt it. Where is the diversity? All I kept seeing was rich, well-to-do, older White men. I didn't see or hear anything during that convention that caused me to even remotely consider joining the conservative movement or The Republican Party! The scene was reminiscent of the 1950s and 1960s. I don't see how this is at all inviting to any groups outside the Republican niche. Rallying your base at the expense of new growth is a stalemate, and stalemates don't win elections. This tactic of White male dominance is definitely dated at best and should be jettisoned at once. The tactic of not wanting change should also be jettisoned, because running into a brick wall shows determination and fearlessness, but it also shows a colossal lack of vision.

The Republican Party resorted to mediocre tactics to fight Barack Obama during the election of 2008. They are very good at spreading confusion, and they were excellent at disseminating misinformation. Instead of elevating their own party platform, it seemed to me that they were more interested in fear mongering. Let this be a memo to conservatives: fear mongering is not a vision. It's often an illusion, a distraction, and eventually the masses will catch on to it. Sensationalism is a fantastic ploy in the moment, but its long-term effects are evanescent at best. It's similar to a sugar high! You feel great for a few minutes, but then you crash and burn. You cannot truly define yourself by strictly trying to redefine someone else. Pointing out the flaws in Plan B does not automatically mean plan A has integrity. Republicans and conservatives can align themselves on the right as much as they want, but I'd like to know what makes them think they are actually on the right. What are they on the right of? Subliminally speaking, I think they are claiming to be on the right side of every issue, but I find that narcissistic, self-assertion to be open to debate, and I would debate that the right is probably right of the true right. Realacrats will take the middle, because somewhere in the middle lies the truth, which is still to the left of the majority of conservatism.

The Republicans' Bad Rap

As Ole Dirty Bastard would suggest, I'm going to keep it real about my traditional African-American views of the Republican Party, which would equate to them being mean-spirited, divisive, elitist, and often uncomfortably too close to racism, but let's face facts here! The overwhelming majority of African-Americans in this country vote for the Democrats. As Al Sharpton once said at the 2004 Democratic National Convention, "We didn't get the mule. So we decided we'd ride this donkey as far as it would take us,"[4] and it has now taken us to the first African-American President of the United States of America, and the first African-American leader of free world. Conservatives have made the argument that the Democratic Party has done nothing for the African-American community; except take their votes for granted. Republicans claimed that African-Americans made little or noprogress under the Democrats, and African-Americans might as well be tossing their support into a political vacuum for all the good that Democrats have done for African-American communities. This is an agenda that only points out what your opponent has done wrong; rather than decreeing what you plan to do right, but the Democratic Party nominated the first African-American for president in history; so much for the Democratic Party not doing anything for the African-American community. That was a lame talking point anyway. Honestly, when I envision a Republican, the image that comes to mind is a racist, redneck, opulent, overindulgent, self-appointed, self-righteous, dishonest, White-culture-superiority-complex-having class monger or some Tea Partier with a racist sign. I am not alone in my views, whether they are right or wrong, because perception is reality! The perception of Republicans held in African-American communities, Asian-American communities, Hispanic-American communities, Arab-American communities, Cuban-American communities, and Native American communities is non-inclusive, snooty, standoffish, and frigid at best.

4 The Associated Press, **Al Sharpton's remarks at the Democratic convention,** http://www.usatoday.com/news/politicselections/nation/president/2004-07-29-sharpton-speech-text_x.htm **(7/29/2004)**

Whether these feelings are well founded is not the point. It is possible that such impressions of Republicans are trumped up more by myth than fact, but the issue remains the same. The GOP brand has been socially and racially tarnished, and it will prove to be painstakingly difficult to rehabilitate. Growing up in the African-American community taught me exactly what to think about Republicans. The general rules about them were very straightforward. Republicans are for the rich, especially rich White people! Republicans are against the poor! Republicans are against African-Americans—rich or poor! Republicans are against all minorities! Republicans pollute the environment with their filthy factory waste just to get richer. Republicans are war mongers! Republicans are religious zealots. Republicans believe God is White! Republicans believe only Whites will get into the White heaven. Republicans have secret alliances with skinheads, the Ku Klux Klan, and the racist law enforcement! Republicans hate gay marriage! Republicans especially hate interracial marriage! Republicans are out to destroy the middle-class, because there are far too many African-Americans finding their way into it. Republicans want to cut welfare to help keep poor African-Americans and other minorities stuck in poverty! Republicans hate to see African-American athletes who manage to accumulate enormous amounts of money playing sports. Republicans believe White culture is the only culture. Republicans hate Darwin's theory of evolution, because it makes all of humanity a porch monkey, not just the African-Americans. Republicans had a secret pact with Hitler! Republicans hold a secret legislation once every 25 years to try and resurrect slavery! Republicans secretly finance the drug trade and funnel it into poor minority neighborhoods, and Republicans are against universal health care, because they don't want poor African-Americans and other minorities to have it.

Here is a joke I heard just the other day. Republicans are all about family values, especially the kind that keeps African-Americans out of their family! Now I know the right is going to be in a firestorm over these harsh accusations, and many will blame their origins strictly on me for bringing it to the forefront! I guess none of these political, urban legends ever existed until I wrote about them in this book. It's Bryian's fault! He's slandering us, which is one more thing that I've heard Republicans love to do; blame the messenger and not the author.

I personally don't give a rat's ass if you blame me. I'm just enlightening the masses, like the Notorious B.I.G. would suggest: "If you don't know; now you know!"

The Essence of Conservatism

Republicans are very much like political hogs guarding the political, slop trough, and they quickly become inflamed when someone other than the status quo slips through the cracks to grab a seat at the political, slop trough, especially if this individual happens to be non-White or a woman. It was the Democrats who first put a woman on the ticket back in 1984, with Geraldine Ferraro running alongside presidential nominee Walter Mondale. The recent undeniable political savvy of Secretary of State Hillary Clinton, who is my all-time favorite candidate, finally forced the Republican Party to re-think its political game plan on women as potential presidential and vice-presidential candidates, and everyone in the country knew it immediately. Hillary Clinton's 18 million votes single-handedly changed the traditional gender based policy of the GOP. Once again, Republicans and conservatives made it a standard to downplay and overlook Hillary Clinton's political prowess, because they would rather pull out their teeth with a set of rusty pliers than to have to acknowledge the building momentum behind the female candidate galvanized by Hillary Clinton. Charlatans of the Republican Party will swoon to Sarah Palin's side to try, and dispute these claims of gender railroading, but like I said before, the world knows it was Hillary Clinton's historic candidacy that unveiled the true possibilities of the female candidacy. She exclusively kicked that door in for Sarah Palin, and for that reason, I was very ecstatic that Sarah Palin didn't become the first, female vice-president. In essence, the Democratic Party set the pace for future political contests, and this includes the Republicans as well, and I don't think, for one minute; that the American people were sleepwalking through all of this. The Democratic Party's tolerance and open-mindedness in the political spectrum has become a game changer, whether the Republicans acknowledge it or not. The American voters have obviously accepted it, and that is all that truly matters.

If by some fluke, Sarah Palin, Michele Bachmann, or possibly some other, female, Democratic or Independent candidate either becomes vice president or president, it will be the great Hillary Clinton's 18 million cracks in that proverbial, misogynistic, glass ceiling that paved the way for it to happen, but not by any stretch of the imagination does conservatism deserve one iota of visionary credit for it! It was John McCain who reached outside of the box in a Democratic way; giving you, Sarah Palin, the jumpstart to your career! The same John McCain who was criticized then, and remains criticized now by core conservatives for being too liberal! You think about that Sarah "The Palinator" Palin! If you can't realize that it was the Democratic/liberal, ideological gesture of the female pick that freed you and every other potential, conservative, female candidate from the ideological shackles of conservative limitations, then you more than live up to the stereotypical, hick-driven portrayals of your character in the media!

And furthermore Sarah Palinator, in case you're too close to the political fire to properly feel the conservative, good-ole-boy heat, allow me to democratically help you get it. Many of those old, conservative men of a certain hue that is strikingly similar to yours aren't as supportive of you as you probably have been lead to believe they are. This was a statement made in a room full of Republicans, Tea Partiers, conservatives, and almost definitely; a few undercover Klansmen. The ringleader of the pick-up truck mafia said this to the group: "That old Barack Osama ain't nothing but a terrorist, a Muslim, and a Kenyan. I ain't voting for that nigger! McCain's too liberal! And as far as that Palin woman goes, I'd cast my ballot in her before I'd ever cast it for her. She's not fit to lead, but she's most certainly fit to lay!" I just felt that you should know that Sarah Palinator!

And as for the Democrats, what more can I say? You come up with a bold, new initiative to reach out to women as political players with Geraldine Ferraro and Hillary Clinton, but then you fail to capitalize on the moment, by allowing Sarah Palin to come within one step of the vice-presidency. The conservative movement will siphon every ounce of female, candidacy credit if one of their conservative women crosses that proverbial threshold of the White House first, and to me; that is the apex of political incompetence and political gullibility by the haphazard Democrats! They come up with the invention, but the conservatives and Republicans steal away the copyright, the patent, the credit, and the political payoff for it! This is one of the main reasons why I became a Realacrat. In my eyes, any conservative, female presidency or vice-presidency is a slap in the face to the Democratic voters, the Democratic movement, and the Democratic, female candidates; and I place the poetic injustice of such a folly squarely on the shoulders of Barack Obama and possibly Howard Dean, because I am absolutely convinced that the Democratic base was ready, willing and determined to launch the female candidate into historical, political orbit. If the conservative movement is able to legitimize the female candidacy with a White House occupation, then you, President Barack Obama, have failed in my book!

As I said before, Republicans haven't exactly led the way on political openness to other ethnic groups. They were slow to move on women, and they were slow to move on African-Americans. Their failure to recruit African-Americans in this country is a monumental flaw. To have a guy like Colin Powell at your dispense for years, and then fail to utilize his political and military resume, is an absolute calamity. Colin Powell was the perfect ethnic candidate and the Republicans had him long before Barack Obama appeared on the scene. Their inability, or reluctance, to be bold and inspiring has come back to haunt them, because there is no legitimate reasoning for not promoting Colin Powell. How does a team have that kind of rare talent and still allow it to remain unused in the safety of political adequacy. Powell is a star quarterback in the making, but his team decides to put him in as wide receiver or fullback. Is this ignorance, or is this purposeful? If it is purposeful, what purpose does it fulfill? Why would you take a leader, and groom him to be a follower? I remember when a high-ranking, Republican Congressman was asked about Colin Powell as a possible presidential candidate for the Republican Party, he replied that he didn't know if Colin Powell was a real Republican. He thought Powell was too much of wild card and a radical. That statement hit the nail squarely on the head. Within the Republican Party, there is a far-rightist, religious zealot ideology that fears change. At that time, this conservative mentality could not, would not, and did not accept the ascent of any African-American, any woman, or any non-White candidate as a would-be selection for the Republican nominee for President of the United States. I call it the Dark Ages movement, because it is stoked in the past and is woeful of the future in a place where the ruling premise is a return to the good-old-days, but exactly whose good-old-days are we returning to? African-

Americans, Native Americans and Hispanic Americans are not prone to finding very many good-old-days in this country. The good-old-days would be prosperous for John McCain and Rush Limbaugh, but the good-old-days for minorities would be distraught by most accounts. It should not be hard to conceive why the majority of minorities want no part of the good-old-days or any party promising a return to them.

The Republicans simply have not had the balls to anoint politicians like a Colin Powell or Condoleezza Rice as their party's presidential candidates, in fear of alienating that enormous conservative, religious zealot base of theirs. Now I see why Bill Maher is so disappointed in religion/religious based politics, because it's only fair at promoting one agenda, by one particular group; a far cry from true democracy. One political group having that much influence is more like a monarchy or a unit dictatorship, and the disinclination to challenge this hysterical, dominating, egocentric, self-righteous, self-serving, close-minded, future-fearing, Jim Crow–longing, White Jesus–imaging, White man dominance–advocating, ethnic-pecking-order–providing, tenebrous-treatment-of-women's-rights–loving coup, is because anyone who dares to speak out against this 800-pound absolutist gorilla is a traitor to the cause, and must be exiled from the political good graces of the Republican Party!

The Punking of John McCain

During the 2008 presidential campaign, John McCain mulled over his vice-presidential campaign pick. I'm sure John McCain was perfectly capable of making this choice by his own accord, at least, he should have been; after all, this was his campaign to win or to lose. He was the GOP nominee for President of United States. The Realacrat ideology would let John McCain, or any other political candidate, make his or her decisions. Isn't that what a president has to be prepared to do? Nevertheless, conservatives all over the country began to bicker about McCain's oncoming pick, which was to be expected. Party members have every right to voice their opinions on whom they believe to be best suited for the vice-presidential slot. But, they do not have the right to impose or enforce their own personal, political, puppet master tactics, with the hopes of squeezing John McCain or any other candidate to do their political bidding at the cost of being blackballed as a candidate in the coming election. Who in the hell do the Limbaugh legion think they are to make demands to John McCain about who he'd better or better not choose as a vice-presidential pick? Now, I can see how the 800-pound gorilla scenario came to pass, which is 800 pounds in politically influencing bullying power. Rush Limbaugh's weight is irrelevant. It is his undeniable iron-claw on the Republican brand that is ten times more intimidating and ten times more important. Realacrats would spend more time addressing Limbaugh's talk radio legions instead of his waistline. As for John McCain, he always touted himself as a peacenik, a non-conformist, and a maverick, but he buckled under the relentless pressure of the Limbaugh legion by passing on Joe Lieberman and Tom Ridge. The Limbaugh legion had already given McCain the thumbs down to both of these candidates. According to the Limbaugh legion, the vice-presidential candidate had to be pro-life, with no exceptions, and they then threatened to lead a revolt against McCain at the polls if he did not heed this dictum. McCain followed his marching orders and tapped a pro-lifer named Sarah Palin as his running mate—so much for the maverick. Mavericks don't buckle, and mavericks don't ask how high when they're asked to jump by some over hyped, overzealous, politically vainglorious windbag.

One of John McCain's best moments during the campaign trail occurred at one of the debates, when he confronted Barack Obama about Obama's constant comparisons between McCain and President Bush. Obama's campaign theme tied McCain to President Bush at every opportune moment on every opportune issue, and it was wildly successful. McCain was slow to respond to Obama's claims, but I think it was during the third and final debate when John McCain finally asserted his strong, non-conformist independence as he shot back at Barack Obama by replying: "I am not President Bush! If you wanted to run against President Bush, then you should have run for President four years ago!"[5] McCain was no longer going to allow Barack Obama to paint him into a corner, so he came out swinging, and I would argue, began to build some momentum. McCain showed the world that he was his own man and not President Bush's puppet or lap dog. This is the type forcefulness we all like to see in a presidential candidate, but

5 CNN, McCain Puts Obama on the Spot in Final Debate, http://www.cnn.com/2008/POLITICS/10/15/presidential.debate/index.html#cnnSTCText (October 2008).

in reality, it is much easier to stand up and assert your strength against your opponent than it is to do the same to dissenting members of your own party, particularly when one of those dissenting members is an 800-pound iron claw that leads with an iron fist. I think the American people wanted to see McCain man up to Rush Limbaugh the same way that he manned up against Barack Obama during the debate, and it did not happen. McCain could not muster the necessary spunk to bite the hand that fed him, even if this was the same hand that was threatening to slap the political conservativeness off of his face if he didn't toe-the-line. Choosing a running mate was a golden opportunity for McCain to show the world exactly who would be in charge of the Republican Party and the executive office; instead, he bowed to more group dictatorship.

If John McCain were a Realacrat, he would have told the Limbaugh legion to shut it, because he didn't owe anyone an explanation about his choice for a running mate. If talk radio hosts were so gung-ho to pick the vice-presidential nominee, then they should have run for president; otherwise, shut the hell up! A statement like this is basically the same concept used against Barack Obama when McCain told Obama he should have run against President Bush. By not doing this, in political terms, he appeared to concede to the conservative pressure! This is why Monday morning quarterbacks always wait until Monday morning before they decide to weigh in with their two cents, because it's certainly easier to make decisions when the consequences of those decisions don't fall on you. Being a presidential candidate is nice and cozy when you have the luxury of doing it from within a radio booth. Limbaugh wants to sit in the stands and call plays where it's safe. If the play doesn't work, the blame falls solely on McCain or Bush. Limbaugh is the type of character who is always quick to remind people just how talented he is through some long, winded conversation, though he's usually conspicuous by his absence, when it's time to suit up and hit the field. It allows Limbaugh to permanently position himself as the criticizer without ever landing in the position to be criticized. I call that the coziest job in the world. Surely, McCain should have seen through this, and surely, other Republicans should have seen through this as well. I will now make another bold prediction. Whoever emerges out of the Republican Party and blazes a true independent path, even if it means blazing right over Rush Limbaugh's political chaperoning, will be the one to lead the GOP in its long-awaited return to glory. I don't see how the Republican Party can have the redemption it yearns for until this happens. As for John McCain's failed presidential bid, he should have taken a page out of Frank Sinatra's book, and done it his way, so that he could live up to his self-appointed maverick status. In the ideology of former Dallas Cowboys coach Jimmy Johnson, if you're gonna talk the talk, then you gotta walk the walk! For John McCain, this statement couldn't be more applicable. Part of being a maverick is having the guts to take risks, having the guts to gamble, having the guts to bet the farm and having the guts to call out the bluff of an 800-pound, political, big, bad wolf, because there is more than a good chance that, as President, you will find yourself having to repeat this same scenario in a competitive world filled with big, bad wolves!

Why I Don't Hope All Republicans Fail

Do you remember when Rush Limbaugh made the statement about Barack Obama's presidency? He said the now infamous quote, "I Hope Obama fails,"[6] but if Barack fails; the country fails with him. Fortunately for Rush, his chums are better equipped to cushion their fall. The average American is already failing, failing miserably, and failing at an all-time high, even without the downward spiral wished upon President Obama by conservatives, such as Rush Limbaugh. I guess Rush wants to see things go even further down the toilet. They say, when in Rome, do as the Romans do, but when in America, the conservatives say, kick a person when they're down and further impoverish those who are already impoverished, and Republicans wonder why they are often tagged as mean-spirited? In the spirit of Eric "Eazy-E" Wright, I must say that I am not an f'n Republican-you know! I clearly am not, was not, and have no future plans to be a Republican, but even as a die-hard Democrat, I never wished for Republicans, such as President Ronald Reagan, to fail. I liked him about as much as I like any other Republican, which is very little to not at all, but hoping for his political suicide was not my game plan. I thought Ronald Reagan did an excellent job in his foreign policies regarding the former Soviet Union. It was the biggest threat

6 Rush Limbaugh, Limbaugh: I Hope Obama Fails, http://www.rushlimbaugh.com/home/daily/site_011609/content/01125113.guest.html. (January 2009).

facing the United States at the time, and Reagan went toe-to-toe with Soviet President Mikhail Gorbachev on many occasions; out dueling him in the end. Reagan exhibited strength and courage during a time of great uncertainty. The proliferation of nuclear weapons created a very dangerous environment, and I thought Reagan met that challenge head on. Reagan's persuasion of Gorbachev to tear down the Berlin Wall was possibly his greatest triumph. In the end, Reagan garners the highest praise from me for one main reason, and it is one of the most misunderstood reasons of all time in regards to governing effectively! The mere fact that President Reagan was willing to at least sit down with Mikhail Gorbachev was a very cooperative, political gesture, and Gorbachev deserves just as much credit for exemplifying the elegance of diplomacy first. In the spirit of the Reagan-Gorbachev summits, President Obama and Iranian leader, Ahmadinejad, should strongly consider following suite. Ahmadinejad might make bizarre threats about nuking other countries, but Gorbachev actually had the nuclear weaponry to back it up, so a long, fireside chat between Ahmadinejad and President Obama should not be out of the question. I also believe that his "Star Wars" project was way ahead of its time and could become effective somewhere down in the not-so-distant future.

I never wished that President George H.W. Bush would fail. I thought he was out of touch with the American people, but I didn't think he deserved to be politically flat-lined for it. I did not vote for President George W. Bush either. In retrospect, I somewhat do wish that he had failed. In fact, I absolutely wished that he had failed, but only on his cataclysmic endeavor into Iraq. I did not agree with the war in Iraq, but I did not wish for an American demise at the cost of American troops, because it is the troops who would be the ones to suffer for it. I wish specifically that former President George W. Bush had failed in his bid to raise public support for his occupying mission in Iraq. Nevertheless, I thought President Bush's push for immigration reform was a step in the right direction to at least begin addressing the situation, and I didn't root for him to fail in that area.

I didn't hope for Sarah Palin to fail in Alaska, and I don't hope that John McCain fails in the Senate, but I do hope that Rush Limbaugh fails to open his toxic waste dump of a mouth to make any more wishes. It's this sort of rhetoric that makes the Republican Party seem childish, erratic, and irresponsible. On one hand, they say they are in it to put the country first. McCain used this phrase as his campaign stump speech slogan. Conservatives rallied around it, but now they all rally around Rush Limbaugh, as they wish failure on that same country they were supposed to put first, all because Barack Obama was elected over John McCain. The Republicans remind me of the neighborhood crybaby from my old childhood days. Remember the snotty kid who would take his ball and go home if you didn't play the way he wanted you to? The Republicans are the same way. They only push hard for the country to succeed when it's their people that are in charge of it. Otherwise, they become the party of no. They take their political football, and go home. For whatever reason, Democrats just don't seem to be as negative about Republicans, and furthermore, Democrats also seem to be more willing to give credit to their opposition when credit is due.

Republican Potential

If I had to begrudgingly pick a Republican candidate for 2012 whom I could actually consider casting my ballot for, it would be Mike Huckabee. He is, hands down, the most logical and most sensible Republican out there. If it wasn't for his religious bias, he could be a Democrat or a Realacrat. I still think he would have been the better opponent for Barack Obama in the 2008 election. If Republicans weren't so pussy-whipped by Rush and his Limbaugh legion, they would have given Huckabee the nomination over John McCain. If I was Mike Huckabee, I would consider becoming an independent!

I think Mitt Romney would have been a fair number two pick for John McCain, because I'm not sold on Romney's ability to be a formidable number one candidate. I don't really care for any of his bland ideas of conservatism, and his religious background does not help him, and I mean; within in his own party, it does not help him. Realacrats and Democrats don't really care what religion he believes in. His economic background should at least be enough to corral him a top cabinet position in the next Republican presidential administration. If Mitt Romney could be trusted to focus solely on economics only, The Realacrat Party would consider sitting down with Romney to have a discussion on economics, but there is one small order of business that would always stand in the way, and that would be the existence of blatant racism in parts of the Mormon doctrine, and Romney's perceived reluctance to clarify his stance on the Mormon doctrine. Democrats may not want to know, and Republicans probably already know, but Realacrats want to hear it from Romney!

Mitt Romney should be called out publicly to make a statement expressing his agreement or disagreement on parts of the Mormon doctrine such as these: "**And the Lord had caused the cursing to come upon them; that they might not be enticing unto my people the Lord God did cause a skin of blackness to come upon them.**"[7] It is one thing to criticize or condemn what could be perceived as a half-assed, governmental, ideological policy that has annually failed to make real change in ethnic communities around America, but it's a completely different ball game to make assertions of God cursing pigmentation with blackness and blessing pigmentation with whiteness! In my opinion, the Mormon religion might as well be saying God Damn the Blacks simply for being Black, and if Mitt Romney either believes this or refuses to stand in opposition of this pigmentation, curse non-sense, then he owes the world an apology for impersonating a human being. Realacrats are not asking Romney to abandon his Mormon beliefs, but we do expect a sane, articulate man to have the ability to realize that certain interpretations of the Mormon doctrine have obviously been corrupted the same way parts of the Bible, and other religious documents, have also been corrupted! Realacrats will never give human DNA a free pass to perfection on any subject, because it is the existence of our imperfections that makes our DNA human!

I think U.S. Senator Bob Corker from Tennessee is full of political potential, and I was not a Bob Corker fan. I supported Harold Ford Jr. for Tennessee senator, and I was not happy when Corker defeated Ford Jr. for the seat in 2006. Nevertheless, I have to tip my hat to the commendable job that Bob Corker has been doing in the Senate. He, like Massachusetts Senator Scott Brown and apparently South Carolina Senator Lindsey Graham, appears to be his own man with his own train of thought, who will vote his beliefs over political talking points. I don't hope any of these senators fail! I hope they manage to get something done that will actually help the people. As much as I dislike most

7 Mormon Racist Doctrine, **Mormon scripture: God curses bad races with black skin, http://www.i4m.com/think/history/mormon_racism.htm.**

Republicans, the courage, professionalism, and individuality needed to work across the partisan isle in today's society should be appreciated apart from party lines!

As for Fred Thompson, I wouldn't vote for him to be the neighborhood dogcatcher! I wouldn't vote for Fred Thompson to be the head greeter/welcoming hand-shaker at Wal-Mart! He needs to return to the back of the line quick, fast, and in a hurry! Fred Thompson reminds me of the conservative Grinch who stole the minority Christmas.

Republicans like Minnesota Governor Tim Pawlenty, Louisiana Governor Bobby Jindal, Congressman Ron Paul, and possibly Senator Scott Brown, who I believe gives the right the best chance to win back the White house, especially if he tells Rush Limbaugh to kiss his ass, all represent new Republican leadership, despite standing in the shadow of more glamorous candidates like Sarah Palin. Even though new contenders such as Ron Paul have far more to offer politically and ideologically, they cannot defeat Sarah Palin in a political beauty pageant, which means in all likelihood, substance will be passed over for style and flashiness. It's more about who looks good in front of the camera than it is about who manufactures the camera, and Republicans have no one else to blame for that but themselves. The Republicans do have some talented candidates left in their stable, but until the Junior Head of the Republican Party, Michael Steele, stops getting his marching orders from the Senior Head of the Republican Party, Rush Limbaugh and his apprentice in training, Glenn Beck, the party will continue to nominate yes men and yes women instead of good, authentic candidates. In my opinion, Michael Steele is nothing more than a "Look, we got a Black one too, America" anti-racism prop. So, the chances of him putting forth any real leadership without dictation from the puppet master is highly unlikely, because there are too many lackeys, footmen, and ideological poltroons marching to the beat. Get me the hell out of here!

Again, this all reminds me of the Colin Powell pass-over. As much as I don't agree with Michael Steele's ideologically, at least not on everything, I am man enough to admit just how intelligent, how upstanding, how strong, how independently thinking, how organizational, and how potentially adroit he could be as a leader—if given the opportunity to do so. The Realacrat Party would never resort to the deployment of someone like Michael Steele as a trivial, gimmicky, anti-racism figurehead. If that's the best the Republican Party and the conservative movement can do, they will continue to dubiously live up to every anti-minority accusation and characterized racial flaw habitually hurled at them. They fear being challenged, because facing one's fears is life, while surrendering to one's fears is death!

And now for Sarah Palin, who as a potential presidential candidate could be the most popular Republican candidate of all time. Well, I can understand why so many like her. After all, she is cute, but that's about it! Besides, I think Todd Palin is the gas that makes that engine run behind the Wizard of Oz curtains, and she is just the pretty face that goes out to sell the product—which just happens to be more of the same old conservative/religious crap, at least some of what Mike Huckabee says makes sense. If Sarah Palin wasn't so pretty, she wouldn't even be in the conversation, because her conversations are severely lacking in political substance, and that is because she is poorly coached. She is the female version of Dallas Cowboys quarterback Tony Romo. All the girls want to be with Romo, and all of the guys want to bed Sarah Palin, but both have struggled significantly to produce winning results when they have been needed the most. It's as if their popularity surpasses their actual abilities more than their abilities seem to surpass their popularity. Sarah Palin can become a formidable political opponent, but she'll need a team far more competent than John McCain's former team, which was a complete campaign monstrosity! Otherwise, she will continue to look like the Alaskan yokel who wrote a hot check to Santa Clause for a used reindeer that she could shoot from a helicopter while looking at Russia on some bridge to nowhere in her own backyard! Palin needs to be surrounded by the right team of handlers who have the political experience to guide her into contention, because being pretty is not enough. She'll need to be just as politically savvy and worldly conscious as she is pretty.

Realacrats see the potential political roadblock that Sarah Palin could provide on the next available route to the White House in 2012, but her campaign is still a work in progress, and the desired results all depend on the Palin campaign's visionary leadership and their packaging creativity. So, while many of the Democrats and liberals promenade around laughing at the current version of Sarah Palin, Realacrats have identified the target audience of this Palin/Republican/Tea Party movement. Sarah Palin's role in the Republican Party is a crafty and cagey maneuver aimed squarely at the re-roundup of White Americans and White American ideology. Daylight for dummies may not get it, but Realacrats can see the whole agenda. After all, it was clear to Realacrat ideology that Sarah Palin was not, under any circumstances, reaching out or talking to non-Whites when she continuously addressed the Joe Plumbers and Joe Six-Packs of the world. President Obama, in a miraculous triumph, was able to acquire huge numbers of White supporters; far more than anyone ever thought he could. Historically, it was thought to be a fact that no African-American/non-White could ever garner such political support, but his Russian roulette maneuver was successful, much to the chagrin of conservatives. If this proves to be a trend and not a fluke, the GOP will be on the fast track to political unemployment. So, they have enlisted Sarah Palin's services to re-attract the pro-Obama White voters back over to the conservative side. With President Obama as the likely candidate of the 2012 Democrat Party, Republicans believe there is no way he can win without the enormous White voting support that Sarah Palin is jockeying him for right now. There are many who often regard Sarah Palin as a loose cannon and a buffoon, but the possible success of her tactical and methodical ploy to weaken the Obama support system is nothing to be laughed at by Democrats.

The Ethnic Dilemma

Not a Minority in Sight

Some of the most important things the Realacrat Party will focus on is tolerance, understanding, and inclusion for all people. I say this because the historical domination of pro-white European culture is being passed off as the only authentic American culture, as if no other culture is worthy enough to make the cut. I pay attention to the world around me, and I have a keen eye for details. I noticed the minuscule number of minority CEOs during the great banking collapse of 2008, and I also noticed the almost non-existent number of minorities representing Wall Street during that same time period. When the CEOs from the big three American auto-companies flew in on private jets to beg Congress for bailout money, I again realized that minorities were noticeably missing in action—and it doesn't stop there. The entire cultural landscape has been broadly painted with a White/non-minority brush. The next time you're in a store, look at the dominant faces on all of the magazines, especially *People*. I call all of this the Brad Pitt/George Clooney effect, the *Friends* effect, the *Seinfeld* effect, the *Everybody Loves Raymond* effect, the Fox News effect, and especially the Bill O'Reilly culture warrior effect.

I witnessed complete White domination in all of these subjects. For example, every year I look at the most beautiful people lists compiled by popular magazines to see if any minorities are included. A couple of African-Americans like Denzel Washington and Will Smith perennially make the list, but other than those two; the huge African-American talent pool goes largely unnoticed, and other minorities go even more unnoticed. When is the last time you saw an established recognizable Native American on a magazine cover? How about an Asian American? If not for extraordinary talents like Jennifer Lopez, Sean "Puffy" Combs, Tiger Woods, Venus and Serena Williams, Lucy Liu, Jet Li, and other strong overachieving minority candidates, it would be a total whitewash of culture and literary opportunities, and this message appears to be prevalent throughout all of this second-class labeling of the non-White community and non-White genetics. It's the inner-workings of a society that always finds a way to apply the ideal standards of beauty to a Brett Farve, a Tom Brady, or a George Clooney, while every other non-White celebrity/athlete is swept under the, "Well, Kobe Bryant looks good for a Black guy," rug. That statement, in my mind, is every bit as racially heinous as calling someone a nigger! It treats my pigmentation like a missing limb or a deformity, and that is nothing more than an old, Jim Crow, scare tactic aimed at societally tarring and feathering any possibility of an African-American as a worthy sex symbol to the White community, especially to the White woman. This country has been systematically set up to know that minorities are present, but at the same time, ignore them to the fullest, until they are forced to acknowledge their existence. This allows Whiteness to be lifted to the apex of American society, further alienating minorities from the table of humanity, including the world of politics.

Every other night I see Bill O'Reilly promoting his icons of American culture, which are almost always White. I have seen Bill Cosby and Demond Wilson represented, because I was curious as to just how long it would take O'Reilly to show an African-American/minority entertainment icon; seeing as how I am bombarded with John Wayne and Clint Eastwood every other week. What is so special about John Wayne? You grew up on John Wayne. I grew up on John Wayne too, because he was the only game in town on the cowboy landscape; a landscape in which Native Americans were not even allowed to play Native Americans. Where are the Black cowboys in your culture warrior fan club? Oh, that's right! Blacks couldn't play cowboys back then either, because they couldn't get the roles. Minorities as a whole were completely shut out of the process. Are these those highly touted good-ole-days you conservatives like hoist up all the time? I find it misleading how White actors are still trumpeted as American heroes with the full knowledge that it was because other minorities were denied the opportunity to participate. It sends out the wrong message. It sends a message of White, cultural superiority. People believe their guys were the best cowboys because their guys were the only cowboys. Now it was either because they were the only ones with amazing acting talent, or it was because of favoritism, and I would argue the latter. Is John Wayne really the best Indian and cowboy killer of all time, or does the distinction belong to Clint Eastwood? Why don't we ask the Native Americans to share their feelings about American, cowboy culture, including John Wayne, Clint Eastwood, and the old Hollywood westerns that infamously excluded them from roles they could have played? Why don't we ask the Native Americans who they consider to be their best Native American exterminator? Those same films used Native American culture as a doormat symbol for all that was evil, barbaric, and boorish, while raising the pedestal of the White, colonial pioneers as God loving, God fearing, peaceful civilians, when they were everything but that, as they ravaged the land, the eco-systems, and the Native American way of life. Remember, it was the Native Americans who provided the first government-like bailout, as they pulled the pilgrims out of total debt! The next time you're having Thanksgiving dinner you should think about that, because I seriously doubt that there are actually people in this country who have ever thought about giving thanks to the Native Americans on turkey day. In fact, I demand that the Federal government immediately begins inviting Native Americans to the White House every Thanksgiving to remind many of the younger, grossly overconfident, and grossly uninformed Americans about the patriotism of the Native Americans, which made Thanksgiving possible. Speaking as a Realacrat, if the country can pardon a turkey, then surely it can show more gratitude towards the Native Americans for pardoning the country!

Hollywood ostentatiously distorted the historical imagery and ethical behavior of the Old West to satisfy and pacify its White constituents. Now Bill O'Reilly's culture warriors are doing the exact same thing all over again, by not exposing the one-sided, completely biased, scandalized, culture discountenance of Native Americans and other minorities, while the American cowboys are painted as patriots of manifest destiny—even though many of them were nothing more than train robbers, cattle thieves, pillagers, scoundrels, rapist, bank robbers, and murderous outlaws. I even saw a question about General George Armstrong Custer once. Does Custer deserve a pass in history, because the United States government employed him? Does this make him a patriot and an American hero too? I can see many differences between Custer, John Wayne, and Clint Eastwood, but I do see one peculiar similarity: they are all White men who tend to receive the patriotic nod more often than not. Are you telling me there weren't any minority actors out there who could have killed just as many Indians and cowboys as John Wayne? Are you saying that if the White audiences had looked up at their screens to see a Chinese cowboy riding into town with a couple of Black cowboys, they would have turned off their televisions? I'll answer that question for you: absolutely! This is why John Wayne gets the go ahead. The audiences he catered to were White. The studios were White. The actors and writers were White. The advertisers were White. The networks were White. The movie theaters were White. The literary critics were White. The themes were White, and the viewpoints were White. This reminds me of the Republican Party today.

In regards to all of this whiteness, it brings to mind this saying, "Power tends to corrupt, and absolute power tends to corrupt absolutely!" John Wayne and Clint Eastwood were given the benefit of the doubt because they were White; the same way affirmative action opponents claim African-Americans may be given a job today simply because they are African-American. I guess you could call it the White man's affirmative action, but the only difference in the African-American's defense is the fact that none of those institutions that helped and promoted the White actors like Wayne and Eastwood were ever pro-African-American/minority. Affirmative action was designed so that the White John Wayne's and Clint Eastwood's could no longer monopolize the markets. It was a microcosm of White domination throughout the American landscape. Without affirmative action or some sense of morality similar to it, I don't believe the White domination would have ever corrected itself. Why would you expect power to self-regulate itself? That would be like expecting a slop hog to regulate itself at a buffet trough. It's not going to happen. Does this scenario sound eerily familiar? Does the 2008 economic collapse ring a bell? Almost 99 percent of the time, an outside independent source is required to stand in and oppose the status quo's greed and decadence, in order to cause any sort of change. If Wayne and Eastwood are American icons, then so are those first African-American/minority actors who made those first important steps into Hollywood, because they had to fight their way in and then fight their way back out, whereas Wayne and Eastwood took the train. The fact that O'Reilly and his cronies continue to brag about this model of American culture is iniquitous, dogmatic, sectarian, and mountainously slanted. I know O'Reilly understands the true history behind this slant, so what agenda is he trying to push here? There is nothing fair and balanced about this. Maybe he should just stick to reciting news-based facts, because the only reason he has the right to pick these White icons is the same reason those White icons were able to be ushered into Hollywood in the first place. O'Reilly is a White man working for a White network, just as Wayne and Eastwood were White men working for White networks. O'Reilly is taking the same train that Wayne and Eastwood rode in on to that exact same, slanted glory he continuously attributes to Wayne and Eastwood. Because he has his own show, it allows him to establish and perpetuate the ever-biased "My generation was the best" thesis. Whether it's the Beatles, the Rolling Stones, John Wayne, Marilyn Monroe, or Elvis Presley, they all get the nod because they were his childhood entertainers, so he has taken the liberty to anoint them as patriots and undisputed American icons. But the question remains: does his blind eye towards many of the minority talents of that very same time period warrant their exclusion from the patriot/American icons list? Are things to which you are not exposed to any less meaningful because of it? Maybe FOX News needs a minority anchor on the network with his own show to do his own alternative version of the culture warriors. I'll bet you that patriot/American icon list would be quite different from O'Reilly's. So which one is correct, which one is more patriotic? I don't know, and I'm not here to speculate on those questions because it does not matter. The Temptations are just as patriotic and just as much American icons as the Beach Boys. The question is not really based on patriotic authenticity or American icon courtship. It is based on one group selfishly propelling its own image as the primary, and in most cases, sole example of American culture, which is just another classic example of extreme, megalomaniacal posturing designed to sustain, attain, assert, and then reassert a historical and often ill-begotten perch atop the mountaintop of American ego-centrism.

As Chuck D of the hip hop group Public Enemy—a group that I hold in just as high of a regard as O'Reilly holds the Beach Boys in—pointed out during a concert in Memphis, Tennessee, that I was attending at the Pyramid in 1991: "If you going to pay homage to American heroes, then make sure you pay it to all of them, including the minority heroes. Elvis Presley and Marilyn Monroe represent true American heroes, but what about our heroes, minority heroes? What about our patriots? What about our American icons? It's high time they garner some recognition for a change, that's what we are sayin"—but this is what I am saying. How can Frederick Douglas not be an American icon? How can Geronimo not be an American icon? How can Dr. Martin Luther King Jr. not be a patriot? And for the record, I haven't seen much about Dr. King on the factor; any idea why? People from many different walks of life have contributed to the culture of the United States, but they are suspiciously absent from most gratitude sessions for some odd reason. It's that same good ol' boy system! The same system used to deny minorities in politics, voting, housing, education, social rankings, religious theory, dating rights, beautification and sexual preferences, employment opportunities, and economic abilities.

Reading Between the White Lines

There are many who would suggest that none of this is newsworthy, but Fox News promotes this agenda, and if they have a right to promote and endorse it, then I have a right to analyze and identify it for what it truly is—and that would be a very subtle, slanted agenda trending towards White American culture. It does not mean that Fox News does not report the news, because it does and so does CNN, but all of these media outlets have an underlying vibe they emit either consciously or subconsciously, and the vibe I get from CNN is one of tolerance and inclusiveness. So is it a coincidence that the majority of people in the Republican Party are White? Is it a coincidence that the majority of people protesting at health care rallies are White? Fox News would have you believe it is just a coincidence, but Realacrats aren't buying it, and neither should you. This is subliminal railroading, the same thing many Fox News henchmen accuse MSNBC of doing, but there is a huge difference between a liberal agenda and a conservative agenda! Within the liberal agenda, there is fertile ground in which to grow and nourish new relationships with new people, especially minorities. Liberal politics may not be the best fit for everything in life, but it is the best fit for race relations. As a Realacrat, I believe the conservative movement is the single most important thing stifling race relations in this country. No matter what Fox News might say, the conservative movement is not a unifying entity. The conservative movement is an ultimatum enforcer where the gates only swing open to strict distinctions devoid of unconditional acceptance.

According to Dictionary.com, one of the definitions for the word conservative is: disposed to preserve existing conditions, institutions, etc., or to restore traditional ones, and to limit change.

To minorities, especially African-Americans, it sounds like the struggles of civil rights movement all over again, and who in their right mind would want to go back to anything even remotely resembling that? It seems as if Republicans don't seem to understand is this one, simple aspect of the world. Their conservative views may work fairly well in the world of business, but as long as those views appear to be deeply entrenched in the dominant White culture at the cost of minority abandonment, you will have one party for White culture and one party for everyone else, which is essentially what we have today. The majority of minorities in this country will not join any party that helps to disable race relations by poorly enabling race relations. Thanks to the White, culture pedestal and the editorialized rhetoric of Fox News, the Democratic Party should have no worries about losing its overpowering numbers of African-American/minority demographic voting blocks.

ETHNICALLY CHALLENGED

First, Barack Obama is a terrorist and a socialist. Then, Judge Sotomayor is a corrupt policy-making judge and a reverse racist, just like Martin Luther King Jr. was a communist and Malcolm X was a Muslim spy. Republicans are masters at two things. They win elections, either by hook or by crook, and they spread misinformation about opposing candidates quicker than a gonorrhea outbreak. Judge Sotomayor is not a reverse racist, as stated by some idiotic Republicans. Now Rush

Limbaugh, on the other hand, could be a forward racist based on many of his distorted views on the rise of minorities to minimal prominence. Limbaugh accusing anyone of being racist is laughable! Rush Limbaugh's GOP, good ol' boy way of thinking has already cost the Republicans the White House in 2008, and If Republican Senators had continued to follow Limbaugh's line of politics on the Sotomayor conformational contingent, they could find themselves in trouble for the next mid-term Congressional Elections as well. Democrats already have control of both houses. What the hell was Rush thinking? The Hispanic vote already bailed on him during the 2008 presidential election. Was he trying to alienate them permanently? Do Republicans actually expect Hispanic-American citizens to get behind them and rally against one of their own? Do Republicans actually believe they can racially profile, racially condemn, and racially oust Judge Sonia Sotomayor, and then turn around and expect Hispanic voters to support them in any upcoming elections? Let me get this straight: a room filled with White, predominately male Senators got to make the historic decision on whether or not a Hispanic woman would finally get a seat at the good ol' boys table. This is America; the land of the free and the land of opportunity; the so-called melting pot of human existence, where everyone has a chance to make it. If this is true, why aren't there any Hispanic-Americans eligible to even have a say in this? Why aren't there any Hispanic-Americans in the Senate? They can't even vote on themselves. The old, White guys will have to let them in, if they are willing to do so. By my count, there is only one African-American in the Senate. The absence of social and ideological diversity in American, high society and American, high government is a strong testament to the severe lack of enthusiasm about drafting different ethnic groups for leadership roles. There is no "I" in the word "team." Incontestably, there is no Hispanic in the word team either, at least not in the American spelling of team--but why? Judge Sotomayor has proven herself in the judicial system. She's done so for many years now. She is no judicial fledgling, but noticeably; her qualifications often appear to be overshadowed by her ethnicity, because in spite of how smart, how highly-qualified, or how decorated a person of ethnicity may be; all such accolades and confidences can be automatically labeled as questionable or unsatisfactory depending on which ethnic background is prevalent, but Judge Sotomayor didn't just walk or swim across the Rio Grande yesterday, and then apply for the Supreme Court today. Yes, I know she's a Puerto Rican. I was only chiming in on the run-of-the-mill, local, yokel, redneck, deliverance doctrine that lumps all Hispanic-Americans into the illegal immigrant, wetback, border crossing, Mexican pool. Judge Sotomayor, like many other Hispanic-Americans, deserves a chance to participate and play for the team. It's time for the White, water fountain to quench some Hispanic-American and other minority thirsts. If you refuse to play alongside Judge Sotomayor due to your own personal, bigoted beliefs, then you are the one who should not be on the team.

The Wise Latina Women Comment

When I first began writing this book, Judge Sonya Sotomayor was only being vetted, but at this very moment she has been confirmed to the U.S. Supreme Court, despite drawing heavy fire from the Republicans about her "Wise Latina Woman" comment. Realacrats believe she made the point about how a wise Latina woman would be wiser than another mediocre, White man who is completely out of touch with the minority populations, especially in regards to minority based, environmental problems. But instead of seeing it for what it was, Republicans branded Sotomayor as a reverse racist, while Realacrats branded her as a true champion of the Hispanic community. Realacrats stand behind Judge Sonya Sotomayor's statement because it is the truth. Who knows better about the struggles of Hispanic Americans and other minorities than Judge Sotomayor; Congressman Joe Wilson, Sarah Palin, Senator Lindsey Graham, or Joe the Plumber? Judge Sotomayor's wise Latina woman comment just means she gets it and will work to make things better; the same way those previous Supreme Court Justices struck down the discrimination laws of 1950s and 1960s to try and make things better. Sarah Palin does not get it. Senator Lindsey Graham does not get it—but then again how could they, when the conservative ideology often downplays the struggles of minorities as welfare based exaggerations! Palin and Graham have faced struggles in their lives, but nothing like the struggles faced by African-Americans, Native Americans, and others similar to Judge Sotomayor. It is extremely difficult for people who don't share your experiences to then turn around and understand the capacity of your emotional pendulum; meaning, it is very tumultuous for someone to truly grasp the gut-wrenching gamut of emotions involved with terminal cancer unless that particular person, or someone in close proximity to that person, has been forced to suffer through it first-hand. It's one of those situations where just telling someone about it can't come anywhere close to mimicking what the actual experience entails. Instead of Senator Graham getting upset about the wise Latina woman comment, because he felt it insulted his abilities as a White man, he should, for once, try to place himself in the economically and politically underrated shoes of minorities—something Republicans avoid like political kryptonite.

If you can remember when Martin Luther King Jr. came to speak on behalf of the striking sanitation workers in Memphis, Tennessee back in 1968, you will recall the hundreds of African-American men marching in protest with signs that read "I AM A MAN," which is the very same fight that still wages till this very day. There is not a day that goes by that I don't feel that I have to prove that I am a person and so does Judge Sotomayor, because it is our minority based struggle that gives a wise minority woman/man more credibility and more common ground on which to deal with minority based issues than the average White, male politician, especially a conservative! Realacrats strongly support Judge Sotomayor in hopes than no one will ever have to march the streets again with a sign proclaiming they are a person too, and there is nothing, and I do mean nothing, the Republicans have done to even faintly make me believe they are willing to help ensure this never happens again in the United States. As an African-American, I'd rather take my chances with a Judge Sotomayor before I'd ever go to Sarah Palin in any attempt to make the problems of minorities understood, and I bet the overwhelming majority of Hispanic Americans and other minorities feel the same way—and why wouldn't they? If it was Father Phleger or someone like him, who was visibly viable in the minority community, it is definitely possible that a wise Latina woman would not be automatically anointed as the spokesperson for minority communities. It also would not be a forgone conclusion that she would be automatically wiser and better equipped to tackle the hazards of the de facto poverty and de facto segregation within many of the minority communities. When someone like a Sarah Palin tries to come in as a regional foreigner, her credibility is automatically terminated. Once again, conservatives have demonstrated hideous, social, bridge building! As the fairly new saying goes, "It is what it is," until someone in the Republican Party becomes a man and decides to march to the beat of a different drum; a drum not dictated and mandated by the Limbaugh legion.

Reverend Wright

The Reverend Jeremiah Wright drew a firestorm of protest in 2008 for his infamous tirade about the chant that reached all the way up to the church rafters and beyond, as the sound of "God Damn America" echoed out![8] The statement was so controversial that it almost cost Barack Obama the presidential election. I hadn't seen White people that up in arms since O.J. Simpson got acquitted. Their basic line of thinking revolved around questions and allegations such as these: "How could anybody say God Damn America? How could anybody think God Damn America? America is the greatest country in world, so why wouldn't this idiotic African-American minister understand that? He must be a traitor or a terrorist sympathizer. He obviously hates his own country and so does Bill Ayers, and I heard Barack Obama is not a real U.S. citizen anyway. I'll bet he hates this country too! America would never commit such acts that would allow rampant, unjustifiable hatred to thrive within its borders. We treat everyone equal in this country. Wright has nothing to gripe about. We even treat most of our niggers pretty good here. What more could he possibly want from this country?" All of this comes from a conversation that I loosely overheard between two White businessmen one day. So how would the Realacrats deal with or translate the Jeremiah Wright ideology?

First of all, you have to understand the point that Reverend Wright was trying to make, because there was a point to be made there, and it was not blind, unbridled disgust and hatred aimed at an innocent America. Realacrats understand full well that African-American disdain is not based on the destruction of America. African-Americans live and work here too with everyone else. African-Americans contribute to and defend this nation just like anyone else. What Reverend Wright

---

8 Brian Ross and Rehab El-Ruri, Obama's Pastor: God Damn America, U.S. to Blame for 9/11, http://www.abcnews.go.com/Blotter/Story?id=4443788 (March 2008).

was tapping into was the underlying, uneasy feeling of America's worst characteristic--racism, which is at the very essence of African-American discomfort towards America. Wright's now infamous sermon was squarely aimed at American racism, not the country as a whole.

Realacrats believe Reverend Wright's well-documented fury was exclusively aimed at the system; a system very similar to the college, athletic, BCS system, where certain entities that are deemed unworthy are automatically herded into an intense obstacle course with the goal of mass elimination. Like the smaller schools, the smaller ethnic groups have been pigeonholed into what amounts to a self-sustaining chopping block, and this methodical mechanism does an excellent job at rooting out the majority of minority groups from contention almost immediately. But with every system there lies a fault, and this undercover, Jim Crow, suppressive, brainwashing therapy is no different, as many African-Americans and other minority groups have found ways to beat the system of scripted-capitalism. But that's just it, in order for minorities such as African-Americans to truly succeed in this country, they have to hurdle the system to do so, because the system is not designed for minorities to be successful, especially African-Americans. This is the reasoning behind the "God Damn America" controversy! For all intents and purposes, he might as well have said "God Damn the racist Jim Crow system that this self-proclaimed greatest nation on earth has allowed to fester and at times flourish, while arrogantly flying in the face of our United States Constitution and our Bill or Rights." The nation of cowards strikes again, as people prove to be very reluctant at recognizing or remedying this corrupt and divisive system, the same system that plundered the Native Americans, the same system that denied women the right to vote, including White women, the same system that continually fails to covet all of its people, and the same system that has given a free good-ole-boy pass to the good-ole-boys, thus creating and sustaining a very real level of resentment from the bottom of society glaring straight up!

The African-American community claims Michael Jackson as a fellow Black man. African-Americans and other minorities flocked to Barack Obama during the presidential elections. Hispanic Americans rallied behind Judge Sotomayor as a potential U.S. Supreme Court Justice. All of this ethnic group rejoicing is to be expected here in

America, because it is that same American system that has created the environment for this type of unified celebration of any non-White success story. Here's an example for all of the Bill O'Reilly's, all of the Sean Hannity's, and all of the Rush Limbaugh's who fail to understand why ethnic triumph trounces American triumph every time. African-Americans have cheered for White people ever since they first cheered for a master at the plantation. I too have cheered and rejoiced at the success of White people in this country. I celebrated the Super Bowl victories of John Elway and Troy Aikman with much glee. It never once mattered to me how White they were, but my merriment at seeing Doug Williams win the Super Bowl as the first Black quarterback dwarfed Aikman and Elway astronomically, because the age-old reasoning behind the stereotypical belief is that Black quarterbacks are too dumb, too ignorant, too deprived, too limited, too unfocused, too unbridled to make sound decisions, too intellectually impoverished to lead, too asinine to be abstract, and too simplistic to cipher complexity, which represents the same clichéd values that are often applied to African-Americans on and off the field. So when Doug Williams won, we as African-Americans felt that we had won with him.

Once again, this is what the "God Damn America" comment was all about, because there is no coherent reason why a nation as educated, sophisticated, and ideological as the United States should ever harbor such buffoonish behavior and dogma, and for some demagogue to question the genuineness of African-Americans when they celebrate triumph over such demoralizing stereotypes is at the zenith of gullibility and ignorance. As long as there are one-sided, empty, intellectually blind, impressionable, non-thinking, propaganda regurgitating, cognitive canvases who are more than willing to have their lines filled in by self-serving vultures of deceit, manipulation, monumental ignorance, and fear; there will always be some aspect of our society engulfed in the sentiments of a "God Damn America" statement, because minorities didn't create the litany of limitations placed on them. They merely celebrate the triumphs over these limitations.

This goes back to Miss California's statement about how she, like many others, willingly took on the belief systems and propaganda handed down by her parents or family, which is fundamentally and intellectually wrong. It's not Miss California that I have a problem with.

I loathe the aspects of the follow the leader, follow the herd, monkey see, monkey do mentality she appears to follow so passionately. I don't give a damn what your idiotic, imbecilic, bigoted parents told you to believe about African-Americans and other minorities, but I will hold you totally responsible for continuing to believe in a fallacy because you are too cowardly to intellectually challenge your Santa Claus, Easter Bunny, Mayberry mindset! I lay the blame on you for not having the chutzpah to develop your own mind and think for yourself. I blame you for being an adult human being who still has to catch it, fetch it, and toe-the-line just to stay in your ignorant family's good graces. If my family told me I had to believe in something that I knew was a bold-faced lie, I would look them square in the eye and tell them to get the hell off my ass! If they gave me an ultimatum to try and force me into some sort of Jim Jones type of intellectual submission, I would tell them to go to hell on a gasoline comet. No one will tell me what to think. No one will tell me what to believe in. No one will tell me what to dream. No one will tell me my limitations, as seen by them. If my family was Republican and I wanted to be a Democrat, then I would be a damn Democrat. If they threatened to disown me because of it, I would beat them to the punch and disown them first. America is supposed to be a country of strength, yet many of its citizens hid behind closed doors, pointed heads, and bed sheets when it was time to confront the fight for equality, because they feared losing their cherished alliances. Realacrats must be willing to shed any alliances that obstruct the progression of rationale and justice, just as we expect NFL players such as Adam "Pac Man" Jones and NBA players such as Allen "The Answer" Iverson to do when they become famous and start getting into trouble. We demand that they shed their negative influences. Well, I think it's about time that Americans shed their own negative influences, and follow the very dogma they are so happy to preach about by disallowing any hindrance of their progression, even if it means telling your old, prejudiced father that you are perfectly capable of making your own decisions, and that you plan on doing so permanently. We expect and demand that our athletes and celebrities distance themselves from any of their past street life negativity; therefore, we must demand the genetic elitist distance themselves from any of their past, present, and future bigoted negativity. If it's good for the goose to relinquish the past, then it's also good for the gander to relinquish the past. You cannot be a Realacrat unless you are able and willing to make that choice. You cannot be a Realacrat unless you are able and willing to sacrifice your personal comfort zone and your familiar baggage for the right to be free.

The large number of close-minded American people who consciously decide to live in the past and fight the future provoked the "God Damn America" comment. Instead of using Reverend Wright as a superficial scapegoat, why don't you all differentiate yourselves from the Osama Bin Laden's of the world, and stop dictating your outmoded, passé, obsolete, genetic, entitlement policies onto your children in hopes of steering them away from certain segments of society deemed undesirable by self-appointed jackasses who are in no position to even make such judgments. You champion and invade other countries to promote and practice democracy, yet you are too afraid to apply it to your own family. Strong words mean very little without strong action to back them up. A law can only be as good as its enforcement. A movement cannot become mobile without participation. A flag stands for nothing if the constituents it represents also stand for nothing. If money is the root of all evil, then hypocrisy is the root of all cowardice. Maybe Attorney General Eric Holder was right when he spoke about a nation of cowards too afraid to address racism.

What Reverend Wright said in his fiery sermon was most definitely inflammatory, but I understand why he preached such a sermon. I also understand why his furious remarks about America are largely misinterpreted. Could Reverend Wright be a Realacrat? The answer to that question is absolutely and here is why! When and if, I ever become the leader of the Realacrat Party and it becomes a major party in this country, I could decide to form my very own version of the Ku Klux Klan and like the Klan; it would be a terrorist organization! It could be known as the Black KKK; a mirror image of the Ku Klux Klan, but opposite on all the issues and especially opposite with their pigmented, ideological origins. Instead of lynching African-Americans and other minorities, the Black KKK would only commit terrorist acts against White people and other American citizens who they felt were in disagreeance. I would bet you a dollar to a doughnut that the infamous Reverend Jeremiah Wright would discourage me from this irrational venture if I brought it to his attention. I also believe Father Pfleger, who was also vilified by the media for his racially charged tirade mocking Hillary Clinton's hypothetical response to Barack Obama pushing her to the limit in the Democratic Primaries, would discourage it as well. I know President Obama, Michelle Obama, Jesse Jackson Sr., Jessie Jackson Jr., the Reverend Al Sharpton, and I would argue that Louis Farrakhan would also discourage it. Hell, I would discourage myself, because ignorance is nothing to be imitated, duplicated, or replicated under any circumstances, and if I had a racist family member who tried to force me into it, I would unceremoniously show that individual the door, and that's more than many of the bigots you conservatives routinely preach to can say that they've ever thought about doing! I think it's safe to say that I, along with the Reverend Jeremiah Wright and Father Pfleger, would agree on finding a more positive pathway for the so-called Black KKK. First of all, the name is asinine, so it would have to go. No group associated with the Realacrat Party would ever engage in lynching, murder, or assault, nor would we go out on any *Birth of a Nation,* White woman, rape sessions either, and that includes all people, because wrong is still wrong even if it's being perpetrated on those who we consider to be inferior and more deserving of it. Instead of riding around waiting and hoping to catch some unsuspecting White person walking alone so that I could harass and beat the crap out of them, I would develop a group dedicated to uplifting young, underprivileged children in crime-ridden neighborhoods that have been long overlooked and forgotten by most of America; programs very similar to the programs already in existence courtesy of Reverend Wright and Father Pfleger, which is again more than many of the conservative elitists have ever thought about doing! Preaching hatred is counter-productive. My goal is to inspire and educate poor, minority kids, in an attempt to re-direct them into the colleges and out of the penitentiaries. These programs would be setup in poverty-stricken areas where at-risk-children could have total access to them; very similar to the way NBA players, NFL players, rappers, wrestlers, and movie stars run such programs. Like Barack Obama, Reverend Jeremiah Wright, Father Pfleger, and other community organizers, the Realacrats would go into these war zone neighborhoods to try and make a difference so that some of these young minds may have a chance to become successes and not statistics. And furthermore, these programs will welcome all young people like: African-American kids, Hispanic-American kids, Native American kids, Arab-American kids, Asian-American kids, and even White American kids. Like Steve Harvey always preaches, we have to put something back into the community from where we came, and the Realacrat Party would be front and center on that venture. I am absolutely sure that the Reverend Jeremiah Wright's and Father Pfleger's would be more than willing to help out with this cause. If I'm not mistaken, they are already involved in similar causes right now on the front lines! Wright and Flagler don't just sit around in some New York studio spouting off conservative rhetoric. They are actually helping communities; those same communities you saw left behind and stranded in a flooded New Orleans during Hurricane Katrina. While some autocratic elitists were quick to call out and criticize the poor for being too poor to properly react, people like Reverend Wright and Father Pfleger have been assisting those impoverished groups for years. If that's not patriotic, then what in the hell is? I guess being deemed patriotic all depends on exactly which group you are helping. Reverend Wright does not hate this country. Reverend Wright simply hates the abandonment of his part of the country, which just happens to be my part of the country as well. America's neglect and lack of acknowledgement for its own communities could very well be its damnation! You can't just give all the pain suffering to the niggas, and just expect it to stay there. After all, love of country is a two-way street, and it takes two cars to get there; meaning, don't expect me to fight for you, if you aren't willing to fight for me, because the righteousness of one's actions should never depend on the ethnicity of another.

Look at it this way! Black ministers have been preaching about Black liberation for decades. Reverend Wright preached it before he met Barack Obama, and I'm sure that he, along with many other African-American ministers, is still preaching it right now. If what Reverend Wright said was so bad for the country, then why aren't conservatives and others still out protesting it? Why didn't more of them protest it before? If Black liberation sermons are the cancerous problems that so many have portrayed them to be, why has it been allowed to fester for decades within the African-American communities? The answer to the question is simple. Either the Reverend Wright sermons truly were not as dangerous as some have made them out to be, or as long as it remains confined to the current, ghettoized communities of African-Americans and other minorities, it's not actually a conservative problem, but when the leader of the free world, who has the authority to make decisions that can and will affect conservative lives is exposed and possibly indoctrinated by these Black liberation sermons, it is then absolutely a conservative problem. If Reverend Wright is guilty of anything, he's guilty of being a victim of the crossover effect, which is the same phenomenon that elected President Obama, and it is also the same phenomenon that causes many of the Reverend Wright communities to mirror the poverty stricken images of the post and pre-Hurricane Katrina conditions in the African-American communities of New Orleans, Louisiana, while more opulent, possibly even more conservative, communities tend to always do much better; prompting the world, renowned anger laced within Wright's fiery sermons! I think the ironic linkage of all of these complexities speaks volumes about the ranking of minority communities on the societal, importance scale. Like it or not, the yellow, brick road to American success or American infamy goes through Mayberry! It alone will decide which one applies to you, and as long as that standard is allowed to be the apex designator of cultural importance, there are bound to be many more fiery sermons arising in protest of it!

Real American vs. African/Ethnic-American

Every time I see or hear this phrase real American, I am reminded of the immortal Hulk Hogan marching down to the ring to do battle with the American flag held high, because there is nothing more fulfilling than being an American. But what exactly does it mean to be a real American vs. an African/Ethnic-America. This is an intriguing question that is much more complex than many of you may realize; particularly if you are a so-called minority in this country, where the social meaning of the word minority translates into non-White. Being an African-American myself, I can attest to this sentiment whole heartedly. Let's take for instance Barack Obama's historic campaign in 2008. He was the first African-American to be nominated by a major party as a presidential candidate in history. He later went on to become the first African-American president in the free world, which was another astounding historical marker. African-Americans celebrated all over the world on election night. Even other minorities celebrated that night for such a joyous and momentous occasion. Now, the question remains: what were they celebrating? Were they celebrating the election of a new U.S. President? Were they celebrating democracy? Were they celebrating for America? Were they celebrating their citizenship in such a great nation? Were they celebrating for themselves, or were they celebrating something entirely different? The answer to that question depends on which group of people you pose the question to. I was happy to have a new President of the United States, and I was happy the Republicans lost, but all of this pales in comparison to my staggering appreciation of seeing an African-American become a champion right before my eyes. That was the single most important virtue for me that night and here today. Not once did I ever utter to myself or out loud how proud I was to be an American. Not once did I attribute anything to Barack Obama's success that even vaguely pointed to his Americanism. I never once thought to myself, this is a great day for our nation. I never once thought about the American flag. I never once thought about the bald eagle. The perception of me presenting myself as a proud American was the farthest thing from my mind, and I never once entertained the idea of my nation with my fellow American comrades living in full acceptance of each other. I think it's safe to say that I had extreme tunnel vision, and I still have it now, and I'm not the only one guilty of it either. I would argue that almost every African-American who cast their ballot for Barack Obama felt the exact same way I did, and I'm sure the Hispanic-Americans, the Arab-Americans, the Native Americans, the Chinese Americans, the Japanese Americans, female Americans, and gay Americans, who also cast their ballots for Barack Obama all possibly felt this way too. By the way, why is it that I rarely ever hear the media outlets refer to Hispanics as Hispanic-Americans or Asians as Asian-Americans, but African-Americans and Native Americans always get it? Nevertheless, I was happy to see an African-American succeed at the highest level, when Barack Obama was elected President of the United States, but I was also concerned about how the country would react to it. Was I then proud of my country? Well, proud is not the word that comes to mind. My feelings were that of the utmost concern, because I felt very uneasy about this election. In fact, let's just say that I kept an ace in the hole that night and kept a watchful eye for any signs of trouble. Believe it or not, I was actually fearful that night. I admit it! I'm still fearful this very day and will remain fearful until President Obama is out of office, and by out of office, I mean able to walk out on his own accord! American pride never entered the equation. Conservatives like Bill O'Reilly will say that I'm loony for being so negative, but my principle concern is not Freddie Kruger, it's still Jim Crow. There are those who will try to convince you that Jim Crow's power is greatly diminished due to Barack Obama's presidency, but I'm not convinced.

Minorities in this country tend to have a different outlook on life, because life in America tends to have a different outlook on minorities! The reason for this is called disenfranchisement. It's the same saga that Barack Obama faced in 2008. Traditionally and historically, African-Americans, Hispanic-Americans, and all other non-White groups in this country have been systematically disenfranchised from wealth, the pursuit of freedom, knowledge, dignity, citizenship, constitutional rights, state rights, local rights, human rights, the pursuit of unregulated happiness and quite a few employment endeavors. I fully understand why the Hispanic-American community has rallied behind Judge Sonia Sotomayor. Like Barack Obama, she now represents an entire conglomeration of Hispanics all over the world. If she wins, they all win, like President Obama's win was a win for all African-Americans and all Black people everywhere. Once again, Ms. Sotomayor's American citizenship means little, if anything, compared to her Puerto Rican/Hispanic ancestry. The fact that she is an American citizen won't even cause someone to blink an eye, but the fact that she has become the first Hispanic ever confirmed to the United States Supreme Court is a definite game-changer that will affect the lives of the Hispanic community forever. The Hispanic aspect outweighs the American female aspect astronomically. America has no one else to blame but itself for its ongoing perception of minority driven success in spite of an atmosphere ripe with bigotry. When you disenfranchise groups of people for years and years, it's only natural that stupendous rejoicing will take place whenever one of these outcasts finds their way into the political, BCS, big dance, championship game.

The Bowl Championship Series (BCS)[9] is a system in college sports set up to accommodate and propel the dominant groupings of big

9 Wikipedia, Bowl Championship Series, http://en.wikipedia.org/wiki/Bowl_Championship_Series.

colleges to the top while keeping the minority groupings of smaller colleges at bay, so when the big schools do win, it's just another run-of-the-mill behemoth beating its chest again. It's always more exciting and remarkable when a small non-BCS school slips through the cracks and clears all of the political hurdles to find its way into contention to be number one. Like the small, obscure non-BCS schools in college sports, minorities have to fight to prove that they belong, to prove that they are worthy, and to prove that they, like the powerhouses, deserve an opportunity to compete. Minorities are those non-BCS schools of society who were never intended to be included at the big, dog table, but parodies have a way of bringing about the unexpected— just ask Hillary Clinton about that. It's the modern day version of David and Goliath, and there is always something at the very core of humanity that makes David a more intriguing story.

Republicans are not happy with all of this minority hoopla. Republicans are against anyone getting selected strictly due to their ethnic background only, and that would be wrong, and I agree. Anyone who is not qualified should not be given any position based on a popularity contest. In the Realacrat Party, the election or selection of a non-BCS candidate will be the norm more than it will be a rarity, as long as the candidates are qualified. Nevertheless, many conservatives and non-minorities feel very uneasy about ethnic groups celebrating their ethnic success and their ethnic identity first, while meekly acknowledging their American roots with a distant second or third. So unlike the Democrats, The Realacrat ideology will now explain exactly why the culture in America is to blame for diminishing its own social importance in regards to minorities. What I'm about to elaborate on has played and continues to play a major role in African-American/minority voter turnout and candidate selection!

I was watching a guy named Lloyd Marcus on CNN in an interview with Don Lemon, where Marcus claimed that he opened up every Tea Party rally that he was a part of with the statement, "I'm not an African-American! I'm Lloyd Marcus--American"[10] I find such a statement to be laughable and quite naïve, and I believe anyone gullible enough to buy into such an idiotic denial is also laughable and naïve!

10 Spydat3k, CNN - Tea Party racist? Not according to Lloyed Marcus - true black American, http://www.youtube.com/watch?v= bLq3vvdGvM (September 2009).

I've encountered many conservatives and Republicans who have openly pushed for a complete omission of the word African being placed in front of American, because just being an American should be sufficient, as we are all one great nation. On paper, it's a unifying idea, but in reality; it's hypocrisy in its finest hour. I can only speak for myself, so I will, even though this will apply overwhelmingly to almost all African-Americans. For every day that I've lived on this planet, I've been Black first and American second, and sometimes the second was questionable or simply non-existent in the eyes of many of these same conservatives who now want to define me exclusively as American at the expense of my African heritage!

It's an argument filled with holes, because I can't sit here and recall a single time in my entire life where I've been addressed as an American by another American. I mulled through my memoirs thoroughly, but I just cannot recall any comment acknowledging the legitimacy of my American, citizenship status. I don't recall anything of that nature, but I'll tell you what I do recall, because I've been called quite a few names during my life, but American was not one of them! Here's a short list of names I've been called numerously and repeatedly during my American experience: the ever popular and number one insult of all time--nigger, The Creature from the Black Lagoon, watermelon, asphalt face, Black, ugly gorilla; Black grease, bowel movement colored blacky, baboon boy, tire people, spook, jungle-bunny, coon, porch monkey, yard ape, Kunta Kenta, colored, charcoal Charlie, spear-chunker, and the always acidic—tar baby! What do all of these descriptors have in common? They are all derivatives of my pigmentation. Apparently, the term American failed to make the cut! I think you now get the picture of why African-Americans are Black first and foremost!

American society continuously promotes and reinforces this racial chatter! How could I be anything but Black first? As an African-American, society pulls you over to the side at a young age just to let you know precisely how Black you truly are. Your entire life prognosis will follow this protocol! One point of view will tell you that you can't accomplish your goals because you are Black, and the other point of view will tell you to go out and accomplish your goals in spite of the fact that you are Black!

For example, within my life experiences, let's say that I've known 100 African-Americans in my life! Out of that 100, I would say that 90 of them believed that my ability would outmaneuver the limitations of the color of my skin, while the other 10 believed the color of my skin would ultimately sink my ships of aspiration! Now, let's say that I've also known 100 White people in my life! Out of that 100, I would argue that at least 50 of them either hoped or believed that the color of my skin would minimize the significance of my journey enough to racially sabotage and culturally marginalize my ability to succeed! But surprisingly, the other 50 either hoped or believed the content of my character would triumph, which shows just how polarizing race is to the totem pole of the human psyche! Whether you think of yourself as an African-American, a Black American, or just an American, race remains the dominant, defining descriptor!

The authenticity of the American label is non-existent, unless you are in the Olympics, out of the country, ideologically obedient to the status quo, or when some bellicose jihadist flies a plane into a building! There is a monumental difference between referring to someone as an American and treating them like an American! If Lloyd Marcus had suddenly decided to change his political views on Obama's health care plan and brought in the assistance of Rep. John Lewis of Georgia to address the Tea Party ralliers and protestors in hopes of convincing them to reconsider their stances on health care, neither of these two men would be considered nor addressed as Americans! They've already called John Lewis bad names, none of which was American! Now what do you think they would have called Mr. Lewis and Mr. Marcus during this shallow attempt at political enlightenment? If he had been walking behind John Lewis with a sign that read support health care, he would have received the same treatment that Lewis got! What Mr. Marcus fails to understand is that his American acceptance is always contingent on his political loyalty to the Tea Party, not his country or his citizenship. Whenever Mr. Marcus decides to cognitively step outside of the Tea Party tent, he will go from American to African-American to nigger almost instantaneously! His American status will always be conditional, because certain political conditions determine whether or not he is granted his American status and how long he is able to hold on to it!

Like I said before, being labeled a real American by some conservative, distortion machine is only important depending on who you ask, because that is one honor I feel I can do without. If being a real American is not based on practicing what you preach, then I agree with John Lennon, you can count me out! If being a real American is the demonizing of anyone who does not look like you, you can count me out again. If being a real American means only the ones who agree with you, then you can count me out again. If being a real American means fearing anything you don't understand, I'm not interested. If being a real American means you'd crucify my ideas just to further crucify my humanity, my dignity, and my acceptance, then I'll have no part of it. If being a real American means you will accept my liver, but not my presence, you can keep your ridiculous label.

If I'm never considered to be a real American, it does not matter to me. My only goal is to beat the system. If I can find a way to accomplish that feat, it will mean far more than falling under any real American label. The never-ending quest to establish my ethnic identity as legitimate renders the real American question irrelevant anyway, and I'm sure the other rarely seen minorities fully understand this dilemma, because being a real American will always be dwarfed by the defining struggle to revoke the specter of second class citizenship. We are not defined by our American citizenship status because it really doesn't mean anything. It just means that we are here. As a minority in this country, we will ultimately be defined by our ability to beat the system or our inability to beat the system. In the end, it's a numbers game with success stories and statistics. Living as more than just another statistic should be celebrated as the quintessential American dream, but it ends up being celebrated as a rare minority triumph instead, and that is America's fault for creating an environment built to harbor such divisive thinking. I remember in the movie *Remember the Titans*[11] when the character called Julius told the character called Gary that a poor attitude reflects poor leadership. Maybe the severe disinterest in the ideology of a real American by minorities is a direct reflection of the well-documented reluctance of leadership to accept minorities as real Americans from the very beginning and even now.

---

11 Boaz Yakin, Director, Remember The Titans, 2000.

This is precisely why I started the Realacrat Party, a place where everyone involved is a real American and where citizenship actually means something. I personally feel that if you are legally a citizen of the United States and the government collects taxes from your household income, you are a real American! In my view, you don't take my money with one hand and then slap me across the face with the other hand by deeming my American legitimacy as generic! And furthermore, the conservative windbags who first tossed around this 2nd tier citizenship notion are nothing more than overrated megalomaniacs engulfed in fallacy! The Realacrat Party will be there to attack any cretinous mooncalf who dares to challenge the validity of any American citizen based on his or her social/ethnic status. We as Realacrats have to try and begin the dismantling of this second tier, fraudulent, American system because there will be no tiers in this party. It's a place where James the janitor is just as much an American as Joe the Plumber. Instead of spreading around wealth, we are first going to spread around humanity and opportunities, because nowhere in the Constitution or Declaration of Independence is there a citizenship, tier system designed to support some group hierarchy based on genetic entitlement, the old class systems of Europe, or slavery. Anyone who suggests that there are tiers of Americanism is unconstitutional and most definitely not a real American. The founding fathers designed the Constitution to move away from feudalism and slavery, even if took another 250 years for that goal to materialize. A tier system of Americanism is about as un-American as it gets, which is yet another reason why I could never join the Republican Party. They worry about owning the terminology of "Real American," while Realacrats strive to become and include real people, because it is the people that make America what it is; inclusive of everyone!

At the Realacrat convention you will see all walks of life and race represented, not just the self-appointed chosen few. The Realacrats will do neighborhood reporting where information from an assortment of neighborhoods will be shared and addressed. We plan to hear personally from Arab Americans on the problems facing their communities and so on. You might see a Native Americans addressing the people, and you might also see Caribbean Americans addressing the people. In honor of Rage Against the Machine, the Realacrat Party will do everything in its power to voice the voiceless and show the unseen, because they are all real Americans, and not just when they're fighting a war so your kids don't have to. It's easy to highly tout a minority as a first tier American when they are in some foreign country fighting a war only to socially abnegate them back down to the second tier when they return home and attempt to date your daughter. In the end, a document full of ideas is no different than a blank sheet of paper. It's the enactment of that idea that breathes the life into it. The less action one displays; the cheaper their talking points will become!

Affirmative Action

Affirmative Action vs. the Good Ol' Boys

There is no doubt in my mind that the United States of America was founded on the good-ole-boy system, and slavery made it that much more profitable. The good-ole-boy network was not hard to figure out. All you had to do was be White, preferably a White male, and you were in it to win it. Membership in this clan would ensure you the best opportunities, the best employment, the best health care, the best education, the best housing in the best neighborhoods and above all else the best financial resources available at the time. The only prerequisite was that you had to be White or at least have the ability to pass for White, because White was everything that was godly and good! If you didn't believe it, you could always ask them, and they would have lynched your ass as they proceeded to tell you all about it. This was a network whose sole purpose was to promote and guarantee prominence for the so-called White agenda, and American, White culture has benefited from it enormously over the past four-hundred years.

Thanks to such great entities and great people, like Dr. Martin Luther King Jr., Malcolm X, Thurgood Marshall, Rosa Parks, Medgar Evers, Al Sharpton, Jessie Jackson Sr., John F. Kennedy, Bobby Kennedy, Ted Kennedy, Linden Johnson, the Democratic Party, Bill Clinton, the Black Panthers, Pro-Black, hip-hop groups, Huey Newton, the Black Church, the NAACP and many others who dared to speak out against the good-ole-boy network of racism and favoritism, many aspects of this good-ole-boy network have been overcome and damaged. A program was designed and set up to help minorities get an equal playing field. The program was called "Affirmative Action," which basically meant that it would be the responsibility of the U.S. government to force American businesses to hire a certain number of minorities, and it also forced universities to enroll a certain number of minorities. Unlike the good-ole-boy system, which sought to completely exclude non-Whites, affirmative action did not seek to totally eliminate White people from the equation. It only sought to afford minorities an opportunity, and at the time, it seemed to be a great response to the old Jim Crow laws of the South. In 2008, the United States elected its first African-American President in Barack Obama. Now questions have begun to surface regarding the need for affirmative action programs in this day in age. Some view President Obama's success as a clear sign that programs such as affirmative action are no longer necessary or feasible in this new, alleged post-racial society, where an African-American man can be elected President.

How would the Realacrat philosophy deal with the question of affirmative action? Well, I believe it is still necessary in this country—maybe not in the shape and form it has at this very moment, but it does not need to be abolished entirely. It could possibly be revamped, but it should not be abolished. The reason that I say this is based on my livelihood experiences and my observations of the world around me. I'll give you some pointers. As I looked around the nation as the housing markets collapsed in 2008, I began to see evidence of things that I already knew about this country. White people are still the undisputed, dominant, economical force in America-plain and simple. When the banks collapsed, I saw rich, old CEO's who were overwhelmingly White; easing out of the back bank doors into their multi-million-dollar, golden parachutes. A high-ranking, Brazilian dignitary accused the White, blue-eyed bankers of the United States of causing the world's poor economic condition. He came under intense scrutiny for his remarks, but maybe he was on to something. When I watched the big American car companies stride into Washington, D.C. to beg for money in front of Congress on high-powered, mile-high-clubbing, private jets. I didn't see any minorities in that group either, if they were there, they must have been left on the plane for janitorial duty. I think the question should be how many minority Bernie Madoff's do you know? How many minority Kenneth Lay's do you know, not to mention all the other high-ranking Enron and Halliburton players who were also White men? The U.S. Senate is almost totally White, and the United States Supreme Court is almost totally White. During the pre-invasion days leading up to the war in Iraq, there were many high-ranking Pentagon officials speaking out and making public appearances. Barring Colin Powell, minorities were noticeably missing again. I assume that there are actually minorities trading on Wall St., but once again, they are well hidden. For that matter, the airline industry seems to be predominately White as well. I will bet you a dollar to a doughnut that the executives of the professional sports industries and the oil companies are also predominately White, because I have yet to see any high-ranking minority associated with either of these multi-billion dollar corporations. All the news networks, including cable news, are predominately White. The entire Republican Party is predominately White. You take any major American corporation in shipping, manufacturing, food processing, automotive, telemarketing and so on, and you'll find a serious lack of minority management; particularly African-Americans, Hispanic-Americans and Native Americans. It's no secret to me or to any other minorities out here in the workforce exactly which group is the blatant, power majority, because the corporate headquarters and the divisional headquarters are almost always predominately, if not entirely, White. Whenever a company or an inspection committee arrives to inspect a facility, they are usually White men, with the occasional White woman. Even on the common worker/operator level, the sheer number of minorities lags far behind the high numbers of Whites. Historically, there have only been a minute number of African-Americans to ever head a Fortune 500 company, and there has only been one African-American president. Ambitious individuals such as these do not grow on trees, and without affirmative action programs, they may never be given the opportunity to be cultivated on any level. Can you sit around and honestly say to yourself that Barack Obama's Presidency could have been possible without affirmative action? Yes, affirmative action has taken a diminished role as of late, and even if it did not fully shoulder Barack Obama recently into the White House, it had to have shouldered the guys who came before him, which inevitably opened the door for him. If all you had was Jim Crow and there was no affirmative action to counter it, there is no way that Barack Obama becomes president, mayor, senator or even a convenient store clerk. Affirmative action shouldn't be retired until Jim Crow has been retired. So I expect the NAACP and affirmative action to be around indefinitely!

The Jim Crow Mentality

The Jim Crow mentality is an equality killer that not only affects the United States but the entire world, anywhere human rights are trampled on, beheaded, or lynched. The modernized version of the Democratic Party deserves the bulk of the credit in this current version of our two-party-system for their periodic and methodical dismantling of the Jim Crow system over the years. The Democratic Party has led the charge against Jim Crow basically on a solo mission, because Republicans were nowhere to be found on this issue. But then, why would any of us expect a party of old conservatives to have the removal of Jim Crow on the top of their list of things to do? The saddest part about this situation is the fact that many of the people affected by Jim Crow have no idea what they are being manipulated by. People cling to their lackadaisical beliefs that it is only African-Americans who suffer from the ills of Jim Crow, which is pure unadulterated ignorance. The very essence of Jim Crow is the denial of freedoms with a self-appointed, hierarchy-based monopoly of scripted capitalism controlling the choices offered and the ability of people to act on them. It is the exploitation of people to further enhance the sustainability of a blatantly corrupt, self-serving power. If you view the fine print of the infamous glass ceiling, it reads "Made by Jim Crow." Adolph Hitler's genetic, superiority scheme was Jim Crow. The denial of voting rights to women and African-Americans was Jim Crow. Slavery was Jim Crow. The Holocaust was Jim Crow. The feeding of Christians, Jews and peasants to the lions during the days of the Roman Empire was Jim Crow. The banning of Facebook and other informational accesses in Iran, China and other nations is Jim Crow. The banning of peaceful protest is Jim Crow. The oppression of Taiwan, Tibet and the Dalai Lama is Jim Crow! Kim Jong-il forcing his own people to suffer for his personal causes is Jim Crow. Osama bin Laden's religious dictatorship is Jim Crow. The genocide in Bosnia and Darfur was Jim Crow. The denial of Haitian refugees was Jim Crow. The pillaging of Native Americans was Jim Crow, and the past and present day assaults on Mexicans and Hispanic Americans were Jim Crow. The Realacrat Party will be the antithesis of the Jim Crow era. The motto will be simply put: "Say no to Jim Crow," because with Jim Crow at the wheel, a true vehicle of democracy will only maneuver within the circles of the abyss. Freedom was created for everyone, not just the self-appointed, self-righteous, self-centered select few, and it will be made a top priority of Realacrats to make sure that happens.

Other aspects besides Jim Crow have also helped to institutionalize discrimination and racism, because minorities have not shown near enough interest in changing many of the primitive, plantational habits that continue to limit progress. What is the real culprit here? Is it the lethargic behavior on the parts of minorities when it comes to business savvy, or is it employment favoritism? The question of affirmative action cannot be corrected or properly addressed until this question is first answered; only then can you accurately decide what to do about affirmative action. So once again, what is the real culprit here? I honestly think that it is both a lackadaisical work ethic and oppressive elimination at play here. I see evidence of the good-ole-boy network continuing to promote unqualified, unsubstantiated, insubordinate, asinine and even borderline retarded workers into the best workforce positions simply because they are White, especially White men, but I've also seen the flip side. I've seen minorities come into the work place and then turn around and willingly exit just as quickly. If I had to pinpoint the single most career-killing mechanism at work here, I would have to say a lack of a decent education, a lack of job skills, a lack of proper employment practices and techniques, a lack of personal responsibility, a lack of responsibility in productive workmanship—in a nutshell, they all seemed to be mentally unprepared for the workforce. This is very problematic within the African-American community, and affirmative action won't fix that problem. The downstream ramifications of Jim Crow not only denies well-educated and skilled African-Americans, but it has denied African-Americans as a whole, which has allowed such economic and social discrepancies to continually stifle the progress of African-American communities across the country.

A New African-American Initiative

We as African-Americans are always quick to put pressure on the employment industry about their employee hiring practices. Most times we are right to do so, but some of the responsibility falls on us as African-Americans, because of our gross non-preparation and our unprofessional approach in the job market. Nonetheless, ideas and views expressed here can be transplanted to fit the needs of all other minorities as well.

As said previously, African-Americans lack many of the desired qualities needed to be successful in the workplace, and there is no doubt that this is in direct correlation to historical discrimination and the Jim Crow mentality. Old habits die hard, but there comes a time and a place where we, as a people, must begin to turn the tide ourselves. We can now look to Barack and Michelle Obama's success for inspiration and proof of non-entertainment related, non-athletic related, non-illegal activity related success. As the great Al Sharpton has continuously pointed out, all we need is an equal playing field, and we can compete with anyone. The key idea in that phrase is "compete." The Obama's competed. Dr. Martin Luther King competed. Malcolm X competed. Al Sharpton Competed. Rosa Parks competed. Huey Newton competed. Jessie Jackson Sr. competed. All of these talented individuals met the challenge of discrimination head on and won. We can do the same thing. Just as we place pressure on the employment industry, we must now put that same pressure on ourselves to better prepare to be qualified in the job market. I do blame the establishment for passing over qualified African-Americans, but I blame many African-Americans for passing over themselves with poor preparation, limited determination, inadequate educational skills, mixed up priorities, a major lack of focus, little or no respect for anything non-athletic or non-entertainment related, treating learning like a dirty word, equating intelligence with Whiteness—which means applying ignorance to us. I blame African-Americans for having limited professional visions, coddling liquor stores, pawn shops, gun play, gangbanging, dope smoking, slanging dope, shiny expensive rims, bling bling, gangsta rap, and the self-destructive definitions of cool to define us. I blame African-Americans for believing the stereotypical hype others equate with us, our crippling inability to appreciate the value of stepping stones, and most of all; for accepting the back seat as our designated destination in life and society. We can blame all of that on American discrimination, but we also have to share in some of that blame. The system does not owe you or me anything. It is up to us to find a way to beat the system, and by beating the system; we will find a way to become a Barack Obama—or at least a microcosm of Barack Obama. In other words, if you can't be President of the United States, then be president of your club or school. A start is a beginning, and a beginning is the pathway to success. You will never go anywhere if you don't start somewhere.

I was watching D.L. Hugely on CNN one day when he talked about his neighborhood. Apparently, he lives by a Hall of Fame singer, a Hall of Fame basketball player, and a world renowned actor. All are African-Americans, and there was one White guy who also lived in the same neighborhood, but he was just a dentist. The key words here are JUST A DENTIST. It is my experience that too many African-Americans, including myself, spend far too much time striving to be those hall of fame people D.L. spoke about. The large majority of us will fail to make it, and end up doing menial or criminal work because most of us don't have serious backup plans that we fully intend to see through, like being a dentist. Hell, the occupation of dentistry should be a viable first plan, as it garners just as much praise as any other professional venture for African-Americans. Everybody I knew growing up wanted be one of those Hall of Fame people and was willing to walk through hell or high water for it. No one I knew growing up ever considered being a dentist; let alone walk through hell to become one. They wouldn't even consider it as a worthy possibility. After all, everybody knows that dentists are supposed to be smart, well-educated White men, with sexy, White women working to assist them; the same way golf and tennis were supposed to be predominately White until someone dared to change that stereotype by challenging the traditional fears of "can't."

Arguably, every African-American kid dreams of being the next LeBron James, who played small forward for the Cleveland Cavaliers, but probably less than one percent will ever accomplish such a feat. I once dreamed of being the next big gangsta rapper. Even though my odds were slightly better, it was still a very unrealistic dream, and unrealistic dreams have plagued the African-American community. I'd rank unrealistic dreams right up there behind racism. Just look at the impact! I, like so many, was willing to forgo all of my educational and job opportunities just to be a gangsta rapper. Why would someone make such an irrational decision is the question you may ask yourself? My answer is simple. So I could get bitches! The money comes first, and the bitches come second. Being a gangsta rapper or an athlete seemed to be the best way to get both at the time; it was either one of those or a dope man/drug dealer. The thought of becoming a Stephen A. Smith, a Roland Martin, a Professor Henry Louis Gates, a dentist, a CEO, a stock broker, or a Realacrat never once entered my mind as possibilities. I limited myself. I have no one else to blame but me, and I'm sure I'm not the only young African-American this has happened to. While White men were willing to take employment in general, especially in the management and operator departments, I, along with all of my homies, was trying to scheme up a way to get some spinning rims, so I could ride clean. We ride clean today, and we walk broke tomorrow. A White man may not be the current President of the United States, but White men in general are very successful within the confines of the workforce, because they are willing to take opportunities that have been given to them, while many African-Americans, especially the younger generations, are systematically denied many opportunities and fail to recognize the ones they do get; even though they are in no position to scoff at any of them. Doors are made to be opened, and your hands are not the only hands capable of grasping that proverbial knob of opportunity. Speaking as an African-American, I've noticed that far too many of us want everything that comes along with the result without putting in the necessary effort to achieve that result, which leaves a highly disproportionate number of people like me living and dying by the Hail Mary instead of a strategic game plan.

Affirmative action or not, you have to utilize your chances in life, because non-preparation will most definitely lead to unemployment. Affirmative action cannot take a test for you, and affirmative action cannot wake you up so you can get to work on time. Affirmative action cannot make you show up for work every day, and it cannot make you competent. Whether it's your local dentistry or Wall Street, more African-Americans have to dare to change those stereotypical, ruinous travel routes. Affirmative action is good, but we as African-Americans also need affirmative progression, affirmative vision, affirmative motivation, affirmative courage, affirmative accountability, affirmative confidence, affirmative prioritizing, affirmative ambition for higher learning and learning overall, and most importantly; the affirmative strength to unlearn our shortcomings. Affirmative action was designed to try and fix a flawed system. It was never designed to try and fix a flawed you or a flawed me, so why would we expect it to?

The Government's Role

With a new global economy, affirmative action must be given a much broader scope to include the proverbial "Have Nots" regardless of ethnicity! Conservatives and Republicans will rail against the financial cost and the inabilities of big government to accomplish this. They would like each state to decide this matter, but I don't believe the states could get it right. On an issue of as much importance as this one, there is no way I could ever trust all 50 states to fall in line and rectify this problem for the good of all people, especially minorities. Everything depends on just how liberal or conservative each state is, and that could become a real headache. This is one area in which the federal government must step in and not only oversee this operation, but it must also implement the main rule of law regarding the new affirmative action. Only the federal government can force all 50 states to get into single file at the lunch line. I'm sure this is the primary reason why civil rights activists such as Dr. Martin Luther King Jr. constantly asked the federal government for equality and protection under the law. Wasn't it the federal government that forced the integration of Little Rock Central with an armed military? The federal government has a legitimate role to play in our society. Sometimes it's big and sometimes it's small, but it must be authoritative. Therefore, affirmative action has to be re-tooled to better cope with the ever-changing times.

The government's job should not and will not be to enforce or create racial quotas. The government's role is not to corral companies into hiring certain interest groups with the intention of enhancing economic advancement for a particular ethnicity. In other words, the government will not ensure that African-Americans or any other group will be guaranteed jobs at any place of employment, but instead; will focus on the hiring practices of employers. The goal will be investigation. If any company shows a specific pattern of employment that falls heavily against minorities, the government not only has every right, but it is also obligated to investigate the area for any forms of discrimination or favoritism. The same rule would apply for any company harboring an overwhelming majority of call back applicants from a particular group. You can't only interview White people, and then turn around and only hire White people. It brings into question the authenticity of your selection process. Either it is a just peculiar coincidence, or it is something much more deliberate and blatant. If investigated evidence appears to be deliberate, then it is the government's job to test this hypothesis personally. A well-educated, well-articulated, well-dressed, highly-qualified individual will be shepherded by the government to apply at one of these one-sided quota companies in a process that could go on for weeks if necessary. If these handpicked applicants are merely passed over for no justifiable reason, the government can then order a complete investigation into the hiring practices of this company. There is nothing unfair or unethical about this type of governmental intervention. No one is trying to force a company to hire more minorities, but there needs to be a program in place to ensure that minorities are at least receiving credible vetting and not being immediately re-routed to file cabinet 13—the secretarial garbage can. I don't care who you are—Rush Limbaugh, Sean Hannity or whoever; you can't convince me that there are no qualified minority workers out there. They should at least be getting some of the jobs. I am not in support of any quota, like demanding that at least 30 percent of all employees have to be minorities, but I also do not support any racial discrimination, under any circumstances. The government's job should be to keep employers honest, not to arrange or re-arrange the employment lists.

Abortion

The New Welfare State

Like gay marriage, this is a fight surrounded by an abundance of controversy. People are extremely passionate about abortion. To me, abortion is a none-issue. The ramifications of abortion are about as important to me as a tapeworm hooked into a man on a hunger strike. When I see these religious zealots, like the morons at Notre Dame University, I feel sick to my stomach. Some religious loons decided to protest the arrival of President Obama in 2009, as he attended Notre Dame's graduation ceremony and gave the commencement address. The protestors were livid at the University for suggesting an honorary degree for President Obama, because of his policies regarding abortion and embryonic stem cell research. I saw some jackass priest being subdued to the ground as he made a frail attempt to play politics with the abortion issue. This all sounds and looks very authentic, but I have to ask myself one very important question. Is it life, or is it Memorex? Now I do believe there are honest, good-hearted people out there who truly want to support the babies, but I also believe there are far too many who are out simply to politicize the issue strictly for political gains, and I strongly feel that politics outweighs compassion, mainly within the conservative ranks. That's just my opinion! Just as conservatives believed Barack Obama was a terrorist and a counterfeit citizen, I, in turn, believe they harbor a rightful contingent of abortion politicizers and sensationalists. The mainstream media tend to shy away from this issue, but this sentiment is real. I'm not convinced it is the ideological monopoly, but it does exist. It is the exact same ideology that caused people to laugh and scoff at Hurricane Katrina victims scurrying through the muck to survive. I've even heard many complain about the over-the-top, saturation of media coverage on Hurricane Katrina by saying: "They're nothing but a bunch of animals and thugs out on the loot; a bunch of welfare recipients too ignorant by their own accord and too economically destitute by their own accord to get out before Katrina hit!" The same gripe has been most recently made about the people of Haiti as an explanation for why the United States should not bail out Haiti after the devastation of their massive earthquake in 2010!

Oddly enough, many of these same crack-potted gurus also despise PETA, and they make fun of PETA on a routine basis by arguing that PETA's alleged grandstanding and self-indulgence far outweighs and overshadows their protective intentions towards animals. From what I can see, PETA has no credibility whatsoever, and their antics are often portrayed as more comical than noble. Radio stations and other media outlets have a field day ripping PETA every time they show up at any event. PETA's problem is simple. They are believed to be out for themselves and not the animals. There are many who have already condemned the organization to this charge, whether it's true or false. What I find mind-boggling is how this same public automatically assumes and believes in the genuineness of any religious, PETA-like organization. For some unknown reason, religious bands get a pass on integrity, because no one has the testicular fortitude to question their motives. This is the number one beef I have with all religious doctrines. They always seem to get the righteous nod from the public, but should they? I say, hell no! Religious organizations are just as, if not more than, capable of grandstanding like any other rogue syndicate—including PETA. In my opinion, religious zealots and PETA should join forces, because they are all serving and protecting the same master, which is self-interest. Whether it's Baptists, Methodists, Catholics, Protestants, Pentecostals, or Mormons, none should ever be given the unregulated keys to righteousness. The same way that many members of the public don't buy the PETA act, I don't buy the religious "save the babies" act! I think one dog and pony show is just about as good as the other. I wouldn't pay my hard-earned money to watch PETA or the religious zealots grand stand any more than they already do. All of those protestors at Notre Dame and all of the protestors at abortion clinics, are grandstanding professionals. Poor, gangland embryos from Compton, California, are not the inspiration for these displays of alleged nobility. The buffoons you see out there getting arrested would be the first ones to sell their homes if fully grown, gangland embryos from Compton, California, suddenly moved in next door to them. I'll even do you one better: if any of these protesting pretenders had a daughter who became pregnant by some of these undesirables, I would bet you more than half would clandestinely seek out or strongly consider abortion or an adoptive release, especially if the undesirable turned out to be an African-American from Compton, a Hispanic American, or an Arab American. This is charlatanism at its best! The message is that we will fight for your rights to exist, as long as you remain a harmless embryo, but once you become a child/young adult who could potentially penetrate our culture or our daughters, we will abort you economically, financially, socially, ethically, religiously, nutritionally, humanly and unlawfully! I recognize this flimflam! To call this disingenuous would be an understatement. This conflicted crusade is not really about embryos—it's only about certain embryos. From studies I've investigated, the sheer number of abortions in this country appears to be skewed in one group's favor, just as wealth and higher educational ideologies appear to be skewed in one group's favor. Is this mere fortuity or something more underhanded? The odds makers in Las Vegas have their legal tenders on the latter! You know, I've always been perplexed at the passionate vigor of conservative and religious movements to ban abortion, when these are the same cliques that despise and loathe the welfare system. Why are they purposely trying to increase the youth population, which will in return, increase the welfare state; which will in return, increase basic health-care needs; which will increase affordable insurance needs, which will in return, increase educational needs; which will in return, increase orphanage needs; which will in return, increase public housing needs; which will in return, increase daycare and nursery needs; which will in return, increase foster care needs; which will in return, increase special needs children needs; which will in return, increase social worker needs; which will in return, increase the need for decent and willing parents; which will in return, increase the need for financially stable, employed parents, which will ultimately fall right back on the very same big government these spurious Republicans routinely rail against—all of it possibly taking place during a bad economy where American jobs are in decline. As Realacrats, we have to take good, long, hard looks at this scenario. Can you imagine how many extra children that will have to be taken care of by some entity, probably the federal government, if the religious fanatics find a way to ban abortion, and 99 percent of all conceived children become part of the population? This would be a massive and colossal undertaking for a system that is shaky at best. Who is going to be assigned with the well-being of all of these children? Do the conservatives not know that this venture will costs millions? How much of it will be footed by the taxpayers; in all likelihood, probably most of it? The welfare state will have to increase its capacities. There is no other way to do it. Orphanages, right now, have kids they can't find homes for, and the shortage of legitimate adoptive parents is a real problem. Cindy Sapsucker can now have ten kids just to give them all away, since abortions will be illegal. This looks like a non-parenting cakewalk. I mean, if you force all women to have all babies, then I guess you are willing to pay for those births, too. I sincerely hope Republicans are not going to force women to have babies and then force them to pay for it as well, all against their wishes. Since Republicans are the ones who want all of these babies, they should be the ones to pay for them. Welcome to the neo-con welfare system. If you ban abortions, you then exert an even bigger amount of responsibility on organizations that deal with unwanted kids, but at the same time, Republicans crusade to cut welfare and limit the number of people who qualify to adopt by such measures as the one to disqualify gay parents just for being gay. Somebody is going to have to help raise all of these new children, and cronyism and the good-ole-boy network are not the answers! I'm sure the religious zealots have an answer for these problems. Maybe they will all pray about it on Sunday mornings. Maybe the Lord will find a way. Maybe he will pay our bills as well. I have no problem with praying, but there will come a time in your life when you have to take action. This situation requires great action in the same way that a failing economy requires great action. Some band of covered wagon, sanctified, Whites only, polygamists doing the rain dance with a cross will not remedy this manufactured cataclysm. While the conservatives and religious nuts promenade throughout the media, criticizing the federal government's involvement in most everything and calling for its immediate downsizing, it will be the federal government who will ultimately have to step in and either run or bail out this new and unimproved welfare state. Who else can do it? I will make that bold prediction right here right now. Hell, I will even go so far as to predict that the federal, local, and state governments will have to create new agencies, new positions, and new businesses just to help curtail the immense pressure of the new welfare state, all to satisfy the same clans who rail against more big government! Maybe you morons don't know the definition of big, because that is precisely what you are asking for.

We're here to Save Your Babies?

Surely the conservatives and the religious right can't be that imbecilic. I know exactly how crafty and artful they are, and I believe they know precisely what they are doing. Previously, I questioned whether or not this entire ploy was purely a coincidence or something more deceptive. Well, after I examined the statistics on all abortions performed in the United States, I found something very nonplussing. The biggest number of abortion cases overall belonged to White women, with African-American women placing in at a distant second.[12] I have always been very suspicious of the fierce opposition to abortion, and I have always experienced a fair amount of cynicism regarding the participants who oppose abortions. I've never really heard any media outlet question this synopsis, but I felt this was a legitimate platform from to do it on. I conceived such skeptical notions even as a teenager, because I just could not be sold on a bill of goods that featured phony, conservative, Republicans attempting to save poor, poverty-stricken, dread-headed kids from the ghetto. In my opinion, the only reason this abortion issue has been so highly visible is due to the race/color of its quarry. If you don't believe me, just think about what happened during the 2008 presidential election. Barack Obama was able to campaign and stump through states that normally voted Republican. Democrats had

---

12 Laurie D. Elam-Evans, Ph.D., Lilo T. Strauss, M.A., Joy Herndon, M.S., Wilda Y. Parker, Sonya V. Bowens, M.S., Suzanne Zane, D.V.M., Cynthia J. Berg, M.D., Abortion Surveillance --- United States, 2000, http://www.cdc.gov/mmwr/preview/mmwrhtml/ss5212a1.htm (November 2003).

rarely ever been true contenders in states such as Virginia, Indiana, and North Carolina, until this recent election, in which Barack Obama was able to outgun his Republican rival John McCain for these former Republican strong holds. They said it couldn't be done, but Barack Obama proved that assumption to be passé. Personally, I believe the Republicans completely understand the reality surrounding Barack Obama's red state upsets. Apparently, demographic changes have now taken place all over this nation that have thrown the Electoral College and the popular vote into a topsy-turvy, political, whirlwind, with every state in the Union inherently up for grabs. There are two main reasons for this demographic population shift. One is the movement of a diverse group of people into traditionally White majority areas and the other is the sheer number of diverse people that now reside in the United States as a whole. Minorities yield a minimal power base when separated and scattered about, but they become a formidable force when united behind one party or one candidate—as was the case in the 2008 presidential election. So while White women appear to be having abortions at a steady pace in this country, minorities, such as Hispanic Americans, are not only descending into America's backyards, but they are also reproducing at a higher rate, which is now beginning to stem the tide and momentum into their voting favor, giving them a brand new stake in the political process! The abortion issue, in the long run, will only continue to change the demographics, and it's a safe bet that religious zealots, Republicans, and conservatives are all completely aware of this new and dangerous possibility. I have my doubts that this argument was ever about the ethics of abortion, and I'm not convinced that God's displeasure at the high number of abortions in this country is a genuine concern. The main concern could very well be the long-term to mid-term and even short-term ramifications abortion will have on plausible voters who could eventually morph into conservatives, when it is a well-known fact that the preponderance of Republicans and conservatives are White. It's obvious to me why the abortion issue is no friend to the Republican Party, because abortion cuts directly into the party's potential powerbase. Why else would it be that the main group of people protesting abortions just happens to be the same group of people who stand to lose the most due to abortions?

Where Does Life Begin?

The other enormous question regarding abortion is the dilemma of pinpointing the exact moment when life begins. I remember back during the presidential debates, Barack Obama felt that it was beyond his pay grade to make such a decision, while John McCain said exactly what his party wanted him to say, not because it was factual, but because it was an easy fix; a Band-Aid on a much larger problem. McCain simply fell in line with the universal conservative ideology that believes life begins at the moment of conception. So, what is the answer? Does anyone actually know? Can anyone ever figure it out, and should we? In today's technological world, we have the power to build I-pods, launch Hubble telescopes, and even regenerate human growth, but deciphering the exact moment where life begins will prove to be far more challenging than we ever expected it to be, if not impossible all together. No one has the true answer to that question, so maybe it is above everyone's pay grade. Conservatives don't have the answer. Liberals don't have the answer. Religious zealots don't have the answer. The media doesn't have the answer. Sarah Palin doesn't have the answer. Hillary Clinton doesn't have the answer. Scientology doesn't have the answer, not even science has been able to find the solution to this one, at least not yet. In defiance of all the rhetoric done by politicians and activists in the media, it's just that: a horde of empty, foundationless, rhetoric! I see loons on television professing their unshakable belief in life at conception. Some even claim their support for this issue is so strong that they would die or kill for it—but that still does not mean they are correct on the issue. It just means they are dangerous fanatics! I find the suggestion that a willingness to die or kill for a cause can somehow make one's stand on that cause more credible to be foolish, shortsighted, cretinous, and derisive. Realacrats would never spend one dollar of taxpayer money trying to decipher such a question, because this question may never come close to being answered. Why waste time on it? The government has more important pawns to manipulate.

The Realacrat Abortion Guidelines

As Realacrats, we would say this about the entire muddled state of affairs regarding the pro-choice argument vs. the pro-life argument.

Since abortions are legal at the moment, I think it would only be realistic and responsible to set parameters based on the safety aspects of the abortions being performed, as it pertains to the mother and the child. I'm not a doctor, but I believe there should be a uniform cut-off marker that ends the time when abortions can be performed and who better than big government to make it all happen? If we're going to tread into this abortion issue, then let's tread cautiously, intelligently, and safely. Once again, I'm not a doctor, but from what I've witnessed regarding pregnancy, it usually tends to take at least a month before most women even know they are pregnant. With that being said, the best the government can do is to try and provide some kind of schedule to federally minimize the number of late-term abortions. This subject could and should be strongly debated by religious groups, political groups, taxpayers, and families. Where is the cut off? Is it two months, three months, four months or so on? Here is the Realacrat plan: there will be no abortions carried out after four months unless the mother's life is in danger. The only exceptions made would occur in cases of rape or incest, which would have to be proven vigorously. I don't enjoy the image of a late-term baby being gashed out of the womb either, but I just cannot bring myself to force some woman, whom I don't know from Eve, to go through with a possibly dangerous abortion after she's either been raped or if she's experiencing life-threatening complications. I know it's easy to sit around and Monday morning quarterback the situation by suggesting a raped woman should simply put the baby up for adoption. That's easy for you and me to say, because we're not the ones dealing with the plethora of emotions surrounding the event. Not only is the woman raped and abused, but forcing her into the trauma of an unwanted pregnancy, where hopefully nothing goes wrong that could endanger the life of her or the baby is arrogant and overbearing to say the least! Then, after all of the labor of having the child, she's just supposed to give it away, give it away, give it away now, and then return home to a normal life where nothing ever happened; living happily ever after with no consequences, flashbacks, guilt, anger, sadness, curiosity, depression, or post-traumatic stress. This could ultimately prove to be a life altering experience, but never mind all of those pitfalls; because God will take care of her--right? Maybe he will, and maybe he won't! That is a shaky gamble at best, but Pat Robertson, Tony Perkins, the Notre

Dame Catholics, and John McCain would all be very proud of her for taking such a great, conservative-friendly risk. She would have just run a gauntlet of emotions and physicality, all to make a band of old, senile, insensitive, imbecilic, megalomaniacal, pig-headed, closed-minded windbags happy. As Realacrats, we understand, as conservatives must begin to understand, that abortions are not going anywhere anytime soon, so it's up to all of us to responsibly deal with them. Instead of touting a religious stump speech, let's attempt to devise a plan to help diminish the window of opportunity for abortions. I believe that a woman should be given about two to four months to decide the outcome of a pregnancy. If the woman is under the age of 18, she must have parental consent. That should be made a federal law! I also believe that no abortion should be allowed to take place without the consent of the father. After all, it's his child too, so he should have a say in it. If a woman fails to produce a father within the two-month period, then she will be forced to have the baby, unless the father is deceased. If he is deceased, his immediate family should be notified, so they can bid for the baby. That's right! I said bid! Once again, I'm not a doctor, but if there is any way possible to have a DNA test on an unborn child to determine fatherhood, then it must be completed before any abortion is performed. This should be a federal law. America can lead the charge on pre-birth, DNA testing. If a woman fails to find out she is pregnant before the first two to four months, she will be forced to have the child. I don't have all the answers, nor do I claim to, but I, as a Realacrat, do have a plan of action that is immersed in reality, not a religious coup! This by no way eliminates abortions, but what it can do is attempt to regulate and gain a much better understanding of the issue. That alone will help lower abortion rates, and lower is better than higher. It's not exactly what conservatives want, but it is far more effective than what they have. This is the core of the Realacrat philosophy. Why exert tons of energy pushing up against resistance, when you can use a minuscule amount of energy to go around it, and get that much closer to your destination? The government is supposed to work like that. It is my belief that the founding fathers kept this kind of model in mind when they designed a government by the people.

MORE BIG GOVERNMENT

A smarter government can beat a bigger government or a smaller government every time, if you can just find people smart enough to run it, and it can serve a useful role in our society, if done right. Despite all the yahooing about state's rights, the federal government has proven time and time again to be the best bet for a uniform policy and justice for all. I thought we had all been through this debate before with the confederate state, succession fiasco. Fifty states all bickering over who deserves the bigger and better seat at the table, bickering over who gets the biggest piece of chicken, bickering over who's going to clean up the mess, and bickering over who's going to pay the bill. This is not democracy! This is grab bag chaos. Fifty states couldn't even agree that they all added up to fifty, because some idiot would say that God told him there were actually fifty-five, and he refuse to participate until it was changed. The Unites States could never truly be united without the federal government or some higher branch of government, to keep things in check, and most importantly; to keep the states from destroying each other.

These same religious zealots who are the main opponents of abortion; are also the ones who hate big government, but it will have to be big government that steps in and puts a stop to this abortion madness. The possible removal of late-term abortions is a subject much too complex and polarizing for all 50 states to deal with on any level. It will require a higher power than Republican governors in the south and Democratic governors in the northeast to solve this one. The federal government, preferably Congress, will have to draw up and pass legislation banning late-term abortions in all 50 states, making it a violation of federal law. This way, if any doctor is found to be performing these late-term abortions, they will be prosecuted to the fullest extent of the law, but not assassinated! I'd rather take my chances with the federal government any day before ever turning my back on some backwater, trigger happy, religious zealot.

LET'S KILL FOR JESUS?

Watching Fox News with Bill O'Reilly, the coverage kept going on and on about all the late-term abortions committed by Dr. Tiller. What is the point? Does any of this matter now? The man is dead! It doesn't matter how many abortions he committed. He didn't deserve to be gunned down for them. If late-term abortions are so bad, then the government or law enforcement should have put a stop to the practice. Harping on the number of abortions performed by Dr. Tiller is nothing more than a blatant attempt to further vilify him, even in death. To me, the message being sent out is one of a righteous killing. Dr. Tiller didn't deserve to die, even though there are many who considered him to be an absolute, murderous, scum bucket. They might as well come on out and say that the world is a better place without him. They might as well come on out and say that his death is vengeance for all of the aborted babies, as they look down from heaven—but this still doesn't mean his murder was justified. If you don't like the laws in the country, then work hard to try and change them for the better. I think President Obama would agree to ban late-term abortions, but please spare me the religious, stump speeches and over-the-top theological rigmarole. What's needed is political reform, not some cheap imitation of a Jim Jones vigilante. I feel bad for Dr. Tiller's family. He became a casualty of an American jihad. How can self-proclaimed Christians have the audacity and the unmitigated gall to call themselves the pro-life party when they sit back and harbor murderers for their cause; similar to the way that some middle-eastern countries knowingly harbor known terrorists their causes? The perpetrator of this hideous crime should be ashamed and the entire right, conservative wing should be ashamed as well. After all, this type of publicity does nothing to revamp the image of the pro-life movement, nor does it help the image of conservatives who are in cahoots with these domestic terrorists, these so-called Christian terrorists, these American terrorists! They may not behead you, but they will put a bullet, or two, or three, or four, or five into your head if God tells them to. Is there anything more dangerous than a fool behind a loaded gun? Dunderheads like this deserve to have their guns and their freedom taken away and replaced with solitary confinement. If I, an African-American, committed this same act against that same doctor, I would probably get the death penalty.

The Abortion Story Featuring God's Will

The fear of an ever-changing, non-political, non-cultural, non-traditional new demographic can present a very serious and very threatening challenge to the reigning status quo. Abortion is fought for political reasons, and Realacrats will not be duped into this charlatan, pseudo-religious puppet show! In closing, I'll leave you with this short story. Another idiotic woman, who allowed her pick-up truck driving husband to dictate her views, said this to me during a conversation about homosexuality.

She said, "How could you be pro-life? You are nothing but a Democratic, baby killer, and God is gonna judge you for this, and he's gonna judge you harshly for it too--buster! You just wait until judgment day, and you'll see what I mean, when you have to stand before God as he asks you the one simple question that will determine the rest of your eternity, and that question will be: why didn't you, Bryian R., stop abortions?" So, I replied back to the holy rolling, Kool-Aid drinker and replied: "I haven't killed any babies, so you watch your false allegations! Whatever party I choose to join is my business, so you can kindly keep your Jonestown nose out of it, and as for God judging me, I would have to say; better him than you. So when God does decide to ask me why I didn't stop abortions, I'm going to reply the only way I know how. I'll say to God: why didn't you stop abortions? I know you have the power to stop anything you want, so why didn't you? Why would you, God, appoint me to stop something that was put into motion through your almighty creations?" According to the Christian doctrine and general, religious doctrines overall, all of these problems were put here by God to come to pass, which is exactly why Realacrats and government should not waste a minute trying to mortally defeat such movements, which are immortal by creation. If all things are possible through God, then that applies to all things that are possible, which may include love, happiness, abortions, and even weapons of mass destruction, and not one of the items mentioned in that list can be legitimately controlled by our civilization. As the old Realacrat motto goes, "We'll save the ones we can and say a prayer for the ones we cannot—and you don't need a bill for that!"

The Gay Issue

The Gay Minister Comes Out of the Closet

Before I get started on the politics of gay marriage, I think I'll share an incident that occurred with a highly religious, self-appointed guru, who claimed to have a direct line to God. Somehow the subject of homosexuality came up in a discussion, and it was all downhill from there. This so-called minister of Christian faith began to explain his views on homosexuality. He believed that God actually hated gay people. In fact, I'm going to be him and give his argument, and here is what he said to me!

"Well man, it's obvious that God hates fags! I mean, I'm sure that's why he gave them the AIDS virus! God's trying to kill them all off. There is no place in heaven or here on earth for gays! There is no such thing as a decent gay. All gays are primitive, sex maniacs. You can never ever trust one. By all means, don't turn your back on one, and I heavily suggest that you don't bend over in front of one either. They are nothing more than a roving band of freaks, outcasts, and degenerates! Society doesn't accept them, as they degrade themselves due to their unbridled sexual appetites. All they ever think about is chasing someone else's feces. The smell of a fetid bowel plastered all over a penis turns these sick animals on. God made Adam and Eve, not Adam and Steve! I absolutely despise homosexuals! The thought of a man getting down on his knees in front of his male lover is just too much to bear. How could he do such a foul and wretched thing? What makes a man want to squeeze and stroke another man? I once saw a gay couple in a park. They were two gay men-of course! The weaker-looking-one got down on his knees and began to operate. The moaning sounds of pleasure and satisfaction made my skin crawl. I would have walked away, but I wanted to witness this abomination firsthand, so I could preach about it. The weaker lover, down his knees, moved quickly on his partner, and the sight around his mouth was disgusting! Before long, the stronger lover wailed loudly calling his lover's name, as he began to jettison his reward. The weak lover simply continued his task. As I watched him looking up at his strong lover masked in biological ointment, I seriously considered killing them. If I had a gun that day, I would have wasted them both, while they were still in the act. God hates fags, and so do I! I would love nothing more than to eradicate the world of all gay people. I believe they should be put into concentration camps, the way the Jews were loaded up in Nazi Germany. We could then herd them all into cyanide chambers, so we could gas them into hell where they belong! They should be stood up on a plateau and executed, so all of our Christian members can watch gloriously as their cold, dead, sin-riddled bodies fall lifelessly into a mass grave to cover their sins in death the same way many of them tried to cover their sins in life, and I, along with my Christian soldiers, would gladly offer our services to pull the trigger. They made a conscious decision to be gay, so we would make a conscious decision to kill them. We would only be doing God's work! God spoke to me and personally told me to exterminate these animals, and that's what will eventually happen."

And following that, with even more of a bombshell, this maniacal zealot made one of the most startling statements, at one of the most inopportune times; quite possibly in all of human history. The raving lunatic then went on to admit to me that he, himself, was a former homosexual. He claimed he was frequently penetrated on numerous occasions by his male mentor. I was floored, shocked, mind-boggled, and vastly bewildered! Then, the unthinkable happened! That rapid fire, all-Christian, all-God-loving, self-proclaimed disciple turned around and winked at me with a devilish grin, licking his lips lecherously. At that very moment, I didn't know if religion had actually helped this hapless soul or indirectly tossed him even deeper into his sexually confused abyss. But one thing was evidently clear to me, and that was the fact that this man was not grappling with the sin of homosexuality. It was the denial of his own mysterious, inner cravings that he'd hoped his newfound religion could help him to erase—but there was obviously no such luck to be had on that front. In my unprofessional opinion, his quest to rest on the righteous, religious, popular side of this issue, even at the drastic expense of selling out and torturing his very core, is the type of primal, powder-kegged confusion that could easily leave an abortion doctor or a gay person gunned down in a pool of blood by some deranged crackpot who may or may not know where their true allegiances lie.

In the end, one has to wonder if the deranged minister was actually one of the lovers in that story, because it sounded a little too personal to me. I'm also perplexed by the Hitler/Nazi Germany references. I find it stunningly ironic that Hitler was rumored to be connected to his hate object, which was Jewish people; the same way that the confused minister was obviously connected to his hate object, which was homosexuality. I also found it quite intriguing that all of his negative, gay slurs were hurled strictly at homosexual men and not homosexual women, but the stigma of the sin does not change based on the sexual orientation of the person who commits it! The more I learn about this anti-gay argument; the more it begins to resemble a corruptive, empowerment tool erected from the victimization of the unjustly vilified and the misunderstood for the sole purpose of even more victimization of the undeserving. It's the old motto of divide and conquer, which lends itself to the goal of oppression and the self-indulgence of power. The so-called protection of the sanctity of traditional marriage between a man and a woman almost seems secondarily pedestrian. Confusion is the environment that nurtures hatred, and it's no coincidence that people like Hitler often rise to power on the backs of those similar to the confused minister, usually on some unjustifiable cause of questionable righteousness, so when either one of these hate-filled, fear mongers decides to journey into politics, their bigoted agendas become law and ethnic and social cleansing becomes the protocol of punishment. Not only should there be separation of church and state, but there should also be a separation of hate and state, because I consider this to be the cancer of politics; and it can devour any political movement blind enough to allow it in.

The Complexity of Homosexuality

Believe it or not, I was not shocked or appalled by any of this. Intolerance of this kind is very rampant here in the South. I've heard these kinds of accusations and ethnic assaults my entire life. The art of judging others has strong roots here in the South, especially when it involves casting judgment on those deemed to be warriors of the societal wastelands. According to Christian beliefs, judging others is a two-way street, but that has done little to curb man's judgment practices. The prevailing idea about homosexuality here in the South is this: God made us heterosexuals right, but he made all homosexuals wrong. But, I thought God didn't make mistakes? The response to that would be: gays weren't born that way; they are trailing the serpent's tail eyeing his anus voraciously. I was watching Pat Robertson on the 700 Club, and the suggestion of homosexuality being a sin choice was front and center, because people have to choose to participate in it. It's a chosen sin, but then again, what sin is not a chosen sin—being born? Maybe you can hang your hat on being born as a sin that you have no control over as a baby, but after that, you are on your own. All you have is your judgment to help you as you prepare to face the maze-like choices life has lined up for you. So, the idea of sin as a choice seems feasible, but not limited, to homosexuality. The choice of sin is life in its bare essence. I don't see any human paradigm that could exist without the choice of sin. In my opinion, the choice of sin is nothing more than God's idea of free will. People are supposed to have free will here on planet Earth. God supposedly made it that way to allow sins to be chosen, because the majority of choices you, or I, make will be marred by sin in some way. I've viewed homosexuality as an option all along! To me, it's just another option for how to live your life. If someone chooses to become homosexual or bi-sexual, and it turns out to be the worst sin they ever commit, I'd say they probably have as much chance of entering into the heavenly gates as anyone else. I think the act of judging is just as much of an abomination as homosexuality is based on biblical ideology, but it is not perceived in such a way by man. If I were God, I would expect my so-called Christians to know better. I would be less-disappointed in the non-religious, gay person, but I would be highly peeved at the very religious, straight person, who is supposed to be preaching and practicing my doctrine, and judging from the perch of immortality with a mortally flawed measuring stick is not a part of it.

I think the real question regarding homosexuality has to do with its status on the sin pole, because different eras seem to cause it to be demonized more intensely. Either so-called Christians are too dumb and don't know this is what they are doing, or they are very artful and cunning in their deliberate attempt to demonize one sin over another. Mathematically speaking, I'd say it's probably half and half! I think the high-ranking, opulent clergy knows exactly what they are doing, but I also believe that the lower ranking, impoverished Joe Six-Packs are clueless! They are merely following the leader! You wouldn't have any opulent clergy, if not for the Joe Six-Packs and Sarah Palinator's of the world. So let's have a look at this sin pole. Where does homosexuality rank on the sin pole? That is the million dollar question. I personally do not know, but I can tell you this much: it's tied with abortion, and judging by all of the attention garnered from this subject, I'd say both of them must rank near, or at, the top.

I remember when the suggestion of a constitutional amendment to ban gay marriage was considered during the former President Bush's 2004 re-election campaign. There have been numerous church organizations around the country that have held anti-gay marriage rallies. I just don't see where the relevance warrants such intense scrutiny. The most dominant sin campaign waged in the past few years has arguably been gay marriage! It is also arguably the most despised sin in the past few years. It appears to me that gay marriage has topped the Hot 100, Sin Chart as the greatest sin in America. These anti-gay crusades are reminiscent of the holy land crusades, as both crusades are based on one idea being superior to another idea. First off, in biblical terms, homosexuality was never labeled as the number one sin or an unforgivable sin. Blasphemy against God and the Holy Spirit is supposedly the worst sin. Do you really want to place homosexuality in the same realm as blasphemy? If so, there are many other sins that need to go along right with it. No one has the right to rank sin according to how they think God sees sin, because no one has any inkling of an idea of how God sees it. For example, I believe that cold-blooded murder is much worse than lying or theft, but that is my opinion, not God's opinion. Homosexuality has been unfairly and politically bumped up the sin pole, in some sort of ideological witch-hunt, because in all honesty, it's a fight that is truly not that important—or at least it shouldn't be that important. People love who they love--end of story!

This is what I refer to as mass hoaxing. Conservatives use the gay marriage issue to rile up and scare the masses with fear tactics such as these: "Well, you know they are going to teach Adam and Steve in your schools now, and your kids are going to be subliminally railroaded into homosexuality. The liberal school system is secretly for homosexuality, and their agenda is to recruit as many children to the cause as possible." The conservative argument will be something simple to this effect: if a school unleashes information to promote awareness about homosexuality, then that school is force-feeding that lifestyle to the innocent. Once again, homosexuality is merely an option. There will always be young people who will be confused about their sexuality. Some of these young people will go both ways, meaning bi-sexual, while others will go the homosexual route or the heterosexual route. This is the reality of the situation. No matter how much we complain about it, there is nothing we, as a society, can truly do about it, and censorship is not the answer, either. You can censor the school curriculum. You can censor your home, but you cannot censor the world, and you cannot censor the right to ideology. You can back a U-Haul up to every school in America and load up all the gay books; take them out to the city dump and have a bonfire, but it will not halt the inflow of the gay philosophy or the displays of the gay lifestyle in the hallways of any school in the country. What are kids supposed to do when they come face-to-face with homosexuality? What are kids supposed to do when their best friends announce they are gay? What are kids supposed to do when the captain of the football team, the captain of the basketball team, the captain of the baseball team, the captain of the softball team, the captain of the swim team, the captain of the debate team, the captain of track and field team, the captain of the golf team, the captain of the tennis team, and maybe even the president of the student council all profess their homosexuality to the world and to your kids? Parents will try to paint gays in a negative light by casting them as freaks, peasants, the failures of society, or the personification of evil, but to younger people, they are just piers. None of these parents actually have true dealings with these gay people, but speak about them as if they do. The kids, on the other hand, go to school with these gay people and know exactly who they are, and what they are. Most times, they are the polar opposite of what's portrayed by angry, bigoted parents. Kids are not imbeciles. Since they spend most of their time affiliating with the so-called demon-seeded gays, it doesn't take long for them to figure out that their parents are actually the ones doing the subliminal railroading, not the school. This is where Republicans and conservatives both go wrong in their arguments. The only thing this empty, mean-spirited rhetoric does is transform gays into discrimination victims in the eyes of many. Instead of rallying against homosexuals, young people sympathize with the gay struggle, and possibly even join in.

I have to side with the liberals on this issue. Demonizing homosexuality is not the answer. There is no answer! Any attempt to legislate the end of homosexuality is misguided and ridiculous. Any politician who promises, or attempts, to use tax payer money to push laws to try and eradicate homosexuality should be labeled a bigot and a financial snollygoster! The conservative movement is always the first in line to complain about big government overspending, but they will waste an enormous amount of time and money on non-issues such as homosexuality. I do not want my hard-earned tax money being squandered on homosexuality! If the idiotic church wants to carry that banner, then let them do it on their own wallets, because I will not contribute one nickel to such a cause! The Republican hypocrisy is fascinating.

I guess it's only wasteful spending if it's a cause that's not on their to-do-list, which brings me to Miss California, the new champion of conservatism. While I do admire her moxie for standing her ground on her beliefs, I do not admire her beliefs. I absolutely despise when someone uses the "That's how I was raised" excuse! This is the one instance where gay rights and discrimination come close enough to actually shake hands, because, being an African-American, I've seen this scapegoat attitude utilized many times in my life. I lost all respect for Miss California, not because she is against gay marriage, but because she still lives her life molding her world views, according to what her family, or her church, has poured into her. I do not care about how you were raised! I am absolutely sick and tired of hearing weak people tell me about how they were raised. That is the biggest cop-out in society, with "The devil made me do it" right behind it. It's not my fault; that's just how I was raised. Bullsh*t, it is your fault! It's 100 percent your fault. When judgment day comes, are you going to look at your maker and say to them, it was not my fault, it's how I was raised. The devil made me do it! I think it's time these poorly managed boxcars step up to the plate to finally take a swing on their own accord for once in their railroaded lives. Point blank, if you are still carrying around ideologies from your family and making conscious decisions based on these beliefs, even though you are now an adult fully capable of making up your own mind without help from grandma, then those beliefs no longer belong to grandma; they now exclusively belong to you. So the next time you make a speech, you might as well leave grandma and the family out of it, because you're now saddling this horse solo. Maybe it's time for you to muster up enough courage and gumption to say, "This is what I believe in. I stand behind my beliefs, which represents me; the same way I represent them." After all, do you think you are the only person who has ever been spoon-fed a high dosage of family driven propaganda, with the intentions of controlling every step you take! I was raised to believe that all White people smelled like dogs when they got wet. A White girl told me she was raised to believe all Blacks had bad breath. I was raised to believe that all White men had small penises. I was raised to believe all White women were forced to have C-section pregnancies, because their vaginas were too small to have a natural birth. A White girl told me she was raised to believe that all Blacks were born with an extra muscle in their legs that makes them run faster. I was raised to believe that White women were filthy, stringy haired, lice carriers, who were terrible in bed, because they all had dried up vaginas that were incapable of bringing a sexually superior Black man to an ejaculation, and I was raised to believe that God didn't make the White vagina deep enough to take the Black man's big, thick penis. There are literally thousands of these axioms, and probably about 99.9999 percent of them are grossly exaggerated and grossly untrue. These suppositions are not taught for their truthfulness! They are taught to brainwash, frighten, and cognitively control the unsuspecting, the willing, and the brainless. So please, spare me from the erroneous aspects of your raisings! If you are against gay marriage because you don't agree with it, then that's okay, but let it be your own rationale and not your grandparent's! I am always amazed at the inability of people to disassociate themselves from their friends or their family, even when there is strong evidence of personal agendas. I am also astonished at the unwillingness of people to even entertain the notion that just maybe their beloved family was wrong on certain issues. Yes, even your highfalutin parents could be, and are, wrong sometimes, and sometimes knowingly and purposely wrong! I figured this out a long time ago, and I'm just a dumb, uneducated, welfare loving Black by most standards! My choices are mine to make, not my family's. Once I became a young adult, I don't even think I was 21 years old yet, I began to see through many of the manufactured illusions, including my family's illusions. Once I see the fallacies of an idea, I can no longer play the game of the dream chaser. I can no longer play the good son, and I can no longer play follow the leader or red rover red rover; send dummy Bryian right over. I knew from then on out that I had to make up my own mind, and I did, with or without the approval of my church or my parents. If they couldn't accept my intellectual independence, then they couldn't accept me. If it meant we went our separate ways, then so be it, but I would not be a sheep to be herded into anyone's flock. I'll find my own flock and my own pasture; thank you very much! This is what Miss California must endure if she is to be touted as a hero. She, like all of us, must be willing to shed her allegiances to the ones she loves dearest in her ongoing quest for the truth, whether she's for gay marriage or against it. The journey towards that conclusive destination belongs to us as individuals, and no one else! The choice belongs to me, and the choice belongs to you.

I was also raised to be against homosexuality, and I was against it for many years of my youthful life. Gay bashing was rampant back in the 80s, and I definitely put in my fair share of it, not necessarily because I disagreed with the gay cause, but because it felt so good to use the bigoted "Hey man, they're a bunch of freaks, but we're not," rationale. Being able to disassociate myself from what I perceived to be an inferior group of people made me feel good about me. I took great pride in being on the right side of the issue, not because it really was the right side, but because it was the popular side. My crowd wanted me pitted against homosexuality, but I didn't have strong feelings for or against it, because my own lifestyle always did, and always does, take precedence over someone else's! I believe there are many more people like me out there. I also believe that there are a larger number of people than expected who are not really as dead set against homosexuality, as they'd like their constituents to believe. As always, the hangers-on are only trying to be positioned on the popular side of the issue, for some form of personal or societal acceptance! I would even go so far as to say that this gay issue is more about making heterosexuals look good than it ever was about making the homosexuals look bad! How else could it be rationally explained? As a Realacrat, it's my observation that this entire fiasco has been poorly managed and poorly designed from the beginning! The key word in Realacrat is real. It's time to deploy a real solution to this saga. The idea of cleansing the world of homosexuality is just not feasible. Why waste time engaging in a war that is not winnable? The eradication of gay culture is unrealistic. As a parent, you can state your case for or against homosexuality, but you cannot culturally enforce it. The decision will ultimately belong to the people, the children. It's their choice to make, not yours. You can try to scare them with the gay boogie man. You can try and use religion to ward off homosexual curiosity. I've even heard of some parents going so far as to commit their children to psychological counseling and even hypnotizing—but after all of these futile efforts have failed; the choice will still remain solely with the individual! Despite what Republicans and conservatives may tell you, the odds are still 50/50. People can either say yes, or they can say no, to homosexuality. It could go either way at any time, and there is little, if anything, you can do about it. Here's my realacratic suggestion: it's your job as a parent to arm your children with all the information about this subject. If you don't, the streets, the schools, the media, and society, as a whole, will! Help your children to understand the consequences of homosexuality! Help your children to understand the consequences of heterosexuality! No matter which one they choose, they will face consequences! Children need to understand this! They must be prepared to make the tough choices regarding their sexuality, because you can't always be there to properly coach them. You can stand on the sidelines and yell profusely, but it's up to them to get out on that playing field and do it! Our job is to have them ready for the moment, because that moment draws closer each and every day.

As for the government's involvement on this issue, they should not even be part of the discussion! The last thing we need is some legislator giving society sexual advice. Lobbying for or against the anus is not an option to be explored-literally! That tax money can be put to better use somewhere else. I'm sorry Rush Limbaugh! I'm sorry Ann Coulter! I'm sorry Sean Hannity! The liberals are right on this one. Freedom of choice prevails! If conservatives are that gung-ho about heterosexual marriages being the only marriages referred to as traditional marriages, then just refer to gay marriages as gay non-traditional marriages. After all, a label is just a sticking label. So why shouldn't the gay guy be able to go down to the courthouse or to a gay friendly church and ask to be bonded in a gay non-traditional marriage? I don't see the big deal over that. Non-traditional just means it's not your typical marriage. We then give the gay couple a gay non-traditional marriage certificate and take their non-traditional money like we'd do with anything else. As far as this issue leading to polygamy or zoophilia, the government can mandate a federal statute that would only allow two adult human beings to be married to each other—no harems and no animals.

The best that any of us can do is hope that our children follow the paths we've pointed them in, but it may not happen that way—that's life! A traditional marriage between a man and a woman is what many of us hope for, but it might not be what many of us get! I hope my daughter marries a man, but I fully understand that it is always a possibility that she may not. I hope my sister marries a man, but I fully understand that it is always a possibility that she may not! All I can do is accept their choices, because I cannot change them, and I will not make them! I cannot eliminate that possibility, and neither can you! Face it, Sean Hannity! Neither you, nor your Republican Party, can control this outcome—nor should you! You can propose any constitutional amendment you like in an attempt to re-steer society back onto the heterosexual highway, but I don't think this is an issue that can be legislated by the government. I do think this issue allows the government the chance to do some highly expensive, highly wasteful grandstanding!

Here is my opinion! It appears to me that the idea of relationships in this country is changing drastically. Once again, I don't understand how one can directionally steer relationships though legislation; seeing as how the ideology of a partnership between a man and a woman seems to be seriously waning at the moment. Same sex attraction is a powerful new trend that actually isn't that new at all. In fact, it's one of the oldest trends in human history, but it really seems to be picking up steam right now. Republicans and conservatives always say they want a smaller government that will remain outside of their personal lives. Well, I don't think there is a government big enough on the entire planet to take on the job of re-instituting heterosexual desires, and then somehow enforcing them. For example, I've noticed a disturbing trend between men and women. It seems that, somewhere along the way, the ideology of manliness has lost some of its luster. I have met a significant number of well-adjusted, well-educated, well-mannered, well-kept, highly thought of, and even sometimes well-paid men and women who just cannot coexist with the opposite sex. I've witnessed guys make attempt after attempt to befriend or start a dialogue with a woman, but for some strange reason, they are met with tons of resistance, skepticism, anger, rejection, insults, demeaning attitudes, extreme standoffishness, and overall rudeness, for no intelligent reason.

The Highfaluting Chili's Woman

I was at a Chili's restaurant in Cordova, Tennessee with a couple of buddies of mine. One was a retired government official and one was a college professor. None of us, including me, were dressed up in million dollar suits at the time. We were just relaxing, drinking, watching basketball, and eating in casual attire. My friend Ed approached this very sexy young lady who took a seat next to us and began a conversation with her about general topics—nothing personal. She never even made eye contact with this man, or any of us for that matter, but she did take the time out of her precious schedule to slam us all by suggesting we were nothing more than a roguish band of poor, broke, trifling, non-ambitious, low-budgeted, uneducated, rent-paying, car-just-got-repossessed niggas—yet my government buddy was White! What she didn't know was that both of these guys, the professor and the retired government agent, were both affluent men who had worked hard and made great gains in their personal and professional lives. For all we know, she could have been the one who'd just had her car repossessed. One thing is for sure. She completely pre-judged and misjudged all three of us. It was there that I saw it. I was Boise State. I was Utah State. I was the University of Hawaii. I was any team besides the national champions in Ms. Thang's eyes. She had already deemed my buddies and me to be non-BCS schools before we ever got a chance to step on her field, automatically eliminating us from contention before we had a chance to even suit up. I guess my friend would have had to flash his championship ring right at the very beginning before muttering a single word so he could have proven himself a candidate worthy enough for her acquaintances. But my question is this: who the hell is she to garner such pre-conditions?

Now, I know what people are going to say here. They will be displeased at my NCAA/sports analogies, but those are the ones unable to grasp the true parallels between life and sports. A struggle is a struggle no matter where it takes place, whether it's at home, at work, or on the grid-iron of some athletic event. Everything revolves around choices and judgments. This is how we are defined on every level. Our ability or our inability to use good judgment in an attempt to make good choices is what determines what we all can and will accomplish, and it also ciphers just how far we all go in our journeys in life. The analogy is not as far-fetched as you might think. Instead of spending unnecessary time bashing and filibustering gay people, the public should be asking what has happened to their beloved society. I know the thought of two men kissing sickens many and causes great concern, but that same concern should be given to the cataclysmic break down of the relationship desirability of men and women. The only thing that seems to be more popular than gay marriage is heterosexual divorce. I don't think homosexuals created this particular hurdle, but this hurdle could go a long way in creating an improved, sociological environment for homosexuality. The reason being, like with the shallow-minded, Chili's woman, there is a new troubling trend emerging between men and women, and it is either the inability based on choice, or it is the inability based on ignorance, to patiently acknowledge, and most of all appreciate, the upsides of both men and women—meaning the potential to become more tomorrow than what you are today, which once was the main characteristic women sought in men. Then, you didn't have to be the national champions 24 hours a day on a year-round basis. Then, if you were a final four participant, or an elite eight participant, or a sweet sixteen participant, or even an NIT champion, women would still consider you as a potential winner with room for improvement. The NCAA, the NBA, and the NFL just to name a few, have all found great success and made billions based on the upside of a potential client; someone who possesses the mindset to dream and aspire, the determination to win, the drive and the courage to compete, the vision to see and seize the moment, the overall ability to rise to the occasion, and a proven track record of being clutch in the face of adversity. This should be the blueprint for every man and every woman's dream lover. Like sports organizations, such as the WWE, if you could find a way to recognize a solid person, and then draft a person with all, or at least half, of these qualities, you should still possess one spectacular mate, maybe not flawless, but great. And for the record, when did just being great become so mediocre that it is often overlooked entirely? This overbearing decadence has driven a wedge between men and women, in return allowing a new option to sneak in the backdoor—literally! All I know is that I, along with my financially comfortable comrades, wasted no time in bidding our rude, voluptuous, gorgeous, and extremely good looking Chili's lady adieu. She turned up her nose and pranced out the door, and we couldn't have cared less. There once was a time when all three of us woman-lusting men would have pestered her unmercifully until she either gave in or left, but today; we were just as content to sit around amongst ourselves, and there lies the problem—there lies the new trend! The snooty Chili's lady didn't care, and neither did we. No one seems to care anymore. People don't seem to care if they date a dude, a chick, the Internet, a farm animal, or themselves, whatever seems to work at the time. Is it really that difficult to see why homosexuality has garnered such momentum during this ethically and socially apathetic environment? Homosexuality has benefited from this new era of apathetic sexuality, but it did not cause this newfound sexual apathy. Homosexuality has become a political football and a scapegoat, but Realacrats plan to punt that football and that scapegoat into political obscurity. It's not so much that I support the gay agenda, as much as it is that I just do not give a damn what people choose to do about their relationship preferences. I just don't care. The government has no business trying to rekindle some kind of biblical romance standard with taxpayer money. As for Republicans, conservatives, religious zealots, and the overall government, you are not the heterosexual, taxpayer-funded, love connection, and you are most certainly not Dr. Phil. In the spirit of Barack Obama's ideology regarding the conception of life on the 2008 campaign trail, I think any endeavor to legislate and enforce parameters on any consenting adult relationship is most definitely above the government's pay grade.

In the end, homosexuality may not even be the biggest threat facing the heterosexual sanctity of marriage between a man and a woman. There could be something much bigger and much more complex. I remember when Rush Limbaugh raised the question regarding the current, welfare system's intrusion into the Black family replacing the Black father; causing the downfall of the Black community in his eyes. Well, I'll take it a step farther! What if technology has replaced the traditional role of men all together? Thanks to technological advances, women don't really need men to reproduce anymore, they don't really need a man to experience sincere sexual stimulation, and they don't have to employ that famed upper-body strength anymore because of technology! As the performance and sustainment gaps begin to close between men and women, the traditional ideology of marriage could be on the rocks permanently, without the over-feared, indoctrinary clutches of the dreaded homosexuality! Could the traditional roles of men be in danger of becoming archaic? Will men become the new dinosaurs? I'd sure like to see how the Pat Robertson's and the GOP's can legislate their maleness back into the female, necessity zone!

So I ask you again: who in the hell was this uptight, uppity, judgmental Chili's woman supposed to be? Michelle Obama, Oprah Winfrey, the Queen of England, Hillary Clinton, Sarah Palin, or maybe Nancy Pelosi? These women have all accomplished enormous success within each of their own rights, but this brazen, uptight, condescending lady at Chili's, who had pre-determined that me and my friends were not quite up to par to her highfalutin, high-hat standards was in no position to be acting all diva-like, because unlike all the skillful women mentioned previously, this Chili's woman, in all likelihood, was no further up the paramount food chain than we were. In all honesty, her resume was probably much shorter than any of ours, but instead of coming clean based on honest and genuine conversation, she slammed the door in all of our faces before we could even raise our hands to knock. She was more than willing to automatically eliminate doors number one, two, and three on her own bigoted, baseless assumptions of a sociological pecking order of which she had personally appointed herself to the top of. So be careful of the knock you ignore, because that knock could be opportunity—a good opportunity that could come back to haunt you.

If you govern your personal life like this, you will fail unequivocally, and if the government or the business world is operated in such a fashion, it will again fail unequivocally. You can't base a sound decision on the unfounded fraction of the whole. The automatic elimination of possibility and potential is the main ingredient in a professional fool. No political party—Realacrat, Republican, or Democrat—will ever live up to its full potential by drowning out logic with blind egocentrism. It is my Realacrat opinion that the same issues that disallow men and women from humility are the exact same issues that cause Democrats and Republicans to be gridlocked within a egocentric, megalomaniacal rut. I believe all parties involved will continue to fail personally and politically until this self-driven, self-sustaining, erroneous, partisan hierarchy is uninstalled from the social psyche. There is no perfect button to push. There is no do-it-all lever to pull, because true progress and real success usually doesn't happen overnight. Any governmental policies bred of such enthusiasm are nothing more than drug-like quick fixes and political Band-Aids. The discountenance of any ideological system based on shallow assumptions and integrated by single-dimensioned intellectuals who attempt to regulate government policy with some knight in shining armor, serendipitous approach must be avoided at all cost. To Realacrats, the act of homosexuality is not a political sin, but the inability to show patience, the inability to recognize and nurture true intellectual talent, the inability to build on and grasp the opportunity of the upside, the inability to honestly self-regulate and the unobservant willingness to permanently slam doors shut that haven't even been opened yet are the quintessential essence of political and humanitarian sin, because you can't just look at a person and find automatic utopia—but you can overlook a person who could be the next best-selling author or the future President of the United States. Realacrats fully understand that appearances are merely possibilities and are not definitives! This is why Realacrats don't just throw stones at the beast; they want to study to gain a better understanding of the nature of the beast, because understanding yields far greater solutions than any blind aggression ever could. Realacrats fight the beast while conservatives fight the boogie man. The unjust notion of a hostile homosexual take-over is boogie man central, and the Realacrats don't have any plans to board that ship of fools!

We're Against Homosexuality—Kind of?

I'll give you another bold opinion: it is to my knowledge and observations that this same sex trend occurs far more frequently on the girl-on-girl side. I think more women have lost interest in men, than men have lost interest in women. I mean, look at it from this perspective: once women begin to find other women sexually attractive, how can a man compete with that? The best-kept secret is out of the bag now. Women have realized just how beautiful and sexy they truly are. There are more beautiful women than there are beautiful men. The ideology of desirability has changed, and that has left a gaping hole in the traditional man and woman relationship model, and there is little, if anything, the government can do about it—so, why bother! Why spend millions of tax dollars trying to unplug an idea that is now self-sustaining? Personally, I call that the essence of insanity! Realacrats will spend no time fighting the wind. Our only responsibility is to ensure that these individuals are not discriminated against.

I see ministers and church members going on crusades to end homosexuality. I've heard some religious zealots claim that God gave them the manifest destiny to destroy homosexuality! I've heard how God hates fags, but what exactly is this trying to say? What exactly is a fag? Who qualifies as a fag? I know ministers who believe wholeheartedly that God does hate fags, but there is a catch, and I've figured it out. The word fag was designed to be hurled at men who date other men. Somehow, this aspect of homosexuality is far more repugnant. When you see tough, macho guys talking big talk about how they hate gay men displaying homosexuality, they are being honest about it in one sense, but you take those same tough, macho, chauvinist guys and put them in a room with Jenna Jamison and Carrie Underwood or Jessica Simpson and Beyonce Knowles or a pre-drugged out Brittany Spears, and these guys would do anything these ladies told them to do. For instance, if

Jenna Jamison, Beyonce Knowles and Carrie Underwood are kissing and clit licking all over each other butt, booty naked, with yummy, delicious, shaved vaginas in full display, along with huge chocolate and vanilla boobs bouncing up and down, neither of these ladies would have to ask any of those macho, homosexual-bashing men to participate. The drooling men would already be there before the women even noticed their presence. I've heard at least four ministers admit privately that this scenario is their number one fantasy. So I asked one of them this question: "How can you indulge in such homosexual behavior—the same homosexual behavior you preach and rail against?" I, personally, thought gay was gay. The righteous minister admitted to me meekly and shamefully that girl-on-girl is different, because it's not nearly as bad as two men. He rationalized it this way: he said God intended for a man to be with a woman, so the man who is caught between two women performing sex acts is not really being homosexual, since he is only behaving in his natural manner. So much for the homosexuality argument being waged for the safety of the children and society, this was never about protecting anyone. This was a grandstanding, social, political, witch-hunt. Gay is okay, as long as it involves multiple women and hopefully some form of male representation—especially if that male is me! If homosexuality is an abomination in the eyes of the Lord, then blatant hypocrisy should also be one. If you're going to torch the gays, you might as well inflame the hypocrites while you're at it. In fact, I would ignite the hypocrites first and foremost. After that, I would strategically lose the matches.

THE FEAR OF BEING CHALLENGED

THE GOD COMPLEX

The arrogance of man has no boundaries! The notion that Joe the Plumber or Joe the Christian knows exactly what God wants leaves me at a loss for words! The notion of God assigning Joe Blow the job of ending homosexuality is laughable and absurd! Then there are the African-American ministers I've seen out marching and protesting the advancement of gays in society. I guess they are just gleeful that Joe the White, Christian male has finally gotten off of their backs for a change and found new witches to hunt. Jim Crow's got a new target now, and the African-American clergy couldn't be happier about it! It's like I said before, it feels very pleasurable to be on the popular side of this issue. Judging down is very satisfying, as long as you are not the one stuck at the bottom! So hear this American churches: it is not your responsibility to end homosexuality! You cannot end it! This is a practice that's managed to survive since the beginning of time. What in the hell on this muck-racking Earth makes anyone believe that they can halt it now? If God wanted it to cease operations, I'm sure that he would have done so by now. I feel safe in saying that God does not need your help to thwart anything, much less homosexuality! God expects these kinds of hurdles to litter our lives—he put them there! By my evaluation, I'd say the best thing that Sean Hannity, Ann Coulter, or anyone else can do is to strive to live their own lives in the fashion that can hopefully somehow earns God's approval! When it comes to other people's lives, we are ineffective at best. I mean, look at it this way: if we were able to control our own destiny or the destiny of other people, there would be no need for a God! We would be our own Gods!

Why would such a powerful entity bestow such responsibility on corrupt man? Why is man so hell bent on trying to assume this responsibility? Here is the startling truth! Man, subconsciously, much like the devil, does not want to bow to anyone or anything, not even God! If there was any way at all possible for man to overthrow God, and replace him as the undisputed ruler of the universe, he would do it in an ejaculatory minute! As Anakin Skywalker said in *Star Wars: Revenge of the Sith*, "We can rule the universe together, and make things the way we want them to be!"[13] I can only imagine where gays and other undesirables would land in that universe. Man wants to be God, because controlling and dictating the universe is the best job ever, and there is nothing more fearful than the helplessness of not being in control and knowing it. Sadly, there are many people within the political realm who have already decided to apply for that universe-ruling job, and we'd all better be praying that they don't get it. I met a Republican jackass once, who was also a preacher, and he made this statement to me about the Democratic Party: "It's that punk ass Bill Clinton's fault! He started welfare in the 90s, so he could give lazy African-Americans and a few lazy Whites a free monthly government handout. If I was God, I would bring about a famine-based plague to starve off all of the poor people who get welfare. The world would be a better place without them. I Thank God for Republicans!"

What this crackpot failed to mention was the fact that he, himself, was only a paycheck away from food stamps and the big government, free-cheese truck making a stop at his house. This is why not just anyone is cut out for God's job. This is also why I could never join the Republican Party. Any Realacrat who believes that they are God or believes they have personally been appointed and anointed to do God's job because he's too busy, will be water boarded until they renounce their membership. One of the most important things about being a Realacrat is to know that you are just a mortal human being; nothing

13 George Lucas, Director, Star Wars Episode III – Revenge of the Sith, 2005.

more and nothing less. Our only responsibility is to do our business, not God's business. God is not a politician and politicians most certainly are not God. If that's not separation of church and state, then I'd sure as hell like to know what is. My advice to Realacrats: govern mortally, prosper, and function worldly, until it's time to move on!

Fear of a Black Planet

I'm sure you're all familiar with *Terminator Salvation,*[14] a movie that apparently failed to impress Bill O'Reilly, despite having numerous fearful and questionable aspects of potential, futuristic, human-based scenarios. The main character, Jim O'Conner, played by Christian Bale, posed a very important question in this movie which was: "What does it mean to be human? Can machines or man ever learn how to clone the human spirit? Can it be replicated in a computer chip?" Conservatives and religious zealots would say the one thing that makes us human is our belief in God, but I beg to differ. The one thing that makes us human is more complex than our beliefs. It's a thing that all governments should take into consideration. It's a thing that no man or government can run away from. It's a thing that factors into all that we think we know; governmental or personal. The thing that makes us human is the X factor. I took algebra one in the ninth grade at Wynne High School, under Mr. Jack Sprat, where I learned about the X factor. X equals the unknown variable. The unknown variable is what limits us to just being human. The unknown is what defines us. The unknown is what challenges us. The unknown is what defeats us. The unknown is what terrifies us. The unknown is what makes us believe, and it is also what makes us not believe. The unknown is what causes us to reach out, and it is also what causes us to pull back. The unknown is what makes us try harder, and it is what makes us give up before we even start. The unknown is what makes us hope, and what makes us pray. The unknown is that which we cannot control, but it can control us; some more than others. Only mortals have the dubious distinction of dealing with the unknown. God has no understanding of the concept of the unknown, because God knows everything. If man could know everything and be free of that unknown variable, then he too would be a God. It's the one thing that holds us back and grounds us in mortality,

14 McG, Director, Terminator Salvation, 2009.

but man still works at a voracious pace to gain as much knowledge as he possibly can on his never-ending quest to be his own God. When man finds all the answers to the universe, he can rule the universe and finally escape the bondage of mortality. By the way, the reason I say, "man this" and "man that" is because man is the one who created and installed all of this crap humanity has to fight through. Maybe one day women will get their chance, and they may do better.

A Realacrat does not wish to rule the universe. A Realacrat knows that just understanding bits and pieces of the universe is an accomplishment all by itself. Any effort to replicate something we cannot see and may never understand through government policy or any other kind of policy is not the kind of ride Realacrats sign up for. The Realacrat ideology is not in the business of knowing what God wants, and it most certainly is not in the business of pretending to know what God wants! Realacrats and everyone else would be better served to focus more of their time and judgments on their own jurisdictions. Our policies have to be designed for humanity, not spiritual absolutes that none of us can ever seem to agree on. Let God rule the heavens, so that we may govern ourselves here on earth! As a Realacrat, I have no intentions of trying to compete against or speak on behalf of something that I have no understanding of, and I think our governmental policies should reflect our lack of expertise on this matter. Instead of divine interpretations deciphered by less-than-divine prognosticators, our governing policies should revolve around common, worldly, mortal sense.

Fear of Humanity

I was watching *The O'Reilly Factor* over the 2009 Memorial Day weekend when I saw Bill O'Reilly questioning Dennis Miller's decision to view the movie *Terminator Salvation*.[15] O'Reilly then went on to chastise and belittle Miller's movie selection rationale based on the alleged simpleton antics of this new Terminator movie. He asked Miller, "Why would you go to see something like this?" Miller then opined that he thought the movie was pretty good. So I got a chance to view this new Terminator movie, and I, like Miller, thought it was very good

15 Fox News, Interview: DENNIS MILLER ON WHY 'JON & KATE PLUS EIGHT' ISN'T GREAT, http://www.foxnews.com/story/0,2933,522682,00.html.

for what it was—but exactly what was it? Obviously, O'Reilly didn't think it was much of anything, because he's not a fan of Christian Bale, due to some of Mr. Bale's questionable personal activities, which have nothing to do with his ability to act. It seemed as if Miller had a certain amount of appreciation for the movie, but he felt too ashamed by O'Reilly to admit it. After viewing this movie myself, I completely understand why the Bill O'Reilly types could not and would not grasp the significance of this movie or any other movie like it, but I think that Miller got it. You may wonder how this movie ties into anything here, but it does. The Terminator movie, like all other alien being concepts, brings in a certain element of humanity that threatens the status quo. The conservative movement is a very close-minded, narrowly-viewed group, where certain questions are not asked because the answers could prove to be too threatening to the genetically entitled, man-made, self-serving hierarchy. The Terminator movie was based on alien machines invading and then enslaving the human race, with the ultimate goal of complete extermination. If you pay close attention, you can see the group called "The Resistance" banding together to fight for their right to survive in the face of annihilation. This rag-tag band of humans was an absolute motley crew composed of humans from all walks of life, from all over the entire planet, at least what was left of it. I saw the young, the old, the deaf, the mute, the blind, women, men, kids, the handicapped, soldiers, African-Americans, Russians, Japanese, Chinese, Hispanics, Arabs, Whites, and so on, all locked into this deadly war against alien machines whose only purpose was to destroy them—all of them! The word all is a very powerful word, because it leaves no one out; and these machines did not discriminate. They killed everyone equally. This meant that the human race, for once in its history, had to be just that--a human race; meaning, no gays, no blacks, no Mexicans, no Americans, no Iraqis—just one united humanity! When we as a people are reduced to nothing more than herds of earthlings in cattle cars, all genetically based, supremacy dreams are permanently knocked off of the top of the food chain. In other words, it may matter who you are forced to live by, but it will not matter who you are forced to die by. Conservatives won't like this at all, but they are powerless to stop it, when and if it ever happens. They can say "One Nation under God" all they want, but when alien or man-made technology pulls the trigger, that one nation will become cosmic dust just like all the other alleged Godless nations.

The appearance of any alien technology here in our world could again prove Charles Darwin, who is despised by most conservatives, to be right again, because if E.T. has enough firepower to cross the galaxy on a full tank of gas, then E.T. most certainly has the power to end our run on this planet, as it would literally, intellectually, and technologically place our species behind the 8-ball, with E.T. holding the pool stick of annihilation. The only thing that could stop it would be the presence of some kind of outer-worldly conscience, but that could prove to be a long shot, as E.T. might reveal itself to be just as vindictive and gluttonous as our civilization, especially if our small corner of the galaxy turns out to be a microcosm of the entire universe, and it won't be good for us if it is! It would be an intergalactic version of "Survival of the Fittest," as the weaker/more imbecilic is consumed by the smarter and the stronger. Darwin wins again!

I don't recall hearing the term America one time in this Terminator movie, because it would have served no purpose against a universal threat. I also didn't recall hearing anything about religion in this movie, because it to would have served no purpose against a universe that was obviously beyond our biblically limited comprehensions. For Republicans, this is blasphemy. For most people, this is science fiction, but for rational human beings, this is a potential glimpse into the future. It's a future where manmade, earthling labels become obsolete, and a new, extraterrestrial hierarchy emerges. This would be Armageddon for all human ideologies, because the confirmation of alien life automatically reduces all of our human belief systems to mud. All of a sudden, our religions, our truths, and our very existences reveal themselves to be not as absolute as we had hoped and prayed they would be.

Visionaries and Patriots of Humanity

The whole exchange between O'Reilly and Miller perplexed me to the limit. I could not understand how or why O'Reilly failed to see the relevance of this concept, no matter how unoriginal it was. It is still a very real possibility. How could a guy from Harvard not see this? It is one thing to be highly-educated, but it is something totally different to be a visionary. Visionary tactics are obviously not necessarily attainable through higher learning. Maybe, the only individual who can lead an individual to the path of a visionary is that individual. With that being said, it is clearly apparent to me that ideologies such as religion and conservatisms are the polar opposites of the visionary.

For example, Jesus Christ was a visionary, but man's corrupt, disfigured version of Christianity is not visionary. The idea of a conservative visionary is an oxymoron. Vision encompasses all that it sees, all that it hears, all that it feels, all that is attainable, and all that is free. Conservative ideology encompasses only that which it agrees with or can control. The very emphasis of conservatism is only engaging a limited amount of ideological structures; structures that serve to regulate the vision, not to enhance it. It all comes down to philosophy. Conservatives believe there is only one true answer, which is usually a solution tied to them or to their belief systems. Liberals are open to anything as a probable answer, and Liberals are open to there being more than one possible facilitator of the truth. Liberals are brave enough to acknowledge unknown variables without ruling them out completely as anti-religious, merely mythical, or the work of the devil. The concept of the human race being one race is visionary, as is the concept of one human race connected through the higher power of a God/higher power is also visionary! It's an old concept; yes, but the acceptance of it remains a vision of the future—a vision that many are struggling to come to grips with even now.

Movies like *Terminator Salvation*, the new *Star Trek*, and all of the *Star Wars* episodes represent what could be interpreted as a liberal point of view about the universe. The mere fact that these concepts are willing to acknowledge any existence of other life forms in the universe again flies in the face of the conservative model of thinking—so, it should be no surprise that Bill O'Reilly and other conservatives have no use for such liberal templates of cognitive suggestion. O'Reilly's lack of enthusiasm for these templates offers up a striking, yet predictable observation. As smart as he and other conservatives may be, they continue to allow their intellects to be stifled and stymied by modern day Puritanism. Why is a smart guy like O'Reilly participating in modern day witch-trials equivalent to the old "the world is flat" teachings? Great thinkers all throughout history have, at some time, been forced to suppress their scientific theories to appease religious egocentrism, and the denial of the unknown is no different! It takes the courage of a visionary to debunk such nonsense, not some pre-historic, Puritan ideology. I just find it astonishing how so many people will follow the church exclusively, but only follow the actions of Jesus Christ sporadically. In my view, religion is a like a crutch. People use it when times are tough, and they forget about it when times are good. They loosely follow what they agree with, and then they completely ignore what they don't agree with, because ignorance sees what it wants to see, and it hears what it wants to hear, and will usually take the path of least intelligence!

Expect the Unexpected

Conservatives and religious zealots have invested entirely too much time and effort into the boogie man blankets of denial, hear no evil see no evil, manly manipulated religions, racial railroading, erroneous pecking orders, and semi-truth hunting. The best thing we all can do is to accept the facts. We are all one earth, and that is our best defense against any heavenly threats. Republicans and naysayers will say that I'm nothing more than a sci-fi loon or some doped-up conspiracy monger by saying: "There is no way that any of this could ever come to fruition, right? I'm a Christian, and I know that God will stop it, because the Bible is absolute, so none of these ideas can possibly exist. I'll just keep praying, and hope it goes away." You do that! You pray, and I'll act. There are millions of astronomers scanning the universe for signs of life. No one can see anything at this moment, which provides a false sense of security and complacency. We can't necessarily see them, but does that mean in any way that they can't already see us? Most animals in the wilderness can see you coming long before you can ever catch a glimpse of them, which is yet another example of the genius of Charles Darwin to study the world around him to form a better understanding of life as a whole. The same principle could apply to the universe. I can't rule it in, and you can't rule it out. As a Realacrat, I want my government siding with the latter part of that statement. All of us have to keep an eye on the sky, whether it's E.T. or a meteor. Your chances of survival are drastically improved when you can see the ammunition that's being pointed at you. People can pray, but the government's job is to be ready for any expected or unexpected phenomenon. The government guys can pray beforehand, but when it's time to punch in the launch codes, pray time and play time will officially be over. The government must remain rational at all times. It can't be overwhelmed by any religious or personal beliefs, and it cannot solely rely on prayer as a savior. It has to rely on investigation and preparation, and it cannot turn a blind eye to any possibility, not matter how trivial it may appear. The government can't remove options from the table based on religious confidences, because it is the government's job to be the eyes and ears of the world, and it almost has to expect something to be out there, which makes the urgency of a contingency plan a top priority, and I'm sure that they probably have one drawn up somewhere, even as we speak, because the government is not as dumb, not as naïve, and not as gullible as people would like to think it is.

The Religious Aspect

Religion

The overwhelming sentiments surrounding my religious ideologies are probably extremely negative, based on my contemptuous desire for separation of church and state, but I would still welcome all religious individuals into the Realacrat Party under the correct circumstances. Your religion belongs solely to you and should never be thrust upon anyone else. The Realacrat Party is based on ideas stooped in reality, and not necessarily religious faith. Let me put it this way: instead of focusing on God's ability to help us and our party, Realacrats will focus on using what God has already given us, which is a faculty of senses, and the ability to think and create. Realacrats are not against God. We are only against handing him any responsibilities that we could possibly take care of ourselves. God gave us a brain, and we should try, if at all possible, to use it whenever possible. Again, we should not expect Jesus Christ to balance our checkbook, or Muhammad or Allah, for that matter. Realacrats believe in being involved with their own lives and their own problems. If a Realacrat is sick in the stomach, the Realacrat will take it upon his or herself to find some anti-acid relief instead of laying it on God's doorstep. In other words, Realacrats don't plan on asking God for anything that they can do for themselves. There is nothing wrong with privately asking God to give you strength and wisdom to make tough decisions. I have called on God for guidance in times of need, but that is just it; I took the initiative regarding my own life, the same way we all have to take the initiative in choosing whether or not we are with God. Without initiative, God would be forced to make decisions for us, and God adamantly opposes that process, and so do I. What is the point of being a human if you can't engage your own initiative? Initiative belongs to the people, and I would argue that one cannot be a true Christian without initiative. I would also argue that the existence of humanity could not be made possible without initiative. Otherwise, we would be robotic zombies or wind-up toy soldiers marching into a dictating oblivion, and God has no interest in simply knocking over human dominoes. To be a Realacrat, one must be able to recognize initiative, and one must be able to make use of their initiative, but as a whole; we will make our choices based on the realities of the moment, which may or may not always be friendly to religion. Realacrats will not be held or pigeonholed into any cognitive, religious slavery. The choice to either go with or against any religious direction will never be removed from the Realacrat table. That is the very essence of separation of church and state, and we all have to make tough decisions regarding what path we follow, so does the government, and those decisions can never be limited by anything, especially religion. It is either yes or no or true or false, but neither the yes nor the no can ever be totally eliminated due to religious dogma. All four options must always be available for choices to be made. Like the founding fathers, Realacrats fully understand how the loss of these options destroys democracy and creates a religious, dictating, monarchy.

No Religion Without Rationale

Religion can be a very helpful tool if it is rationally understood for what it is. Bill Maher, who is my favorite thinker, disagrees with this theory, but I am not yet *Religulous.* Just because Realacrats refuse to be lassoed by religious manifestoes does not mean that we are willing to totally throw away all that religion has to offer. This is what makes us intellectually unique. Unlike the religious zealots, who are quick to throw away all that Charles Darwin researched because certain aspects of it are in direct contradiction with some prominent religious teachings, Realacrats fully understand the importance of both Darwin and religion. Both Darwin and the Bible share some excellent lessons, and knowledge is knowledge apart from whom or where it originates, whether it is antagonistic or not. Realacrats take great pride in their ability to listen and learn from all sides, and sometimes even their opposition. This is specifically why Realacrats will not do away with all religion teachings, because we know that somewhere within the many topics lies vast knowledge about life.

Now, Bill Maher has repeatedly made fun of Biblical passages on his show on HBO, which I watch religiously! How ironic that I would use that word. He loves to make fun of the talking snake scenario and belittles it the way the religious zealots belittle everything and everybody who does not believe in the talking snake. So somewhere in the middle must lie the truth, and it is the Realacrats that will attempt to uncover that truth once and for all. It is my background in literature and poetry that has ultimately allowed for me to have a special insight into societal institutions such as the Bible and its relevance, but Darwin's scientific research and observations of living creatures in their natural habitats cannot be denied. If you don't believe him, you should go out into nature and make your own observations. Your results will further confirm Darwin's theories. Hunters have relied on Darwin's observations for years now, even though they will never publicly admit to it due to their religious limitations. What Bill Maher may not understand is the symbolism or the metaphorical and allegorical life tribulations in the Bible, which continues to hold the admiration and trust of so many. Let's take the infamous talking snake incident, for example. Non-believers and atheists will point out that the idea of an actual talking snake as ridiculous. They consider a talking snake slithering over to Eve and selling her some anti-God propaganda as astronomically risible. The idea of a Water Moccasin or a King Cobra coaxing Eve into an apple eating tour is the epitome of absurdity to many religious opponents, but there may be some validity to this story if it is understood for what it truly is--a symbolic allegory.

How would I know this you may ask? Well, I studied poetry, journalism, and literature in college for many years and unbeknownst to many of the literary deficient minds, the Bible is a book of literature, allegories, symbolisms, metaphors, oxymorons, paradoxes, puns, hyperboles, apostrophes, soliloquies, verbal ironies, situational ironies, allusions, personifications, and overall poetry—and that does not mean, in any form or fashion, that the truth is not strongly represented. The snake or serpent has long been affiliated with evil and is still a symbol of evil even today. Whether it was a snake, a raven or any other vilified animal, it is the existence, the communication, and the mesmerizing power of evil that caused the irreconcilable damage to Eve by tempting her to pursue something that, on the outside, appeared to be delicious and harmless, but on the inside was rotten and corrupt to the core. Looks can be and usually are deceiving. This reminds me of old sayings like, "Everything that glitters ain't gold" and "The grass ain't always greener on the other side! You might find weeds when you get there." How many times have we seen this storyline play out during our very own lifetime? Have you been tempted to do something that you knew was wrong, but at the same time some subconscious, non-vocal voice deep inside of you continually coaxed and prodded you to do it anyway? At times, it almost seemed enthralling, as the voice eventually convinced you that what you were about to embark on was actually not that bad after all, and no one would ever know about it anyway, and it'll be for just this one time only, so just go ahead and do it. I promise I'll never tell, so let's have some fun! Who can sit here with a straight face and say unequivocally that this has never happened to them? This tribulation is just as authentic and just as genuine as Darwin's observations. Therefore, neither Darwin's studies nor the religious aspects should be eliminated from the intellectual discussion. Realacrats will not place either one on an integrity chopping block, because both are reasonable mechanisms for decision making.

You Don't Have to Be Religious to Learn From It

The reason I bring up this controversial manifesto is to try and open doors to a broader way of thinking. This broader way of thinking is the doorway into the Realacrat Party, which could possibly include religious believers and non-religious believers, such as atheists. Yes, that's right: I said atheists! The Realacrat Party will recruit the best minds available, including religious skeptics and atheists. Unlike conservatives, Republicans, and religious zealots, you don't have to be a Christian to be in our party. You don't even have to be religious. Now, I've already expressed my personal belief in Jesus Christ, not Christianity—but Jesus Christ. I believe that Jesus Christ had the ability to tap into a greater subconscious of an unknown power. I think we all have glimpses of this power, but it appears as if Jesus and others were able to tap that power more than any of us can, at least for the moment. I think any ideology of a potential, unknown power is not as irrational or farfetched as some tend to think it is. What is farfetched is the notion that it can be definitively explained through the mortality of our abilities.

That belief is private, and it affects me only, not my party. The guy sitting next to me may be a follower of Buddha or Muhammad, and that is perfectly acceptable. So look at it this way, if you can learn a lot from a dummy, then you can retrieve valuable insight from anywhere, including other religious theologies with which you may be unfamiliar with, or you may disagree with, but you cannot credibly debunk everything unrelated to your religious comfort zone without severely limiting your ability to cognitively evolve beyond where you are right now, and nowhere is it written that being a slave to your limitations makes you a better Christian, a better Muslim, or a better atheist. So it seems to me that thinking and learning beyond your self-imposed limitations does nothing to sway you one way or the other, so why not learn all you can? We may or may not have a God in common, but we do have a humanistic, academic, and economical recipe for success in common, and that is all we really need. The same recipe applies to the atheist. As long as that individual can learn anything objectively from anyone objectively, I can absolutely co-exist with that individual in the Realacrat Party. For example, I believe Jesus Christ was the son of God; although, I am not convinced that he was the only one exclusively connected to God, while atheist believe there is no God. We can agree to disagree, but it does not end there. Remember, objectivity and flexibility is the quintessential and fundamental nature of a Realacrat. So let's not dwell on Jesus Christ as the son of God. Let's dwell on Jesus Christ, the teacher and philosopher of life. As with Darwin's theory of evolution and the talking snake allegories, you can't just toss out all that Jesus Christ spoke about purely because you don't believe he was the Son of God—or that there is a God. Buddha had a vast and knowledgeable arsenal. Muhammad had a vast and knowledgeable arsenal, and Jesus had a vast knowledgeable arsenal. Realacrats plan on raiding all of these arsenals, not just one, because I don't have to become a Buddhist just to agree with Buddha.

Here is another allegorical and symbolic example of why Jesus Christ the teacher and philosopher must be reckoned with. A woman who had allegedly been promiscuous with many men was sought out for judgment and punishment. Apparently, this woman was a prostitute. The self-righteous, self-appointed, egocentric, public mob decided to take justice into their own hands as judge, jury and the executioners. Whether this woman had been sexually promiscuous for a day or a lifetime, it did not matter to these bloodthirsty, punishment-mongers. They didn't care about the consequences that had pushed this woman into her alleged lifestyle of prostitution. The only thing this pompous, braggadocios band of hypocrites cared about was looking down on someone who was obviously less fortunate, with the hopes of doling out their brand of unwarranted and severely questionable hedonistic punishment, not so much to teach the woman a lesson, but to parade their own inflated ego-maniacal righteousness. Jesus Christ stepped in and questioned these marauding, two-faced, hypocrites. After hearing the charges levied against the woman, Jesus Christ argued a lawyer-based defense for the woman by questioning the moral authority of this band of ethical thieves and attitudinizers to sentence this woman to death for something they themselves had more than likely participated in; many of them, probably with this very woman at one time or another. So when Jesus Christ raised doubts about the moral authority of those sinful judges and sinful executioners in doling out punishment on a fellow sinful individual, it brought into question the ability of one wrong to fairly judge another wrong. Needless to say, the stoning execution was thwarted! Once again, how many of us can say with a straight face that we have never either experienced or witnessed this storyline play out in our lifetime. Jesus Christ the teacher had a fabulous intellect; leave God out of it. The lesson Jesus taught and fought for here was a life lesson, not a heavenly lesson, and that lesson is: the gross, unwarranted, arrogance of self-righteousness can be just as corrupt as the corruption it intends to dismantle. The lesson is: self-righteousness is corruption in and of itself. The lesson is: everyone deserves to have some form of defense when brought before a jury for a trial, and everyone deserves to at least have a trail. Otherwise, anyone accused of anything would be and could be convicted and possibly wrongfully sentenced or executed. The lesson is: no one has the right to force any kind of condition on you that they themselves have been unwilling or unable to sustain. The lesson is: the only true corruption you can ever hope to remedy or abolish is the corruption that exists within you, the man in the mirror; anything else is a witch-hunt, and witch-hunts are not intended to remedy or abolish corruption. Witch hunts are intended to empower the powerful and to remove power from the powerless. Even if you are a staunch atheist, Muslim, Buddhist, or Jew, how can you possibly dispute the remarkable authenticity of Jesus Christ's life teachings of humanity? This does not prove that he is the son of God, but it does prove that he was intellectually empowered with a strong desire for fairness and truth. Is there anyone out here who cannot see the appeal of such principles within the Realacrat Party? Fairness and truth are not limited only to Christianity. They can be and should be applied to all of humanity. If you take the time to explore the themes of these other religions and non-religious philosophies, you will find elements of such ideologies prove that they are not exclusive to Christianity, which means that we all can share them for the good of humanity regardless of a religious pecking order. This can be accomplished, and the Realacrat Party should be the first to tackle it. The same principles of learning, truth, and fairness of Jesus Christ's teachings could always be applied to include other religious leaders, who were also just as scholarly within their own teachings. The only reason I did not indulge the teachings of Muhammad is because I am not familiar enough with them to speak on them, but there is one thing we should all agree on, and that is: none of these religious philosophers were dummies, and as long as you can prove that you are not a moron by choice, we should all be more willing to accommodate possibility.

I can see why someone like Jesus Christ was labeled as a radical. He brought forth a new, radical approach to religion, and he called it the New Testament. This was a drastic leap of faith away from the previous testament, which represented a major policy change and drew intense scrutiny ironically similar to the negativity being hurled at the entire leftist ideology today, because the success of the liberal, open-minded era does have something in common with Jesus, and it's called change, which sometimes, like now, can represent something completely different than anything that has come before it, very similar to the social rise of Jesus. Republicans and conservatives will be highly upset at my comparisons of the left to the White, blue-eyed Jesus, but I have every right to make any comparison, even if it means using Jesus, because he belongs to me just as much as conservatives believe that he belongs only to them. I'm just as much of a shareholder in the Jesus stock as they are—we all are! So was he the original socialist/activist?

Was he the original liberal/moderate/radical? Judging by the standards of his peers, they deemed him as all of the above and also deemed him to be a definite threat to the status quo. Jesus Christ had to be radically liberal; otherwise, there would be no New Testament. If he were a strict constructionist/conservative, he would have continued on with the teachings of the Old Testament. Now, statements such as these will, again, infuriate conservatives, because they self-servingly, exclusively, and deceitfully feel they own 99 percent of the Jesus brand, but they are sadly mistaken. Anyone can have something in common with Jesus Christ, and it does not necessarily have to be in a religious sense, because being a game changer or a visionary is not exclusive to religion.

The plight of Jesus Christ is a metaphor, which symbolizes the fickleness of human nature, the willingness of the sheep to be led, the unappreciative dogma of human nature, the corruptive influences of hedonism, selective vilifying, the severe lack of patience in human nature, the hypocrisy of violence dressed up as peace, the friendly hand that puts the knife in your back, the suppression of freedom; the injustices of life, and the fear of being challenged. Oddly enough, none of these ideologues hinge on the question of whether or not Jesus was the son of God, because knowledge is multi-dimensional, even if your faith is not! This is the world we live in, and these are the obstacles we face, which gives life to our politics! I think the plight of Jesus says more about us than it does about him or God! In all fairness, I think religion in general says more about us than it does about God, and I think that is the real significance of religion, not some simpleton game of follow the leader, or my God is better than your God!

Separation of Church and State

The founding fathers always spoke about a separation between church and state. The idea of a religious monarchy was the very thing they were trying to get away from. The founding fathers knew of the ills and perils of a religious few having the power over society, especially the government. There is an old famous saying that says, "Power tends to corrupt, and absolute power tends to corrupt absolutely." I will probably have to use that quote a few times in this book. This could not be more discernible than by looking closely at any area where one religious component is the rule of law and government, and everything else is oppressed into ideological submission. Let's face it! The church has not been a glowing model of fair and balanced government throughout human history. I would even argue that there has been no bigger failure within the governing process than the mishandling of the church. I would also argue that the church has been, and still is, one of the most, if not the most, corrupt organizations in human history. People have used the church to finance and enhance everything under the sun from murder to rape to slavery, because a dishonest select few have often been left unregulated due to the fear of being challenged, as their departmentalized quests were allowed to become the face of the whole. As Bill Maher explored in the movie *Religious*,[16] religion is not based on science, and it is not based on rationale. Religion is based solely on faith. Faith is a very useful thing for the individual, but it is not necessarily useful for a group of individuals, because the term individual suggests differences, and religion does poorly when faced with differences. Religion is at its best in a uniform, unilateral, homogenous environment, where all parties involved are in agreement, but then again, most groups, gangs, or organizations are all at their collective apexes in such environments of consistency. Religion is a very personalized ideology. People often feel as if they actually own their religious aspects, and they feel as if they are spiritually connected to religion better than anyone else, based on the religion for which they are willing to live and die. Such strong passions do not, under any circumstances, allow for the legitimacy of any skepticism or tolerance. Duality is not usually welcomed with open arms here. Once again, I'm reminded of an old saying: "It's my way or the highway!" I think that is religion in a nutshell. Maybe, this is one of the many and main reasons why the founding fathers were so unwilling, so reluctant, and so cautious about integrating or merging the church and the state. Whether or not Jesus was the son of God is not really the issue at hand, the issue at hand is the balance between personal beliefs and

---

16 Larry Charles, Director, Religulous, 2008.

practical beliefs, because contrary to religious misconceptions, there is a colossal difference between the two. Once again, I'm reminded of an old saying: "It's only business--never personal." But religion is personal, and it should not be a business. It was never designed to be a business. The idea of business was crafted and developed by man to better assist in the pursuit of riches and wealth, and religion should have no part in that. In plain English, there will be no shops in the temple! I now understand why Jesus tore down the shops in the holy temple. Here's a new one for you! Maybe Jesus was saying there should be a separation of state and church, while the founding fathers were preaching for a separation of church and state, but in the end, they were all embarked towards the same solution. Jesus once told a Jew to give to Caesar what is Caesar's and give to the Lord what is the Lord's.[17] To me, what that statement says is very clear-cut. Caesar's worldly possessions and God's soulful possessions were then and are now two totally different things. It's like having God's apples and Caesar's oranges, the government mule versus God's holy stool. The government mule has no right to deny you access to God's holy stool, while God's holy stool has no interest, desire or relevance in man's government mule. It's only when you attempt to combine and intertwine the two that you run into serious discrepancies. Obviously, Jesus knew the dangers of using the holy temple as a business outlet to gain profit for man. The exchange of wealth within any temple would only further the economic and corruptive power base of man, not the righteousness of God! The temple is supposed to be a personal place of worship, and worship is for God, not money or power. This behavior leads to the rich becoming richer, and the powerful becoming more powerful, to the point at which man can began to dictate God's relationships with his own people. When the opulent clergy begins to decide who deserves access to the temple, they are attempting to also decide who has access to God. Business always equates to the exchanges of money and power, and both will find a way to corrupt any religious compartment with which they get involved. The government is a business, and its business is to make, collect, and spend as much money as it can possibly get its greedy hands on. This aspect alone is enough to warrant a separation of state and church.

---

17 Bob Deffinbaugh, God and Government (Luke 20:19-26), http://bible.org/seriespage/god-and-government-luke-2019-26.

Government is a Business

The founding fathers obviously knew this all too well, because they spoke against the combination of church and state from the beginning, and for good reason. The government is a business, first and foremost, and must be treated as such. It is an economic, financial entity that is based on the imports, exports, and the inner/intra-state commerce of goods and services for a profit. Once again, the idea of a financial profit should eliminate any inclusion of religion or church. The government's job is to make money. If the government fails to do so, then the country goes bankrupt. The world goes bankrupt! Business is a job, not a personal belief system or some faith-based initiative. Have you ever heard the saying, "It's a dirty job, but somebody's got to do it?" Well, that saying is affirmative, because the next statement you'll hear after that will be one that goes like this: "If you refuse to do this job, then we will find somebody out there who will," because the show must and will go on with or without you or any of your religious deliberations. The operation of a functioning government is often a dirty job, and somebody has to do it while leaving aside any personal or religious ethics. If you can't do your job due to some religious restrictions, you will be replaced, and your paycheck may find its way into someone else's pocket.

A classic example of this mentality is our military, which operates on what I refer to as a willing suspension of religious doctrine for the further proliferation of a specific agenda. Yes, the United States was founded on Christian principles, but those principles are methodically tucked away by our military troops, our government officials and by us, the American citizens; whenever the time calls for the dirty job of killing, whether it's provoked, unprovoked or accidental, there is obviously a time to be religious and a time to face the real world. Your job as a human being is to first survive, and you cannot survive without a means of income. Last time I checked, prayer did little to ease the pains of starvation. The "give to Caesar what it is Caesar's" statement means you have to get up and go to work to support your family, pay your taxes to the government, while giving your personal time and your soul to God. Expressly, God and Caesar don't mix! I know there are laws in this country strictly based on the Christian Ten Commandments, and that is not a real problem. Wishing someone a Merry Christmas is not a real problem. Holding a Christmas parade or a Christmas play is not a real problem. Wishing someone a Happy Easter is not a real problem. Reciting the words "One nation under God" is not a real problem. It just means we are one of the nations under God, not the only nation under God! I know many arrogant, genetic-entitlement-based people who believe that they are the only nation under God, but they are severely blinded by their own megalomaniacal dreams of grandeur. I call that fantasy land! The only real problem happens when any traditional Christian-based beliefs or overall religious based beliefs are legally forced on the entire population. If the government and the 700 Club passed a law that forced all Americans and all non-Americans to recognize Jesus Christ as the sole religious icon; only then would there truly be a serious threat to pure vintage freedom. You can't force all Americans and all non-Americans to officially recognize Christmas, Easter, Jewish holidays, Islamic holidays, or any other religious holidays. If the federal government wants to shut down to acknowledge a Jewish or Islamic holiday, they have every right to do so, but they cannot under any circumstances force me or you to follow suit. That is the undisputed essence of the separation between church and state. And furthermore, we as Realacrats are not intimidated or offended by the governmental recognition of holidays of different faiths, and we are more than willing to participate and celebrate them as well, because Realacrats know that simply acknowledging an event or a tradition does correlate into dogmatic indoctrination. Realacrats don't fear intellectual expansion, religious or otherwise!

The Torture Debate

Torture

Before I get started on this torture issue, let me say this to all of my leftist friends, who are unconditionally against torture. If I told you guys that I had Rush Limbaugh locked-up in a room, where he was forced to watch a White, Christian woman have liberally indoctrinated, sexual intercourse with an African-American man, who just happened to be a Muslim, with a huge table of his favorite prescription drugs, and a stack of triple cheeseburgers, just out of his reach; a television placed on CNN, and a guy dressed up like former Philadelphia Eagles quarterback Donavan McNabb kissing a woman dressed up like Laura Ingram, you can't tell me that you all wouldn't pay money to see that. I don't necessarily believe in physically hurting someone, but I am more than willing to mess with somebody's mind!

The question of torture is a polarizing subject to most Americans and politicians. Republicans/conservatives tend to be for it, while Democrats/liberals tend to be against it. As a Realacrat, I believe that some of the torture tactics deployed by the Bush Administration were viable, and if I were President, I'd allow for the continuance of some of those policies—but only as a last resort of a dire straits situation. Here is where I disagree with the Democrats and liberals. As a Realacrat, we will not be indebted or bonded by any of the groups, not Moveon.org or any other political band. It seems to me that if you are a Republican, you have to toe-the-line to receive Rush Limbaugh's approval. If you are a Democrat, you have to toe-the-line of any liberal media conglomerate or fringe publication. Neither of these political horses can lead me to water, nor can they make me drink! Speaking as a former Democrat, I disagree with the liberal positioning on torture! Since when did war become a sportsmanship contest? During times of war, the tough get going and the captured get scared. As a detainee, your job is to talk and release information. I don't want to torture anyone, but extenuating circumstances call for extenuating actions. I believe in the three strikes approach when dealing with detainees. We will be kind and courteous the first three times we question you, and we would even go so far as to offer you food, water, conjugal visits, and even time to speak to your family via phone, but when we ask of your participation during interrogations, we expect to be remunerated with sufficient and useful information. If you choose to be non-cooperative, water boarding will always be an option, similar to a pocket veto, because we can always reach into our back pocket and utilize it when needed. This is not a first line of defense; nor is it a desirable one, but it will be a potential one, and the potential is always present! We will do everything in our power to derail these proceedings, but there will be times when these actions must be, and will be, implemented. I feel that if the President, the CIA, or the FBI knows of a formidable plot to attack the country, it's their patriotic duty to coax that information from the detainee by any means necessary, short of killing that individual or placing them in a vegetative state! I would have water boarded the September 11th mastermind myself to get him to talk. If there was even the slight possibility of a sequel, I would not only water board this guy, I would have 2-by-4 boarded his ass! If a government man was clandestinely responsible for this, then he would get water boarded on his way to the electric chair! I would have utilized anything in my repertoire to make the perpatrator's life that much more uncomfortable, even if it meant giving him uppers so he couldn't sleep and then forcing him to listen to music by Dan Fogelberg and John Tesh! When American lives are at stake, mainly mine, sportsmanship goes right out the nearest window. There is only one goal worth fighting for at that very moment, and it's called survival! Survival is a goal that must be met at all costs, even if it means death, as some must die in order for others to live! I know it sounds brutal, and it is; but you can't save everybody. What we can do is save as many people as we can! If water boarding achieves this goal, then I suggest the detainees make preparations to take a cognitive swim. I'd approve it, and sign off on it without batting an eyelash! We don't condone torture, but we don't condemn it either. To me, it's just another option! As for the rest of the world, I would explain it this way: do not attack my country, and I will not attack yours! What's so hard about that? I find it riveting how many of the same people who applauded the dropping of the atomic bomb on Japan causing the deaths and crippling of hundreds of thousands for generations are now up in arms over water boarding! You don't have to look any further than Darfur to see real torture at work every day, while the entire world remains reluctant to get involved. This was never a question about the morality of water boarding. This is a frail attempt to appear to be the good guys. I don't care if it looks good to China or Pakistan! This is business, not personal! There is that quote again. I think the other countries around the world get it, even if a majority of Americans fail to grasp this concept. I don't believe that public opinion polls should be dictating our detainee policies. Acts of war are as serious as it gets, and cannot be taken lightly. Prisoners of war in other countries are made to talk via whatever methods are available. If you don't believe me, just take a trip to China! The Chinese government has been known to torture its own people, as well as foreigners. You do not want to become imprisoned in China. Britain also has stiff punishments for those who play hard ball with their interrogators, and I don't think that anyone in America wants to find themselves at the mercy of the Russian KGB. Hell, you don't even want to go to jail in Mexico, for that matter. And by all means, none of you want any part of being interrogated in North Korea. Kim Jong-il would probably give you electric shock volts up the anus while personally water boarding you. You can't allow an unwillingness to commit to tough interrogations to cause the United States to become limited in data gathering, while these other countries continue on with their rough shot collections. The safety of the nation is not something that can be compromised on some flighty ethical issue. There is a big difference between going to war and playing cowboys and Indians in the backyard.

I never liked President Bush's Iraqi agenda, but I did attempt to give him an objective look at first, after the attacks of September 11th.

When he sent troops to Afghanistan, I felt it was the right thing to do. His policy of undertaking preemptive strikes against the enemy was a crafty maneuver. I had no problem with the idea of going on the offense instead of sitting back and waiting to play defense. I give President Bush all the credit in world for such actions. Bush and Cheney attacked the terrorists in hopes of disrupting terrorists from attacking us; that is a brilliant and shrewd business plan, even though the invading and occupying of another country is a very demanding load, especially a Muslim-based, hostile country. I knew then that it would be a long, hard battle, but I also knew that the American psyche is no shape to deal with war time conflicts here on American soil. These hicks would be more concerned with trying to make sure the races don't mix in the fox holes than actually fighting the enemy! War should always be the last option, because there are many other aspects that come along with it—one being torture! When other terrorists from other countries such as Iran, Syria, Saudi Arabia, and Afghanistan started to join in the fight against us by utilizing guerilla war tactics, the odds of torture became a shoe-in certainty. War produces torture, and guerilla war simply escalates it. There is no good way to successfully fend off guerilla combat. The need for strategic information becomes a lifeline, and torture becomes a very effective way to achieve that information. In some cases it may be the only way to do it. If you're not ready and willing to make these kinds of sacrifices, then a ground war should not be an option for you. Stepping into any situation that you are not totally prepared for is a fool's move. Fighting a torture-less war on terror is about as asinine as trying to drive a car with no fuel—you won't get far.

Although it is possible, I don't think that it is very likely that Nancy Pelosi was left out of the loop on all intelligence information. I believe the information she received from the CIA was fairly accurate, with fairly being the key word. Ms. Pelosi just does not want to be associated with torture at this time, because it is bad for her leftist image. She's between a rock and hard place. She knows that enhanced interrogations could have been effective, but she also knows her constituents would not be happy about it. Her constituents represent her voting support, so Ms. Pelosi has to toe-the-line on this issue. This is the classic Washington two-step, where a politician dances to their party's music, rather than what's best for their country. Ms. Pelosi is no worse than any other politician in Washington, and she is not alone in her pandering. Once again, the reasoning behind these misleading allegations is unrealistic. The CIA is a counter-intelligence, intelligence gathering, misinformation dispersing, clandestine-mission-planning, highly classified and highly deceptive organization that manages top-secret foreign policy projects with superior espionage tactics. The CIA lives and dies through its world-class, highly classified espionage programs. Intelligence gathering is a very serious and very treacherous business, where good men and women come up missing never to be heard from again in attempts to gain and report back sensitive information that could change the face of the world. Every civilized nation is part of the information age, and every civilized nation keeps a close eye on its friends and its enemies. Every nation is looking to gain some kind of an advantage, some form of an upper hand. If I was a betting man, I'd say that all of these nations will go through extremely harsh measures to achieve their objectives, even if it means using torturous type activities. The espionage business is a very dirty, very crooked, cut-throat business. If you are too naïve to play the game, your nation falls squarely in the danger zone. The spy business was built on murkiness. When a CIA operative's cover is blown, it's curtains for that individual. The CIA has no other alternative but to operate within a cloak of darkness and secrecy. I mean, you just can't announce to the world what country you plan to infiltrate and spy on, and then send your people into a waiting buzz saw. Intelligence gathering must be cloaked, even if it means cloaking a Congressional member or two temporarily. Transparency inside the CIA is a paradoxical statement, because the two are polar opposites. The CIA's job is to be deceptive, even to some of its own constituents. I would imagine that the CIA has to absolutely shoot straight with only the President and Vice-President. With that being said, the idea that Nancy Pelosi was told a plethora of half-truths and watered down events by the George Bush/Dick Cheney-CIA is not that unfathomable. I think Dick Cheney himself would give out murky explanations to anyone he deemed to be a non-teammate, and that would definitely include Democrats. But still, Washington DC is a very gossipy town. It's like the old saying goes, "Tell a friend, tell a phone, tell a Congress!" Congressional members, Pentagon members, White House staffers—they are all very loose lipped about damn near anything. The public may not know about it, but government officials always leak information amongst themselves first, before it ever leaks out into the media. Even if Nancy Pelosi didn't get the full Monty from the CIA, she would have eventually gotten it from other government officials, preferably other Congressional cohorts. In a realistic world, the CIA has to operate on an "It's only illegal if you get caught" premise. A Realacrat would instruct the CIA to do whatever it had to do to get the results needed, without getting sloppy. For example, if CIA operatives find themselves in a position to make some roguish corrupt world leader who is an exemplary threat to the United States and its global interests, suddenly become a missing person, they would be advised to do it, but cautiously—meaning no loose ends. This is standard CIA operating procedure. They could not be successful with a "tip-toe through-the-tulips" approach. This business is a dog eats dog business at its worst. All the presidents recognize this, and so should all other government officials, especially Congress—and I'm sure all of them probably do. We must adopt the Realacrat philosophy regarding our intelligence agencies. Transparency and ethical questions have no bearing and no place in the discussion. The public is better left in the dark until the situation has been neutralized. The media's job is to report and gain ratings to make money, not necessarily national security. It is the government's job to make sure it knows as much about what goes on in the world as possible. The government cannot afford to be left out of the loop. There could be grave consequences for such actions; therefore, the CIA must be on top of its game at all times, and deception is not out of the question. The average Joe on the street could not handle the enormity of a classified agenda, and the media would report it for sensationalism to bolster the ratings. For example, everyone wants to know what exactly is at Area 51 in Nevada. What is the organization? What is their purpose? These are all good questions that may have answers that you might not want to hear at this moment. I remember talking to a religious woman who was convinced that Area 51 was a hoax. She thought it was merely a remote desert airport. She told me in distinct terminology how she knew there were no aliens, no robots, no weapons of mass destruction, and no extra-terrestrial aircraft in existence because God would not let it happen. She said it was all a stunt to promote science fiction budgets of the government. So I asked her a simple question: "What if you are wrong?" She became infuriated! She lashed out at me and said, "My

God rules! Don't you ever question the power of my God again! You'll burn in hell for that blasphemy! You make me sick! You're nothing but an infidel!" I was like, "Damn lady, calm down. I don't care what's in Area 51, just forget it!" This just goes to show firsthand why the CIA and other top secret organizations must remain top secret organizations; sometimes even from fellow government officials. As for that dingbat, religious zealot of a woman, it is only science fiction for two reasons, you clodhopping hick. Number one, they haven't created it yet, and number two, they have created it, and you just don't know about it yet! Why don't you go and grab a seat at the Jim Jones Kool-Aid bar, so you can order yourself a nice cold shot of the Jonestown Cherry Surprise. I hear it will help you relax more than you could ever imagine; trust me!

The War on Terror

Unlike abortion or gay marriage, the torture issue is a legitimate one, and taxpayer money is well spent debating this issue. It's that serious! No option should be taken off of the table, including enhanced interrogation. I will make another bold prediction: if terrorists attack this country again, water boarding do-it-yourself DVD kits will be on sale at Wal-Mart! I will repeat the Realacrat policy on torture. Any form of enhanced interrogations can be, shall be, and will be utilized at any time during a time of war. Detainees may be made to feel uncomfortable by various means, but there will be no crippling, no butchering, no beheading, no death causing starvation, no limb removal, no body puncturing or anything causing irreversible damage to another human being. No detainee will be forced or punished into a comatose or vegetative state, and no detainee will be murdered without a fair trial. I might not physically hurt you with a torture mechanism, but I will religiously scare the living crap out of you by any means necessary!

Otherwise, do not declare war if you are not willing to deploy wartime ideologies. Do not declare a war that you are not willing to fight! Do not declare a war that you are not intending to win! Do not declare a war that you are not patient enough to see through! Do not declare a war that you are not totally prepared for! Do not declare a war without a sound and feasible strategy! Do not declare a war with no exit strategy! Do not declare a war because it's the popular flavor of the month! Do not declare a war if you are not willing to kill civilians, including women and children! Do not declare a war if you are not willing to deploy your own children! Do not declare a war if you are not willing to deploy yourself! Do not declare a war if you are afraid and unwilling to accept high casualties! Do not declare a war if you are afraid to accept ridicule! Do not declare a war if you are not mentally sound enough to fathom the reality that your judgment will cause immense pain and suffering to numerous families! Do not declare a war based on any personal vendetta! Do not declare a war, if its main or only benefits are geared only towards some elite group! Do not declare a war with the expectations of a quick and easy victory! Do not declare a war if you are not prepared or willing to counter and defend against guerilla war maneuvers! Do not declare a war without the understanding of another military entity possibly getting involved, and do not go to war without any provisions set in place to deal with such an event! And most of all, do not declare a war, if you are not 110 percent behind your troops. War is not a daffodil collecting contest. This is serious business regarding life and death scenarios. War is ugly! War is hell! War is dangerous! War is unfair! War is murderous! War is costly, and war is torturous! Might I suggest that anyone who does not have the tolerance for torture, in all likelihood, should not be declaring war on anyone. It is not possible or rational to support war, but not the basic fundamental activities and inner-workings that come along with it.

The war on terror is not the same as a war in which two sides line up against each other and shoot it out until the last man standing is declared the winner. Many people here in the United States are still enamored with the mythical superiority of brute strength and flexing muscle, but muscle alone may not always be the answer. I don't think the war on terror can be solely won by dropping bombs. The idea of simply building more bombs or bigger and better bombs may be an effective strategy, but not necessarily a winnable strategy, because military muscle, like any other strength mechanism, can be nullified.

This reminds me of the old Superman versus Lex Luthor storylines. If you think about it, Luthor was very similar to the modern day terrorists, with his dreams of world domination and his chaotic, annihilatory means to attain those dreams. He was always clandestinely plotting his next move, and he was just shifty enough to outmaneuver the goliath Superman and always remain a few cognitive steps ahead, despite Superman's superhuman strength. The average hick/yokel would see Superman flying and be impressed by that alone, but Realacrats like me saw something else. Amazingly, despite all of Superman's titanic strength and all of his alien, acrobatic abilities, it was his ability to think that allowed him to defeat the brainy Lex Luthor. The message I got from that was crystal clear. Muscle is genetically built to enact physical activity, while the brain is genetically built to direct that muscle in its enactment of physical activity. Without the distribution of the cerebral marching orders, muscles are merely sleeping giants.

The same scenario comes into play today with our latest war adversaries-the terrorists. The Superman-like United States has all of the flexing muscle, but the Lex Luthor-like terror cells have a cunning, guileful, disciplined, team oriented strategy of execution and a more useful familiarity of their enemy, which keeps them on the offensive and the United States on the defensive. The war on terror is really more like a contest of wit, and it will take even more ingenuity from organizations like the CIA to combat and counter the treacherous complexity of the terroristic threat. Fighting harder and longer, posturing bigger, and praying to a higher power for salvation will more than likely not lead to a win; another scheme is needed, because there is far too much time being allotted on trying to dictate who people choose to love, when there are real threats out there to be concerned with! People in this country routinely underestimate the terrorists' abilities to assemble, to learn, to engage, to plan, and to attack on multiple levels. The current, western education doctrine has enabled a pseudo superiority veil to pose as protection against an erroneously perceived notion of a lesser, diminutively educated opponent. Nevertheless, the historical success of the attacks perpetrated by this so-called diminutive opponent has undoubtedly proven these notions to be grossly fallacious, and it has cost the United States dearly.

I saw a movie called *Vantage Point*[18] not long ago, and I wrote this review based on my interpretation of the theme of the movie.

> This movie raises many questions about our government, our Secret Service, and our weak and often predictable foreign policy. This is more of an informative movie

18 Pete Travis, Director, Vantage Point, 2008.

> than a blockbuster, because this could be a precursor to the future. What if the terrorists could infiltrate our Secret Service and sabotage our government from within; using our own people? This plot reminded me a lot of 9/11, which was a well-developed plan filled with willing and competent participants who carried it out almost flawlessly. I think what this movie was saying is this: it's going to take much more than just being tough on terror. The United States is going to have to be smart on terror, a lot smarter than the terrorists, in order to keep America safe. In this movie, the terrorists simply out-gunned, out-thought, out-planned, and out-executed our governmental forces. The U.S. is going to have to be more strategic and more cunning to either win this war or just break even.

The reason I have decided to bring this state of affairs to light is to stress the importance of its future possibilities, because the purpose of information is to be processed, and the results of that processing usually develops into an ideology, which could then develop into action, which means the plot aspects of this movie could soon become a reality. I think it most definitely is a precursor of future terroristic tactics, and the United States government should be viewing it the same way, because like cancer, early detection saves lives. If I, a local hick from Arkansas, was able to recognize this movie as a montage on the creation and execution of a much more sophisticated terror model, I'm sure the professional plotters and 9/11-like masterminds of the terror cells have also seen this movie and figured it out! In a move similar to one taken by the most recent President Bush, the United States should try to be more offensively minded and get out ahead of the curve, instead of waiting around in a defensive posture.

Welcome to the Terror Dome

The closing of Guantanamo Bay (Gitmo) has become a lightning rod for President Obama, largely due to this issue dispersed around torture. President Obama promised during his campaign to close Gitmo. Alleged allegations of torture and the mistreatment of detainees prompted many on the left to push for the vacating of Gitmo. This makes no sense to me. I don't see the importance of closing Gitmo. It almost appears to be some sort of symbolic gesture of goodwill to the rest of the world. The closing of Gitmo accomplishes nothing, in my eyes, but I would find a way to use this problem as an opportunity to come up with a plan on how to deal with and house terrorists. The GOP, conservatives, and some Democrats staunchly oppose the closing of Gitmo, and further oppose the re-deployment of these terrorists and terror suspects to American soil, but I see an opportunity to make something useful out of this possibility. It's what I call "Operation Welcome to the Terror Dome." The housing and detaining of terrorists could prove to be big business, seeing as how the world will always have a terrorist problem. Why not be creative and bold, and at the same time make some financial gains in the process? Since finding and targeting terror cells will now be a priority for the United States, and the world, a stratagem will have to be drawn up to help manage this new operation. The media and the GOP all suggest that no Americans want terrorists to be held on the mainland, but these terrorists will eventually have to be incarcerated somewhere. If the closure of Gitmo is inevitable, then now is the time to develop a new and improved terrorist prison system; a placed called the Terror Dome, where terrorist do hard time. This place will be a huge, maximum-security prison that can be enforced by some form of military or government agency. Either way, it will give the economy a boost and create jobs as well. It will be a place where water boarding is a possibility, and the workdays will be strenuous. Now, the question is where to put it. My preference would be somewhere in Alaska, but other destinations such as: Antarctica, Siberia, Greenland or northern Canada would not be out of the question? These are all selections where any route of escape could only be useful during the brief warm summer months. Otherwise, the cold and brutal winter gusts would cut escapees up like a shredder, not to mention the colossal icing and snowfall amounts, which would make the area almost uninhabitable without some sort of shelter. If other countries such as Russia, China, Israel, Pakistan, or India wanted in, then they would have to help foot the bill to build it and maintain it, and they would also have to take turns at guard duty. This could be a microcosmic outline of NATO—only this time, we could actually make it work. After all, the United States is not the only country in the world with terror issues. This is not just an American problem.

This is a world problem, so why not concoct a worldly solution, with the possibility of worldly cooperation? The common ideology surrounding such an initiative is usually one of skepticism, but I believe this idea could work to benefit all parties involved. The Terror Dome is the type of structure that, if successful, could spawn other terror domes. I think a world council should be formed consisting of all nations who are willing to take part in this penal experiment, because it would not be run by just one dominant entity, but by all parties involved. This world council would be set up similar to our supreme court or our Olympic games. Yes, our Olympic games! High-ranking officials from an infinite number of countries would hear the cases, and then make determinations on the fates of the would-be terrorists. Like our Olympic games, this council will be a bi-partisan, worldly panel. I think a worldly group is necessary to help convince all nations to fight and prosecute terror. I know there are many citizens in the U.S., especially Republicans and conservatives, who deride any sort of world cooperation because of NATO's past debacles, but this is a new world, a new day, and a new millennium, with new threats that will require a world effort to stop them. If it's okay to ask for world participation on one of our occupying or dictator removal operations, then it should also be okay to ask, and accept, world participation in the construction of a terrorist-only penal system. This can be erected through NATO, or it can be erected through other alliances. It does not matter to me, but I do lean more towards an alliance separate from NATO. NATO can bring charges against any suspected terrorists, but I do not have confidence in current or previous NATO policies on foreign involvements. The criteria for incarceration are simple: the individual must be tried and convicted of a terrorist act with intent to harm or kill. Mandatory sentences would be at least 10 to 15 years, minimum, depending on the seriousness of the act, or the individual's aptitude for danger. In other words, the more dangerous the terrorist, the more likely they are to remain in the Terror Dome for a long, long time. The terror dome would not be called a "terror" dome for nothing. Going by the torture rules I've previously laid out, the Terror Dome would not be a cakewalk or a country club, under any circumstances. Our goal would be to lessen the number of repeat offenders. Life in the Terror Dome will not be something to which detainees will clamor to return. I don't see any other way to effectively operate it.

THE WORLD ABROAD

U.S. FOREIGN POLICY

I was watching Bill Maher on May 1, 2009[19] when an interesting story came on. Originating out of Saudi Arabia, it reported that a 50-year-old man was about to be divorced by his eight-year-old wife. Yes, the girl was eight years old! Now this kind of behavior does not surprise me. The Middle East has a different culture. I don't want to participate in it, and it's not for me to call it socially diminutive, but I can plainly see that it is not my Realacratic cup of coffee. Maher posed a question regarding how it is acceptable for the U.S. to do business with Saudi Arabia, while turning a blind eye towards Cuba. According to U.S. policy, Cuba has a terrible human rights record, but after hearing about that child molesting Saudi man, it appears to me that Saudi Arabia is right there with Cuba, if not worse! I think it was during the G8 Summit that President Obama appeared to bow to the Saudi Royal Prince, [20] and the entire nation was worked into an uproar; people here in the U.S. were outraged! They called President Obama an ass-kissing wimp and a sell-out! Apparently, the President showed weakness to Middle Eastern dominance. The entire world would now look down on the U.S. as weak and ineffective. With all of this political, posturing ballyhoo towards President Obama, I was reminded of President Bush when he kissed this

19 HBO, "Real Time With Bill Maher," 1 May 2009.

20 Fox News, Controversy Over Obama's Saudi Bow (Full Story!), http://www.youtube.com/watch?v=ihCGy6YuFH8&feature=related.

same man on the cheek at his Texas ranch, and then held his hand, as he escorted him. This is the same President Bush who once proposed a constitutional amendment to ban gay marriage. It would have been an amendment that would only recognize a marriage between a man and a woman. So, I beg to question: did President Bush's questionable; less-than-macho antics with the Royal Prince make America look weak or just gay? Unlike Republicans, who hate President Obama, we Realacrats completely understand why President Bush did what he did. Gay had nothing to do with it. I was only playing devil's advocate. President Bush kissed this man because he has something the United States desperately needs- oil! To me, there is no point in bashing President Bush or President Obama for doing the petroleum rain dance for the undisputed God of oil! The problem with America is simple: there are too many blind bus drivers! These bus drivers are not blind because they cannot see. They are blind because of what they refuse to see. All of this mumbo jumbo about human rights records is just a load of crap. When the Saudi man comes to town, let the ass kissing begin! When it comes to big money made off of big oil, Jesus, ethics, human rights, integrity, discipline and intelligence go right out the window! The United States is a business, a corporation, a store, and a home! It must be treated as such. The sooner people in this country come to grips with that, the better off everyone all will be. It's time to eliminate the blind bus drivers, for more qualified drivers who actually know where this country needs to go to be financially successful. I'd rather have a Donald Trump behind the wheel than a Pat Robertson! The battle of the economy is not a religious issue. The Ten Commandments being posted in a local courthouse will not solve our economic woes. Economic ideologies, and not religious ideologies, must dictate U.S. foreign policy. Jesus Christ will not balance your checkbook! He won't pay your bills on time either. You can go to church seven nights a week, but the Repo Man will still pay you a visit, and all of the rats will come back, if you fail to pay the piper. Business is business! The United States, at one time, was much like Wal-Mart in the financial world, but now it's more like a mom and pop shop, and that's pathetic, which brings me back to Cuba.

CUBA

The U.S. relationship with Cuba has been terrible, but there is no legitimate reason for it to remain that way. Cuba could be a great opportunity, if it's orchestrated correctly. I can recall when businessmen had to ship their products to other places around the world in a secretive maneuver to eventually get their products sold to Cuba! It's these kinds of red tape business decisions that have ultimately tanked the U.S. economy. Castro is no saint and neither is the Saudi Royal Prince, Premier Putin, the Chinese Government, or any U.S. President! Why not make an attempt to do business with Cuba? Why let Putin or the Chinese find a way to come all the way across the ocean to make a profit, when we are a mere 90 miles away. Well, we don't do business with communists—bullsh*t! You can go and tell that to the Chinese government, as they continue to laugh all the way to the bank! We should get involved with Cuba. We should work out some sort of deal with Castro's brother Raul, who represents the new figure-head of Cuban government since Castro's health has become an issue recently. I'm sure the airline industry, Wal-Mart, UPS, FedEx, the auto industry, U.S. agriculture, and most importantly, the tourism industry would all love to establish and develop a new market. It would bring jobs to Cuba, and it would be great for the U.S. I don't care if the Hiltons of the world have to line Raul's pockets with a nice profit to do it. It would be no worse than lining the pockets of Wall Street and the banking industry's rich fat cats, and we've all seen how that turned out! The airlines and even the cruise industry also have a lot to gain by doing business with Cuba! I would argue that travel between the U.S. and Cuba would be non-stop, not to mention the nice beach investments U.S. companies could get involved with. It could be another Caribbean Cancun, because whatever is being developed in Cuba at this moment could be proliferated significantly by U.S. involvement. If there is fertile ground on which to grow money, then it must be cultivated. The United States cannot continue to allow opportunities like these to fizzle! The majority of naysayers would argue that a country like Cuba is too small and too insignificant to add any value to the U.S. economy, but Realacrats would argue back by saying that every little bit helps. Some is better than none! While it's true that these would be humble beginnings, the future possibilities could bode well for the U.S. Realacrats will not live in the past! What happened in Cuba back in the 1960s was then, this is now! Our motto believes that people should learn from the past, not live in it. We have a chance to live in a brand new day, and we should seize the moment!

Some Democrat met Fidel Castro back in 2009 and began bragging of how intelligent he was to have survived all of the U.S. pressure created to oust him. Republicans on Fox News blasted that Democrat for saying anything good about Castro. There were even some who characterized Castro as a dimwitted, thuggish, dictator with a horrid and wretched human rights record. This is the alleged reason the U.S. does not do business with Cuba, but I know, and you know, that if Fidel Castro was living in Saudi Arabia even with the same vague human rights record, the U.S. would gladly do business with him. They would simply turn a blind eye like they do for other resource rich countries. The economic-based sanctions placed on Cuba aren't really meant to teach Castro a tough democracy lesson, but more a tough, capitalism, make sure you dance to our music lesson. If a big oil well gushed out of Castro's backyard, he and the U.S. would be nothing short of Facebook buddies.

Mexico

The United States and Mexico have had their problems in the past over land disputes; namely Texas and other southwestern regions. Oddly enough, the U.S. and Mexico are still having border problems today. So, what do we do about Mexico? There is not an easy solution to be had here. Presidents have come and gone, and very few, if any, have had much success with the Mexican border crises. Now there are dangerous drug cartels on the Mexican border; some have even crossed over into the United States, bringing the violence with them. There are two major questions here. Who's at fault, and what should be done about it? Everyone loves to talk about how the U.S. is the greatest country on earth, especially the Republicans and Fox News. Well, part of being the greatest country on earth is the ability to take responsibility for any problems to which you contribute. The U.S. contributes to the drug markets of Mexico! There is no other way of putting it. We are more than likely their biggest consumer and also their biggest ammunitions vendor. I will probably be called a traitor for saying this, but someone must say it. Living next door to the U.S. is best thing that could have ever happened to the drug cartels. It's the perfect setup. Realacrats, unlike Republicans, are willing to take a good, long, hard look at reality in order to find the truth. If you can find the truth, then you can eventually find a solution to the problem! The hopes of sweeping a wooly mammoth underneath a political rug is simply not feasible. After all, you can sweep the mammoth underneath the rug, but you cannot keep it there! Eventually, it's bound to get out! I would argue that it's already out, even as we speak. Instead of trying to coax this mammoth back underneath the rug, I think it's time we re-route the mammoth somewhere else. This is not just Mexico's mammoth. It belongs to the U.S. as well. The sooner we deal with this reality, the better off we will all be. There are many people in the U.S. who believe that just ignoring the problem will allow it to go away. They believe the violence and poverty will remain just south of the border. Somehow, the U.S. is supposed to have the moral high ground on this issue. We are too high and mighty to be locked into some low-class struggle with an inferior neighbor such as Mexico. I think this is the major reason why many refuse to acknowledge our involvement in this situation. Since Realacrats operate based on reality, I think it's time to take a realistic look at this problem.

First off, why don't we address the war on drugs? The U.S. war on drugs has been a success on some levels. It has kept the U.S. prison yards full; making the penal system a booming business here in the U.S. There are so many criminals that we simply can't build the prisons fast enough! This is similar to infrastructure, as long as there are prisons, there will be businesses revolving around the services of those prisons. In other words, incarcerating the masses is very lucrative in this country. Prisons bring jobs! People need jobs! Prisons need a supply, and the war on drugs has done that! I have always had my doubts about the so-called border drug problem. Apparently, the U.S. Border Patrol Agency is under-funded. This is a bad economy, and people need jobs. Why not draft these out of work people who are struggling to make ends meet and living in tents to join the border patrol? It's a good job, and it pays good money. If it doesn't pay good money, then make it pay good money; that's what stimulus friends are for. If building a fence, which would also be a monumental task that would take years to accomplish and would employ a huge number of people, is too outlandish to become reality, then why not significantly up the number of border patrol agents. In a time when people need jobs, it would be reasonable to start working on some of these programs that have been collecting dust on some politician's desks, instead of distributing money to finance some measly outpost project over some remote creek in Montana. This new stimulus plan should be put to work on major, necessary projects—projects the entire country can benefit from, projects that help to keep America safe financially and physically. The time of Americans working to rebuild their country from the ground up is long overdue here. It's time for us to revamp our own country and get paid for doing it.

It sounds like a good idea to me, so why isn't the government doing this? There is supposed to be a boatload of stimulus money floating around, so much of it that certain governors are turning some of it down. These states don't have major projects that need to be financed? I know Louisiana still needs recovery help from Hurricane Katrina; looks like a job for stimulus man! The job assignments are out there, but the actual movement on these assignments is anywhere from slow to non-existent. Why is that? Who is running this show? This reeks of failure on a local level all the way up to the federal level. I have to contemplate the possibility of the Mexican government lining the pockets of politicians to keep this border fiasco going, because there is no rational reason why nothing is being done about it, especially when such work could help to employ a nation scarce on jobs. I heard a conservative Republican blame the Mexican border situation on President Obama. He claimed that Obama cut the border patrol to help out his Mexican/terrorist buddies so they could get a free ride in the United States, but what this low-budgeted Forrest Gump failed to realize was this: no president has done much of anything involving this border topic except make speeches about it. The damn fence could have been built two to three times over by now, but I don't think the government wants to build a fence along the border, and I think the Mexican government, along with all those deadly drug cartels you've been seeing on the news lately, have a much greater influence within the American government than we realize. There is no other rational reason for this lackadaisical effort to work on what all walks of government have labeled as a legitimate American security threat. It seems as if the only time the border fence discussion ever gets a real audience is during an election year, like the recent 2010 John McCain Arizona senate re-election ad, where he says, "And complete the danged fence!"[21] Any fence that stretched the entire length of the U.S./Mexican border would be one big ass, danged fence, and a big ass fence will require a big ass government, with some big ass government oversight and some big ass government intervention! This would be a great project for the stimulus package!

Mexico and Illegal Immigration

Speaking of Mexico, the enormous problem of illegal immigration has to be addressed as well. As I just stated previously, no president has ever done much of anything to clean up the Mexican-U.S. border problem, and illegal immigrants continue to cross over into the U.S. like human, ant trails. I wrote about a guy in this book that I once worked with, named Paco. He was from Mexico. I don't know how he got here. First, he was alone, and then a few weeks later there were about 25 others all living in one house and working. I liked Paco. He could barely speak English, but he was a great co-worker. He worked as hard as he could and as much as he could, then he would send money home to Mexico to the rest of his struggling family. This is how he was able to help get his 25 friends and family into the U.S. within a few weeks. I personally knew of least 10 other Mexican individuals who also went through these same channels to help bring up their families from Mexico. I even met one Mexican lady who was fine as hell. She spoke very little English, but she was able to tell me point blank that she had just entered into the U.S. by crossing the Rio Grande River in Texas, where her family was waiting to pick her up at an undisclosed location. Her family had already opened up a restaurant and a job was waiting for her. If this is happening in my small, insignificant neck of the woods, I can only imagine how much of it has already implanted itself throughout the rest of the country.

So, let's get one thing straight right now! I was not mad then, and I am not mad now at the people from Mexico with whom I've met and worked with. They have all been very nice people to me. To be brutally

---

21 Jason Linkins, McCain's 'Danged Fence' ad mocked by Joe Scarborough, John Shadegg…Basically everybody(Video), http://www.huffingtonpost.com/2010/05/13/mccains-danged-fence-ad-m_n_575068.html (May 2010).

honest, many of their family values make the Republican version of family values look like used, bubble gum stuck to the bottom of a pair of farm boots. Their loyalty and commitment to each other is awe-inspiring and so is their uncanny ability to dramatically appear in this country and immediately start to economically lap people who have lived here their whole lives.

The only question Realacrats have is in regards to the taxable, citizenship, inventory accounting, because if illegal immigrants are allowed to send money back to their homeland, they should also be paying some in to the U.S. as well; something like a host tax. They should pay to be here. I'm not suggesting that the government unfairly tax this group, but I am suggesting the federal government receive a portion. This would generate enormous revenue for the economy. The responsibility would fall squarely on the employers of these illegal immigrants. The government can either compensate the employers to come clean and document their illegal immigrant workers for tax purposes, or it can always drop the legal hammer and begin prosecuting these employers, whichever way works best, even if it means taxing any employer who refuses to cooperate at a higher rate than usual. The employers would be forced to do a much better job of documenting their illegal immigrant workforce. I guess this is where my view comes ideologically close to conservatives, but this is what I would do as Realacrat! I'll have more to say about the long-term goal of such documentations later.

In Border States like Arizona, the problem of illegal immigrants is obviously not going anywhere in the near future. With that in mind, maybe a national registry for illegal immigrants could be set up to specifically deal with the issue of undocumented individuals in the United States. People aren't going to like what I'm about to propose, but Realacrats know through experience that there are no abundances of exit strategies between a rock and a hard place! So I ask this question. Why not offer immunity and amnesty to all illegal immigrants/undocumented individuals? I think that is more feasible than some Rambo style round-up or some modern day trail of tears where the Hispanic community replaces the Cherokee, but it doesn't end there! Any illegal immigrant/undocumented individual who signs up with the national registry will not be arrested; barring they haven't committed a serious crime, and they will not be deported. What they will be subjected to is identification documentation and the possibility of embarking on the road to U.S. citizenship, but there is more. Once an illegal immigrant/undocumented individual is in the registry, they will be forced to wear some sort of ankle/arm bracelet very similar to those worn by house arrest detainees for tracking purposes only. As soon as U.S. citizenship is achieved, the bracelets are removed immediately.

The flip side of this deal will go as follows: any illegal immigrant/ undocumented individual apprehended by authorities, who has been found to be in the United States over 30 days, will be detained and deported, unless that undocumented individual has already signed-up for the national registry. If any illegal immigrant commits a serious crime/ felony while applying for citizenship, it would automatically terminate any citizenship application, and that individual would be brought to justice or deported; depending on the nature of the crime. We'll even go so far as to set up a national hotline where you can turn in any suspected illegal immigrant activity for financial compensation. We'll call it 1-800-GET-THE-MEXICAN, because that is specifically what this is about! No offense to the Hispanic community, because I'm only joking about the 1-800 hotline to make a point, but based on the newly signed Arizona immigration law of 2010; the joke has become a reality! I've heard some delusional conservatives actually claim that the illegal immigrant situation in states like Arizona is not really geared towards Hispanics. According to these more than credible conservatives, some of the main targets of the illegal immigrant sweep are Middle-Easterners, Chinese illegal immigrants, warm weather Eskimos, other illegal Asian immigrants, and anyone who looks funny, but not even Beavis and Butt-Head would be gullible enough to believe that one. Make no mistake about it my Hispanic friends. 1-800-GET-THE-MEXICAN was just my way of being sarcastically and politically funny, but there is an eerie element of truth surrounding it. Regardless, none of these proposals will be effective to any capacity if the U.S./Mexican border is not beefed up enough to at least drastically diminish the numbers of illegal crossings to around 5 to 10 percent.

I'm sorry if this sounds harsh to the Hispanic community, who has never done anything of ill-will to me personally, but a plan is going to have to be hatched by someone at some point in time, and it probably is not going to favor Hispanics in the least bit. My proposal is not daffy dills in the daylight or Kum Ba Ya with a Krispy Kreme Doughnut, but it at least gives people a fighting chance. Unlike many of the cowards of the county who reside and hide behind their religious snobbery, I don't get intimidated by people who don't look like me! Even though a Hispanic illegal I once worked with told me that he forbid me feverishly from dating his sexy ass, Mexican daughter because I was Black. I still don't dislike Hispanics, and I will not support legislation aimed at signaling them out for persecution, although I did strongly consider calling the INS (Immigration and Naturalization Services) on my illegal buddy for telling me I wasn't good enough for his super, hot daughter! But in the end, you can't fix stupid, and you can't introduce the gift of sight to willingly closed eyes.

And as crazy as it may sound, there is a certain element within the undocumented, Mexican population that honestly believes it is a step ahead of African-Americans, with citizenship being a non-issue. You'll never hear this story from Democrats, Republicans, or the mainstream media, but what I'm giving you now is the truth straight from a Realacrat! A serious and heated discussion took place at an undisclosed location between three undocumented, Mexican workers; another African-American, and me; about the possibility of a race war due to the mounting hatred of President Obama by certain segments of the White population. The three Mexican workers were convinced, beyond a shadow of a doubt, that they would be given a pass by the Ku Klux Klan, Skinheads, and other racist groups, because they were light-skinned. The guy who didn't want me dating his daughter made this statement, "I'm not legal, but I'm not Black either! They hate you more than they hate me. We, Mexicans, can just lay low, and they will overlook us. Besides, most of us are light enough that we can pass for tanned White and gain limited acceptance. I'm sorry my friend, but that's your fight, not ours!" Well, wherever you may be in life, Mr. "It's not my fight," I truthfully hope that you have been watching what's been going on in Arizona in 2010, because it is now officially your fight too, but you will never hear me say that it is not my mine! That is the difference between you and me, because I understand that there is no difference between you and me.

Again, some people are not going to like the comparison I'm about to make here, but I am independently democratic, and no one dictates my comparison distribution. I was listening to talk radio recently, when I heard the statement "All of you Mexicans had better get your papers ready or else!" I was then reminded of an event I once watched on the critically acclaimed, yet largely forgotten, *Roots* series. There is a scene where a character named "Chicken George" was freed from slavery by his master. George then went up north to live as a free man! One day George decides to return to the slavery riddled south where his remaining family lived, still enslaved, to visit. In a town where 100% of the Black population were slaves living in poverty, here comes Chicken George ridding into town on a big, white horse dressed cleanly with an aura of freedom emanating from him! Needless to say, he was racially profiled immediately, as some of the White, slave owners retained him for questioning. They asked him who he belonged to, and George told them he belonged to no one, because he had been set free by his master. The infuriated, White, slave owners first laughed in his face, but then got serious, by demanding that George produce his freedom papers or else! Lucky for George, he had his papers ready, as he handed them over to the insecure, White, slave owners. What happened next will be eternally etched in my mind for the rest of my life, which is part of the reason why I can recant this scene so vividly without having to ever see the *Roots*[22] series again. The White, slave owners looked over Chicken George's freedom, documentation papers with the ultimate disgust, as they tossed his freedom papers on the ground like trash in front of him. As George got down on his knees to pick them up, the hideous, White, slave owning cowards looked Chicken George right in the eye and told him that any nigger who remained in that particular region for more than 30 days would be automatically demoted back to regular, old nigger again, with slave duties mandatory! I can still see the augustly image of Chicken George waving goodbye to his enslaved family on the 29th day of his visit, as he rode out of slavery for a second time!

So to the Hispanic population, listen to me well! Do everything in your power to attain, sustain, and produce, at the drop-of-a-hat, your freedom papers, so you too can ride off into the sunset with your freedom just like Chicken George did! Ironically, and thanks to CNN's Soledad O'Brien, I learned of a sign that hung in Jonestown, Guyana that read, "Those who do not learn from the past are doomed to repeat

22 Marvin J. Chomsky, Director, Roots, 1977.

it!" As a Realacrat, I think the idea of freedom papers in the year 2010 speaks volumes about that.

Now I'm going to tell you how I feel. For almost 200 years, old, arrogant, White men have been in charge of the government on every level. Most of these self-proclaimed heroes have never let up in their egotistical crusades to tell the whole world why they, alone, should be number one! After almost 200 years of spoon-fed power, is this supposed to be the best that you glory hounding prima donnas can muster? Every president pre-dating President Obama has had an opportunity to fix this border/immigration problem, but no one has managed to produce anything beyond "Jack Squat," which means, "Not a damn thing!" This won't be President Obama's failure until he is out of office, but it is each and every one of the pre-Obama presidents' failure right now. It seems to me that you guys let your ethnically induced identity write a check that your "Everyday people abilities" could not cash, but now, all of a sudden, since President Obama is in the White House; people like Arizona Governor Jan "Vinegar Lady" Brewer have decided to take matters into their own hands through some premeditated, vigilante, political plot to discredit the federal government under the current watch!

Hispanic American populations and Hispanic populations, listen to me good once again! People don't come after you for nothing. There is something that you have that your oppressors want, and if I was a betting man, I'd say it was voting demographics. In a way, it almost seems as if a certain, bigoted, conservative segment of society blames you for the wild card votes that pushed President Obama over the top. This would explain why a drastic reduction in your populative numbers is so desperately sought-after! Remember, if what you have is worth somebody's effort to try and take it away from you, then it should unquestionably be worth your efforts to do everything in your power to keep it!

ISRAEL

The topic of Israel is one of the most controversial, hot button issues of all time. I know people here in the United States that are die-hard Israel fans. Even Democrats are die-hard Israel fans. For all intents and purposes, Israel might as well be the 51st state of the union. I wonder how long it will take the other nations in the Middle East to figure this out. Hell, I hear more about the plight of Israel than I do about some of the states that are physically in the union. Conservatives and Republicans always take pot shots at the media for their slobbering love affair with President Obama, but now I'm here to take pot shots at the conservatives, the Republicans, the religious zealots and the media for their boot licking affections towards the state of Israel.

Whether it's money, weapons, security or verbal defense, we, The United States, take good care of Israel. They are always in good hands with the United States. Every religious zealot I know loves Israel to death. I had a long discussion with this Christian preacher about Israel, and he explained to me why I, as a U.S. citizen and a loving, God-fearing Christian, should not only care about what happens to Israel, but I should utilize everything in my power to stand with Israel against the infidels of Islam. He told me that it was my Christian responsibility to do so. He then went on to say how his congregation believes that God is looking out for Israel—but if this is true, and God does have Israel's back, then why is the U.S. needed? His logic was simple. The United States is buying their political/international/Christian stairway to heaven by protecting Israel. Every time the United States lends a helping hand to Israel, God puts a proverbial feather in the hat of the United States and its interests. This is like a Christian, stock market, and the United States is determined to buy as much of that stock as humanly possible. The preacher basically professed that America was spiritually obligated to be Israel's personal bodyguard, because this is what God wants.

I have to admit it: the preacher made a very compelling case for his cause, but that's just it. The cause belongs to him and not necessarily to me. Apparently, he had purposely discounted the fact that some of us here do not share his strong compassion towards Israel or his Christian beliefs. Personally, I have nothing against Israel, and I also have nothing for Israel, either. My passions don't run deep for Israel like the preacher's passions do, because Realacrats like me are able to separate Israel's symbolism from its Israel's politics! Instead of a blindly misguided love affair with Israel, I have a tough question to ask: Mr. Israel, give me one good reason why I should align my tax dollars with your pockets. Why should I care about you, Mr. Israel? For that matter, who are you, Mr. Israel? Have we ever met before, Mr. Israel? Tell me this, Mr. Israel. Republicans, like Bill O'Reilly, and Democrats, like Hillary Clinton, have done everything in their power to convince me to be more financially generous towards you. What, Mr. Israel, have you ever done for me? I'm not talking about any encouragement you may have bestowed upon the United States government. I am inquiring about me personally as an African-American/U.S. citizen. Seriously, have you ever spoken up or stepped up on behalf of African-Americans? The same question could be addressed on behalf of all the other minorities, as you should be aware of at this point, and shame on you if you are not, but African-Americans in the United States have caught hell since the 1600s. The true progress of racial equality didn't make any significant gains until after the 1960s civil rights era. During this tumultuous time period, did you, Mr. Israel, ever offer up any financial assistance or verbal support towards our movement for racial equality? A movement that would allow us, as African-Americans, the right to vote, the right to attend any educational program we choose, the right to live anywhere we please and the right to eat inside of a restaurant like everyone else, in other words, basic human rights! Where were you when all of this was going on? Did you ever ask the United States government to do a better job in its support of African-Americans? The reason I ask these questions of you, Mr. Israel, is because I have never heard anyone reference you as a supporter of African-American civil rights. I don't recall any civil rights activist tossing around the name Israel as a supporter. I'm just saying that I have never heard it, and I'm sure that I am not the only one who has never heard it. I, like other African-Americans and other minorities, would like to know exactly where you stand on civil rights, which are the same basic rights my tax dollars go to you to support your right to exist without unwarranted persecution. I'm just asking a few simple questions. I don't really know the full extent of this, but I think it's time we all find out. If Israel has contributed to the cause, we should not hesitate to remunerate. If Israel has not contributed to cause, then maybe it's time they do so. The next time the United States tries to lecture Israel about its questionable treatment of Palestinians, Israel should counter with the same lecture, and tell the United States to clean out its own closet first, because both countries could use improvements in that area. Hey, I'm waiting Mr. Israel; make a statement, if you haven't done so already. If you expect me, as an African-American, to back you, then I expect you to back me; meaning, to stand firmly against the unethical treatment of minorities in the United States. It's the least you could do, seeing as how you are happily spending my tax money.

Realacrats don't hate Israel. Realacrats just want Israel to be more vocal in a humanitarian sense towards all Americans, not just certain ones. If Israel has not yet reached out to the minorities of the world and the United States, then now would be a good time to do it, because to Realacrats, there is no Israeli side and there is no Palestinian side. There is only the human side, and our politics should reflect this, because two wrongs don't make a right, just as two oppressive forces often fail to find peace.

The Peace Initiative: Gaza, Israel and the West Bank

Well, in the long line of Middle Eastern, peace initiatives, there have been few shining moments and numerous failures, because trying to mediate peace and logic between two different countries is difficult, to say the least. Former Arkansas Governor Mike Huckabee has now weighed in on the situation with his plan for peace in the Middle East by suggesting that any ideas of a Palestinian state be vacated immediately because they are unrealistic.[23] In fact, he even goes so far as to suggest that any Palestinian homeland should be removed from the area completely, leaving only Israel. No one knows exactly where this somewhere else is supposed to be, including Mike Huckabee. Maybe, Huckabee and his Christian brigade are going to make a pilgrimage over to the West Bank to personally escort the Palestinians out of their homeland. If that happens, the United States will be fighting three wars instead of two. Who gave Huckabee, who I actually agree with on some issues (not this one, of course), the moral, high ground or Holy Roller authority to decide who goes and who stays? There is nothing more genuine than a non-ethnic, religious westerner drawing up plans for a Muslim-based trail of tears. It's like I questioned previously! Who gave

23 Matthew Duss, Will Huckabee Pay a Price For Rejecting the Two-State Solution?, http:// http://www.prospect.org/cs/articles?article=will huckabee pay a price for rejecting the two state solution (August 2009).

Israel the moral right-of-way, while at the same time attempting to give Palestinians the old manifest destiny boot? This is precisely why you cannot govern fairly through religious dogma, because Huckabee would never suggest that Israel pack up and leave. No westernized politician would probably be crazy enough to ever suggest that as a solution.

THE REALACRAT MIDDLE EAST PLAN

As a Realacrat, we know that packing people up and carrying them away in a NATO U-Haul is not the answer, but it is definitely a way to start World War III. The Realacrat strategy would take another route, because other countries, like people right here in this country, have to learn to live together. That actually sounds like John Edwards. People try to minimize him because of his personal improprieties, but as with Darwin's teachings, you can't just throw out the entire John Edwards platform on humanity based on his transgressions, because his transgress don't de-legitimize his ideologies! It's very similar to the way some cultish idiots try to discredit the theories of Darwin because some of it clashes with traditional, Christian dogma. The behavior of an individual and the ideological inventions of an individual are two separate things. Thus, Realacrats will call this the "John Edwards Approach," because he is the one who really tried to hammer home the humanitarian side of politics. I, like Edwards, believe that humanitarian politics can lead to humanitarian behavior abroad. When Edwards spoke about living together, he applied it to African-Americans and other minorities neighborly mingling together with their fellow, American, White counterparts; much to the chagrin of White, God, fearing conservatives, but when Realacrats speak about living together, they will indulge a new initiative based on the Middle East; mainly Gaza, Israel, and the West Bank, which is something the international community has failed to do.

The Realacrat battle plan will consist of a model called the "Neutral Zone Project." Instead of trying to move the Palestinians out of their homeland so others can make a profit, a neutral zone would be set up using part of Israel and part of the West Bank. Hopefully, the United Nations can walk and chew ideological gum at the same time, because their role will be instrumental in helping to secure the area in order for this bold and gutsy maneuver to have a chance to work. We know the

United States would get involved, because they always get involved, but since peace in the Middle East concerns the entire planet; just maybe, other nations will offer to take the initiative and get involved in a humanitarian cause that could prove to be historic. This would be a great time for idle China and idle Russia to get involved in for a change and exert some international leadership. This is not just an Israeli problem. It is a world problem, and Realacrats believe a strong world front could prove to be a game changer—only this time for the better.

The neutral zone will be geographically part of Israel and part of the West Bank, but other worldly dignitaries, including dignitaries from Israel, the West Bank and other nations would oversee it. The plan will bring in schools, colleges, living quarters, places of worship, commerce, and an international governmental environment. The call will go out to any and all people who wish to engage in this new international community where Israelis and Palestinians will actually get a chance to live together, alongside other nationalities as well. It would be the equivalent of establishing an Air Force Base in a small town in America, because all of the military and government officials would become part of that community. Realistically, you could have Palestinians, Israelis, Americans, Gazans, and other nationalities all learning to live and govern together. As I've said before in this book, sometimes what you've been raised to believe and what actually is are two totally different things, and this interaction can be used to prove that. Sometimes when you get a chance to look your perceived evil right square in the face, you then realize that it is more perception than reality, and the other person is really not that much different from you. Separation allows fallacious perceptions, devious confusion, mindless propaganda, groundless myths, and indoctrinating principles to thrive and flourish. In the end, I think you'll find that Gazans, Palestinians, and Israelis all want the same basic thing, which is opportunity. If we can offer families on all sides of the issue economic opportunities, people will show up for this; because ultimately, bills are not paid by heavenly rhetoric.

An internationally based academics program could be used to teach the youth about Islam, Christianity, western culture, Middle Eastern culture, and all other cultures abroad. I think that if the strict, constructionist, religious ideology could be revaluated; there could be a real chance for a new understanding in the Middle East. Again, you don't have to believe Jesus Christ was the son of God, and I don't have to believe and pray to Muhammad. Where is it written that the guy next door to me has to share my political and religious views, or I'll get to suicide bomb him? I'm sure there is much that I can learn from Muhammad about life right here on planet Earth, the same way Muslims can learn much from Jesus, without the "Son of God" proclamation being made on either side. Both men had a vast array of knowledge, and it would be unwise to minimize either one of their teachings due to this "Son of God" aspect, just as Israel has much to offer and the West Bank and Gaza also have much to offer, as long as people don't allow one dissenting facet to dictate and destroy the entire ideology. There is no reason why this can't be the norm in the neutral zone. Just because you learn about something outside of your normalcy, it does not mean that you have to adopt it as policy. If Christians, Jews, and Muslims all had as much faith as they all claim to have, they would allow their children to learn about all of their options and then make their own choices. I know it's a long shot, but peace could arise out of this rationale, and the neutral zone could be the springboard. If we could just get one community of Jews, Christians, Muslims and others to coexist, it would be a major accomplishment and a great omen for the future. It would prove once and for all that it could be done. As a Realacrat, I truly believe that showing an actual, functioning, international community would go a very long way towards the re-evaluation of the old, traditional, stereotypical philosophies of belligerent separation. The proof would be in the pudding, and people would have to take notice, because it would really deflate the sails of the naysayers and the fear mongers of the exclusive God club.

Fear Inhibits Progress

There is no doubt that this will be a very dangerous, uncharted venture, but everything in that area is already dangerous. Naysayers will say the threat of violence will be great, but the violence is already great. The current culture of violence that exist right now is counter-productive to any real, potential progress, so maybe a little new, potential violence can change that. Republicans and conservatives will probably say this plan is too risky. Other Middle Eastern leaders will probably also say it is too risky, but everything in Middle East is too risky. They will say it won't work, but we Realacrats will say that nothing has ever worked. It has just as much of a chance as all of the other previous debacles. But one thing is for sure, throwing rocks and armed Israeli soldiers and numerous suicide bombings have only made things worse, and the last time I checked; a spoonful of sugar beats a spoonful of vinegar every time.

Realacrats have seen U.S. presidents invite leaders from the Middle East to the peace table with little or no results and usually just more of the same. Realacrats believe this is a problem that must be solved by the people and not necessarily by presidents and prime ministers. If we can commit to send troops into Iraq, then we can commit to send a motley crew of brave Americans to this neutral zone. Instead of always taking the Israeli perspective, the United States can take the world perspective. Fear mongers will say it's impossible, but what if it works? This is a risk that the Realacrat nation believes it is time to take. Look at it this way: for every idea that turned out to be revolutionary, there was always someone trying to talk the inventor out of it by saying it would be too risky or just outright impossible. Think of all that would have been missed if the majority of inventors had listened!

Engaging Hamas and Others like Them

None of this is even worth discussing without the interaction of groups like Hamas, Hezbollah, and the international community, including the United States. Now I understand how the United States does not make deals with terrorists, but I also understand how they just find common ground behind closed doors, and I have no problem with that. Hamas would be addressed in a very simple way. To groups like Hamas, we Realacrats would say no more suicide bombings. It's time for a truce so that a deal could be made. The question to Hamas would be as straightforward as possible, and that question would be: would you like to participate in the peace movement or would you like the United States to enforce as many economic sanctions on your country as humanly possible while we give Israel even better resources to fight you with? You can reap the same benefits of a U.S. affiliation as Israel, but you have to come to the table with cooperation at the forefront of your agenda. The U.S. has nothing to gain from the destruction of your country of your religious idealisms. Whether Hamas is here today or gone tomorrow, our economy will still be in and out of the recessional pit, our people will still be uninsured and unemployed, and neither of us will be any closer to finding out the secrets of heaven than we already are right now. All over the world millions of people are praying, and have been praying for eons, for peace in the Middle East with little or no results to show for it. It's apparent to me that neither Muhammad nor Jesus Christ have had much successful involvement in this process, judging by the severe lack of progress made on it. So does it really matter who's in charge when conditions only continue to deteriorate? Has it ever occurred to you, Mr. Hamas or to you, Mr. Israel, that maybe, just maybe, the Supreme Being wants us to work it out on our own, because he knows we can? I can't prove to you that he does, but at the same time, you can't prove to me that he does not, but one thing is for certain; fighting and warring over who the supreme prophet of the same God is has failed in the past and continues to fail in the present, and without some new form of understanding, objectivity, humility, and cooperative intervention, will continue to fail in the future as well. However, what if Hamas could be the first Islamic, Middle Eastern organization to be part of the solution for a change? Some would raise the question--why Hamas, but why not Hamas?

Why can't Hamas be part of a solution that makes sense? Why continue battling and warring over a positioning controversy that none of us can actually grasp any certainty of? Why are so many of us willing to lie, cheat, steal, kill, occupy, pillage, squander and behead innocent victims over a heavenly seating chart, when none of us know what the arrangements are? Is Jesus two seats back, or is he one seat back? Maybe Muhammad is two seats back, or could he be one seat up? People have been fighting for decades in the Middle East to try and establish exactly who possesses the only front row tickets to the God concert when it is transparently evident to me that there is a strong possibility that Jesus and Muhammad are both at this concert. The question is, who sits in front, and who sits in the back? My question is; does it really matter, and should anybody care? Instead of squabbling over where Jesus and Muhammad may be sitting in heaven, I think people should spend more time pondering where and if they will be seated in heaven. The other two appear to already have their seats!

I ask this because Muslims can't prove that Jesus is not there and Christians can't prove that Muhammad is not there, because no one has looked God in the eyes to find out and then lived to tell about it. Yet we are willing to kill hundreds of thousands because of this faith-based, comfort-zoned, personalized guessing game. We don't know who sits on the right-hand side of God, and we don't know who sits to the left-hand side of God, either! What if God changes his mind and his seating chart--then what? People can only speculate. Most of these buffoonery specialists don't even know who is sitting at the right-hand side of themselves here on Earth, so you know any accurate human deciphering of heaven's seating chart is completely out of the question. We all seem to jump at the chance to fight about what we don't know, but when faced by a catastrophe like Darfur, which is something we all know very well because we've seen it played out time and time again throughout our recorded history, we suddenly become reluctant to tango! This is a senseless disagreement, so why don't we work together to end it?

As a Realacrat, I am even ready to come out of my Westernized comfort zone to enter into yours, a place where Muhammad is the chosen one, not Jesus. I'm not converting to Islam, but I am willing to listen and learn because the acquisition of knowledge is not meant to convert but to inform. My Christian lemonade stand should not be feared any more than your Islamic orange juice stand. The entire world knows about both of them by now, so it would be totally asinine to try and hide or suppress either one. Within these neutral zones, both stands will be made available, and it will be up to the people to decide which one they support, and no one will be brainwashed or converted in either direction. This means that Israel will have no right to come in and destroy it, and neither will you--Mr. Hamas! If I told Muhammad that we Realacrats had a plan that could drastically improve the livelihood of Muslims without, under any circumstances, compromising their Islamic core, faith, and belief systems, do you, Mr. Hamas, believe that he would look down from heaven and say no? Do you think that he would destroy the neutral zones, because I do not believe that he would, and if he wouldn't destroy them then why would you? You can't tell me that the freedom of Muslims to practice their religion is not the goal of Muhammad. So tell me this, Mr. Hamas, where is it written that the humanitarian cooperation between religions will erode one's core belief system, because shaking hands with a Muslim does not diminish your character as a Christian, and shaking hands with a Christian does not diminish your status as a Muslim?

If you, Mr. Hamas, are not willing to accept the existence of the other side then you are no better than the infidels you rail against so passionately, no better than the evil you attempt to suicide bomb, no better than the ugly, prune-faced, highly religious, White woman who said her God was White and also said that he didn't want the White cows to walk with the Black cows, because the Black cows were clandestinely tied to the evolution of apes! Somebody has got to step up to challenge these pseudo-religious, self-entitlement policies. If Israel seems willy-nilly about it, then you, Mr. Hamas, can show the entire Christian world why labeling groups as barbaric can be highly inaccurate; highly offensive; and highly unproductive.

Why rail against the flaws of another when those very flaws are your flaws as well? No one has God in his or her back pocket, no one has Jesus in his or her back pocket and no one has Muhammad in his or her back pocket! No one has a cell phone that they can just whip out and dial up the Supreme Being for a morning chat, not the United States, not Israel, not Russia, not Pakistan, not the West Bank, not the Republicans, not the conservatives, not the liberals, not the Democrats, not the Realacrats, not anyone, so any notion of some religious superiority is nothing more than a trumped up dream of mortal grandeur that should be jettisoned immediately. In my Realacratic opinion, the sooner people will admit that they do not possess God's or the Supreme Being's personal roadmap to heaven, the more likely peace can be achieved in the world, even in the Middle-East. However, it will take more honesty and less judgmental arrogance disguised as faith, because peace cannot be legislated, it has to be orchestrated, not by suits and ties, but by everyday people like you and me, as Rage Against the Machine so eloquently stated in their song "Renegades of Funk."[24] The Realacrats are willing to try. What say you?

---

24 Rage Against The Machine, "Renegades of Funk," Renegades, 2000.

It has become clear to me that religious doctrine is just as sensitive, if not more, in the Middle East as it is here in the United States. So, any self-righteous attempt to belittle or discredit these doctrines will probably be met with some serious resistance and force. Keeping this in mind, pedestal-perching your belief system at the expense of other belief systems is a terminal cancer in the peace process. As long as all parties involved remain unwilling to relinquish their death grip on a faith-based absolute, the misinformation, misrepresentation, and stereotypical warfare will only grow stronger. It's time for all of us to unlearn our absolutes because; after all, both Jesus Christ and Muhammad were both men of infinite Godly wisdom. If we only continue to fight each other without learning to be better Christians and better Muslims, then what have we truly learned from either of these visionary prophets who we claim to follow and emulate so closely? I believe the success of these all-inclusive neutral zones could be the beginning of a new era if we can just locate true citizens of God, not just a specific brand of God, who are willing to try to make the world a better place by placing their religious egos to the side. Realacrats believe there is enough power and money in this world for Muslims, Christians, and Jews to all experience and participate without the destruction of one just to benefit the other.

AFGHANISTAN

What can I say about the Taliban and Al-Qaeda? I absolutely hate to agree with the Republicans on anything, but I have to stand with them on this particular issue. I don't know who I trust less, but I'm giving The Republicans the benefit of the doubt--this time. I think Bill O'Reilly is correct in his presumptions about the terrorists. I agree with him. You cannot trust these guys! I also agree with Bill Maher about religion destroying the lives of millions of people for eons, but there is more to it than just religious loons trying to convert the masses into Christians or Muslims. Back in the 1800s, White Christians tried tirelessly to convert African-American slaves and Native American tribes into Christians, which on the surface does not appear to be such a bad thing, but underneath hides an ugly and well-camouflaged agenda. It was never really about making new friends for Jesus, the same way it is not about making new friends for Allah. Economic, financial and cognitive control is the real motivating factor at work here. Do you remember when your mother used to put apple sauce in a teaspoon with your medicine to get you to take it? The same dogma applies here. Religion is the apple sauce, and the loss of your freedoms is that horrid tasting medicine. The religion, like the apple sauce, is only used to mask the deception. We need a party that understands this tactic. No matter which side of the pond you live on, money still talks, and bullsh*t still walks! The mere fact that the Taliban and Al-Qaeda are faith-based initiatives makes me extremely skeptical of their integrity. The Taliban has no right to enforce their theocratic doctrines on anyone who does not choose to participate in them. You can't just go around speaking loudly, carrying a big stick, and then bashing out the brains of whoever disagrees with you. There is no Christian insurgence to quell in Afghanistan or Pakistan and there is no real threat to Islam there. This is all about the Taliban's treatment of its own people in an effort to severely limit the choices made available. Unlike many of the religious sheep in Afghanistan, I will not bow to the Taliban or their religious tirades. The same thing goes for Al-Qaeda. You will not intimidate me into membership; that's gangbanging, and like the gangs here in the United States, and around the world, it's not about their culture, it's about control and power, where they gain and you lose! I only wish that there were others in the Middle East, as well as here in America, that could find their way to this conclusion without being duped or intimidated. To be a Realacrat, one must be about freedom of choice. It's everything we believe in. Totalitarian theocratic dictatorships must not be allowed to run amuck! I saw the footage of the Pakistani couple that was murdered by the Taliban for committing adultery. They were taken out in a field and gunned down in cold blood. I say screw the Taliban. I'll bet you a dollar to a doughnut that the guys pulling the triggers also have succumb to many improprieties in their own right, but since they are in cahoots within the organization, no one dares to question their integrity, and anyone who does may come face to bullet with their own destiny. The Taliban didn't do this to help uphold the righteousness of a committed relationship. They did this to instill fear into the masses, to keep the troops in line, to make an example, to quell any future challenges before they can even be waged, and to exert their will and dominance! This is not a war on Islam. This is not a war on Muslims. This is a war on good ol' fashioned corruption—the very same corruption that every nation is forced to deal with. I hear people in this country making fun of the 40 virgins in paradise after-life model. I hear people making fun of turbans. I hear people making fun of camel jockeys. I hear people making fun of praying seven times a day. None of this mockery amounts to a hill of poo, because this is not Christians versus Muslims in a hand-to-hand in the sand battle royal. The sooner we begin to attack this situation as more of a corruption machine than a religious square off, the more effective our attack will become.

Any idea of a religious, Christian-based cleansing at the expense of Islam is preposterous. In my opinion, the best the U.S. can hope do is replace the current corruption with a more business-minded corruption, because Afghanistan and Pakistan are no different than any other corrupt country with which the United States has dealings with. In my view, both of them might as well be the same country, because I don't believe you can fix one without fixing the other as well. This could prove to be a daunting task; just ask the Russians about that. Whatever strategy the Russians deployed in Afghanistan is clearly not the strategy the United States wants to utilize. There are some people here in the United States now questioning our involvement in Afghanistan the same way others have questioned our involvement in Iraq! The question is simple: are we helping or hurting in Afghanistan and Pakistan? My question is: does it make a difference? Most military endeavors are trials by fire, which means that years of hurt could be endured before a better plan emerges that could begin to turn the tide towards peace. We can always ask the Russians about that. They failed to out muscle the Afghans, and as long as Pakistan is a willing enabler, the United States will also fail to out muscle Afghanistan. Whoever devised the blueprints to the Sunni awakening in Iraq will be needed again in Afghanistan and Pakistan, because one way or another, their populous support system has to be disabled and then redirected, and this could take much longer than previously expected. As long as the people are willing to lay down for the Taliban and Al-Qaeda, the United States will continue to follow along in the footsteps of the Russians, leading to a stalemate, at best. The citizens of both countries have to be convinced that the Taliban and Al-Qaeda are not looking out for them, but only looking out for themselves. The United States propaganda has to be more convincing than the Taliban propaganda, and the U.S., Muslim, warlord payroll will ultimately have to be more potent than the Taliban's and Al-Qaeda's. Personally, I think many citizens in both countries know exactly how corrupt the Taliban and Al-Qaeda truly are, and that is why they are so afraid to oppose them. A lack of confidence in the international community and public executions has the people of both countries between a boulder and a hard place. When you see what happened in Iran just over protests, it's easy to see why people in the Middle East are reluctant to confront the powers that be. Corruption cloaked as religion has been a problem ever since the beginning of time and today is no different. These cloaked leaders must be challenged and held accountable. If you are willing to commit suicide bombings against what you perceive to be outside corruption, then you must also be willing to commit suicide bombings against what you bashfully know to be inside corruption, which is the freedom-robbing corruption that will linger long after the United States is gone from Afghanistan. The common and accepted belief regarding the people of the Middle East is their fearlessness in facing death to preserve what is right. That same courage will be needed to confront and expose corrupt religious leadership.

The Infidels

I am about to do something that will make my entire sociological base question my core integrity, because I am about to endorse one of the most hated men in the western hemisphere, the diabolical and sinister Osama Bin Laden. That's right! I'm officially endorsing Osama Bin Laden. I'm championing Osama Bin Laden. I'm about to encourage the world to follow Osama Bin Laden. This is highly controversial, but it is time that we all give Bin Laden the credit that he so richly deserves. Bin Laden is 100 percent correct in his desire to fight the infidels. He couldn't be more right about this sentiment, and I agree with him unmistakably. Yes, we should all fight against the dreaded infidels of society, but what Osama Bin Laden failed to eloquently explain was the tiny matter of exactly who or what a true infidel is. So, while Osama Bin Laden is correct in urging opposition towards the infidels, he conspicuously omits the greatest infidel in decades from the infidel list, which is he--himself. Yes, Osama Bin Laden is an infidel, in the same way that Hitler was an infidel, as they both conducted pseudo-crusades against the tyranny of the dreaded infidels. Bin Laden is quite possibly the worst infidel walking the face of the earth right now as we speak. When Bin Laden deploys his followers to fight against the infidels, they all need to walk about five yards before turning around and attacking him, because it is he who has done more damage to their respective freedoms than the rest of the world, most notably the United States. Bin Laden is the type of controlling character who will teach and train you how to wage the good fight, but against the wrong people. Like Hitler, and every other infidel, Bin Laden gains and retains his power of persuasion over the weak, the sick and the ignorant. It's more Darwinism at its best, or worst, depending on how you view it. Infidels are fabulous manipulators, and the apple doesn't fall far from the tree in Bin Laden's case. He has used his warped interpretations of Islam to mentally enslave his opponents. Muslims in the Middle-East firmly believe they are supposed to fight and destroy the infidels who invade and occupy their homelands and have domineering plans to extract all aspects of Islam; replacing them with Christianity. Muslims believe their very culture and ways of life are in jeopardy. Muslims believe they are about to be religiously and socially railroaded into the White, blue-eyed Jesus, train station, and they have decided they are not going down without a fight, which is identical to what would happen if the shoe was on the other foot, and Muslims were coming here, to the United States, to forcefully convert Christians to Islam, and to say that it would be a blood-bathed catastrophe would be an understatement. Bin Laden has convinced the people that the U.S. only exists to strip them of their religious identities, but Bin Laden is no better than his rhetoric. He and his posse of henchmen, the Taliban and Al-Qaeda, are what I call the Bin Laden league. They routinely deny the people an opportunity to decide for themselves. This is why they try to ban the internet, certain books, overall debates, religious freedoms, certain forms of music, certain clothing and controversial forms of education, basic human rights, and many other mind-freeing tools. It is simple as a box of rocks. If the United States is an infidel for trying to force Christianity, then the Bin Laden league henchmen are just as much the infidels for trying to suppress it.

Infidels cannot be successful without a hefty, willing herd of human cattle to lead astray. This is why Bin Laden and his Taliban, Al-Qaeda forces crusade religiously, while trouncing the freedoms and rights of the masses in their respective countries, because if you control the choices of the people, you control the actions of the people, and if you control the actions of the people, you control the people. The same tactic was used during the slavery era right here in America to control the Black slave population. The more information you can deny someone, the more you can lead and manipulate that individual. It's easy to herd zombie cattle, even if you're leading them into the slaughterhouse, because sleepwalkers don't site see! They don't know it's a slaughterhouse; for all they know, it could be a bath house, and the infidel wants to keep it that way. It's good for business. The cattle do all the work, and the infidel drives off with all the money. How many times have we seen that scenario play out? Infidels are notorious for leading their counterparts in erroneous expeditions, like Bin Laden leading his followers out to fight against the U.S./Christian-led infidels, when in actuality, the Bin Laden league is not really fighting for Islam; they are fighting for themselves, their own personal interests. This is about money, power, deception, favoritism, sexism, manipulation, and dominance. The Bin Laden league is not out to promote Allah. They are out to promote themselves. In Realacrat terminology, the world, not just the United States, has to make every attempt to alleviate the Middle Eastern desire to drink the infidel Kool-Aid, which alleges that we, as Americans, all have a vested interest in controlling their freedoms, when we clearly do not! If we could somehow find a way to tear down this wall of manipulative blindness, we may have a chance to diminish this misguided propaganda.

THE REALACRATIC RESPONSE TO SEPTEMBER 11TH

What I am about lay out in front of you now will be the most controversial material regarding September 11th, and it will most definitely be the most controversial material in this book. First, I will speak as an African-American regarding September 11th, then I will speak on what the Realacratic response should be to this event.

Long before I ever had the idea to start the Realacrat ideology, I was awakened on September 11th by the sights and the sounds of horror on CNN, and I will admit to the world right here and now that I was afraid. I thought nuclear war would be next. It was, without a doubt, the most horrific event I've ever witnessed in my life. But here is where the ugly truth comes in. I never once thought the attacks were aimed at me personally or others like me. Yes, I said it, and I'm not the only one. Other minorities have also discussed this, but not on camera. I will boldly state that the outright majority of Asian Americans, Hispanic Americans, Cuban Americans, Haitian Americans, Native Americans, Arab Americans and African-Americans did not, and still don't; believe that Osama Bin Laden and the terrorists were sitting around the Middle East plotting a scenario aimed at the destruction of Juan, Julio, Hakeem, Mafutu, Chief Red Feather, Won Wong or Tyrone! I'm sorry, but there is nothing, absolutely nothing, that Senator Lindsay Graham, former President Bush, Bill O'Reilly, Sean Hannity, Ann Coulter, Hillary Clinton, Bill Clinton or even President Obama can ever say or do to convince me of that one. This was not the shot heard around the world aimed at minorities. Minorities did die in the September 11th attacks, but they were the metaphorical body that had to be targeted in order to wound the head. They were just a by-product of the attack, and here is why. All any of the minorities had to do was move back to their ethnic homelands on September 10th of 2001, and they would have been automatically morphed into bystanders and not participants, with about a 90% chance of never even having their lives directly affected by Osama Bin Laden. If the rich, elite, European/Caucasian, Christian, power players were no longer the self-appointed, self-approved bearers of global instigation and global ego-centrism, the country, in all likelihood; would never have been attacked on September 11th, because minorities were virtually non-existent during the pre-Obama/pre-September 11th days. With the recent election of President Obama, this is the first time in American history that a minority actually has the power to make decisions that can and will affect the whole world, and not just the impecunious, drug-infested, crime-riddled, gang-run neighborhoods of the customary African-American/minority communities.

You want the cold hard truth behind the lies and propaganda? Well, here it is! There are people in the United States resembling a Rush Limbaugh, a Sean Hannity, or a Liz Cheney who view themselves on a much different, much higher, much more powerful societal and political plateau than that of African-Americans and other minorities. Apparently, the terrorists had that same view. I guess that's why poor minorities in slumlord hoods failed to make the cut as targets of the terrorist attacks.

I mean seriously, if your goal was to economically, socially, or physically maim the United States, would you attack inner-city areas like those of Compton, California; Orange Mound, Tennessee; or the old Ninth Ward of New Orleans? I think the terrorists, like everyone else, have figured out that if you want to hurt the head fat-cats in charge just follow the money, and I'll guarantee that you'll end up in the World Trade Markets/Washington D.C./Wall St. vicinities a million times over before you'd ever find your way to Orange Mound, Tennessee or the Ward 4 of Wynne, Arkansas. There is a huge status differentiation between being a neighborhood terrorist and being a global terrorist. One thing America might want to do is go back to school so it can attempt to finally learn the difference between a threat to one's life and a threat to one's egocentric pecking order in the social and economic distribution.

I'll go even further. I could go to Afghanistan, Pakistan, Venezuela, Cuba, North Korea or any other disgruntled country and emerge less-feared and more trusted than previously thought, because African-Americans don't have a real history or real beef with any of these nations, and most of the minorities in this country also fall into that same category. The disenfranchisement from power also affords the disenfranchisement from the ramifications based on the usage of that power, because conflicts and rivalries are based on engagement. Fortunately or unfortunately, African-Americans and other minorities have never been granted the luxury or prestige to be a rivalry or an adversary to anyone outside of the United States. All we've ever done is donate money to Israel while watching disinterestedly from the worst seats in the house! This is a Realacratic analysis. No other political party would ever dare to discuss such a volatile ideology.

Out of the ashes of disenfranchisement arises the Realacrat, who brings forth principles based in humanitarianism and not vengeance. This is the Realacratic response to September 11th. Speaking as a Realacrat, I had no idea who those people in the World Trade Center were. None of them were personally linked to me. Some of them could have very well been the types of people who would not get into an elevator with just me in it, but that is not important. What is important is the right to live, and that is a right that was brutally taken away by anger and treachery. Realacrats don't have a problem with the Middle East, but we do have a problem with the unwarranted, genocidal-like attacks of September 11th. If you hate the United States, and you want to pick a fight with the U.S. military, that is one thing, but when you attack innocent, working people who are just trying to bring home a paycheck, you've gone too far. If you have a problem with management, then you take it up with management, but you don't use employees as guinea pigs of decimation, because you believe the boss is screwing you and your girlfriend! After all, neither President Bush nor Vice-President Cheney ever consulted with me on any Middle Eastern, foreign policy. If any of you jihadists would like to know the Bryian R. views on any of your doctrines, just pick up a copy of this book, because I don't mince words. This is my ideology, not the foreign policy of George "The Wannabe, Texas Cowboy" W. Bush or Dick "The Oil Vampire" Cheney! Like me, the working people killed on September 11th at multiple locations were not out to enforce any U.S. foreign policy. They were only trying to pay the bills, eat, and survive. New York Firefighters are not the reason your Middle Eastern country is in economic turmoil, and those passengers on those ill-fated U.S. planes had no desire to recruit Muslims into Christianity, regardless of who was actually behind the attacks.

I have associates, who are truthers, and I have people that I know that are Islamophobic, but this is how a Realacrat stands! If I knew for certain that President Bush had no idea about the September 11th attacks and had been totally honest about everything, I would have been out there, if at all possible, trying to save lives; and the politics of Democrat or Republican would not have mattered. If strangers from abroad or local hicks in the U.S. held Sarah Palin and Rush Limbaugh at gunpoint and threatened to behead them if they did not submit to some religious doctrine, it would be my Realacratic, American, humanitarian duty to act on the behalf of Limbaugh and Palin, because no one deserves to be forced into any ideology; regardless of one's political affiliations! The victims of September 11th didn't deserve it and neither do you or me. Realacrats would not fight to say that any ideology is wrong, but we will fight the violent, unjust force-feeding of it to those unwilling to swallow the propaganda! This is how our government and our democracy are supposed to work. This is what the Founding Fathers had in mind.

This entire notion of force-feeding is counterproductive by its very nature, so if you are looking for someone to blame for your livelihood woes, I believe at least half of that blame falls on you Mr. Extremist. I know the United States has not always been flawless in foreign or domestic efficiency, but then again—neither have you! One does not have to relinquish their Islamic distinctiveness to be civil, and contrary to tyrannical beliefs; cooperation is not a sin or a sign of weakness. It's actually a show of respect. If you want better conditions for your area of the world, which most sane people do, then you will have to learn how to become more tolerant of others in the business world, as well as in the religious world. Flying planes into buildings is not, and never has been, a coherent means of establishing a foundation for economic opportunities with other countries that are in position to bestow such possibilities. The same problems you face before you fly a plane into a building will be the same problems faced after the plane has hit the building. The self-detonation of a bomb on a plane or in a building that kills everyone around, including you, just so you can teach one guy who disagrees with you a lesson; is the epitome of the ultimate dupe.

I thought the benefits of getting even with an adversary were based on the one seeking and deploying the revenge leaving his intended target in ruins. If I have to detonate myself into gory dust just to make sure that I detonate you into that same gory dust, I would in no way consider such an action to be a circumstantiated version of retribution. In my old neighborhood, we call that a draw, and a draw is one of the least effective ways that one can achieve payback. I'd rank it a step ahead of forgiveness. How many rich, prosperous, happy suicide bombers do you know? It's very hard to ride off into the sunset after a self-detonation. This is why the smart, rich, prosperous people focus on living, so they can remain rich and prosperous, while the weak-minded, impoverished sheep wait to cash in their chips at the death bank on 40 Virgins Avenue. These are not real solutions. Burning down your own neighborhood or breaking your own toys as a child represents the same played-out crusade tactics that have continuously produced more of the same, rather than feasible possibilities for progress. Anything that undercuts your own ambitions should be jettisoned at once. And for the record, anyone plotting to bring down or destroy any form of public transportation should be automatically eligible for the death penalty!

If you want to become the next China, you have to acquire a China, business plan and not a death plan! The reason many of the countries in the Middle East struggle is due to supreme corruption cloaked in religion and hypocrisy. The Middle East needs to leave God at home and take the laptop to work. They should give to Caesar what is Caesar's and give to Allah what is Allah's, because, as I've already pointed out, neither Caesar nor Allah want the same thing. Caesar wants a momentary pay-off, while Allah looks for the eternal pay-off later on down the road. In other words, pay Caesar with your money and pay Allah with your soul, because these barbaric, misguided, problematic, resultless, crusades of bloody carnage and despair do little to help create solutions.

If I went to the Middle East and killed over 3,000 people, I would unequivocally get the death penalty, either by trial justice or by beheading justice. The terrorists that were originally set to stand trial in New York should suffer the same fate for placing thousands of lives in a murderous deathtrap for the sake of making a point that serves no purpose, if they are solely responsible. For example, any theory suggesting the murder of innocent people as a justifiable pathway to a righteous heaven is nothing more than an erroneous, fallacious tool of manipulation built solely on the willingness of the weak. Any theory suggesting there are entities within the acknowledging presence of God almighty that would order chaos, death and destruction revolving around the diversity of a point of view is a theory based more in an earthly, worldly, man-made reality than anything even remotely resembling a heavenly one, and any theory based on the premise of sacrificing thousands of lives for political, social, economic, and religious augmentation is rivaled only by the crapulent, power-hungry lust of Adolph Hitler himself.

The Iraq War

Realacrat behavior was built on questioning those who have unceremoniously self-appointed themselves into a hierarchy. No one is above questioning, not even the religious. Your belief system does not give you a pass on accountability, and silencing the messenger is not an option! I am reminded once again of the invasion of Iraq, when President Bush went on worldwide television and demanded that Saddam Hussein relinquish his power and his entire country. The timeline basically said to Saddam Hussein: "You have 48 hours to get out or else!" [25] I bring this up for one reason. During that time, there

25 CNN, Bush gives Saddam 48 hours to leave Iraq, http://www.cnn.com/2003/

was tremendous ambiguity over the planned unilateral invasion of Iraq. Not everyone was for it. There were many who did not share the President's enthusiasm over removing Saddam Hussein. There was also a huge amount of skepticism over the possibility of weapons of mass destruction allegedly lying in wait somewhere in Iraq! Illinois State Senator Barack Obama characterized it as a dumb war based on partisan intelligence.[26] Republicans, conservatives, and Christian, religious zealots had a field day going after Obama and anyone else expressing a lack of confidence or leeriness over this dictator removal plan. Not only were Democrats concerned about the ethics of this planned invasion, but they were also concerned about the financial aspects of it to the American people, as well as the casualty factors of such a large-scaled invasion. Democrats and the media were unmercifully attacked and scrutinized by conservatives and Republicans for questioning its legitimacy. There were even talks of making any criticism of the President a criminal act. Any Democratic leader who stood up and spoke out against President Bush's military incursions was branded a traitor! Just ask Natalie Maines of the Dixie Chicks about that. Media outlets were unjustifiably labeled as liberal, weak, soft, terrorist lovers, who hated America and wanted to see it attacked again. Since when did criticism become an act of sedition? It's the job of our elected leaders and our media to ask the tough questions and hold people accountable for their actions, especially when those actions involve the lives of our military and our citizens. It's the very motto Fox News and Bill O'Reilly tout so proudly nowadays. I had every right to question President Bush. No dictatorship is a good one, not even a political/economic/religious dictatorship. The Realacrat platform will never be about forcing anyone to do anything at any time. No one is forced to stay, and no one will be forced to leave over any rational ideological disagreement. Anyone can criticize the policies and directions of the platform whenever they feel the need to do so. We welcome debate; because we don't believe in becoming a dictator just remove a dictator!

Speaking of debate, I still can't get over the Iraqi invasion rationale. I sit around and ask myself quite often just how we, the American people,

---

US/03/17/sprj.irq.bush.speech/index.html (March 2003).

26 Barack Obama, Remarks of Illinois State Sen. Barack Obama Against Going to War with Iraq, http://www.barackobama.com/2002/10/02/remarks_of_illinois_state_sen.php (October 2002).

sheepishly allowed President Bush and his administration to pull off such an immaculate con-job. The removal of Saddam Hussein was supposed be an issue of national and international security, yet other nations were more than reluctant to participate in this political, yet personal, witch-hunt—and for good reason. The Republicans and conservatives were boasting loudly and boldly about their military intentions to save the world and the country from the dangerous Saddam Hussein. His alleged, mythological weapons of mass destruction were the stuff of legends. They were like Bigfoot sightings, Loch Ness Monster sightings, or the numerous UFO sightings around the world. There is no substantial proof that any of these things truly exist, but there are many who feel so strongly about it; they are willing to believe in it no matter what. I always had serious doubts about Saddam's weapons of mass destruction. Even though some Democrats, such as Hillary Clinton and John Kerry, were on board with the Bush administration's dictator removal plan, I was never fully convinced of its legitimacy. It always sounded more like Politics 101 to me. People in my camp were under the impression that President Bush was on a revenge tour aimed at eliminating Saddam Hussein for allegedly putting out a hit on President George H.W. Bush. So we believed that Bush Jr. had decided to go in and finally finish the job his father started about nine years earlier, and the events of September 11th were the keys that slid open the door for Bush Jr. to do just that. Again, I could not understand the reasoning behind removing Saddam Hussein due to the ramifications of September 11th. To me, this just seemed like a misguided plan of action, and I was staunchly against it, and I didn't care in the least bit how much all of the gung-ho Republicans and conservatives tried to brand me with the traitor logo. The Republicans were just toeing-the-line like good party members. In the Realacrat Party, we only toe-the-line when we believe in it, and we step across that line when we don't. There will be no political Kool-Aid passed out here.

Nevertheless, I was not a fan of President Bush's plan to launch preemptive strikes on our enemies at first, but I began to come around to it the more I thought about it. Maybe President Bush was on to something when he suggested we fight the terrorists over there so we don't have to fight them over here in the United States, which actually was not a bad idea, because I have no doubt in my mind that the

United States is not ready to wage war on its home court! I don't think the American people, including myself, have any idea about the demanding toll such a measure would take on this country! So when President Bush launched attacks on Afghanistan and went after terrorists full steam ahead, I never once criticized President Bush's Afghanistan offensive. I was very leery of American troops being placed in Afghanistan, but I knew it was a necessary hazard that had to be waged. In fact, I don't remember many, if any, Democrats speaking out against the Afghanistan offensive. For the most part, President Bush had the support of the country. He and his Republican brigade were all given the benefit of the doubt.

It was only when he decided to go after what I perceived to be an unrelated issue that I began to question the morality and practicality of his terrorism, battle plan. However it may have happened, I, under no circumstances; would have ever agreed to an invasion of Iraq! I also never believed there was any primary connection between Saddam Hussein and September 11. There was a ton of partisan information being released and touted to suggest otherwise, but I was not buying it. Barack Obama felt it was a dumb war. I agreed then, and I agree even more now. It was and still is a dumb war! It was never about national security. This Iraqi invasion was all about political vengeance and oil, and it was waged on the American taxpayer's dollar. President Bush may have felt safer knowing that Saddam Hussein's days were numbered, but I didn't feel any safer because of it. Knowing Saddam Hussein was captured and in custody did absolutely nothing for me, and many other nations felt the exact same way. The worst evidence against Saddam Hussein was his previous actions, not against the United States, but against his own insurgents in his own country. People like Vice-President Dick Cheney condemned Saddam Hussein for his violent and unethical treatment of his own people, like the Kurds. It went from a national security issue to an issue of justice for the Kurds. This entire campaign was supposed to be about weapons of mass destruction, which would give Saddam Hussein the power to strike the all mighty Israel, but the more I watched the coverage of the Iraqi invasion, the more I began to suspect that there were no weapons of mass destruction. Look at it this way: the Republican Guard was getting trounced and routed on a daily basis. If there were truly any weapons of mass destruction available, they would have been quickly deployed and utilized.

Put yourself in their shoes for a minute. If some foreign dude appears on national television and hands you a 48-hour ultimatum to vacate your home or else, what would you do? If a Muslim/Iraqi/Middle-Eastern/non-American organization gave the United States a 48-hour ultimatum to vacate the premises or else, Americans would flip out into complete, chaotic, war preparation. Every Joe Blow, Joe Six-Pack, and Joe the Plumber would be armed and ready with their fingers on the trigger. If there were any biological weapons, chemical weapons, or weapons of mass destruction available, they would be on the table locked-in and loaded, and Saddam Hussein was no different and neither are you or me. If some stranger came to remove me from my home to seize weapons of mass destruction that I may or may not have, that stranger wouldn't have to worry about finding my weapons of mass destruction. The stranger would have to worry about my weapons of mass destruction finding him! The more Saddam suffered losses on the military front, the more I came to the realization the weapons of mass destruction was a lot of political smoke in mirrors. The longer it went on, the more obvious it became just how militarily impoverished Iraq actually was, when lined up against a superpower like the United States. It also became abundantly clear that Saddam Hussein was not much of a threat to the United States or anyone else, except for his own enemies in his own country. In the end, Saddam Hussein was captured, tried and then executed. I assume that President Bush had finally achieved his goal, but at what cost to the American taxpayers and the American military? This dictator-removing journey has cost billions, and in the summer of 2009, it is still ongoing and costing even more millions. Osama Bin Laden is also still out there alive and kicking; releasing new audio material whenever he feels like it. As I sat and viewed the last moments of Saddam Hussein's life with a rope tied around his neck, it felt like one of the most hollowed, most insignificant, most unimpressive, and most uninformed, alleged, American victories since the pushing of helicopters into the South China Sea after the ending of the Vietnam War in 1975. I don't think the same could have been said if it was Osama Bin Laden who was executed. The American people would have felt far more vindicated by Osama Bin Laden's execution and rightfully so. Neither the military occupation of Iraq, nor the cancellation of Saddam Hussein's run-of-the-mill tyranny has managed to make the majority of American people feel any safer, but it has made them feel the economic pinch of the costly dues of a long-term, occupational invasion. The Iraq war should be called the Iraq distraction, because it has caused the United States to be engulfed in a manufactured, generic crisis when there are many more pressing events and many more treacherous unknowns that have yet to be resolved or decided. We are still there in Iraq at this very moment, and as the price tag for this phony September 11 retribution scenario continues to mount, the American people will have to find themselves a 7-foot, Crawford, Texas mirror and take a long, deep look, as they ask themselves these simple questions: Was it really worth it? Did the ends justify the means? Has the input produced a sufficient output? From my viewpoint, the answer is a resounding and reverberating no! Like the Republicans have always barked in response to other domestic, economic, government operations, it is my philosophy that our military capabilities should be used wisely, efficiently, effectively and only when necessary. War is not something you wage when you get tired of channel-surfing. War is not something you wage when the guy down the street calls you a pinhead. War is not something you wage when some idiot calls your best friend a stinking corpse and threatens to kick their ass. As I learned from the streets of the African-American community, fools that talk a lot usually turn out to be the ones who fail to do a lot, because talk is cheap! There is an exorbitant difference between punching some idiot in the face for trash talking and launching a nuke or declaring a war on some idiot for trash talking!

As for the botched effort to locate those infamous weapons of mass destruction, it's evident to me that somebody played dirty pool with the intelligence gathering, but dirty pool is Washington's version of grand theft auto. I'm not a fan of Dick Cheney, and if I were prosecuting him or the entire Bush administration, it would only be based on my extreme displeasure at his ideologies in general and that's not a legitimate reason to do it in my eyes or with my taxpayer money, but I will say this. Whoever was in charge of intelligence gathering about those infamous weapons of mass destruction should be dragged up to Capitol Hill and grilled like the baseball players and the auto execs were grilled, and if it is found that the intelligence used to prompt the invasion of Iraq was politically trumped up to the highest degree to achieve a specific political result; prosecutions should be in order!

Iran and Ahmadinejad

It is the summer of 2009, and the Iranian presidential election between the incumbent Ahmadinejad and his upstart challenger Mousavi has just taken place, and it appears to the entire world that the fix was in. By all appearances, it looked as if Mousavi was well on his way to defeating the crafty Ahmadinejad. He had even been advised to prepare his victory speech. The tech-savvy Mousavi had used a page out of Barack Obama's playbook by tapping into the power of the Internet to corral potential voters. For a short time, things looked good for Mousavi and the U.S., despite the sly and guileful Ahmadinejad blocking out Facebook and much of the internet just prior to the election, but the more I looked in the slick, used-car-salesman face of Ahmadinejad; the more I had a sneaking gut-feeling that he was going to find a way to cozen the election away from Mousavi, and he accomplished that feat with ease. I don't live in Iran. I'm not Arabic, Muslim, or Iranian, and I've never been to the Middle East or Iran, but I could still see through my westernized, American eyes; a monumental hoodwink in the facial expressions of Ahmadinejad, which just goes to show how some aspects of humanity takes precedence over political, geographical and religious divisions, and dishonesty is one of those aspects that you can just sense and feel even if the guilty party is of a much different background than you. Ahmadinejad looked guilty and fraudulent from the very beginning. He never acted concerned over Mousavi's well-orchestrated challenge. It was as if he already knew he was going to win, and undoubtedly he did. If there is one thing the American people should learn from the turmoil in Iran is one humanly incontestable point, and that would be that you are only as righteous as your representation. In other words, your kindness and understanding can be literally canceled out if you have a corrupt, deceitful, deranged, greed-monger speaking for you. The flip side of that axiom is that one bad apple can undeservedly become the face of the good apple franchise; constantly and consistently tarnishing it. I, like many in the United States, had a very negative opinion of the nation of Iran due to past conflicts. The hard-line posturing of Ahmadinejad and the influx of the terrorist mindset caused me to view the people of Iran as the purification of negativity, but after witnessing the events that have unfolded after the botched, shady win of Ahmadinejad; I have developed a new-found respect and admiration for the people of Iran and for all Muslims in general. I'll say it again. There are certain aspects of humanity that can transcend petty, religious, political differences; and the struggle and fight for freedom is one of them, if not the most important one of all. I fully support the people of Iran, including the ones residing here in the U.S. I once thought Iranians were evil. I once thought Iranians were crazy zealots. I once thought Iranians were mean-spirited. I once thought Iranians were full of hatred for me. I once thought Iranians were out to destroy the American model of democracy, and I once thought Iranians were out to destroy and disparage Christianity, but I now see that I was wrong and extremely stereotypical, and I'm most definitely not alone! I, along with many others, should have known better than to buy into those us-vs.-them distractions. The ruling powers use distractions such as these to keep the people divided and unfocused. This allows for misguided aggression, misguided hatred and misguided confusion, which allows the ruling elite to retain full control over the masses.

I think Hitler perfected that battle plan, along with Jim Crow and the Klu Klux Klan. The people of Iran have now been forced to read the writing on the wall of their livelihoods and their very existences. No one can sell you anything that you don't believe in, and Ahmadinejad can no longer sell the people of Iran a distraction passed off as progress. Once the Iranian people had their own version of a Sunni awakening, the freedom cat was out of the bag and running free in Iran. You can only dupe those who are willing to be duped, and the people of Iran are no longer willing. This was never about preserving the Muslim creed from the infidels of the West. This was never about Westerners riding in with the cavalry to indoctrinate poor, unbeknownst Muslims to the corruptible spell of Christianity. This was never about protecting the Iranian heritage from the outside world's infidelity. What Ahmadinejad has proven here is that he is just as roguish and corrupt as any Western nation out there. After all, the west is supposed to be the poster child for religious and political corruption. So, where exactly did the mighty and righteous Ahmadinejad learn how to fleece and rig an election?

I think he's learned to appreciate much more from America and the west than he's allowing to be known. Maybe we should send Katherine Harris to Iran, so she can personally appoint Ahmadinejad President of Iran the way she did for President Bush in the Florida, voting fiasco of the year 2000. Ahmadinejad's only goal is to remain in power, and all of his brainwashing mechanisms were designed for one purpose only; to ensure that the ruling class could continue to rule the minds and wallets of the Iranian people. So to the Iranian people, Ahmadinejad, like Osama Bin Laden, is not trying to help you! He is only interested in controlling you. Facebook, knowledge, intellect, education, the media and Western nations are not the enemies to your freedoms. As a Realacrat, I am not here to oppress whatever it is you may believe in, and I'm not here to ban or censor information from anyone at any time. Now that's the best deal most of us will probably see during our time here on this planet, and you won't have it offered to you by many either. Do you think Ahmadinejad, the supreme leader, or Osama Bin Laden would ever offer you that deal; much less live up to it? As the legendary Steven Tyler of Aerosmith would say, "Dream on!"[27]

My heart bleeds for the people of Iran, especially the brave women of all ages who have taken to the streets, putting their lives in danger to stand up and fight for what they believe in, alongside the multitudes of freedom-seekers in the streets of Tehran and the rest of the country. Standing up for what you believe in, along with standing up for your freedoms, is about as American as it gets. In the spirit of the 13 original colonies, Native Americans, American women, homosexuals, Cuban refugees, Haitian refugees, Asian-Americans, Hispanic-Americans, and most of all, African-Americans; the protestors in Iran are all patriots of humanity. I feel such sadness for the young students and all of the other protesters who have been unmercifully gunned down by their corrupt government. I don't know what it is, but when I see people fighting enslavement I am compelled to act, and I would join the protesters if I could, because they are right to aspire to be free. I sincerely hope Neda's death can inspire the people of Iran to fight for their rights!.

When the loving and caring Ahmadinejad called the nation of Israel a stinking corpse and drew tons of fire from the Jewish community and other world communities, he also referred to the Holocaust as a phony

27 Aerosmith, "Dream On," *Aerosmith*, 1973.

event, and further enraged even more people. There were some in the United States who wanted to go to war with Ahmadinejad to strike down his aspirations of a nuclear weapons program, fearing that he might decide to eradicate Israel once and for all which, in my opinion, is a genuine concern, but I think America and the rest of the world missed the bus on this issue. While yes, it was inappropriate for Ahmadinejad to make such disparaging remarks about Israel, it actually was not the most despicable act in my eyes. I find it funny how some people want to attack Ahmadinejad for his Israel comments, but then suddenly become much more reserved about the deplorable treatment of his own people. Didn't we just remove a rogue dictator a couple of blocks down the street because of the vile way he treated his own people? Why is it okay to remove one dictator and not the other? Didn't we just remove a dictator because we thought he had weapons of mass destruction that could be used to kill innocent nations like Israel? Ahmadinejad told the world of his desires to produce a nuclear power and defiantly continues to work towards it. I don't think the previous dictator we removed had weapons of mass destruction, nor was he working towards weapons of mass destruction, yet he was terminated! Can you say the words politically biased? Saddam Hussein was removed from power because of his alleged weapons of mass destruction and the harboring of terrorists, while all along it appears that Ahmadinejad has been indulging in both. If Ahmadinejad is capable of harboring uranium, then I'm sure he has probably harbored hordes of terrorists, if he wants to! So in honor of Sarah Palin's empty, stump speech, rhetoric: "How's that hopey changey remove Saddam Husseiny thingy working out for you now?"

No matter how tough on terror conservatives may claim to be, blind, misguided, vendetta-driven aggression will nullify its productivity in a heartbeat! It's ironic that one of the last things Saddam Hussein ever talked about was his concern regarding Iran's military ambitions.[28] Evidently, Saddam was more concerned about Ahmadinejad than the United States. In hindsight, it looks as if Saddam Hussein had more sense than any of our high-dollar, high-powered, yet faulty in the end, reconnaissance scouting of the Middle-East. Nevertheless, we went into

28 Associated Press, **Saddam Hussein Wanted Iran to Fear WMDs: Saber rattling was aimed at neighbor; dictator "miscalculated" Bush plans, http://www.nbcdfw.com/news/archive/Hussein-Worried-About-Iran.html (July 2, 2009).**

the Iraq War to deliver democracy and freedom to a group of people that were not clamoring to receive it or our presence. We basically force-fed it to them whether they were ready for it or not, and we have been paying the human and financial price for those actions ever since. Now you have an actual uprising by the people of Iran who have taken to the streets to fight for that very same democracy we pushed onto the Iraqi people, but this time; we are nowhere to be found. We merely report on it and say it's a local problem to make the case to stay out of it. If that's the case, why are we still meddling in Iraq? This could turn out to be one of the most important missed opportunities in human history. While the people of Iran text message and send videos in English to the United States in hopes of gaining support, we are forced to sit back and twiddle our thumbs because we are so bogged down in Iraq. Ahmadinejad's Israel comment was horrid. There is no doubt about it, but his blatant and outright rigging of the election, and his unwarranted banning of the internet, media and journalists is beyond the pale, and his government crackdown that killed fellow Iranians, like Neda, is certainly beyond the pale. I cannot believe the unmitigated chutzpah of this tyrannical Narcissus. Who in the hell does Ahmadinejad think he is? The Iranian people don't need father Ahmad to tuck them in at night so the American boogieman won't get them, and they don't need a dictating chaperone either. The banning of all journalists and media from reporting on the events in Iran in hopes of covering everything up is a futile attempt to sweep another political mammoth underneath the corruption rug. Hey Ahmadinejad, here is a word of advice for you! You can always declare war on the future, and you can always fight the future, but you cannot stop the future. You can only hope to delay the inevitable. Not only is he killing people, he is killing dreams, human rights, knowledge, creativity, justice, progress, and most of all; the freedom to pursue one's own happiness.

People haven't quite realized the amazing details of what has happened in Iran. Yes, the murder of protestors in the streets by a grotesque, dictating regime is hideous and heinous to say the least, not to mention unacceptable, but there is something even more astounding at play here. The Iranians turned out in record numbers for this election in hopes of having a voice or say in their lives and government, and there is absolutely nothing wrong with that. In fact, they should be commended for their bold, fresh aspirations, and it doesn't make them any less religious or less Islamic because of it. The desire and passion to be free should never be used as a status indicator of anyone's religious convictions. Freedom is not a sin! It is simply the right to sin, which is a right given to all of humanity by God, the Supreme Being, Mother Nature, or whoever; regardless of religious background. Contrary to popular, Middle Eastern beliefs, the United States does not own the copyrights or patents on the freedom of sin choice. Ahmadinejad's fruitless quest to deny the Iranian people the freedom of sin is not for him to decide. This is why God/life gave us the option to choose, because it allows us to be in control of our own destinies. Maybe Ahmadinejad should spend more time touching up his highly touted, religious teachings, because right now; I'd put him squarely on the same level as a Jim Jones. The Iranian people are expressing their identities of humanity. This does not make them American puppets on a string, but this can make them the new sole controllers of that string, which was their string to begin with. The newly found courage to venture outside of their personal and religious comfort zones is a historic milestone for the Iranian people and the entire Middle East, and you'll never guess who is partly responsible for setting this ship afloat. That's right! It is partially the fault of the West, America in particular. So when Ahmadinejad accuses the West of influencing the Iranian people he is actually onto something. The West, through the options of technology, has affected the people of Iran, which is clearly evident by this latest election and its aftermath, but only because the Iranian people have chosen to be affected by it. Now, Republicans will never admit to it. Conservatives will never admit to it. The religious zealots will never admit to it, and Fox News will never admit to it, but the election of Barack Obama as President of the United States of America was a game-changer, not only here at home, but globally as well. The image of an African-American son of a Kenyan who just happens to have a Muslim name leading the United States and the world has caused a magnificent transformation in perhaps millions of people around the planet. America has boldly gone where no country has dared to go before and the results could possibly change the course of human history. It's not about President Obama so much as it is about what his election represents and symbolizes to minorities and different nationalities around the world. The Iranian people had made up their minds to follow in the footsteps of the Barack Obama presidency by daring to try and change all that had come before them, and it appears that they had successfully used the power of their vote, not their religious tendencies, to honestly bring about this change. If the alleged, evil empire can do it, then so can we, thought the Iranian people! Despite all of the historic, traditional, long-term, deeply rooted negativity surrounding the alleged infidelities of the incredulous United States, it was the United States that was able to bring about a change that was once thought impossible, and that was to prove that people can make their own possibilities if given a chance to do so. The Iranian people witnessed it here in America, worked hard for it in Iran, voted for it, and by all accounts; should have received it. However, the ruling regime and the deplorable Ahmadinejad squeezed the life out of the Iranian people politically and figuratively! Ahmadinejad didn't do this to save Islam or the Iranian people. He did it to save himself, his ego, his riches, his power and most of all his control. Because Ahmadinejad has chosen to do what is best for him, instead of what's best for his country, I think it's time the Iranian people choose what is best for them, including the removal of Ahmadinejad if that is what they truly wish to happen.

You want a Realacrat solution for a possible showdown with Ahmadinejad? I would shut down the Iraqi occupation starting immediately. All diplomatic options with the current Iranian regime would now be on the chopping block. I wouldn't hesitate for a second to criticize the Iranian leadership, because they wouldn't hesitate for a millisecond to criticize the U.S. I would not lose any sleep over the negative feelings Ahmadinejad had about my questioning his election credentials, because it is obvious that he is only out for himself. I would do everything in my power to help other nations and the Iranian people see Ahmadinejad for what he is. His anti-West propaganda would be countered on every front with anti-Ahmadinejad propaganda. Ahmadinejad's credibility has already been severely diminished, and this advantage must be utilized to the fullest. If Ahmadinejad's miraculous comeback victory is determined to be fraudulent, I think the international community has a responsibility to put economic pressures on his regime in hopes that the Iranian people will continue to be defiant until the Ahmadinejad regime is removed.

As for Ahmadinejad's nuclear development program, it does not seem likely that the United States or the rest of the world can realistically prevent Iran from eventually acquiring some sort of nuclear power—possibly a weapon. With that said, a renewed policy plan for missile defense will be needed. Without the strong cooperation of both China and Russia to try and help quell Iran's nuclear ambitions, I strongly feel that Iran will inevitably develop nuclear power, if they haven't developed it already. What they choose to do with it is unknown, but there is one thing the entire world knows, and that is the fact that Ahmadinejad will do just about anything to keep his narrow-assed, narrow-minded, underhanded, erroneous, grubby, gluttonous hands in the cookie jar. This means that even if I negotiated a deal with him to dismantle all nuclear weapons; I would always have a nuclear ace of up my sleeve at all times, and a missile, defense program might be out of sight, but not out of mind!

Being a Realacrat, I would go to the United Nations and propose a new guideline in regards to civil unrest. Taking a page out of the President Bush/Dick Cheney playbook, I would incorporate what would be known as my "Subjects of Sanctions" list, which is based on the "Axis of Evil" list first introduced by the Bush administration. While the Bush administration sought out and added certain countries/regimes to the "Axis of Evil" list due to their political and social improprieties, the Realacrat "Subjects of Sanctions" list would include any country that broke these rules of engagement.

The Assed-Out Rule

This would be a new rule implemented on behalf of all the megalomaniacal dictators around the world. Consider it the Ahmadinejad/Kim Jong-il sanction, because there is so much concern over the nuclear desires of both Iran and North Korea due to the many antagonistic remarks uttered by the North Korean government. In the past, Kim Jong-il has threatened to wipe out the United States entirely, and he has also threatened to launch a nuclear attack on Hawaii, South Korea and possibly even Japan; notice he made no such threat against China. The international community has highly condemned these reckless threats made by Kim Jong-il, but they are very aware that threats of this nature cannot be simply tossed out as dictator mumbo jumbo. In a Realacrat society, we deal with problems realistically, and realistically; it may only be a matter of time, money and the right connections before North Korea finds a way to attain its long-awaited dream of nuclear weapons. So how will the United States and the rest of the world deal with this looming reality? Economic sanctions would continue to be imposed against a nation like North Korea, but we would need something much more trenchant in order to thwart an actual North Korean, nuclear attack. Therefore, I propose the "Assed-Out" rule. Any nation that sets up and then proceeds to launch an unprovoked, unwarranted, unjustifiable nuclear attack on any country will be dealt with accordingly and not strictly by the United States, but by the entire international community. It's time for other nations to carry their own load, because they, too, have a vested interest in the proliferation of nuclear weapons by trigger-happy crackpots. The rule will be simple. If you launch a preemptive nuke at any nation or group of people, the international community reserves the right to coordinate, consolidate and militarily combat your country with William Tecumseh Sherman-like force, which means the complete annihilation and eradication of the weapons and all of its launch sites on land, sea, and air. However, it will not stop there. All human rights will be suspended and all citizens of that nation will be automatically deemed as terrorists. An offensive will be put forth that will target all military, all civilians, all plant life, all animals, all economic structures, all educational facilities, and all government facilities. The civilians will be given a certain amount of time to vacate the nation or move to another part of the nation. They will be forced to adopt refugee status, hide out, or suffer the consequences of total war. After the launch of nuclear weaponry, a strategy similar to the total war/Civil War strategic tactics will be implemented, as all non-nuclear efforts will be utilized and exhausted to destroy all of the service routes, rapidly choking off the entire nation from all supplies and necessities. After the conflict has been resolved, the rebuilding of the nation can take place, but only under a newly formed internationally-based government. If the international community is going to foot the bill and manpower to rebuild a nation, then the international community will have a say in what form of government will oversee that nation. In other words, there will not be more of the same. Speaking of rebuilding war-torn nations, unlike the rebuilding and reimbursements of the Iraqi occupation, it is the international community who will finance this juncture, not another solo undertaking by the United States. I know there are many who will be shocked at the severity of this application, but the launching of a nuclear weapon is a destiny-changer, a game-changer, and a game-ender; second only to the wrath of God! The nuclear business is a deadly business! and there is no easy way to deal with it once it starts.

The Weapons of Mass Destruction Rule

The weapons rule is based on the Bush era. President Bush used faulty intelligence to further his own personal military agenda in a veiled attempt to remove Saddam Hussein from power in some sort of vendetta-driven, aggrandizement kick. Now let's revisit the Russian invasion of Georgia back in 2008. Numerous nations and world leaders, including the United States, strongly supported the condemnation of the Russian, military aggression towards the country of Georgia. There were calls from all sides for Russian leader Premier Putin to disengage and withdraw from Georgia, as the Georgian president begged and pleaded for international help, specifically U.S. help. Republicans such as John McCain and Democrats such as Barack Obama took firm stands against any forceful occupation by any nation, yet at that very same moment, the United States was simultaneously occupying Iraq. I guess it's understandable why Putin laughed at the United States' request of non-occupation. It is the existence and execution of double-standards like these that call for new international rules of engagement.

The weapons of mass destruction rule will be patterned after the Bush administration's monster quest/witch-hunt into Iraq for those infamous weapons of mass destruction. The new international rule will be precise. If any nation invades another nation for whatever reason, whether it's weapons of mass destruction or some trumped-up charge of alleged terrorism, the invading nation must provide an astounding amount of credible evidence, and that evidence must be made public to the world. In the event that the evidence turns out to be politically one-sided or fraudulently bogus, the invading nation must vacate immediately. The invading country will also be financially responsible for all reimbursements of damages and reconstruction. The international community will offer available resources and manpower to the victimized country, but it will be financed by the invaders. If the invading nation tries to overstay, occupy or annex the victimized nation, the international community reserves the rights to economically sanction the invading nation by cutting off all resource avenues immediately. If this process fails to convince the invading nation to withdraw, then the international community can carry out the old, Gulf War tactic; a tactic that used military force to remove Saddam Hussein from the unlawful occupation of Kuwait, by which President Bush Sr. strategized, executed and exited the premises much more effectively than his son was able do. The world should have the right to assist the removal of any unlawful occupation, especially if the citizens under occupation are unable to fend off the unwanted domination.

The Genocide Rule

This rule must be put into action immediately; given the number times we've seen entire groups of people slaughtered in a veiled or blatant attempt to purge the world of an undesirable group or race of people. For as long as the world has existed, there have always been superiority freaks hell-bent on rough-housing their warped agenda on the innocent, whether it is religious intolerance or genetic entitlement. From the plight of the Jews in Egypt, the Jews in Germany, American slavery, the plight of Native Americans , the Bosnia conflict or the present Darfur genocidal conflict, the world has been and will be faced with this dilemma of ethnic eradication by the hands of oppression! As in the case of the Darfur situation, thousands of innocent people are murdered in the streets and forced out of their homes and into refugee camps with nothing more than the clothes on their backs with little food or water. The public will get wind of it through media reports, and the outrage and calls for help will begin to grow louder and more intense. The governments around the world will hear these outcries from within their own ranks, but will usually drag their feet in response to it. Most countries are reluctant to interfere in the affairs of other countries and rightfully so, but any execution of genocide must outweigh and trump any reluctance to interfere. The international community must reserve the right to immediately impose economic sanctions, or the use of military force on any nation that practices genocide. Genocide must not be tolerated under any circumstances.

The Neda Freedom Fighters Rule

I base this rule on the current situation in Iran, the former situation of American slavery, and manifest destiny. For all we know, Ahmadinejad could be using a manifest destiny thesis to justify his continuance of power in Iran as President, taking a page out of the plantation owner's manual, as he tries his best to control exactly what his flocks are allowed to read, write, tweet, e-mail, report, say, hear and pursue. As I've said before, if you control the choices, then you control the people. No one knows that better than African-Americans and Native Americans. They can tell you first-hand what it's like to have no choice or say in matters that directly concern or dictate your very existence. Absolute power can only be sustained by suppression. It is for this reason that I propose the "Neda Freedom Fighters Rule," which gives the international community the right to assist any group of people around the world that are oppressed and fighting for their rights to be free. All people deserve the right to fight for their human rights, and all of us deserve the right to help the fight for those human rights. In my opinion, God gave all humans the right to be free, and he gave all humans the right to seek out that freedom. In other words, I don't believe that God will hold it against anyone who fights to be free. I think God is freedom.

I base this on the beautiful, young woman named Neda, who was brutally gunned-down in the streets of Tehran, Iran in 2009. When I saw Neda lying in a pool of blood, the death filled expression on her lifeless face spoke volumes to me. It no longer mattered that she was Iranian, and I was American. It was never any clearer to me than it was at that very moment, as I mentally absorbed the humbling truth that we are all the creations of a creating force, regardless of what you personally believe that force to be. Nationalities are nothing more than useless labels meant to divide and conquer the human spirit! I felt sorrow for Neda like I would feel sorrow for any young life violently snuffed-out, whether it's here in America or in Iran. So I dedicate this rule to you Neda, from one American to one Iranian, because human policy trumps foreign policy in my eyes, as it should in all eyes! Hopefully, some version of "The Neda Freedom Fighters Rule" will become reality at some point in the near future to ensure that no one else will suffer the fate of Neda in hopes gaining what should already belong to them anyway!

The Katherine Harris Rule

Once more, this rule is based on the current situation in Iran, although it does not necessarily require the usage of any military action. When Katherine Harris,[29] who just happened to be a Republican, tried to appoint George W. Bush as the President of the United States of America by certifying the state of Florida's 25 electoral votes for him, her authoritative tone gave me the democratic runs, but there was nothing I could do about it. Maybe she was just doing her job. I don't know, and I no longer care. The rigging of elections to pre-determine the outcome is the charge that has been most recently leveled against Ahmadinejad and the Iranian government. The engineering and gerrymandering of democracy is an abomination, and it must be ousted at every opportunity. And with that in mind, the international community should reserve the right to question any suspicious outcome, especially by a known suspicious dominion. For example, if Ahmadinejad is found to have been erroneously re-elected into office, the international community reserves the right to politically scrutinize his regime, to deny all diplomatic relations with his regime, and impose economic sanctions on his regime. The media has the right and the obligation to report on it, and expose it to the rest of the world for what it is. Hell, I would go so far as to suggest hearings in the United Nations on the issue. Consequently, any duplicitous, swindling, phony, counterfeit regime could be and should be voted out of the United Nations until an authentic and veritable authority can be established.

North Korea

If it's one thing that absolutely gets on my last nerves it's a loud-mouthed bully who likes to wave, and pull his gun on unsuspecting people, because they don't yet know that this fire-breathing windbag is only touting a gun with no bullets; although, I do strongly believe that any hand that is wrapped around a gun is always capable of using it. Nevertheless, this idiotic numbskull continues to make idle and unwarranted threats against numerous groups that have done no wrong to this loony sociopath. These kinds of individuals have mastered the art

29 CNN, Florida Secretary of State Katherine Harris: 'I just followed the law', http://archives.cnn.com/2001/LAW/01/17/harris.lkl/index.html (January 2001).

of trash-talking intimidation. Even though it is all totally established on a bogus concept, the browbeater has his bluff firmly entrenched, as long as no one challenges the threat, because his entire survival depends upon it. Whenever someone finally does step up to this egomaniac, and they find out the coveted pop-gun can only shoot blanks, the jig will be up, and the domineering dolt is now out of a job. The flip-side of that argument is what happens when the dolt finally gets a handful of bullets.

This description fits Kim Jong-il like his own personalized straight jacket, which he has obviously slipped out of again. Like the infamous Ahmadinejad, Kim Jong-il is the latest angry enigma who just happens to be a world leader. North Korea suffers from what is known as little dog syndrome. Do you remember the old Looney Tunes cartoon in which the little, junior chicken hawk was always going after the much larger prey known as Foghorn Leghorn? North Korea is that little chicken hawk, and the United States is Foghorn Leghorn. Unfortunately, on a psychological level, the chicken hawk and Foghorn were almost evenly matched, although Foghorn seemed to have a minuscule advantage allowing him to routinely slip past the ambitious chicken hawk. Optimistically, the United States,' foreign policy towards North Korea will be much more effective than Foghorn Leghorn, because unlike the Looney Tunes and unlike Saddam Hussein's Iraqi arsenal; there is a real possibility of weapons of mass destruction looming in the balance, with death threats of nuclear annihilation being tossed around like radioactive jumping jacks!

The supreme brazenness of North Korea causes one to wonder what the catch is. Either North Korea has an economic and political death wish, or they have an ace up their sleeve they are not yet revealing. Kim Jong-il waltzes around with as much confidence as Ahmadinejad had when he was up for re-election against Mousavi. What is it that makes Kim Jong-il so sure of his abilities, when all of his nuclear tests have been less than stellar, to say the least? I'd sure like to know precisely where China and Russia stand on this complicated issue. The United States cannot rule out the possibility of either of these countries being in bed with North Korea to deliver some type of global, neighborly, financial, military bailout. It may sound farfetched, but I think it has quite a bit of validity to it. Ask yourself this very simple question: out of China,

Russia, and North Korea, which one can you ever really trust to not pull a Jesse James and shoot you in the back of the head when your back is turned? So again, I make the point, why spend millions of dollars on removing Saddam Hussein in Iraq, a guy who wasn't threatening a nuclear holocaust aimed at the United States, when Kim Jong-il sits around North Korea working on weapons of mass destruction and his very own American-based hit list?

Kim Jong-il spends an awful amount of time trying to develop nuclear weapons and threatening the United States, but why? Why would a small and seemingly insignificant country like North Korea arrogantly pick a fight with the mighty United States? By Realacrat estimations, there are a few possibilities that do emerge. One is; maybe Kim Jong-il has finally flipped out. Is it possible that all of the sanctions have finally caught up to him, and the strenuous economic pressures placed on his country has backed him into a corner, causing him to throw all caution to the wind and just go for broke. Have we pushed Kim Jong-il to the economic breaking point, where he is now willing to bet the entire farm in some last-ditch effort to force the hand of the United States? Could Kim Jong-il feel he no longer has anything left to lose? If this theory proves to be true, the United States has a very real concern. The antics of a desperate Kim Jong-il could be fatal if he can muster the means that would allow him to do some serious damage.

Maybe President Bush was right to place North Korea on the Axis of Evil list. Realacrats would rename it the Axis of Danger, with North Korea, China and Afghanistan at the top of the list. Yes, you heard correct, I said China, because they are the 800-lb. pink elephant in the room that no one wants to tackle or acknowledge, as having a dog in this fight, but I'm afraid that they just may have one. I am not convinced in the least that China does not have a vested interest in the fate of North Korea. Could North Korea be the little cousin who goes out and smarts off to the big guys on the corner, because they have inside information about big cousin China's reinforcement plan? I don't think this idea is beyond the pale at all. The more reckless Kim Jong-il becomes, the more I see a potential strategy or hidden agenda in the works. While there are many Americans and other nations who consider Kim Jong-il to only be a foolish man with a big mouth, who is full of hot air and empty threats, Realacrats are not among them. Maybe there is a definite plan of attack, and I have an idea of what it could be. All roads and arrows, in my opinion, point towards South Korea. Could Kim Jong-il be the new George W. Bush who takes it upon himself to finish what his father couldn't? It is my opinion that the first thing on Kim Jong-il's to-do-list is the invasion and possible reunification of South Korea, and there is only one real threat standing in his way—the United States. Kim Jong-il doesn't want Hawaii, he wants what he feels is rightfully his, which is South Korea. He probably feels he has more of a right to intervene in South Korean affairs than some Western country like the United States. Maybe this is North Korea's version of manifest destiny, and this time we, the United States, are the Indians of the old Wild West. I only wonder if China feels the same way as Kim Jong-il. Secretly, I'll bet they do, and this is why the United States cannot rule out the possibility of a second Chinese intervention if the United States attacks North Korea, either provoked or unprovoked. There are many here in America with legitimate concerns that the United States will never be able to pay the debt owed to China. Well, maybe the Chinese government feels the exact same way and has no inhibitions about hitting the United States in the mouth for a second time. This could help explain the brashness surrounding Kim Jong-il's arrogant attempts to coax the United States into some form of military action. Kim Jong-il must feel fairly confident that with China to back him up that he can finally claim South Korea and unify the two countries once and for all, making him just as great and just as highly regarded as his legendary father, and I believe Kim Jong-il is counting on Chinese intervention to distract and weaken the United States. However, I do not believe that Kim Jong-il is convinced that he can accomplish this feat alone; not even he is that pretentious. With the United States military spread out thinner than a poor man's mustard from Iraq to Afghanistan to Pakistan, Kim Jong-il appears to be systematically picking his attack positions because North Korea feels that if they can somehow develop weapons of mass destruction, a unified Korea is that much closer.

I have to ask myself if the occupation of South Korea is worth it. Do the people of South Korea still want the United States there? If they don't, then it's time to say good-bye. If South Korea desires to be one country again, I think the United States has to honor that, and reluctantly begin to relinquish our empire. I just hope that South Korea knows exactly what they are getting into if they choose to take that path, but the choice is still theirs to make. On the other hand, what if South Korea decides they want no part of being North Korea's red-headed step-child? In this instance, the United States is faced with another tough dilemma that basically involves the same plot and circumstances, which would again be the very real threat of Chinese intervention, but in this case the United States will have no choice but to meet it head on. The United States cannot afford to live in fear of conflict. Fear cripples progress, and progress has to be made in spite of who is standing in the way of it. According to the Realacrat protocol, China would receive one phone call about North Korea and that conversation would be precise and terse, and it would sound similar to this: "The United States is in South Korea right now, and we will only leave if the South Koreans ask us to. If North Korea attacks South Korea while we are there, it will be considered an act of total war, which would also apply to anyone who decided to get involved in the attack. An attack on Alaska or Hawaii would enact the same total war declaration. China, you need to talk to your neighbor, because I'm done talking, as long as North Korea feels the need to threaten my country in nuclear terms! I know we owe you a ton of money right now, but that is not the point. North Korea needs to cease with the threats of nuclear augmentation and aggression towards the U.S. Kim Jong-il is a perplexing individual to figure out, and we feel that you may know him better than we do. I'm simply trying to avoid World War 3. The United States is willing to engage diplomatically with North Korea, but the nuclear threats have to end now! The check is in the mail; have a nice day China!"

Do-Nothing Russia and Do-Nothing China

Both of these countries are very similar when it comes to dealings with the United States. I've already touched on China's bear-hug on the U.S. economy, so let's talk about Russia. I find it quite ironic that the United States finds itself in the same economic shape during a similar time of war with the exact same country-- Afghanistan, which is the very country that gave the old Soviet Union all it could handle. And like the old Soviet Union eventually discovered, Afghanistan will prove to be a very tough road for whoever attempts to travel on it. The Russian

President and Prime Minister have agreed to allow the United States to ship weapons into Afghanistan via Russian airspace, and some in Washington view this as an act of cooperation between nations, and maybe it is. But then again, it could be looked at as a better-you-than-me type of gesture, as the Russians know all too well what the United States is getting into. The war in Afghanistan is one of those wars where it's much better to be on the outside looking in. This is exactly where Russia is, and where they plan to stay. After all, the old Soviet Union went broke fighting the wars in Afghanistan, while the U.S. used it as an opportunity to sell weapons and make a profit off the situation. The U.S. was able to make money and eradicate Communism, all at the same time.

Today, I think Russia's only goal is to now reclaim its perch as a superpower, more specifically a financial superpower, because it appears that the world economic markets are the new arms races. As the old Soviet Union learned the hard way, you can build and produce as many nuclear arms as you want, but arms don't pay bills. The biggest military in the world can always become the most destitute military in the world. I know there are many who think Putin is a moron, but I believe he has traded in the Soviet uniform for a new Russian, fat, cat wallet. The old Gorbachev days of trying to outspend your enemies appears to be over, which will entail more economic competition for the United States, not to mention the many other European countries and other nations, such as India, who are chomping at the heels of the United States on the global markets.

Now China is the slickest one of them all. China is similar to the Michael Jackson type of celebrity; very secretive, very entrepreneurial, very savvy, very shrewd, very narcissistic, and very dominating. As with Michael Jackson, the Chinese know exactly who they are and what they are worth, rendering Western, constructive criticism ineffective at best. Michael Jackson obviously received just about anything he wanted. He had money and power, and there were few willing to stand up and question his demands. Money and power allow one to do that. China is the exact same way, and there are even fewer who are willing to stand up to the Chinese government, and that includes the West. The West attempting to dictate policy to China is like a doctor or a nurse trying to instruct Jackson on some of his questionable, self-medicating behaviors; as both are laughable at best. Bill Clinton once spoke about how you can't make tough demands to your bankers, benefactors and sugar daddies, because you can't throw your executive producers off the set, nor can you dictate your personal policy, your philosophy, or your ideology to them either. You can suggest, and you can request, but you cannot bring it to rest. You don't bite the hand that feeds you. You don't spit on Superman's cape, and you don't talk down to the money that's financing you. So when I see these dignitaries traveling to China with the hopes of convincing the Chinese government to adopt a more Westernized, cerebral, political context, I just think to myself, what a tremendous waste of the taxpayer's money. While we, the United States, look to teach China about democracy, politics and human rights violations, they literally take us to school on industrial manufacturing, banking and the transfer of wealth from us to them. They must laugh all the way to the bank; a bank they probably now own that once was ours.

If I had to personify Russia or China in real-life, allegorical terms, I would do it this way. In my youth, a group of guys and me used to exert a ton of energy to perform, and perfect this crazed new dance called the "Gangsta Walk." It was a blistering routine that required an enormous amount of energy to display. This is why most couch potatoes declined from participating in it, but I was always spirited about doing it, and I often led the charge out onto the dance floor. One night a couple of old pals came down from Fort Smith, Arkansas. As they were regional foreigners, we took upon ourselves to show off our newly found, gangsta-walking maneuvers to assert our creativity and performance dominance for all to see, especially the girls, who never seem to be that impressed by our grand-standing antics anyway, yet we still pushed that envelop. Our favorite song came on, and we beat ourselves to death out there on the dance floor. Everyone else just eased out of our way and allowed us all of the narcissistic space we needed to completely drain and wind ourselves like the arrogant fools that we were. The next thing we knew the tone had changed, and it was now time for some slow jam music, so the guys and gals could cuddle up and dance together, but our crew was so winded and exhausted from our egotistical and self-absorbed rain dance that none of us could muster up enough moxie to even whistle at the girls. We just stood in front of them, bent over, having mini-asthma attacks trying to catch our breath and retain our composure. At that very moment, our friends from Fort Smith, Arkansas, who had reserved all of their energy and resources, stepped right in and swept our girls out from under us as we were left hunched over and powerless to stop it. Even though the Fort Smith guys had done absolutely nothing, except sit back and watch, they are the ones who drove off with the hot, sexy girls that night, while my loyal friends and I continued to attack the dance floor in a battle that no one seemed very interested in outside of us. Eventually, we exhausted all of our time and energy, and we were forced to retreat home in confusion and defeat. My exhausted friends and I were the United States, while the two slicksters from Fort Smith were China, Russia and the rest of the world. The United States does all of the fighting while China, Russia and the rest of the world drive off with all of the money and power. The entire scheme reminds me of the WWE. China and Russia remind me of the WWE superstar Edge, while the United States reminds me of the WWE superstar John Cena. Very much like Edge, both China and Russia are the ultimate opportunists, while the U.S. is very similar to John Cena; full of strength, vigor and always searching for the next cause to champion. And like the WWE, the Cena-like United States constantly pushes itself up against the wall and into the ground in honor of its core beliefs. The Edge-like China, Russia, India and other up-and-coming nations hang around in self-concerned limbo; steadily increasing their power, status, global connections and overall wealth, as they patiently wait their turn. And with all of the improved technology, the world has now become a much more level and equal playing field, which has severely limited the old, geographical advantages of the past. Now the remote areas are just as informed and just as involved as the more modern, metropolitan, opportunistic hubs of society. For the United States in particular, this means getting ready for some up-and-coming, hungry, highly competitive company.

The U.S. vs. the World

Realacrats deal with reality, and the reality of typical, U.S. foreign policy has the United States out to fend for itself, because it is glaringly apparent that neither Russia nor China have any plans to get involved with much of anything that doesn't involve making more money off of the United States. These two countries are more interested in building up their economic clientele than enforcing world policy, and it appears that other would-be nations are following suit. This tells me that other countries are also only out for themselves. They would be more than happy to sit back and watch the United States go further and further into debt, fight two or three wars at the same time, and go through all the money they can lend us like a ghettoized welfare recipient. The United States is dangerously flirting with becoming the new, global, section 8, unemployed, welfare queens, who sit around; and wait for the first of the month for Chinese checks to come in. America as a whole has become its own version of the poor and its own worst enemy all at the same time, while China has become our mean-spirited landlord. If the terrorists do decide to attack our Chinese-funded rent house, it will have to be us; the hapless Americans, who will be forced to take care of it, while the Chinese, the Russians, and other countries go on a cruise together. The bottom line is that America will never have leverage until it corrects its economic calamity, and China will continue to do whatever the hell it wants because broke leaders have few followers. The United States will have a tough time trying to establish, and then enforce; a moral leadership base over an economic leadership base within this current, global economy.

In light of all of this economic jockeying for power, some have begun to label China and other aspiring nations as industrial enemies of the West in some kind of economic Axis of Evil, but is this a fair characterization? I thought it was just good, old-fashioned capitalism. The Republicans yell loudly about it all day, but what they fail to understand is that capitalism does not function on racism, favoritism or genetic entitlement. Capitalism draws its greatest successes from all outlets, not just a few. I wonder where China and other countries learned capitalism from. The world may never know. Basically, China has taken our playbook and simply outgunned us with our own plays, and the sad part about it is that most Americans don't even recognize the plays when we are the ones who first developed them. Capitalism is like the atomic bomb. When used in your favor it is the best asset one can have, but when used against you; it can reduce your power to that of a third world country. This is where I must slam Republicans, conservatives, and religious idiots again, because you can't be capitalistic on one hand and then be conservative on the other! If the love of money is the root of all evil, then capitalism is the desire and the means which allows it to be cultivated and collected, and Republicans, conservatives, Democrats, religious factions, and Realacrats all benefit from it! By Realacratic interpretations, capitalism is the economic equivalent of Charles Darwin's "Survival of the Fittest" hypothesis! If you discredit Charles Darwin, then you discredit yourself and your society, so shut it!

While I hear the vast numbers of redneck, banjo-thumping, NASCAR-loving, keep-my-daughter-away-from-the-Blacks, hillbillies aiming their anger and dismay at African-Americans, especially President Obama; gays, and Muslims/Arabs, the much smaller numbered, higher educated, more affluent people completely understand the full scope of the global threats to this country, with economic dangers being the most concerning threat. While the morons in of country continue to try and live in the past, other nations around the world are more than happy to churn ahead into the economic future. While rednecks and hillbillies seem more content to work diligently on choice segregation to keep little Amy and Misty Anne chocolate-free, China is working diligently to get little Amy and her estranged, chocolate undercover lovers all into the checkout line at the nearest Wal-Mart or any other retail store to purchase even more of that great Chinese ingenuity. Maybe they should just hang up a sign in front of retail stores that says, "Made in China!" While Americans choose to fight and bicker over why God is White and evolution is ethnic, the world continues to close the American dominance gap a little each day. I guess the Joe the Plumber/Joe Six-Pack nation won't actually recognize it until a Chinese guy comes over here to America and wins a NASCAR race. Then, and only then, will they realize that the world has caught up to them.

This is just like basketball or baseball, as both were at one time completely dominated by the United States. Do you remember the Dream Team? That was us economically at one point in time. We, as a nation, were the Dream Team, and the world could only sit, watch, and hope to play catch-up. But as the years went on, other nations began to creep closer to our talent level, eventually catching us and on occasion surpassing us, and it would take years for the United States to produce the Redeem Team, and reclaim their spot on top of the basketball mountain. The reason I say this is due to the asinine ideology shared by a certain group of people in this country, who believe they can just magically get back into contention with the rest of the world anytime they desire, because living in this country, America, makes them so great that they can be like Nike, and just–do-it whenever they want to. That is the precise patriotic, theological, geographical bias that has allowed other countries to pull even with the United States in sports like basketball and baseball. The same thing has happened economically. Other nations are hungry for success and will stop at nothing to get it, while America is a victim of its own success, because other nations have seen the numerous triumphs of the United States, and they now want a piece of the pie too. America has become economically complacent like a fat, out-of-shape, heavyweight champion who foolishly believes that things will always be the way they are right now. Complacency breeds arrogance and arrogance breeds upset and defeat. Isn't that how the tortoise beat the hare? President Obama is absolutely right to be concerned about the global economy, because this is no longer a chess match between two superpowers like America versus the old Soviet Union. Much like baseball, there are new players in the game now from all over the world, and you can't underestimate any of them, because they all can play, and China is just one of many. America needs to forget about the Babe Ruth days, the Ronald Reagan days, and the Dream Team days, because those days of dominance are gone. Success can no longer be based on how badly you can defeat poor African-Americans from across the tracks. Now you have to defeat the world, and the world does not appear to be intimidated.

The fear of being challenged is one thing, but the arrogance of non-preparation and the refusal to acknowledge an oncoming threat is pure insanity. This is all reminiscent of the Ghost Dances of the late 1800s, where the Native Americans had been duped by desperation into believing this mythical, folkloric ritual would give them spiritual protection from the U.S. cavalry's bullets. This was supposed to ensure the final triumph of the Native Americans and the final defeat of the U.S. cavalry, but it did not happen that way. It failed the Native Americans the same way it is going to fail many of the conceited and misguided Americans who believe their prayers to the White, American, conservative God will defeat China and all other foreign threats once and for all, bringing back the good-ole-days when they were the only superpower in town. However, wishful thinking, wishful hopes, wishful dreams, wishful myths, and wishful abstract manifest destinies will get bludgeoned and annihilated by good-old-fashioned, cold, hard cash and ammunition every time.

Judging by my life experiences, I would have to conclude there are no good-ole-days that exist outside of memory lane. I think the best, and only, thing that any of us can do is to focus on creating some good, new days; and that begins with the willingness and the courage to move forward out of the old and into more self-reliance and less self-centeredness.

AMERICAN MAKE-OVER

THINKING GREAT VS. BEING GREAT

Everywhere you look in the media today, there will be someone trying to convince you of how great America is. Lesson number one is that greatness does not have to be pushed. It pushes itself. Always beware of anyone who is constantly trying to trumpet themselves as great, because usually the end result is far less than previously advertised! The same thing goes for America. You can't just sit around, and crow about how great you are when your entire economic and social infrastructure is crumbling to the ground in front of you. That is pure insanity! Chris Rock made a good point on HBO one night. He questioned the whole God Bless America idea. Why just America he asked? Why not God bless the world? That would still include America. The reason for this arrogance is rooted in the very self-righteousness that has fueled this country since its inception. America is not the only country in the world worth blessing, but there are certain aspects of America that believe it is. Contrary to popular belief, there is no nation on the face of this earth that holds the key to the high road. Don't allow the reflection you see looking back at you in the mirror to taint your view of your own importance. The blue eyes you spend so much time adoring in every mirror you pass do not give you the genetic entitlement to God or the world. Believe it or not, both of them have to be shared by all! You can't be a great country until you first realize that greatness is not exclusively yours or anyone else's. Greatness is something that can be earned and achieved by anyone at any time. The highness of you horse can often cause you to miss out on the greatness of others if you continue to arrogantly refuse to get down off of it. The more you learn, the greater you can become. The more you appreciate, the greater you can become. The more you learn to acknowledge, the greater you can become, and the more abilities you have to accept reality, the greater you will become. A nation cannot be greater than the sum of its own parts, which means that only taking care of the wealthy few, while the less fortunate majority become more and more disenfranchised is not a sign of greatness. Failing to contain the spread of poor education and poverty within low-income, minority neighborhoods is not a sign of greatness. Turning a blind eye while your children drop out of high school and enter the penal system is not a sign of greatness. Failure to recognize these children as your own due to a discrepancy in skin color or class is not a sign of greatness. Unbridled fear of anything you do not understand, either by choice or by ignorance, is not a sign of greatness. Snarling down your nose at the less fortunate is not a sign of greatness. Promoting the culture of one over all other cultures is not a sign of greatness. Disguising or abandoning the truth because it forces you to think is not a sign of greatness.

This entire fiasco reminds me of the part in Snow White [30] where she asks, "Mirror, mirror, on the wall; who's the fairest of them all?" but in this case, the partisan, media savvy mirror replies back, "You are, of course," but what it fails to tell you is that the voice and the mirror are both made in China.

It's still the summer of 2009, in the month of June, and I just watched Liz Cheney and James Carville go at it over the alleged greatness of America. People like Liz believe America is the greatest country that has ever existed. So, how great is America? What is the relevance of such a question? Does it really matter, and why is there so much mammoth, global chest-beating going on? I think I know why Liz Cheney and others like her, mainly conservatives, truly believe this country is the greatest of all time. It has far more to do with that beloved reflection they see in the mirror than it does the actual country and its policies. Let's just cut to the chase here. Whenever I hear conservatives like Liz Cheney

30 Jacob Grimm and Wilhelm Grimm, "Little Snow-White," http://www.pitt.edu/~dash/grimm053.html (Revised November 2005).

spout off their American superiority speeches, I completely understand that under no circumstances were they even remotely referring to me or anyone ideologically opposed to them. This is all part of the "God-is-more-like-me-and-not-at-all-like-you" syndrome! The alleged greatness anoints itself from here, and the seats in this chariot all say conservative America. There are actually people who truly believe they've inherited competency, while others have inherited the obligated duty to follow this inherited competency. However, the greatness of America will arise from the multiplicity of the rainbow, not the baseless monotony of the ego, because true greatness makes each of its compartments better, not just the head compartment!

There is no doubt that America has made progress, but it still has miles to travel, because it is very difficult to achieve greatness, but it's even more difficult to consistently sustain it. But for the most part, America has made a certifiable effort to try, which is a vast improvement from the not so distant past of the early to mid-1900s. I think America deserves tremendous credit for having the courage to elect an African-American as its president. It's a sign of a possible change for the future, but that is about as much as I can honestly give it at this time. Overall, America is a great country with many great expectations, but great expectations do not make greatness, it is the fulfillment of great expectations that solidifies true greatness. America is headed in that direction, but it is not going to be a cakewalk by any means, so don't fool yourself into believing it will be a hop, skip and a jump out of the negative past and into the bright, new, post-racial society. If it was that easy, people would have achieved it a long time ago.

The Nigger Jim Scenario

This will be a very difficult process. The scenario reminds me of the many exchanges out of "The Adventures of Huckleberry Finn" by Mark Twain between Huckleberry Finn, Tom Sawyer and Nigger Jim.[31] Huck and Sawyer knew a Black man who was their confidant, who often accompanied them on many of their adventures. They called him Nigger Jim, and he was a reasonable, older Black man who tried to look after the young, rambunctious duo as best he could. To Huck

31 Mark Twain, The Adventures of Huckleberry Finn (Charles L. Webster And Company.1884), Ch. 31,34.

and Sawyer, Nigger Jim was just a common, harmless name, and to Nigger Jim it was indeed very common, but not very harmless, judging by all of the social baggage and negative consequences that came along with being one. To Huck and Sawyer, Nigger Jim was all they'd ever known. Their families had all referred to him as Nigger Jim, so the boys were only doing what came naturally to them. They were only going by the environment in which they were raised. The two boys probably thought Nigger was Jim's actual first name, because everyone in their circle addressed Jim that way. The two boys were rightfully ignorant of the negative impact of their treatment of Nigger Jim. They were only following traditional family protocol, and there was no harm intended. Nigger Jim understood the plight of the young, misguided boys. They were only kids doing what kids do, which is the repetition of the grammar and actions they see in their society. So when Nigger Jim was captured the two boys began to realize just how much Nigger Jim had meant to them, and they devised a plan to risk everything to try and free Nigger Jim. Despite all of the negative stereotyping done by society and the young boys' families, their personal experiences with Nigger Jim had allowed and forced them to re-evaluate their ideologies about him. Huck and Sawyer had to find a way to unlearn all they had once thought to be true, as they would now have to rebuild the foundations of their character, as they prepared to try and free Nigger Jim. They would now have to begin the strenuous, uphill trek against all of the one-sided, self-serving, classless, false, misleading propaganda that had been methodically and systematically bred into them by the people they loved and trusted. They slowly began to chip away and erode the partisan ballyhoo that had shaped and molded them throughout their young lives. It took remarkable and extraordinary courage for both Huckleberry Finn and Tom Sawyer to attempt to walk away from the past and into the future. For that, they are both patriots of humanity and Realacrats, because they were gutsy enough to stake their own claim based on their own doctrines, even in the face of possible disciplinary actions by their very own loved ones—and society as a whole. They were willing to place their livelihoods on the line for what they believed in and not what society and their families had hoped to program them to believe in. This is what makes an individual great. America is Tom Sawyer! America is Huckleberry Finn! America is being forced to unlearn all of its racism, bigotry, relationship parameters, economic parameters, neighborhood parameters, political parameters, employment parameters, all of its favoritisms and all of its fears. Huck and Sawyer resigned their membership in the good-ole-boy's network, as they began to let go of Jim Crow. They both stood steadfast against the realm of ignorance, and they both refused to continue riding on their high, White, self-righteous horses. It is a colossal task, but America will have to follow in the footsteps of Huck and Sawyer. It takes sight to read the writing on the wall, but it takes vision to understand it, and it takes gallantry to go out into world and enact it. Unlearning that which you hold to be true is much harder than learning it, but you cannot grow without the ability or willingness to execute this option. Unlearning requires one to take a substantive look in the mirror, and most people want no part of cleaning out or retooling their sacred closets, but it must be done during times of change, because change waits on no one. You can deny its existence, but the change is still there, and the results of that change will be absorbed either by choice or by force. One way or another, we all have to face it, and deal with it, and if or when America finally does climb that hill, it may truly be the greatest country ever. The ability to overpower racial inhibitions and elect Barack Obama was a monumental step into that future.

It just goes to show that you cannot base or build relationships on spoon-fed, biased, propaganda beliefs such as fascism or racism. You can't get to know a person by staying behind your fearful, bigoted, fences of ignorance. People have to be given the opportunity to display their own identities, not just the ones we judgmentally conjure up for them. We can't have cooperative progress with people in our own country or people in other countries without humanistic communication. One can only imagine what Huck and Sawyer would have gone on believing about Black people if they hadn't actually spent time with Nigger Jim. The same thing applies to the United States in regards to other nations and other world leaders, and President Obama has done an excellent job at trying to communicate openly and avoid pecking order conditions with other world leaders, because sometimes what you've been raised to believe and what actually is are two totally different things. The Realacrat motto would be, "Talk when you can, and fight when you have to." After all, the cognitive darkness of a willing stubbornness is not necessarily the best synergist for understanding, because true greatness is rarely reluctant when challenged to change a current course or adapt to new and unfamiliar environments in a world that often appears resistant to change through the toys of restriction, which only provide more of the same.

American, Inc.: The New Industry

Nevertheless, there are real, legitimate problems facing this nation right here and now, and race should not be one of them, when Americans of all walks of life are losing their jobs and their homes. It reminds me of the song "Allentown"[32] by Billy Joel, and the song "My Hometown" by Bruce Springsteen[33], where they both sing about the loss of employment and how it devastates the community. As Bruce Springsteen said, "Foreman says these jobs are going boys, and they ain't coming back, to your hometown!" This was a strong concern back in the early 1980's, and I find it astonishing how relevant it still is today. But Bruce and Billy both make a good point; those industrial jobs are not coming back. I agree with President Barack Obama, T. Boone Pickens, Ralph Nader, and even Al Gore. We can't manufacture or drill our way out of this situation. I know how much conservatives have made fun of Al Gore's ideas, but I believe some of what he's said has to be taken seriously. This world needs a new economy. This world needs new industry, and it's quite possible that the green technologies could be just what the world needs. If nothing more, it's possible they could help to lower energy costs. Al Gore may not be the total quagmire that many seem to believe he is. It's simple! If the wind turbine industry can be expanded throughout the United States, then it should be at least examined as a possibility. The windmills will have to be operated by a workforce, and our workforce needs a source of new employment right now. As they used to say back in the day, this could be just what the doctor ordered, not to mention, the potential savings that could be acquired by this the new, free-flowing energy source. To me, the concept is a no-brainer! What's the point of having a stimulus package that fails to stimulate? The windmills should have been at the top of the stimulus list. This is one industry that we don't have to have manufactured in Mexico or

32 Billy Joel, "Allentown," The Nylon Curtain, 1982.

33 Bruce Springsteen, "My Hometown," Born in the U.S.A., 1984.

China. We can do this one on our own. Every wind turbine should be completely owned, operated, distributed, and manufactured right here in the United States, because there is nothing wrong with being energy efficient—although government penalties, fines, and forced mandating is not necessarily a good way to bring about energy efficiency to the less fortunate, who continue to struggle financially. Okay, I'll tip my hat to the Republicans on that one, even though I know their main concern was for the rich corporations, not the poor.

The American people love to experience and witness positive, progressive, economic results; meaning, the American people will quickly grow tired of empty promises of energy efficient results and prospects with no tangible follow-ups. So the government shouldn't just say green jobs can work to save energy, it should go out and prove that green jobs can and will save energy, which equates to more dollars and savings in the wallets of the consumer. The government could pick one of the worst economically hit communities in the nation and install a windmill farm. If those windmills could find a way to employ the community and save energy-based money for that community all at the same time, to the point where average citizens can detect a noticeable decrease in their monthly to weekly billing, they would immediately and voluntarily rethink their views on green technologies. Not even racism or some of the bigoted hatred shown towards President Obama could undercut the satisfaction of cold, hard, cash being re-funneled into consumer pockets. The government has to develop a way to benefit the people and not the just the stockholders and investors who stand to acquire substantial amounts of money if the windmills are successful as some of us believe they can be, and it doesn't have to stop with windmills either, because we should always be investing in the exploration of new energy sources. This should be the Democratic plan of attack.

I know Republicans will argue about how small this first step is and how ineffective it will prove to be, but the majority of first steps are often small, but that does not mean they have to remain small. Like the old saying goes, "You have to crawl before you can walk." These new wind turbines can be our nation's crawl back into industrial contention. Green jobs don't have much support in this country, but it can't hurt to try. They just may work. One thing is for damn sure! Sitting around praying, complaining, finger-pointing, scapegoating, and continuing with our outmoded, Trojan horse battle plan is not the answer.

Homeland Job Security

Homeland security is not enough. We need a new plan of attack, a Realacrat plan of attack known as homeland job security. It's what I like to call American Inc. It's time to re-incorporate our country—a re-incorporation that includes all who are qualified. There will be no discrimination here. Anyone who is an American citizen or anyone who is in the country legally will qualify. No exceptions will be made. Americans are living in dire straits, and they must be given the economic opportunities to better their situation. I feel bad for the illegal immigrants, who have risked their lives to get to America in search of a better life, but this time we have to help ourselves first, or we may be the ones risking our lives in search of better employment. The government will not own American Inc. The government may be instrumental in getting the ball rolling, but after that; it will be up to the private sector to find the winning combination. If the private sector does not need government assistance, then so be it. Some might argue that this idea is pathetic and will not work. Some might argue that the idea of promoting yourself and your own products is irrational, yet I see other companies here in the United States, and abroad, do it all the time, because the less you know, the less you can participate in. Here is a perfect example.

I was at a Best Buy not too long ago looking to purchase a new television. I was only there to find the television with the best picture for the cheapest price. My aunt called me and asked me to try and find an American-made television, so I began to check the backs of all the television sets in the aisle, and I could not find one. I found televisions made in Mexico, China, Japan, and Canada. I would have strongly considered buying an American-made television, but there were none. Now who is at fault here? You can't blame the American people for not buying American, when there often is no American product to buy. If it wasn't for ESPN radio's amazing Colin Cowherd and his informative commercials about American electronics companies like Vizio, I would still be in the dark about my purchasing options, if I had any intentions whatsoever about checking for American based products first. Cowherd is an in-sourcing patriot, and ESPN radio is doing what the federal government should be doing; promoting American ingenuity!

Furthermore, the brand of America has been severely tarnished over the years. Whenever someone speaks about anything that is American-made, two things come to mind. Usually, it's how rare it is to actually see a product that is American-made, and the other is a huge concern that this American product could very possibly be a real hunk of junk! This national economic epiphany over the amazing lack of consumer confidence in American products caused me to take a serious look at my own purchasing habits, and the results startled me. I decided to inspect my property for manufacturing location, and I found that over half of my possessions were made in China, Mexico, other Central American countries, Middle Eastern countries, and southeastern Asian countries. I was flabbergasted! I had seen "Made in China" stamped on the back of products all of my life, but it never struck a chord with me—until now. Our importing of Chinese manufactured goods is occurring at an epidemic pace, along with many other countries from which we import. We obviously owe China a ton of money, and at the same time, they are getting rich off of our import consumption. This transfer of wealth is very similar to the transfer of wealth that is happening between the U.S. and the Middle East in the oil business. I can see why the country is going bankrupt. We are like a porn star getting it from both ends. All the bailouts in the world won't help to ease this fiasco.

I was recently at a manufacturing hub visiting a friend, with a room full of conservative minded people who absolutely loathed President Obama. They rode him like a government mule/welfare Yugo. They blamed him for everything except the Holocaust, and I believe that was coming next. While the Obama piñata was being pummeled as usual, I started to look around at the office supplies, and you'll never guess what trend I stumbled upon. Anywhere from 75 percent to 90 percent of all office supplies were made in China or some other country such as: Canada, Vietnam, South Korea or Mexico. What really caught my attention was an ink pen. Yes, a measly ink pen! As I stared at that ink pen, which was similar to every other ink pen in the department, I read the inscription, and it said: "Made in China," which has been quite the reoccurring theme as of late. So while the angry, conservative, Republican led White people were busy labeling President Obama as the anti-Christ and the next Hitler, I was having an epiphany, an economic epiphany, about why so many Americans are out of work nowadays when the majority of our products are of Chinese origin and not just major appliances either. This was no coincidence to me. This was much more than dumb luck or over-hyped skepticism. Then it hit me, another epiphany: like most of the people in this country, my White conservative, Republican, fanatically, religious counterparts were clueless to the economic, one-way street onto which we are all being railroaded. The Chinese government could have come in and personally picked all of their conservative/Republican pockets clean, and they would have still continued to bash Obama, while fearing the thugged out Blacks with their pants on the ground and the turban-wearing, camel jockeying Arabs, as the Chinese government is driving off with all of their money, leaving only a mountain of debt in the rearview.

I'm not mad at the Chinese government for being opportunistic. That's what Republicans call capitalism, but it just seems to work much better, when they are the beneficiaries. As I looked over the Chinese ink pen, an official company ink pen, I began to feel bamboozled. I felt let down. I felt ashamed. I felt demoralized, and I felt sorry for America. Are you kidding me? The Chinese even have the ink pen market cornered? You are telling me that the United States of America is not competent enough to mass produce and distribute their own ink pens; particularly, when the nation is begging for jobs? Americans need the work, and we continue to buy ink pens from China—not to mention that we owe China financially, despite the fact that we are probably their number one customer. This reminds me of the old sharecropping schemes of the late 1800s and early to mid-1900s, where the same guy you worked for was the same guy you purchased from, who was the same guy who you rented from, which just happened to be the same guy you were eternally indebted to. It's great for the boss man, but it's beyond detrimental to the sharecropper. Institutionalized debt is what it all amounted to, in a system where you could never quite catch up enough to be financially free. America knows the ending to that storyline all too well, and I find it ironic that America now finds itself in that same bind. If the United States does not have the know-how to become economic contenders again, then it will be the most gut-wrenching, self-inflicted debacle I've witnessed in a very long time.

If we can't be successful at making our own ink pens, we deserve to be economically duped out of existence. This is unsatisfactory leadership at its best, or worst, depending on how you look at it. There is no good reason why we shouldn't take this industry back. We don't have to put China out of business with a knock-out punch, but we can at least show up to throw a manufacturing punch. An idea such as American Inc. could be put to good usage in a scenario like this one.

It most certainly beats the hell out of a religious scenario set up by some scatter brained goon, when he assured me that the White, Christian God would foil China's quest to be a superpower! Instead of physically trying to match-up with China, this goof ball suggested that we all pray to his God, and ask him to personally sabotage China's efforts to be a top manufacturer! According to him, he had already asked God to quell China, and the great red nation was losing steam even as we speak! Well, it's obvious to me that someone forgot to give China the memo, because they haven't lost a step!

Why not invest in your own country? Why not put out an American product built by American people, to be sold everywhere possible, but especially right here in America? Is it the fear of failure, or is it the fear of Asian technology? Either way, recruiting has to be considered. Take a page from the great college coaches of the NCAA, coaches like Chris Peterson. Peterson took a small non-BCS school like Boise St. University and turned it into a perennial powerhouse capable of not only competing with the bigger schools, but also defeating the bigger schools, and he did this by recruiting. He recruited big-time players to make big-time plays, and the United States can do the same.

If you go back and take a look at the financial and commercial assets of Northern Mississippi and compare its current economic status with its past economic status, the results speak for themselves! Before the emergence of casinos, Northern Mississippi was often considered to be one of the poorest regions of the Delta, but you wouldn't be able to tell by looking at it now! Yes, the filthy, sinful, home wrecking draw of gambling has proven to be the difference between the obscurity of poverty and the hustling and bustling of commercial progress! While it is true that gambling may be a political, add-in sin to the Bible that hopes to eliminate competition in the money collecting business, the entice of gambling is usually good for the overall, economic business of the community. Now there are plenty of religious followers who would try desperately to convince you that Northern Mississippi was right on pace to have every bit of that phenomenal growth with its tired, passé cotton fields, but you and I both know that casinos trump agriculture all day and every day! The idea to bring in/recruit the gaming industry to Northern Mississippi and the state of Mississippi as a whole has proven to be a game changer! If you don't believe me, just take a straw poll of Mississippians and ask how many of them would rather go back to the empty cotton fields and dusty roads!

When the United States decides to get serious in the global markets, it will have to follow a similar business oriented game plan. If Asian technology is too much for our cognitive confines at this moment, then we should do the next best thing--recruit! Either recruit the top Asian technological talent away from Asia, or recruit the top Asian-American talent presiding right here in our own backyard. It's time to 86 the disenfranchisement of the Jim Crow policies of the past for fresh, new, talented people, who can get the job done. As Martin Luther King once preached, it's time we started looking towards the content of character, and as I preach currently, we should always look towards the ethics of responsibility, the assets of accountability, the willingness to try, the desire to succeed, the hard work to win, the ideas of the future, no bright mind left behind, and the resilience of rebounding, even if it means embracing new faces previously relegated to sideline duty!

The government can be the first business in the country to be Americanized! Who better to spark this regenerative process than the federal government? Starting immediately, all government offices will be totally Americanized; meaning, that all supplies, all materials, all clothing and all transportation—as many things as humanly possible—will be converted into American based productivity made with American ingenuity. In other words, every department in the White House, Congress, the Pentagon, the Supreme Court, and all other government branches will only use American products, including all uniforms and accessories. American Inc. manufacturing sites would be set up in the communities hit the hardest by the economy, even if it meant picking them via a lottery draft. These new economic sites will be completely responsible for servicing the federal government. The idea of Americanized productivity would then be transferred down to the state and local governments as well. I would even go so far as to transfer it all the way down to all American industry, educational facilities, and health care industries, if at all possible. In Realacrat terminology, this means that there would be no "Made in China" ink pens floating around. There shouldn't be anything on Capitol Hill that reads "Made in China," "Made in Mexico," or made anywhere else but in America. We have to take a page out of Apollo Creed's playbook! He was the African-American boxer from the Rocky movies who always wore the American trunks and the American top hats. He was great at promoting himself and his patriotism. Now, it's time for America to do the same.

Again, in honor of the immortal slogan created by Nike, we should all just-do-it. I know it's a long shot, but even long shots are meant to be taken, as long as it's the right time—and the time is perfect for taking a shot. Now some will call an investment like American Inc. too insignificant, but you have to start somewhere. And what better place to start at than American Inc., which would manufacture American bikes, American shoes, American electronics, American automotive, American ink pens, American infrastructure projects to revamp American transportation, American outdoor apparel, American clothing lines, American uniforms, American food processing, American mechanical parts, American packaging, American shipping, and American overall industry. Basically, the idea is to incorporate more American involvement into all of these previously mentioned areas of commerce, so the American people will knowingly have an authentic, visible American option to compete with other global competitors in the market with the hopes of convincing the American people to re-invest in their own country and their own domestic agendas. Ask the American people to follow you onto the new road to recovery, a road that is paved by America, with roads built for all Americans.

This will be what I call the "Guinea Pig Project." We can go to Michigan or California—anywhere there are people living in tents or on the streets, and find the community with the highest unemployment rates, which will also have a high number of uninsured people as well. If done right, we can successfully thwart two birds with one stone. Let's say that American Inc. decides to invest in the production of American-made, workman boots. If the media and the Internet can be utilized effectively the way Barack Obama used them during his

2008 presidential campaign, the American people can be informed of this economic revitalization plan to reinstitute manufacturing here at home, starting with this particular community. I think the federal government, who may help to finance the startup, but will not own any part of this operation, can use those media outlets to coax the American people into reinvesting in American manufacturing. We could then strongly suggest that huge retailers such as Wal-Mart, Target and Sears to promote and sell this American footwear. Personally, I would hope that retailers would want to promote their fellow American producers without being told to do so, but not everyone is a patriot or the kind of ambitious person who believes they can turn loses into gains. The next step is to try and persuade even more American companies to buy this American footwear. Any company willing to go under contract with American Inc. for a lump sum supply of footwear for their workforce would be given a home investment tax credit from the federal government. The next step would be a massive media campaign to target the American people. I firmly believe they would respond, as this would be a chance for them to personally help their own economic future and the future of fellow countrymen, because when you buy and support American manufacturing, you are buying into your own company's stock and making it stronger. If it is successful, you could possibly even go after foreign markets. The government does not have to own or run these types of operations, but it can promote them. It would be quite an accomplishment for the federal government to be able to hold up an actual impoverished community to the nation and show the amazing economic turnaround. The morale of the country would begin to rebound drastically. In fact, other businesses in other states would probably find a way to install that same ideology into their own ailing economic communities. The government's job should be to come up with a plan that works; a road map to follow, so that the private sector will then join in. Instead of being the CEO of these new American companies, the federal government could regulate and inspect these new companies to ensure that only the best quality is being produced and the correct guidelines are being followed. The government could be very helpful here. This is one way to decrease the number of uninsured people by increasing the numerical percentages of employer based insurance. If this strategy works, a similar one could be used to overhaul the health care industry one segment at a time. The American brand has to be restored to respectability, and then people will believe again. The same principle applies to health care, car care, pet care or anything else. People will buy into new prospects, even if it means starting small, as long as they have a promising reason within sight. It doesn't matter how small it starts; it only matters how successful it can become.

Republicans and conservatives will be the first to call for my head with a statement such as that one, but it is an ugly reality that must be effectively dealt with. Confidence in American products is not very high right now. In fact, I can't remember when it ever was very high during my lifetime. Even as a kid, the word on the street and in the media was always how much better and technologically superior Asian-based products were, especially electronics and automotive parts. Once again, who receives the blame for this? The Asian markets function like well-oiled machines. Japan supplies the technology, while China and South Korea supply the labor. If you've ever watched the movie *Remember the Titans*, you may recall a scene where Coach Yoast walks past Coach Boone and says, "He's a mile ahead of you," in regards to their opposition, which was a highly touted and well decorated, former champion named Ed Henry! That particular storyline sums up our dilemma. America is Coach Boone and Asia is Ed Henry. And right now, they are a mile ahead of us, if not more.

Energy Efficient Cars

Here's a good example of it. It's what I call "The Corolla Experiment!" Back a couple of years ago when gas got all the way up past $4 a gallon, during the Bush era, I found myself, for the first time in my life, driving a foreign car--a Toyota Corolla; even though I also drive a fairly new, Dodge Charger. Originally, I had driven a Chrysler Concorde, but the decision was made to trade it in for the Corolla in hopes of attaining better gas mileage to help ease my commute back and forth to work, which was about 90 miles a day. I had always heard about how good Toyotas were, but I'd never ventured out to try one. Toyotas, like other foreign cars, were rumored to get better gas mileage, have a lower depreciation value, require less maintenance, and have more overall durability than American cars. Speaking of American cars, I heard the exact opposite about them, and I heard it from other Americans, not foreigners. I have to be honest. I fell completely in love with the Corolla. It is a great car. It outmaneuvers my Dodge Charger, and it gets much better gas mileage, which is almost 40 miles-per-gallon on the highway, even though none of my pseudo-patriotic associates like the Corolla or Toyota in general. They accuse me of being duped by Al Gore's global warming hoax! Global warming or not, the energy efficiency of the Toyota Corolla is saving me money at the pump, and I'd sure like to see these Paul Revere wannabes beat that! The Corolla has a quick pick up, and it's so easy to park. As of yet, I have had no problems to speak of involving the Corolla, and I would go out tomorrow and buy another Toyota, despite the recent sticking, gas pedal controversies, which seem a little too conveniently suspicious for me. I now have plans to own a fuel efficient/foreign car from here on out.

I also had serious doubts about owning another American car again, and this was before the big three American-auto collapse. I'm sure that I'm not the only person who felt that way at the time. My confidence in the American automotive field and in American manufacturing, as a whole, was trending towards non-existent, but then a funny thing happened that would cause me to have to rethink my new found expectations. Due to an unexpected car accident involving my Dodge Charger, I was forced to use a rental car, and the rental car just happened to be an American car by Chevy called an HHR. I was very unenthusiastic to be in this car, but I had no choice. To my surprise, the car was excellent, and I'm not a Chevy fan. It got about 30 miles per gallon on the highway, and it had just as much technology, if not more, than my Corolla. Some of the gadgets and devices were better than those in my Corolla, and it handled and rode like a charm. I was more than impressed with the new Chevy brand. And remember, this was before the big collapse. I thought Chevy had done a fabulous job of re-inventing itself into a sleeker more up-to-date version of itself. These HHRs should be flying off the lots. I thought Chevy had found its niche and was headed for a comeback. I mean, I would definitely strongly consider purchasing a Chevy product now. But for whatever reason, GMC sales continued to slide, as the big collapse grew nearer and nearer. Media outlets had slammed Detroit hard, and so had the American people—including me—but maybe we should have done a re-evaluation, because these newer American cars were better than the world was giving them credit for. What could the problem be? I think I've already displayed ample evidence of the problem in my previous statements about American ingenuity. Perception is reality, and the perception of American ingenuity was in the toilet. So it really didn't matter how much the new American cars had improved, because consumer confidence was also still in the toilet, and simply building better machines was not enough to raise confidence levels at that time. The brand had lost its luster, and ominous signs of an oncoming collapse only dampened it further. The government tried to help by passing a bill to bail out the big auto companies, but that did little to help resurrect consumer confidence; in actuality, it probably hurt it more than it helped. So the question remains. How do we re-establish consumer confidence in American manufacturing? Until this trend is somehow reversed, American products will continue to lag behind, and American industry will remain stagnant at best.

The government has been highly criticized for getting involved with the American auto-industry. Republicans are quick to accuse President Obama of trying to be the new, green CEO of the American car industry, so he can force his radical, leftist, green, car/hybrid, auto agenda on the country, but just maybe, the new green technology is the way to go. After the collapse of the Big Three, it surely can't hurt much more than it already has. I do agree with the President on his new vision of Detroit. A vision of a much leaner and much meaner auto-industry; an industry that can and will compete in the world market; an industry that can and will begin the defense of its own home court here in America from other foreign car companies who have literally manhandled American manufacturers. When President Obama tries to promote his new vision of Detroit, he is often met with huge amounts of skepticism and leeriness. After all, the United States has depended on foreign oil for decades now, and big oil has an infinite amount of power, money, and financial influence coupled with the reality that Americans, like most people, are very reluctant to change. The average Joe Plumber is happiest as long as things remain the same as they have always been. The word conservative means little or no change at all, or more of the same, but more of the same during these uncertain economic times could mean disaster for us all. Like the great T. Boone Pickens, I think it's time for the world, including America, to set a new and improved course of action notwithstanding our age-old fears of the unknown. As in the concept of science fiction, things are only unknown due to the fact that no one has dared to make them known as of yet, but as always; eventually somebody or something will. You are only in the dark as long as you choose not to look for the light switch. It is time for America to start searching for the light switch in hopes of getting a better and clearer vision of its economic future. Now is the time for courage and creativity, not fear and squeamishness! Just because something has always worked well in the past, it does not mean that it can and will continue to prosper in today's economy or in the future. Part of growing is the ability to face and engage the next bend, whenever or wherever those bends may arise. I understand the uneasiness of the new. I understand the uneasiness of the untested. I understand the uneasiness of risk, but I also understand that not taking a risk can sometimes be just as or even more risky than the risk itself. America was founded on a risk. America was the unknown. America was the new direction. If those early explorers had been afraid and turned back, where would the world be? We would probably still be trapped in the mentality of a flat earth, as we limited our exploration due to the fear of going too far, and falling off of the earth. It appears to me that all throughout human history, people have found ways to make unprecedented moves into the future. Today should be no different. When all is said and done, our greatest successes and our greatest inventions have all arisen out of uncertainty and doubt, with no shortage of disbelievers constantly chiming in against them, saying it would be too dicey to try.

The new green technology is the modern day version of the man will never fly weltanschauung, but people only say this because they fear that which they do not understand. Can green technology work? Can hybrids become a staple of the auto-industry? Can hybrids shoulder the American load? The President thinks so, but many of the American people do not share his enthusiasm. Personally, I am in favor of hybrid technology, hydrogen technology, flex-fuel technology, Brazilian sugar cane technology, natural gas technology, or even electric plug-in technology, and I think the government would have been a very good place to start off this new green technology. If government offices could have been successfully operated and sustained by green power, it would definitely have bolstered consumer confidence. Take the Hummer for an example; it was first a governmental military production where it was very advantageous. It was then released and distributed into the civilian population where it sold well. Forget about the fact that it got horrible gas mileage and look at the experimentation factors of how it was first implemented by the military/government before it was later released to the public. Why not use this same test run model on the hybrid theory/green technology theory? President Obama wanted a plan similar to this, but I do believe his plan was abandoned. If this is true, it needs to be re-introduced and re-evaluated. This green technology could possibly help the government cut costs and save energy at the same time. Isn't that what the Republicans always bark about it--cutting costs? Why wouldn't they be on board with this plan? If government cost could be cut by at least 20 percent or better, it would be an improvement and a start. It would also display great leadership by our elected officials and begin to restore confidence in their loyalty to their country, and not their lobbyist/campaign fund donators.

I've heard many conservatives and Republicans take firm stands against the hybrid theory. The motto of 2008 was the "Drill Baby Drill" chant when gas was over $4 a gallon, and the economy teetered on the verge of collapse. Once the economy collapsed, for a fleeting moment in time, people actually began to entertain the thought of hybrid power. It seems that drastic times call for drastic measures. While Barack Obama and T. Boone Pickens were lobbying for the green technologies, such as wind, solar, natural gas, and bio-fuels, John McCain was championing more offshore drilling. But surprisingly, it was Paris Hilton, usually given little intellectual regard, who suggested the government do both, which is not a bad idea at all. The hybrid theory is usually mocked and scoffed at, but during the 2008 gas heist, the American people started to trade in their behemoth SUVs for smaller, more efficient cars with better gas mileage—even hybrid sales felt an increase. You could actually see hybrids on the highway and in parking lots. By my evaluation, the economic stability, or lack thereof, determines the demand. If gas skyrockets to over $4 a gallon again, President Obama won't have to try to sell his hybrid theory! The theory will sell itself, especially if the price of gas remains over $4 a gallon for an entire year or more. Even the staunchest conservatives will have to search for alternative fuel methodology. As a Realacrat, I say why wait until the big oil companies decide to rape us at the pump again—because you know they will. Why not make a move now?

What would it take to convince more people to invest in hybrids? I have an idea. The American people are notorious for getting behind a cause only when there is something in it for them personally. If denting their wallets and checkbooks can sway consumers to at least consider a hybrid, then maybe padding their wallets and checkbooks can do the rest. Let's just hypothetically say that I get about $300 for my end of the year tax returns, which does very little when the price of gas is high or and many other prices for that matter. If I went out and bought a hybrid, how much would you be willing to give back to me now Mr. Government? I would make the case for about $1,000, or slightly more. You give me anywhere from $1,000 to $1,500 added on to my end of the year tax return, and I will morph into a hybrid driver instantly. The old Cash for Clunkers program could be re-implemented and re-vamped, because people just can't afford to buy a $50,000 hybrid/natural gas/hydrogen car. I'm sure this will do nothing to inspire Oprah Winfrey or Bill Gates to buy one, in case they haven't already, but these individuals don't make up the majority of the population. The overwhelming majority of the population is not Paris Hilton. It is comprised of lower to middle-class people who could absolutely use that $1,500 in a tax refund. Yes, I said $1,500! I couldn't care less about some whiney Democrat or some elitist Republican getting all bent out of shape over somebody like me receiving $1,500 for a hybrid, tax write-off. I can hear it now. Some conservative blow-hard will be up in arms calling it auto welfare, but I disagree with that sentiment totally. Why is it that when the rich, fat cats of the corrupt, private sector get the big financial breaks; it's called stimulating the economy, but when regular, working people like me can manage to receive a decent, financial, tax break; it's called a welfare, government handout? This is not auto welfare. This is the poor man's bailout, seeing as how so many of the politicians who had no quarrels about fattening the pockets of Wall Street execs, big oil, big bankers and other rich fat cats who helped run the country into the ground while they slid out of the crashing plane using a golden parachute marked with a federal logo. I'd sure like to witness politicians bailing out their economic, gormandizing, fat cat buddies without my taxpayer money. If you can cushion the negligence of irresponsible CEOs, you can cushion the wallets of the taxpayers who made it possible. Anyone who owns a hybrid will get around $1,500 back, because money talks and elitist bullsh*t walks. The American consumer needs a, "what have you done for me lately," reason to get into a hybrid, and I just gave 1500 reasons that will continue to be distributed to the recipients, as long as they are able to meet the requirements, which is the ownership of a functioning hybrid and the proof of its usage!

Helping the Commuters

My next installment is the commuter's bailout. Like me, there are millions of Americans who commute to work five to six days a week, and the average commute is usually at least 20 miles or better. I, like the greater part of all the American commuters, spend the bulk of my drive time going back and forth to and from work. The clear-cut lion's share of my gas purchases is work-related. I would say that my work commute encompasses about 90 percent of my gas consumption. Lucky for me, I don't own an SUV. A gas-guzzling car is the last thing the consumer needs when facing five to six days of commuting. Back when gas was $4 a gallon, it was the commuters who got economically murdered at the pump. I was one of them. I was averaging about $95 a week in gas purchases, which was almost $400 a month in fuel alone—and you wonder why the economy collapsed. The prices keep going up, but the wages do not. That kind of navigation leads to bankruptcy. It's time for the commuter's bailout; a creative new way to make commuting more efficient. Once again, we go back to hybrids or high mileage vehicles. Since the big three auto manufacturers are in the re-tooling phase, their new products should include a commuter line, which would be a slew of high mileage cars—the highest mileage possible. These automobiles would be built specifically for commuting. If we could cut commuter gas consumption in half, it would save tons of energy and money, plus help the environment. The government could provide some sort of financial assistance for those willing to participate, possibly some purchasing assistance and/or a good tax return, like the one previously mentioned. I would also give a $500 end-of-year tax cut to any non-hybrid, non-green, traditional gasoline car that charted at least 30 miles per gallon. All of these tax cuts previously mentioned would be added on to what you already receive in tax returns.

The second part of the commuter's bailout is revolutionary at its core. Again, I say that if the government wants consumers to get behind the new technology, they will have to give consumers a distinct advantage, because we consumers love price breaks and discounts. What better place to have a permanent discount than at the pump? Yes, I said a permanent discount at the gas pump, but not for all cars—just the ones that meet the fuel efficiency requirements. This plan is a simple one. If you drive a vehicle that gets 30 miles per gallon or better, you will receive a numerical discount on each and every gas purchase you make, though this would all hinge on the price of gas on any given day. It is universally understood that the price of gas will always fluctuate. There is nothing that can be done about that, but this program will help to alleviate some of the pump pain when the price moves into the $4 a gallon range again, due to the Hurricane Katrina effect, which now happens whenever any storm travels throughout the Gulf of Mexico, hampering or temporarily shutting down the off-shore oil rigs. Now, Exxon Mobile and BP track hurricane season harder than the Weather Channel. The discounts are not there to eliminate these sensationalized price spikes, but they can not only ease the pain at the pump somewhat, which is better than nothing at all, but they can also spur on the further development and usage of higher mile per gallon automobiles. It would definitely be an incentive to consider a Toyota, a Hyundai, a Honda, a Nissan for your next new car. I know I have left out the American car companies. Maybe cars like the Chevy Volt can compete, but Detroit is going to have to ante-up and revamp, come out firing on all cylinders because right now they are still behind the eight-ball. Nonetheless, after the bailouts and the Cash for Clunkers program, the American auto industry has begun to make a comeback. If so, President Obama deserves major credit, because he was lambasted for his involvement in the auto industry. As for all the SUV lovers, anyone interested in purchasing an SUV should be able to order one from the Big Three American car companies. A special, much smaller SUV line could still be kept in operation, but the bulk of assembly should be potent high-powered fuel efficient cars to go after the foreign car competitors who have been mauling the American car companies for years. The agenda is not to force anyone out of their SUV. The goal of this plan is simply to encourage and support fuel efficient cars as the new mainstay of American culture, preferably the new American fuel efficient cars, because these automobiles could be manufactured, assembled, test driven, designed and shipped right here in the United States.

Another additive to this plan would be the regulation of the gas stations, through the actual monitoring of all price changes in gasoline. Right now, gas stations in the United States are free to change and moderate their prices in an unlimited manner. The price could start out at $2.15 a gallon at 6:00 a.m., be up to $2.55 a gallon by noon and then later move up even more to a hefty $2.75 a gallon by 3:00 p.m., with no explanation as to why. Websites devoted to help consumers find the best deals on cheap gas prices are hard pressed to keep up and stay relevant in real time with so much lawless price fluctuation. The driver is at the mercy of whatever particular traveling radius he or she is in at the time. You just have to pick the nearest gas stations and roll the dice, knowing full well that after you've filled up you could always spot a 10-to-15-cent discounted price a mile down the road. If there was some way to know and control the times and frequencies of the prices changes, gas friendly websites could actually stay much more accurate and become more helpful to the consumer. So, I've devised the "Regulators Not Speculators Bailout Plan." With this interactive plan, all gas stations would have the same set times at which to adjust pricing. For example, gas stations could be delegated the time slot of 6:00 a.m. until 6:30 a.m. to set their morning prices, and these prices could not be adjusted until the next allotted adjustment time, let's say 2:00 p.m. until 2:30 p.m. After that, the prices would stay locked in until the next allotted time change, which would simply start all over again at 6:00 a.m. the next day. At each of the designated adjustment times, it would be the sole responsibility of the gas station to go online and enter its current pricing into a government owned and operated website system where the price setting and price fluctuation would be monitored for any sudden, unprovoked spikes. All gas friendly websites could then become permanently logged into this government system, from which they would then receive the latest gas pricing updates. With this new regulation, the government could keep tabs on reckless speculators who attempt to drive up the price of gas, because all spikes would be recorded and investigated. The government has all the mechanisms necessary to implant such a system. All they need is the leadership and vision to develop it.

Speaking of mechanisms, a new one will have to be drawn up and installed in every gas station, or at least every major chain, to make these permanent pump discounts a reality. Right now they are merely science fiction that only exists inside my mind, or maybe someone else's. There is probably someone somewhere saying: "it will never happen! It can't be done! It's too complicated! It's too risky! It's too hard to install! No one will participate! It will surely flop! It's a stupid idea! We should just keep things the way they are now; in my recognizable comfort zone! We don't need this! Gas is not that high right now!" Actually, some of this negativity is correct. It will be difficult to re-tool our fuel efficiencies, but it is difficult to re-tool anything. Once changes are imbedded properly and sufficiently, the gains can be tremendous and rapid; nevertheless, America has to start somewhere, even if it is perilous at first. So here is my idea for the commuter's bailout discount. All cars capable of displaying at 30 miles per gallon will be given an engraved code very similar to a navigation GPS tracking chip. This coded chip will contain all the mileage information about the vehicle. A specialized infrared scanner will be placed at all gas stations beside all pumps. It will be permanently attached to the pumps. The scanner will be movable, but it will not be able to be removed from the pump without breaking it. The scanner will work almost identically to the grocery store scanners; once it reads the coded information, the appropriate discount will automatically be factored into the price, giving the consumer a lower price. For safety purposes, another sensor will be installed at the top of the pump. This will be known as the cheat sensor, in case some idiot tries to scan his fuel efficient car first, then rapidly drive it forward, so he can then have an accomplice pull some big, gas-guzzling behemoth up to the pump to cipher the discounted gas strictly and exclusively designed for fuel efficient cars. As soon as anyone pulls up to a pump, the cheat sensor will acknowledge a vehicle in the pump position so the code can be scanned. If, for any reason, the car moves, and the sensor beam is broken, the transaction will be automatically terminated. Furthermore, the sensor will sound an alert to the cashier of a possible fuel theft. An alert of this kind could also be used to trigger all gas station security cameras to record immediately, in order to catch the thief. Anyone caught doing this will be prosecuted. In honor of Anderson Cooper, we are keeping them honest.

Here are the proposed discounted ratios:

GAS PRICES PER GALLON	DISCOUNT
1. $1.5O and under	$0.10
2. over a $1.50 to $1.99	$0.15
3. $2.00 to $2.40	$0.20
4. over $2.40 to $299	$0.35
5. $3.00 to $3.50	$0.50
6. over $3.50 to $3.99	$0.75
7. $4.00 to 4.50	$1.00
8. over $4.50 to $4.99	$1.50
9. $5.00 to $5.50	$2.00
All rates are adjustable	

More Bailouts For the Little Guy

There is no doubt that the great financial bailouts of 2008 and 2009 were utterly infuriating to many American taxpayers, mainly because of who was getting bailed out. These were rich, affluent, prosperous individuals; the kinds of high rollers who rarely ever seriously hurt for capital. I was never personally offended by the great bailouts of the rich fat cats. Most of them were probably major campaign contributors. I just believe in turnabout being fair play. As a Realacrat, I think it's about time that the government hands out a few well-deserved bailouts to the average Joe Blow, Joe the Plumber, and Joe the Taxpayer. Republicans were speedy to piggyback on Joe the Plumber during the 2008 presidential campaign, as if they were the party who was going to look out for the little man, the small business owners, and the average, working class, taxpayers, but in the end; it was the rich, fat cat, Wall Street Execs and CEO's who drove off with all the money. Now it's time to remunerate the little guy; the one whose hard earned taxpayer dollars financed many a golden parachute for reckless fat cats to glide away from failures and into some hefty payoffs.

Support Bailout

I think it would be a good idea to bail out the child-support-paying dads, because they are getting hosed in the worst way. Child- support-paying dads are definitely not jumping out of the plane with a golden parachute. They are being thrown out of the plane with a rusty anvil reminiscent of the well-known Wild E. Coyote fall! The overwhelming consent surrounding this state of affairs is one of non-sympathy and deserved swindling. Due to the sensationalized vilification of the dead-beat dads and fathers in general, whenever a man questions or speaks out about his child support condition, he is automatically labeled as a whiner who merely wants to escape his financial obligations. As a man, even if you are getting screwed, you are supposed to shut up, and take it for the betterment of the child and the mother, but I disagree unreservedly, because getting screwed has absolutely nothing to do with being a father. The sentiment that fathers deserve to get screwed is preposterous. First of all, the government is taxing the child-support-paying parent, who is usually is a guy, for the total amount of money earned, when the paying parent is not receiving that full amount. Taxes will decrease the amount but so will child support. You might be making $30,000 a year, and you are taxed for $30,000 a year, but you are not getting $30,000 a year. If you pay $60 a week, that amount totals out to be $3,120 a year of child support payments, which is directly garnished from the paying parent's check. The payer never sees a nickel or dime of that money, not a penny of it, but the government will still tax that payer as if they have received it, while the receiving parent, usually a woman, will actually be the one who collects, at least a portion, of that amount, and it will be tax-free money. The question is exactly how much of that $3,120 did the mother actually see in a year? She should have received every penny, but this is not always the case! Secondly, the paying parent who is being taxed for grossing $30,000 a year is actually only getting about $26,880 a year after the $3,120 child support deductions alone, which does not include regular taxes, not to mention the fact that the paying parent rarely if ever gets to carry the child support recipient as a dependent.

So, here is the "Paying Parent Bailout." The parent who paid that $3,120 a year in child support will now be placed in a lower, tax bracket in the same way as having a 401k can place one into a lower, tax bracket. The government can continue to tax the paying parent throughout the year in the normal regular fashion, but at the end of the year that parent will be given a tax break by being dropped down to a lower tax bracket, so even the paying parent can reap a small benefit from having a child. The paying parent who earns $30,000 will be automatically lowered into the $26,000–27,000 tax bracket, and if no back child support is owed, the paying parent can receive the full benefit.

Spreading the Wealth Around

The next bailout should go to the workforce, because they are the ones who drive the economy and the country as a whole. This will be called the "Slashing Bailout." After all, it is no big secret that Washington spends a tremendous amount of money on crappy, lackluster projects known as pork barreling or earmarks. John McCain and President Obama campaigned hard against these baskets of economic goodies for special interest groups and lobbyists, but today little has been done to stop it, which includes little from Democrats and even less from Republicans. As a Realacrat, I would take it upon myself to, in the ideology of Sean Hannity, tighten their belts in Washington! Increasing taxes is one way to raise revenue, but slashing government spending on junk is also a viable solution. Every month a horrid government pork barrel project, like $50,000 for a tennis court touch-up in South Dakota, should be identified, critiqued and potentially eliminated. I would draft a pork barrel czar or pork barrel sheriff to enforce it, and it would only take 50 Congressional members (25 Representatives and 25 Senators) to vote yes to have the pork barrel project slashed. I would even go as far as creating a bipartisan pork barrel committee, and their only responsibility would be to tag pork barreling. Every month the worst pork barrel project would be brought to trial and eliminated or at least shaved. That money would then be shuttled out to the people as a surplus bonus, which would then generate more tax revenue through consumer purchasing. The weeks leading up to Thanksgiving and Christmas would turn up even more pork barreling and spending. Both weeks would have at least two pork barrel projects slashed or discontinued; giving the American people a nice, Thanksgiving bonus and a nice, Christmas bonus from the government, and like the Bush tax cuts; these bonuses would be tax-free. The goal would be to give from $500 to $1,500 back to the taxpayers on both occasions. People receiving government assistance would get $500, and all single payers who made between $75,000 and $100,000 a year would receive $500. Single payers making under $75,000 a year would receive $1,500. Couples with combined incomes over $100,000 a year, but under $175,000 a year would also receive $500, and all unemployed workers who had held a job within the past year would receive $500 as well.

Blue Collar Bailouts

The second part will deal with the plight of the American worker who is working longer, harder and for less, while thousands have been laid-off and are not working at all. Nevertheless, this is based on the work related experiences of a group of people who worked for this major corporation located in the northeast part of the United States, and it involves the issue of an employee's personal time off/ PTO. We'll call it the PTO shake down hustle, where greedy, unfeeling corporate bastards are constantly budding new ways to hornswoggle employees out of their well-earned and well-deserved PTO. For example, the average worker gets a minimum of 1 to 2 weeks for vacation/personal time off/sick days, which is nominal, but better than nothing. The problem occurs when these mega-factories have to shut down; sometimes for weeks at a time. The worker is forced to burn up all of his PTO to cover this corporate, down-time, because most people survive on the regular arrival and the regular amount of their paycheck; meaning, if the workers didn't use their PTO to cover the days they were forced to be off, they wouldn't have received a check for that week. Now, the flipside of that argument is; most corporations don't even give the worker a choice in the matter. They force the workers to use their PTO; however much that it takes!

Now, let's flash forward a couple of months into the future. Those same workers who were mandated to use the bulk of their PTO to cover industry, related down-time could suddenly find themselves facing a family crisis; requiring the usage of PTO, despite being forced to use most of their PTO earlier in the year by the company. The worker is forced to take off anyway and does, even though it now means he/she will not be getting paid for that week. And furthermore, the worker will be documented for the absence and potentially punished because of it, by either withholding a coming raise or the distribution of a blue slip. Workers who discipline their PTO efforts should not be forcefully stripped of it due to industry politics. Realacrats would push for a new law where all workers must be paid for any industry related, down-time caused by that industry. If your company tells you not to come in for 2 weeks, then they are accountable for your pay for those 2 weeks, even if you have PTO to cover it, because PTO belongs to the worker's discretion, not the company's. They can file it as a tax write-off, and the government can financially reimburse them at the end of the physical year. Realacrat policy would also include a 4 week, paid vacation for all full-time employees who have been employed for at least five years, with a 5 week, paid vacation for all full-time employees who have been employed for multiple years. Furthermore, all employees grossing under $30,000 a year can submit one vacation package per year to the government and receive $1,000 dollars for one or two people and $2,500 for a family of 3 or more, because asking or suggesting that people earning at, just above, or under the poverty line go on vacation is the epitome of being out of touch with the Main St. working class, who most of the time, just will not have the resources to make it happen. You file a vacation claim and the government puts the financial credit on the bill leaving you to pay the lesser amount.

The Bilingual Issue

The Language Barrier

The American people are far too caught up in themselves, far too caught up in the hoopla and ballyhoo of their exaggerated self-images of grandeur. Instead of meeting the rest of the world halfway, they expect the entire planet to meet them all of the way--their way, and no other way, because a significant amount of American culture is reluctant, resistant, and outright afraid to think outside of the box or outside of the traditional, cultural, comfort zones. For example, I love to eat Chinese food on the weekends. I usually frequent the Red Sun Buffet in Cordova, Tennessee. Their selection of seafood, rice and noodles is exquisite. I also love to visit the Mongolian Grill in Jonesboro, Arkansas. There you can find an excellent variety of seafood, pizza, chicken and salads. I also visit the China Express in Wynne, Arkansas. They have great rice and stupendous frog legs. The other Asian restaurant I love to visit is the Osaka, also located in Cordova, Tennessee, which has fantastic shrimp fried rice and a superlative sushi bar. Because I go these kinds of places so much, I've become closely acquainted with many of the employees, and they are mostly Asian and Mexican. The more I got to know these individuals, the more striking similarities I began to see. All four restaurants have one thing in common besides the great food. The overwhelming majority, about 99%, of the employees had the barest ability to speak the English language. They were all very well-mannered people, and they were all substantially friendly, but it was a difficult task to comprehend anything they were attempting to say. I actually witnessed numerous orders being turned in wrong due to poor communication. The employees appeared to make every effort they possibly could to take in as much information as possible, but the language barrier was just too high for them to make decent progress in the short amount of time that they have lived in the United States. One night I was in the Mongolian Grill, and this tall, White man was experiencing the same problem I just described. The language barrier was becoming a hindrance, and this guy was not at all happy about it. He looked at me and began to rail about the Mexicans and Asians not being able to speak English like they are supposed to. He went on to explain his disdain for foreigners, and their below average linguistic I.Q.

He said to me and another White guy, "What a bunch of morons! You'd think these slant-eyes and wetbacks could've learned to speak the English by now. If you can't learn our language then you need to go back where you came from. Nothing here but a bunch of Buddha-loving chinks and sweaty, thieving wetbacks who feel that they are too good to learn our language! It's all that Barack Obama's fault! We got a sorry President who allows these English-defiant border-jumpers to infiltrate this country, and take our jobs away! This kind of crap never happened under Bush or Reagan! These lazy, ungrateful immigrants refuse to learn our language, because they are probably too dumb to grasp it. They should all be deported!"

Then, another person decides to chime in by saying this, "All of these taco-tossing wetbacks and all of these stir-fried, rice-chunking Orientals don't want to learn our language, because they have been sent here by the Chinese and Mexican governments to indoctrinate our children with second-rate languages and cultures such as Spanish, Asian, Cuban and Communism, and if that's not enough; you have all of these Sand Niggers (Arabians) coming over here to further indoctrinate our children with the help of the media and that immigrant- and foreigner-loving Barack Obama! All he ever does is try to make friends with all of these second-rate world leaders and countries, and by doing so; he validates and authenticates the world's trash that is clearly beneath us. I am a southern, White woman, and I am a proud conservative and Republican, and we don't indoctrinate our children to try, and bring down their culture! The main thing I try to teach my kids is to never date outside of their race, never date or trust anyone who is not an American, the Mexicans are taking all our jobs, the only country that is truly not on the Axis of Evil list is America, just because you are born in this country, it does not mean you are a real American; evolution don't apply to us White people, slavery wasn't as bad as people have made it out to be, God hates fags, God hates non-Christians, God is American, and God speaks English! We don't indoctrinate over here."

So I said to this egocentric woman, "We don't indoctrinate over here? Then what in the hell do you call that *Mein Kampf*[34] expository you just laid out?"

Then, she said, "Mein who? What I said was not indoctrination, because it was Christianly righteous! This is why my kids will never learn to speak Spanish, German, Arabic or any of your dog languages, and if that Marxist Barack Obama tries to dictate his Marxist propaganda to our pure American children and their pure American virtues, our strong Christian faith gives us the right to bear arms, and fight back against the mongrels and infidels who have come here to try, and reprioritize our values and our American Christian core. The Second Amendment was placed there by our founding fathers to give us a chance to destroy our enemies, and that is the main reason why the foreigner-loving liberals and that Communist Barack Obama are dead-set on revoking it and taking away our guns, but I'm not worried. I know our God will give us the strength to defeat these mongrels and their lower-class culture! I sure do miss the good-ole-days when we were the only game in town."

I would like to say that I was shocked to hear such hateful rhetoric, but I was not! I hear comments such as these almost every day, especially from misguided, misplaced, discrimination-practicing megalomaniacs who seriously believe that their sh*t does not stink, with all of it deriving from the mere threat of American students being required to learn two languages instead of just one. The ability to be bilingual is not a threat to anyone, but you would think it is the equivalent of being injected with the Aids virus, judging by the way some people are so distraught about it. I asked one of my sexy, Asian waitresses exactly how long she'd been in this country. She told me she'd only been here a few months and that she came directly here from China. She admitted that her

34 Adolf Hitler, Mein Kampf (July 18, 1925).

English vocabulary was very limited, and she was catching on as fast as she could. According to her, there was little or no opportunity to gain or experience any English training in China where she lived, so she was forced to learn all the English she could randomly, when she arrived here in the United States to work and live. She then explained how all the other employees had encountered similar fates on their journeys into the United States. She told me that the ones who can speak English fairly well in the restaurant are the ones who'd been here the longest.

The more I listened to the plight of my sweet, adorable, Asian waitress; the more I began to understand that there is not a system in place to help deal with the language barrier. In a linguistic sense, these Asian and Mexican immigrants are being thrown to the wolves and left to fend for themselves. Now, my question is this. Who is the real dummy; the Asian and Mexican immigrants with limited linguistic resources or the pompous clodhopper who went on his belittling tirade? Instead of criticizing the employees, he should have been more critical of the non-existent system that makes all of this possible. As a Realacrat, we should make every effort to develop a plan to help rectify this quandary. Instead of railing against people with blind and unwarranted hatred, I decided to sit down, and talk with some of these immigrants to try and attain a better understanding of the problem so I could then possibly develop a better understanding for a possible solution. Talking down to people from some self-appointed societal totem pole is like giving a true or false answer on a discussion question that requires two or three paragraphs.

Once again, I know how much Americans hate the idea, but the reality of our existence is rapidly becoming global, so maybe it's time to start looking beyond the borders of our country and our beliefs. Somewhere down the line there is going to have to be a world language. I mean a language that the majority of nations on planet earth can speak, so everyone can communicate with each other, even if it is on a limited basis. Now some will call me biased or partisan, because my suggestion would be to use English as the universal language of the world. This is not my idea of linguistic imperialism! This is not an attempt to ramrod English through while driving all other languages out. The Chinese will still learn Chinese, and the French will still learn French, but they will both learn English to go along with it, at least enough to be vocally viable. The ability to speak two different languages or be multi-linguistic is an asset, not a liability. With that said, I also believe students here in the United States should begin learning to speak a second language as well, either Spanish or some other language. Once again, most Americans loathe this idea of teaching their children to be bilingual, because they believe Spanish will remove English as the dominant language here in the United States, which is incongruous. Being able to speak Spanish could prove to be very useful depending on where you find yourself located. The world is becoming more globally oriented, and the United States is no exception, with Spanish culture leading the charge. Unlike the buffoon who dreams of building a fence that will halt the influx of multi-cultural aspects, I'd rather take a more realistic approach to it. Because culture cannot really be halted, I think it would be beneficial to find creative, new ways to meet this new challenge, and being able to install some form of communication with this new culture would be a rational gesture.

So in true Realacrat fashion, I would require that all American students be taught to speak Spanish and English starting from day one. This new, Realacrat, linguistic, global curriculum would also mandate that two years of an additional foreign language be a prerequisite for all high school, graduation standards in this country, and those foreign languages would more than likely be an Arabic or Asian tongue. I know simpletons and bumpkins like the two oafs in the Asian restaurant I spoke of previously will be furious over such proposals, because in their dimwitted minds exposing American kids to other languages somehow devalues their American identities, when in reality it is only helping to prepare them for the global challenges here at home and abroad. The days when the greatest challenge to American, White culture was simply finding a way to deter your White children from Black culture and its influences are gone, and new players and new challengers have arrived on the scene to force more competition. All this is happening right now, which is similar to the pro-argument for the government-run, public option, health care push; and Realacrats see this clearly. Why follow the Republicans on some half-hearted, ill-advised pilgrimage down memory lane in hopes of becoming reacquainted with the old, covered wagon days when it is painfully evident that the global community is beating down your door and is camped out in your backyard? Why not get these American children mentally and physically prepared for the new, hungry competition that awaits them?

The goal of having American children learn more than one language is not to harm or indoctrinate them. On the other hand, just think of the harm your White American daughter would face if she was approached by two Spanish speaking individuals who just happen to speak Spanish, if she wasn't able to, at least, speak and comprehend basic Spanish! The two people talking in Spanish could openly talk about robbing Misty Anne, and she wouldn't even have a clue about it. The same scenario could also play out using Arabic, Chinese and other languages. Also, in a global marketplace American competitors who speak only one language are at a disadvantage when pitted against multilingual competitors. As the old saying states, the more you know the farther you can go, and it makes no rational sense whatsoever why becoming bilingual should even be debated. I guess it's the fear of a changing world, a changing demographic, a changing ideology, a changing social and political glass ceiling, changing challengers and challenges, or a fear of change itself. If you are afraid to change, then you are afraid to learn, and if you are afraid to learn; then you are afraid to grow. If you are afraid to grow, then you are afraid to live, and if you are afraid to live; then you are already dead, so long live the Realacrats!

Progressive Learning

The next Realacrat academic proposal will be the most contentious one of all, because fear induced by a lack of understanding only works in favor of a more diminutive understanding, which seriously limits the possibilities for solutions. It becomes excruciatingly evident that we should require all American students to learn about Islam or the societal status of religion as a whole around the world, similar to the class I took during my years at Wynne High School, in Wynne, Arkansas. The class was called Global Studies, and it was taught by a man named Coach Westbrook, who was one of the best, if not the best, teachers I've ever had the privilege to learn under. At the time, the class was only an elective, but in today's world; Realacrats would push to make it mandatory for all high schools in the nation, because Realacrats do not believe that learning about other cultures is an indoctrinary threat, but they do believe it is a way for American students to become more globally literate. All the way back in 1989, I knew all about the meanings of such words like jihad, pilgrimage, Mecca, Hinduism, Yin, Yang, Kwanza, Hanukah and Ramadan. I learned a significant amount about other religions, especially Islam. I learned enough back then to know that Islam was another extremely strong, faith-based religion like many other religions in the world that could be used to make peace or to make war! Christians should unquestionably be able to relate to that part. I also learned how Islam acknowledges the existence and the supernatural abilities of Jesus Christ, and that is totally different from the imagery of blood-thirsty Muslim extremists in search of American and Christian flesh to devour. Such fears have become the primary reason why so many Americans fear Islam despite knowing so little about it, but that limited mentality will have to change if the U.S. plans to continue on with its occupying, nation-building, Islamic terrorist hunts, because there is no rational reason why Americans should be opposed to learning about Islam. It's simple! If you're going to do business with the Middle East then you might want to know all there is to know about the business of doing business with people of Islamic faith, who reside in the Middle East. Therefore, it would be mandatory that every student in the United States school system learn about other religions, including Islam, in order to graduate, and I couldn't care less about who this offends. I know there will be mad Christians, mad conservatives, mad Republicans and even a few mad Democrats, but this is something that needs to be done, because being informed is not a crime or a sin. Learning about different viewpoints does not mean an automatic translation into indoctrination or conversion. The United States should not be about the cloaking of information with the intent to deny the freedom of acknowledgement or acceptance. I call it theological capitalism, and anything that limits it is theological Communism! The fear of being challenged is one particular fear that must be overcome if there is ever going to be an unadulterated face-off against any form of terrorism, whether it's global or domestic. Pointless, blind aggression based on pointless, blind assumptions developed from pointless, blind, misinformed fears only serves to lead the lost and the weak even further into belligerent confusion, and that goes for players on both sides of the global pond.

THE BUBBA CHRONICLES

One of the main components of being a Realacrat is being able to state, observe and process the obvious. For far too long, the main two parties have been shrouded in lunacy and denial. Some of it is due to religious pandering and some due to personalized ignorance! Either way there is too much egocentric behavior on display most of the time in this country. In a story similar to the one about the buffoon who hated immigrants, this one is about another absurd idiot who hated Mexicans, gays and African-Americans.

BUBBA VS. THE MEXICAN

I was once working at a seasonal job. It was an assembly line job near Augusta, Arkansas. There were about ten of us on the crew line. One of them was a tall, lanky, big-mouthed, wanna-be cowboy/bull-rider named Bubba! I knew from the very beginning that Bubba and I were not going to get along very well, seeing as how the first thing he ever said to me was, "I didn't know they hired your kind in here." So, I asked of him, "What kind is that?" He then replied back to me, "You know--blackies!" I wanted to get him right there and then, but it was my first day on the job, and I needed the work badly, so I took the high road, and looked past his arrogance and his ignorance; but it would only get worse from there. Work on the line was very demanding and very filthy, and the job turnover rate was always sky-high. This left the door wide open for anyone who might be seeking a job, and one day a Mexican guy named Paco joined the crew. He wasn't a very big man, and he wasn't a very tall man either. He was probably about 185 lbs., and his height was right at 5'3", and I think he was 48 years old. His communication was extremely constrained because of his minuscule ability to speak English, but his work ethic was unbridled and unmatched. He was the kind of man who would continue working through his breaks, and he never slacked off during his shift. Needless to say, Bubba hated this man with a passion. Bubba was so arrogant and such a braggadocio that he wouldn't even converse with Paco directly. He would always ask me or someone else to explain the orders to Paco, because he refused to talk to a Mexican. Bubba had been raised to believe that America was White, God was White, Jesus was White, and right was White. He told me his father taught him all about how lazy, trifling, good-for-nothing Blacks and Mexicans were ruining the country and taking all the good jobs away from the White man, but how can lazy, trifling people take away jobs that require them to not be lazy and trifling? Nonetheless, he characterized Mexicans as some of the worst non-working sleaze-buckets on the planet. He truly believed that they were good for nothing, but a funny thing happened on the way to Bubba's paradise. Every day the assembly line started up like it usually does, and we all went to work. Low and behold, Paco jumps on his job the first day and begins to work well. In fact, he works so well that he passes and then laps Bubba. This went on for about two or three months. Bubba was so infuriated by all of this that he approached the crew leader and asked him to investigate Paco for possible removal. The crew leader asked me how I felt about Paco's work ethic and I told him, "If I was going to fire someone for a poor work ethic, it would be Bubba!" This made Bubba even more infuriated! He confronted me and asked me how I could back a Communist Mexican like Paco? I said to him, "So, now he's a Communist?" I then said, "You are just mad because you've been one-upped by a Mexican. Every day that we have come in here to work, Paco has smoked your ass like a cigarette. It hasn't even been close. Paco is stomping you on this line, not because he is a Mexican, he is not even a U.S. citizen, but because he is a man, while you are just a mouse with a big mouth. You're all talk and no action. The bottom line is this! A 48-year-old Mexican man stomped a mud hole in your redneck ass and then proceeded to walk it dry." I then told Bubba that he was too prejudiced and too biased to give credit when credit is due. He didn't know a thing about professionalism. All he knew was ignorance and unfounded fear.

Bubba vs. the Alleged Homosexual

I wasn't even going to tell this story, but I feel the need to do it. It involves the idiotic Bubba again—only this time his arch-nemesis was an alleged homosexual guy who Bubba hated even more than he hated Paco. By the way, did I forget to mention that Bubba was a tried-and-true religious zealot, a Republican, and a conservative who never missed going to church on a Sunday? His rationale was basic and brutal. Since God hated fags, it was perfectly okay for him to hate and regularly admonish and punish all homosexuals just for breathing. It just so happens that we had a gay, African-American guy who also worked with us. He didn't work in our specific area, but occasionally, he would fill in if a regular didn't come in that day. Once again, the battle lines would be drawn. It would be Bubba versus the gay, Black guy in an "I'm-better-than-you" match, and just like the Mexican man; the gay guy would out-work Bubba by a mile. The gay guy was like a well-oiled machine as he constantly moved product for deployment, while Bubba, slowed and stricken by cigarettes, found himself winded and lagging. He spent the majority of his time cursing the gay guy and belittling homosexuals because that is all Bubba could find to belittle him about. He certainly couldn't belittle him about his poor work output. Bubba had the poor work output category permanently nailed down, and he knew it, but then again; so did everyone else. The gay guy routinely defeated Bubba to the point where I got tired of paying attention to it. But then, it occurred to me how Bubba could be so full of confidence yet so devoid of ability. To Bubba, it didn't matter how hard the gay guy worked, how hard he tried, how impeccable his attendance record was, how focused he was, how efficient he was, how humble he was, how quiet he was, how under-the-radar he was, and most of all, how dependable he was, because Bubba truly believed beyond a shadow of a doubt that he was genetically and religiously superior to the gay guy, the Mexican man and me; the African-American man. Bubba didn't have to work hard in preparation because his Whiteness gave him the edge naturally. All he had to do was show up, and collect the trophy in his mind, because it was rightfully his; despite the fact that he never did anything to earn it. Bubba's greatest fear of being beaten outright by a non-White second-stringer consumed his life enough to make him hate, but not enough to make him prepare, because his counterfeit genetic entitlement told him he didn't have to. If America rallies behind this same entitlement arrogance but on a global level, it too will suffer the same crushing defeat that bludgeoned the ill-fated Bubba. If homosexuality is an abomination, then genetic arrogance has to be one too! If it's not one, it most certainly should be.

The saddest thing about this entire superiority debacle was the fate of the gay guy. First of all, no one truly ever knew whether he was actually gay or not. No one ever asked him either. People placed that label on him, because he was mentally challenged and different, and they knew they could get away with it. I question whether or not the poor guy actually knew what the word gay even meant. Honestly, the only thing we ever knew with any amount of certainty was that this guy was mentally challenged; that much was strikingly obvious. His elevator didn't go all the way to the top, and people punished him unmercifully because of it. This man was gay-bashed for being weird and misunderstood, when in all honesty; he should have been given the key to the city for his work ethic. The fact that this guy could somehow find an employer that would hire him for a job that he could actually understand and maintain was nothing short of a modern day miracle. After all, this guy could only muster about five words on a good day, but he showed up for work every day and worked very hard. Unfortunately, he ended up losing his job, because once again; the gay question arose, as some homophobic hooligan literally beat the living daylights out of him over a misdiagnosed stare. Both of them were terminated, even though the allegedly gay guy never threw a single punch. I don't think he quite understood what was happening to him at that time. He just took his ass-whipping like it was part of the job. The management used this as an opportunity to get rid of him, because they knew he lacked the mental ability to challenge it, and that was the end of the gay guy who, for all intents and purposes, may not even have been gay at all. This scenario, again, reminds me of the Caesar assassination, because he was punished for what he may have been, not necessarily for what he truly was. The bigoted buffoon claimed he felt unsafe around the gay guy and was merely protecting himself, but this witch-hunt was not about the protection of self. It was about being on the popular side of an issue and in the end, this misguided, macho, fallacious allegations-hurling fool cost an innocent man his job and his livelihood based on the fear of being challenged!

Money Talks

Taxes and the Economy

If there is one thing the majority of people in this country do not like, it is taxes. No one likes or wants to pay high-ass taxes. I suppose it's always been that way. Even during the era of Jesus Christ, his fellow disciples and other citizens would complain about the steep hill of taxes. Some even took their complaints to Jesus Christ personally. We all remember the Boston Tea Party. That was blatantly over taxes. And during the run up to the Civil War, northern states wanted to tax the southern states' booming, slave-based, agricultural trade causing bitter dissention between the north and the south, because people take taxes personally. Presidents have been elected into office because of taxes, and presidents have been run out of town because of taxes. I think it was Benjamin Franklin who once said, "But in this world, nothing is certain but death and taxes,"[35] and I believe wise old Ben was right. Taxes are a necessary evil of our society. Our lives as we know them cannot be sustained without taxes and revenue—but then again, what society can be sustained without taxes and revenue? Obviously, taxes are here to stay, but maybe we can find a more efficient pathway to utilization. I don't think it's the idea of taxes that leaves such a foul taste in the taxpayers' mouths. I think it's more about the collection procedures, the questionable executions, the murky authority figures who decide

35 Benjamin Franklin, Famous Benjamin Franklin Quotes, http://quotes.liberty-tree.ca/quote_blog/Benjamin.Franklin.Quote.FE5B (1706-1790).

who, what, and how much; the nonchalant attitude about drafting and enforcing new taxes, the reckless spending of tax revenue, and a complete disregard for the financial status of those individuals being taxed! I'll say it again: the government is supposed to help the people, not help themselves at the expense of the people.

There is no doubt that America is in heavy debt at the moment, and tax revenue will be used towards paying down that heavy debt. New taxes will be created, and old taxes will be raised. In the African-American community, namely the television show "Good Times," They called it the Washington D.C. boogie, where they let you get ahead one step, but then they tax and drag you back two, while the debt and the spending continues to spiral out of control. For example, a worker gets a nice raise in pay, along with a some much needed overtime during the year which provides some extra cash to either put back for hard times or potentially pay off or pay down a delinquent credit card or two, only to see his income moved up into a higher tax bracket at the end of the year, as he's now forced to pay in instead of receiving a refund. Taxes can be effective in the march against mounting debt, but they have to be used creatively and efficiently. Furthermore, a large percentage of taxes can't be collected or raised from people who are unemployed. If your workforce decreases, you payroll taxes decrease with it, which also means overall sales taxes decrease, because people just don't have the money. Does this storyline sound familiar to you? I have to agree with the Republicans. If workforce payroll taxes, which are responsible for a majority of all economic purchases decreases, it would be unwise to then go and increase the overall tax burden. In essence, your bills become greater than the amount you bring home, which could ultimately lead to bankruptcy, depression and recession, and there goes the neighborhood, literally! Once again, does this storyline sound familiar to you? Have you ever heard the old saying, "If you don't work, you don't eat?" Well, that saying is not as farfetched as one might think. The American economy is just like you and me, if we lose our incoming assets, we would more than likely lose the majority of our possessions and be forced to go on welfare assistance—but that very assistance is footed by the working, income-earning force that pay in the taxes that provide the welfare assistance. Once again, if the sheer number of working people decreases and is then forced onto welfare, the number of people requiring assistance will outweigh the number of people who pay to provide that assistance. It's called going broke, and somebody will have to pick up the slack, and that somebody will have to be the federal government, which represents the last line of defense or the critical control point! If the government can't raise enough taxes from a beleaguered and shrunken workforce, it can always whip out the magic printing press and create some more money, or it can borrow it from China! The same ideology could be applied to social security, Medicaid, and Medicare.

I'm not a business major, but to me; it appears that merely raising and creating taxes is not a total solution, and it might even be more problematic than helpful. Taxes are only as sustainable as the incomes that provide them. Hell, we could tax the sun and the moon if we wanted to, but it would accomplish nothing, because the only goal of a tax is to raise money, which means the only object of a tax is something with the means to bring in money. A tax is like a car, and the income is the gasoline, and the tax will not run without it. With this in mind, I would again remind you that I am not a businessman, but to me, it appears that focusing on the tax issue is like treating the symptom and not the illness. The illness here is the inability to legitimately generate money. Maybe we should be focusing on that aspect of the game. Here is simple math. The more employed working people you have; the more taxes that can be collected. It seems as if we should cultivate as many business seeds as we can; all with the potential to expand and grow. We leave all the harvesting details to a locally operated workforce, and then hope for the Wal-Mart/Goldman Sachs mother lode! I think the best thing the government can do is to strive to be just as much of a catalyst for the beginning of this process as it is more than willing to be a financial collector with an overzealous intent to gain off of the end results of this process! Again, I'm not Ross Perot or Donald Trump, but maybe the lack of employment opportunities is not only bad for Main Street, but Wall Street and Pennsylvania Avenue as well.

Stimulus Projects

Right off the top, I have to say that universal health care should not the first line of business. Again, I have to agree with the Republicans on that issue, although I am not against a new health care system. I just don't feel now is the time to incorporate universal health care. The first order of business has to be jobs, because jobs translate into to tax revenue, and tax revenue translates into the financial means to fund government endeavors. So how about some infrastructure to get things going? I've heard that many of these early infrastructure projects have been remote highways, remote and obscure airports, remote bridges, and proverbial bridges to nowhere. Following the Realacrat train of thought, it's not necessarily a bad venture to embark on infrastructural improvement, but it is wasteful and useless to mismanage these opportunities. Democrats have a valid point to pursue these junctures, and Republicans are narrow-minded to criticize to entire idea simply due to partial mismanagement. The government is notorious for being reckless and out of control at times; destroying perfectly valid ideas that could actually achieve something good. Unlike the Republicans, Realacrats realize that it is the lack of true leadership that is at fault, not the ideas themselves. I thought the president was supposed to be a visionary, a leader, a businessman, a decision-maker; and a legislator. Why can't the president pick his/her own policies for the stimulus plan? If you are the President of the United States, you should not have to ask governors, mayors or any other localized, broom pushers for the final say on any legal activity financed by the federal government. If I was President of the United States, I would find my own stimulus projects in each and every state. I would then list them in a hot 100 list—the exact opposite of Sean Hannity's 101 executive waste list.

For example, let's say the Hernando Desoto Bridge in Memphis, Tennessee—no, better yet, the old I-55 bridge connecting Arkansas to Memphis, Tennessee needed some serious overhauling—which it does, because I haven't traveled across anything that rickety since I last rode the old "Zippin Pippin" roller coaster at the now defunct Libertyland. I, as President, would contact the Governor of Arkansas, all Arkansas Congressional members, the Mayor of Memphis; the Governor of Tennessee, and all the Tennessee Congressional members, to inform them of my federal intentions to overhaul the old I-55 bridge connecting Tennessee to Arkansas. Now the mayors and the governors might try to pull a Governor of Louisiana Bobby Jendal or a Governor of Mississippi Haley Barbour by trying to discourage such new stimulus intentions by arguing how the overhaul is unnecessary, but I, as President, would already have done my homework and research, and would know for a fact that the bridge does need work. I would make a bipartisan attempt to work with these local dignitaries, but if they refused to play ball, I would remind them of the Minnesota bridge disaster from a few years back and proceed to literally go over their heads on this issue to put my plan into motion, because there is a time for politics and there is a time to act. These weakened bridges and other pieces of infrastructure are constantly endangering American lives. I believe that a domestic threat should be dealt with just like a terrorist threat. Bottom line: the Memphis, Tennessee I-55 bridge overhauls would commence. This is a major transportation artery in the United States, and it must be maintained. Republicans would be hard-pressed to call this a bridge to nowhere. In actuality, I would more than likely build another bridge over the mighty Mississippi River just south of Memphis, Tennessee creating a bypass that could be utilized as a Tunica, Mississippi exit and a direct route to I-55 South, which would also be a direct route to U.S. Route 78 headed towards Tupelo, Mississippi. The same bypass would extend westward into Arkansas as it merged into I-40 West just south of Forrest City, Arkansas, headed towards Little Rock, Arkansas. The second part of this bridge to nowhere bailout stimulus would encompass another bridge just north of Memphis, Tennessee somewhere in the Millington, Tennessee, area. It would head towards Jackson, Tennessee and then merge with I-40 East on route to Nashville, Tennessee. The flip side would extend west into Arkansas, merging into I-55 North somewhere near the Jonesboro, Arkansas U.S. 63 exit. It would then curve southwest back towards I-40 West, meeting somewhere west of Forrest City, Arkansas to create an I-55 Marion/West Memphis bypass towards St. Louis to the east and towards Little Rock, Arkansas to the west. Another badly needed project would be the hotshot transportation route, which does not include a bridge to nowhere. Old Highway 64 West between Beebe, Arkansas and Conway, Arkansas is a heavily traveled highway. People have been complaining for years about the need for a four-lane upgrade, but progress has been slow. I, as President, during this stimulus era, would not only upgrade the highway to four lanes, but I would make it a short hotshot interstate connector, as it would connect U.S. Route 67 to I-40, completely bypassing such towns as Vilonia, Arkansas among others. I would also build another badly needed interstate hotshot connecting the bustling industrial community of Jonesboro, Arkansas to I-55 North to the east and U.S. Route 67 to the west. And one more thing, I would re-open the Air Force Base in Blytheville, Arkansas. I'm sure the highly intelligent powers that be can find a new and innovative way of utilizing it—be creative!

A stimulus package is just like a man's penis; proper placement and timing can make all the difference in the world, and bigger does not always translate into a desired and satisfactory result. Stimulus can work, if distributed correctly. A stimulus should always be used to meet a challenge or opportunity and to make much-needed improvements. The results of a stimulus plan should have the potential to make positive gains from its development, especially economic gains. I know that there are many who will criticize me for my regionalized examples of infrastructural stimulus, but I am only discussing that which I know from my personal experiences. I am not in position to detail any infrastructure problems in Alaska, because I know very little about Alaska. That would be a job for the Alaskan Governor. I'm only giving you a model to follow. I'm sure every state in the union has just as many, if not more, infrastructure problems as my home state. What governors, mayors, and local legislators should be doing is the same thing I just did, which is identifying the most necessary infrastructure projects and working with the federal government to implement them. After all, some of these projects could take years to build, which would give much needed employment stability and tax revenue to the country. If the state leaders do not like the projects receiving the stimulus, then it is up to them to locate other worthy projects. The federal government should be willing to compromise for a more positive result. And again, the need for strong federal government is evident and clear. If the federal government uses its vision, it will do everything in its power to oversee and assist all 50 states in being more productive for their people, but it must be for the people. The federal government, above all else, must uphold a strict obligation to the people, even when the states become self-serving. If the federal government maintains all of its focus on the needs of the people, it will greatly diminish partisanship.

Red Wolves vs. the Razorbacks

Speaking of revenue, this part of the book that I am about to discuss is literally being added in for the sake of being added in. I am quite literally ramming this section in at the very last minute strictly because I can, I should, and somebody has to! The University of Arkansas in Fayetteville, Arkansas is one of the most storied universities in the nation, and the most storied in the state of Arkansas. My Alma matter, Arkansas State University in Jonesboro, Arkansas; is only a distant second at best. People all over the state have been pushing for years to see a meeting of the minds between the Arkansas Razorbacks and the Arkansas State Red Wolves, especially in football. Here is yet another reason why the stench of broad conservatism sucks!

The state of Arkansas is not exactly a cash cow, and our universities are not exactly amongst the big boys in regards to other powerhouse conferences with much more money. Both of the major universities in the state of Arkansas could always use an increase in revenue, so you would think that an economic, cooperative endeavor would be just what the financial doctor ordered, but not necessarily! What we end up getting is a selfish, conservative agenda meant only to preserve the status quo and the elitist hierarchy that comes along with it, but less money for the state means less money for the state, even if the big dog is still getting more than the not so big dog, who looks to one day pull even with him.

Every year the University of Arkansas Razorbacks will schedule a non-conference team from a much smaller division, but usually; there will be a couple of Sun Belt Conference schools like Louisiana-Monroe, North Texas, or Troy. These games are almost always played in Little Rock, Arkansas; so the smaller, less-revenue stacked, Sun Belt schools can claim the attendance towards their attendance record, not to mention the fact that these Sun Belt schools are also getting paid a huge amount of money just to come Arkansas and play the University of Arkansas Razorbacks. There's your cooperation!

Backwater buffoons would rather pay schools from rival states, who routinely outspend and out-recruit them, to come in and play non-conference, tune-up games against the Razorbacks, instead of playing an instate, non-conference, Sun Belt school, and keeping all of that revenue money within the state of Arkansas. It sounds like a good idea, but pick-up truck driving hicks say no. They want things to remain the same; the way they've always been, because that's what they are accustomed to. They don't want to threaten the pecking order, even in the face of financial gains within a bad economy! Conservatively speaking, since these two schools have never met in football, we should just keep it that way, but liberally speaking; counter-productive traditions should be abandoned for newer ones that have the potential to be productive. Why hold on to a dog that won't hunt, when you are in the business of selling dogs that do?

Play the f*cking game! Replace one of the other Sun Belt schools from out of state with the Arkansas State Red Wolves, and give them those same breaks that the Louisiana-Monroe's have been getting, at the expense of the state of Arkansas. Stop trying to live in the stone ages of the University of Arkansas, Northwest/Central Arkansas, good-ole-days, where only the Razorbacks do well, because the athletic, Jim Crow system has been rigged to ensure that they do. I've heard rumors that Arkansas Governor Mike Beebe, an Arkansas State alumni, like myself; was going to push to make this game happen, but rumors only create talk, not results! So as we say in the streets—"Governor Mike Beebe; man you ain't showed me nothing," at least try to get a statewide dialogue going. Play the f*cking game! Bryian R. said that to you!

New Revenue

Everyone is so concerned about the United States' growing deficit. I even heard Glenn Beck speculate that it is now so out of control that we won't ever be able to work our way out of it. Maybe we can! Maybe we cannot, but we most definitely aren't making any progress with our current directions. Even if we can't work our way out of it, we can still work on it, depending on the directional ventures of the leadership we've entrusted in Washington—which at this moment looks bleak. I'll agree with Glenn Beck on that observation, and I'll also agree, to a certain extent, that the United States, in all likelihood, cannot work its way out of this enormous debt, although I do believe doing something is better than doing nothing. I believe some progress is better than no progress. The first thing I would do is drastically cut spending in Washington. Until we do that, it truly will not matter what programs we develop, because any gains made by the new programs will automatically be consumed by massive spending on crap. This is like trying to lose weight. It doesn't matter how much you diet, and it doesn't matter how much you exercise. Until you cut your caloric consumption, the weight will not come off. So the spending has to go first. After that miracle is accomplished, I will incorporate what I call the "Fed Lottery!" Yes, you heard it right; a lottery owned and operated by the federal government, but funded by you and me. It could be held once a week or once a month, but the proceeds would go to either the deficit or health care. Do you remember the big sign that was once put up to display the national debt? The numbers on it were constantly increasing to show the nation how fast our debt was growing. Well, I would copy that same sign, but my sign would be decreasing the numbers to show the rate of how much we are paying it down, even if it means we are only slowing the rate of its acceleration; that's still better than what we have right now. If state lotteries can raise tons of money for educational scholarships, roads, and government official's salaries, then why can't a federal lottery raise money for the debt or health care? Some will say that it will not work, but it is already working. Some will say they don't like the government sponsoring and endorsing gambling, but I say that it's time to act, even if it means the government moves into the gaming industry. The American people love to play the lottery anyway. Why not allow them to play towards their very own debt? Taking a page from the NBA, NFL, and MLB playbooks, a salary cap will be installed on this federal lottery. Let's say the winner can only receive 10 percent to 25 percent of the total earnings no matter how high the big payoff goes, but that number is flexible, and it will be non-taxable income for the winner. Therefore, once the federal government has garnished its part, the remaining 25 percent will belong strictly to the winner without any further taxation. I would guarantee the winner a minimum lump sum of at least $2 to $10 million no matter what, but then again, these numbers are not written in blood. The bulk of that money will go towards the debt or health care, as its primary purpose. I would also allow for companies to donate money to the "Fed Lottery," as if it were a charity. Any company that offered up a donation would be given a charitable tax break. I would also make it mandatory that all government employees, at every level of government, would have to participate financially, including the President. If politicians can go on junkets to China and Broadway shows in New York, then they can most certainly contribute to this cause. If the winner turns out to be an elected government official or a government appointee on the federal, state, or even local level, the winnings would be distributed to the taxpayers of that individual's home district. The details can be tweaked and re-arranged. I'm only giving you a model. There would have to be a government website overseen by the finance committee (or some other committee) to make sure the American people can log in at any time to see their lotto money being plugged into the debt or health care. This program can be successful, but it has to be overseen correctly by the government. Finally, some sort of legislative restriction would have to put in place to disallow the distribution of this income towards anything except the national debt or health care.

Vice Profits

It's no secret that medical marijuana has been legalized in states like Colorado and California. Nevertheless, the federal government has not legalized it and on occasion has put legal pressure on medical marijuana vendors in these states. Republicans always stomp for state's rights, but not necessarily on this cause, due to their follow-the-leader mentality and their self-righteous, religious backers, who oppose it, because they think it is a sin. When in all honesty, running up the national debt for the next generation should be an even bigger sin, whereas remaining economically inactive twiddling our thumbs about it because of erroneous, religious fears should be an even bigger sin than the previously mentioned sin. Religious, toilet scrubbers will argue that God does not like medical marijuana, and we should abandon it completely. Did God tell you this personally? Well, in that case, the next time you talk to him; could you please ask him for a debt-solving portfolio from Heavenly Financial? Maybe they can figure out how to solve our economic problems. I mean, let's get real! God hates marijuana, but he endorses cigarettes and alcohol? You will never find the Puritan business plan on Donald Trump's desk, on Bill Gate's desk, or on Vince McMahon's desk. There is a time to go to church, and there is a time to go to work. The economy needs revenue, not prayer. In the Realacrat world, now is the time to brush all religious idiocracies to the side in favor of more economically based thought. Drastic times call for drastic actions, and this is one of the most drastic economic times in American history. It's now time to free ourselves from the religious shackles that have severely hurt our ability to raise revenue, due to trumped up Christian ethics. So I propose the vice profits agenda. Others have suggested this as well, but I would not only endorse it, I would employ it immediately.

Just like the Fed Lottery, all revenue raised from these vices would go directly to paying down the debt, supporting health care, or some other urgent economic need, whether at the state or federal level. Once more, we find ourselves right back here at the intersection of state rights vs. the federal government, because there will be states that will not want any vices made legal in their jurisdictions despite the current economic difficulties being suffered at the time. These are the types of individuals who believe they can pray their problems away. These are the types of individuals who believe that Jesus Christ will melt the financially frigid hearts of the bill collectors and the repo-man! No branch of government should be publicly buying into this theory. Now, I don't think we ought to go around murdering people to raise money, but I do believe that medical marijuana should be made available in all 50 states. I would even go so far as to legalize marijuana all together! Of course, that would open the door to further debate, but that's just it. This issue deserves to be seriously debated and rigorously weighed as a valid, economic option. It is not the church's job to chaperone you or me. That job is ours and ours alone. The government already grows its own marijuana. I would rather buy government-grown marijuana before I'd ever purchase it from Johnny- Cum-Lately in the alley. The federal government would be in charge of all of the transportation, distribution, and cultivation of medical marijuana, or marijuana in general. The same laws and restrictions that apply to public alcohol consumption dangers could then be applied to marijuana as well, which in return would significantly increase tax revenues through sells and fines!

And speaking of alcohol, all outdated, outmoded laws about the prohibition of alcohol sales on Sunday would be overturned at once, whether states liked it or not. Not selling alcohol on Sunday is a religious-based doctrine, and it should have been thrown out years ago. You tell me what the difference is between being liquored up on Saturday, Monday, or Friday, as to being liquored up on a Sunday.

Hell, most people are liquored up on Sunday anyway. You just aren't allowed to legally purchase any alcoholic beverages on Sunday, because it's the seventh day—but wait a minute! Sunday is the first day of the week, and Saturday is the seventh day of the week. So what kind of logic are we dealing with here? Let's see if the vendors are down to stop sales of alcohol on a Saturday, since it is the true seventh day. I'm sure that one will fly like an ostrich on a titanium zeppelin, which brings into question the authenticity of this whole argument. The seventh day prohibition is okay to parade around in some dog and pony show—as long as it doesn't fall on the biggest alcohol purchasing day of the week. So to remedy that, we just simply moved the seventh day to Sunday. This wasn't done for Jesus. It was done for business and profit. Well Realacrats would do the sober, Sunday, bootlegger enhancers one better by abolishing the seventh day prohibition of alcohol nationally, and we wouldn't be doing it for Jesus either. We would be doing it for the same reason that Sunday became the seventh day—for business.

Other vices could allow for even more money to be raised. I was once a heavy gambler, a strip club frequenter, and a whore house regular. There is no doubt that I was a very lonely man looking for human contact or social interaction. The funny thing about this scenario was the fact that no matter when I frequented any of these so-called morally, hideous establishments, I always found myself surrounded by legions of lonely guys, and more recently--gung-ho women. My point is this. There is a need by lonely people like me that could be filled legally and for profit. I, like many others, risk my freedoms to satisfy my urges quite often, which means that someone is profiting opulently and driving off with all the money. I'd say it's probably going to be the underground market. Why not have it go to the government, where it could be taxed and utilized towards health care or the debt? Like Amsterdam, we should treat some of these vices as business and not character markers. I mean, how is it any more acceptable to journey out into the Nevada dessert to satisfy these same vices than it is to satisfy them regionally? This is more religious hypocrisy. Some of the very Christians from the Bible belt who campaign staunchly against vice gratification go straight out to the state of Nevada, Mississippi, or any other state with gaming or vice options and indulge themselves under the cover of obscurity and the 150/500 mile rule, which is an unwritten rule used by hypocritical bigots who claim to be religious, where they are allowed to indulge in unlimited sin, as long as it is at least 150 to 500 miles away from their home base!

It's time to remove the veil. First, we apply the happy ending vice code. Any massage parlor that wanted to participate in granting happy endings would be allowed to do so. It would be operated in a similar fashion as the bunny ranches. Outercourse should not be illegal, which means any sexual gratification not involving the exchange of body fluids into any orifices and no penetration of any kind. The government does not have to force any state to install any of these vice-oriented places, but the option should be available for any state that wants to pursue it; meaning, the states could enact it at any time, because the federal government would make the option legal in all 50 states. The key word is option. Realacrats, unlike Republicans, conservatives, and religious zealots, are unafraid of options. Options are choices, and choices belong to the people. We don't need some Puritan, Pat Robertson, 700 Club chaperone to tap my hand with the blue-eyed, White Jesus, witch-hunt ruler every time I reach for a slot machine or a call girl. It's time for religion to get out of the sexual chaperoning business.

Term Limits

I know there is a strong chance that none of these programs or ideas will ever see the light of day, but what if they do? What is the purpose of enlisting creative well-thought-out plans when the next airhead will just waltz right into the White House in the next four years and practically dismantle them? Naturally, there are pros and cons in any system, and this is one of the cons in our current system. While limiting the number of terms that any president can serve is a great tactic to combat dictatorships and monarchies, it is also a horrible tactic when pertaining to the preservation of any incumbent successes. In other words, our permanent cycle of politics could always resemble this: four to eight years of prosperity and cooperation followed by four to eight years of debt and recession. One guy puts it up! The next guy comes in and tears it down. With this gridlocked scenario, any progress made will automatically be cancelled out by the next buffoon waiting in line. All it takes is some idiotic mooncalf drunk on religion, greed, or power to come in and halt any program he or she deems too inappropriate, like the half-witted preacher who said he'd rather have the country broke economically, but completely with God morally. I say we should be economically prosperous at all costs, because we're about as close to God as any of us are ever going to be, while here on earth. I mean, realistically: how close can you really get to God without dying to prove it?

It's time for some new ideas specifically designed to deal with an ever changing world. Because of that, I would incorporate the "Don't Rock the Boat" rule, which would basically say that any program that has been proven to work in the past and continues to work in the present will be given the opportunity to continue working into the future. For example, if we are able to construct an economic plan that begins to put dents in the deficit, improve health care, and improve the economy as a whole, then that particular plan will be amended to continue its course as is, even if it is in defiance of the next president or the next Congress. It's already pitiable that we often have to trade in a diamond for a dime or a donkey for a jackass. Just because an individual can only serve two terms should not mean that his or her potential economic surpluses should only be allowed to serve two terms as well.

More Efficient Economical Government

No one group has the all the answers, not even close! I know there are quite a few who like to beat their chest meaninglessly, but they are nothing more than blow hard puppets. I shudder to think about the alleged righteousness of either political party in this country. There are many who like to argue about ethics and religious convictions, but these ideologies can become a serious handicap in the world of business, and the United States has to be seen as a business! The Realacrat motto is simple: "Take care of your business, or your business will take care of you!" The same way that Republicans are steadfast about water boarding a terrorist, I'm steadfast about making sure the country makes more than it spends! In this new millennium, we need a party that will quickly look past any outmoded laws that could be overturned to create economic stimulus. Instead of investigating whether or not to remove the slogan "In God We Trust" from all currency, we should be creating new industry to help people earn even more currency, whether they trust in God or not.

As Erdell Revoner once questioned me, "Why hasn't the government done more in the realm of the fixable?" Some of these areas are definitely fixable, but very little has been fixed or done. She speculated that the corporate-driven, uber-rich controlled government has no real intentions of creating more jobs in any significant capacity. It appears that this old dog is relying heavily on an old trick commonly used to make sure that the rich stays rich and to make sure that the non-rich and the poor are contained, especially in regards to minorities. Just look at the historical and perennial unemployment statistics for them as opposed to that of Whites! We might trust in God, but we live and operate for the preservation of the man based status quo, because there are just too many missed opportunities at play here.

While conservative politicians stomp for a constitutional amendment that would make the only legal marriage: a marriage between a man and a woman, I say legalize gay marriage and make money off of it. There is no right or wrong here, as far as I am concerned. There is only surplus and deficit! The use of taxpayer money to investigate whether or not Bill Clinton got a blow job is an absolute deficit! We spent millions of dollars to find this out, when I could have told you that for free! It does not matter who instigated this, whether it was Republicans or Democrats. What matters now is that it has to stop—pronto! No more taxpayer-funded investigations into steroids in professional sports. You hear that Joe the Plumber? The government, including some of your Republican cohorts, spent our hard earned tax money investigating the possible consumption of steroids in professional sports, when I, again, could have told them that one for free, and you wonder why the country is bankrupt. Then, we hold high paid hearings on Barry Bonds' and Roger Clemons' ability to tell the truth. The total cost of those congressional hearings on the Mitchell report should be tallied and sent back to the taxpayers. The more I watched it, the more it felt like and smelled like a political, grandstanding earmark, because the federal government had no business getting involved in baseball. I guess Bud Selig was too impotent to get it up, so he dialed up an order of Congressional Viagra, and we paid for it—what a joke and a waste of time! If Bud Selig can't do his job, then he needs to be fired; plain and simple! Selig should not be getting paid millions of dollars to hide behind a big, fat desk when the truth comes out. If the government has to step in and clean up the steroid era, then what in the hell do we need Bud Selig for? I now understand why conservatives don't want big government; although, I don't think big government was the problem here. Even if it were only one congressman participating in all of these egocentric hearings, that would still be one congressman too many costing the taxpayer another dollar too many. It isn't size that caused congress to hold these imbecilic hearings. It was the misguided leadership in Washington. The government needs to be far more efficient, more energy efficient, more financially efficient, more emotionally efficient, and more militarily efficient.

This is inefficiency at its best! What we have here is gross decadence and a severe loss of reality— Realacrat reality! The government should spend more time creating riches for the people, not becoming rich off the people and wasting their hard-earned tax money congruently. Political witch-hunts waste millions of dollars on bullsh*t! The hiring of Ken Star was all about politics, not at all about a truth-finding mission. Such investigations are political grandstanding amplified as another diversion to ward off logic. If I can mesmerize the sheep dogs into passiveness with a distraction, then no one will ever notice, as I raid and pillage the economic hen house. It is the one thing that I agree totally with Glenn Beck, Lou Dobbs, and Bill O'Reilly on. The governmental hosing of the American people has to end, and the citizens of America have to stop sleepwalking.

Conservatives believe a smaller government would mean instant gratification, but I'm not convinced! First of all: you can capsize a Jon boat, if you have an incredulous cretin for a captain. Size does not guarantee anything, but quality, on the other hand, goes a long way on the road to success. The tragic sinking of the Titanic didn't happen because it was too big to fail! It happened due to apathetic observations, poor planning, reckless behavior, and a grossly over exaggerated sense of self-absorbed greatness, which is the equivalent of some farfetched idea of self-regulating egocentrism, which sounds eerily similar to economic meltdown of 2008! The asylum is only as sane as the inmates who run it. The same sentiment can be applied to Congress, because many members of congress have received their status from other ideologies, not necessarily common sense or rationale.

The search for true elucidation is not always giving what's wanted, but sometimes giving what's needed, instead of some popular party-based answer that inspires a thundering applause from political constituents. Usually these responses are more of a scripted stump speech than a credible solution. Big government is the villain of the month right now, and the conservative movement will vigorously trumpet anything hurled at it, because this is not about finding the truth; this is about finding a leader to get behind. The truth is more of a question than an answer. How is it possible to have an efficient government that's not too small and yet not too big, but is just the right size to be effective enough to function at a high level while delivering a satisfyingly, pleasurable result? Even though some say women don't belong in government, this particular question is one that they have been grappling with for centuries—only in another dominion. They may be able to find a plausible solution regarding this matter much more effectively than men.

I'm not a woman, but I'm also not Forrest Gump either, because as the old Prince song goes, "Something in the Water Does Not Compute!"[36] I don't understand how sane, articulate, educated people can sit back and make the assumption that big government is incompetent just by its very nature of being big. Since when did the definition of big translate into ineffective? Just because something is big, it does not mean that it does not or cannot work, and you don't have to be a rocket scientist to figure this out.

The corresponding view of this too big to work argument is the idea that small things automatically translate into production, which is also insane. The only person who would suggest or guarantee anyone that simply downsizing to a leaner version will automatically resolve any problems of ineffectiveness is probably a used car salesperson who just happens to have an unusually high number of sedans vs. gas guzzling SUV's. Smaller government can't always be the answer any more than expanded government can always be the problem.

This entire argument is deficient of basic logic, which leads me to believe that there is something more here than smart conservatives

36 Prince, "Something in the Water Does Not Compute," 1999, 1982.

trying to pass asinine ideologies. I do believe conservatives think smaller government is better, but not for the reasons previously stated about efficiency and effectiveness. In my opinion, the smaller the government becomes, the less the tax burden should become, because a smaller government just will not have the functioning capacity to demand the same heavy, tax burden as big government. The government could still be as ineffective as it ever was, but people will be happy, because they will be able to keep more of their money, which is a good thing to a certain extent. But any way you look at it; certain programs will have to bite the dust! Sure, there would be no more corporate bailouts, but that also creates the possibility of a severely diminished Hurricane Katrina bailout as well. Keep in mind; I witnessed quite a few snobs laughing at the poor, dumb Blacks stuck in New Orleans during Hurricane Katrina. If the government were any smaller during that fiasco, who knows what would have happened? I don't think it's any secret that social programs would be on the chopping block first, foremost, and often, because it's most definitely not going to be the military. So anyone receiving government assistance should be concerned. We've all heard Republicans, conservatives, and Tea Party members go on and on about President Obama and his socialist agenda to spread the wealth around to his ethnic buddies in the welfare lines, but if the Tea Party and the Republicans can find a way to drastically shrink the government, you won't have to worry about the wealth getting spread around to anything outside of the rich and the powerful. The economic discrepancy between the rich and the poor will skyrocket. We'll probably end up with an economic system somewhat resembling Haiti, where there will be multi-million dollar mansions on the affluent side and pitiable huts on the other. There will be very little in between. It could turn into every man, woman, and state for themselves! Some other entity will have to step in and take up the slack for a weakened federal government or all hell could break loose.

Republicans will be quick to point out the role and the strength of the private sector, as they argue for more business and far less federal government interference. Between 2008 and 2010, the banking industry has faced monumental collapses, monumental bailouts, monumental greed, and now monumental disdain for their unethical, arrogant chutzpah to be stingy about lending out the very same taxpayer money that bailed them out in the first place. Remember, the private sector is supposed to be good, according to conservatives. It's supposed to straighten itself out, as long as the corrupt government stays out of it, but the banks aren't straightening themselves out—they only appear to be lining their pockets with our money! In my eyes, the private sector is just as vulnerable to corruption as any other sector. The private sector is only in business to serve one purpose, and that is to increase dividends. Anything else is suspect, which leaves America with an intriguing dilemma. Who is going to watch the cookie jar? Inevitably, I think it will have to be big government. In the end, you'll probably have Kenneth Lay watching Bernie Madoff, but that's still probably a better than worst case scenario, but with new, upstanding leadership like the Tea Party, maybe the government can become less like a Kenneth Lay and aspire to be more like a Pete Rose! It's reminiscent of the bear story, in which a bear is chasing two guys through the woods. The question is a simple one! How fast do you have to run to escape becoming the grizzly bear, lunch buffet, and the answer is: you only have to run faster than the guy behind you! Well, the same principle applies here. In order to stabilize the economy with jobs and prosperity, we need to eliminate corruption, at least to the point where the government is corrupt-free enough to contain and regulate an economically corrupt industry.

For instance, it wasn't the private sector that ended American slavery. The private sector got rich off of American slavery! Their only question revolved around how much cotton could be sold and how much cotton should be taxed! It was the federal government that eventually ended slavery, because the private sector will support business first and morality last—dead last—and even though the federal government was just as motivated by economic prosperity as the private sector, it, at least, did the right thing by ending blatant slavery, despite the strong possibility that if the South had not seceded its economic resources from the union, slavery would have probably not ended, at least not during that cycle of history. The government, under Abraham Lincoln, proved that it could be less corrupt than the private sector and have more of a conscience than the private sector. I think that when the government ceases to be any aspect of a conscience for the people, it will truly be game over for the United States in regards to all political parties!

THE HEALTH CARE ISSUE

THE HEALTH CARE QUESTION

I remember well when Bill Clinton was elected into the White House back in 1992. I voted for Bill Clinton. He was from my home state of Arkansas, and he was governor for most of my adolescent life. I felt that his ideas could turn the country around, and I also felt that he would bring a different perspective on American life, a new equation to work for the American people in a brand new day. There was nothing more radical at the time than First Lady Hillary Clinton's nationalized health care plan. When I say this was extremely radical at the time, I couldn't be more serious. Just the idea alone was enough to send social shockwaves throughout the political spectrum. Republicans, conservatives, and many religious zealots were up in arms over the mere possibility of nationalized health care. The Clintons might as well have been peddling cyanide to children, the way right-winged politicians carried on about it. It was already more than apparent that Republicans and conservatives hated First Lady Hillary Clinton, and they despised her health care plan that much more. The plan of nationalized health care intimidated the Republicans, the conservatives, and the rich, in fear that it would potentially afford poor, ethnic groups better health care. Also, the fact that an intelligent woman most certainly had drawn up such a plan intimidated these groups, and shook their White-male-dominated hierarchy to its core. This all but ensured the demise of Hillary's health care plan from the very start. I remember when Rush Limbaugh, who had a television show on at the time on which he mocked President Clinton, used this hideous rap song to desecrate Hillary's health care plan called "Womb to the Tomb," [37] where he belittled Hillary's health care efforts as nothing more than socialized medicine put together to give medical welfare to the poor and the lazy. The thought of every American being able to afford universal health care overseen by the government royally pissed off Rush Limbaugh and his constituents. In the song, the lyrics basically implied that truly impoverished people who really do need some financial assistance to help cope with high medical bills should be forced to fend for themselves. It's not the government or the taxpayers' responsibility to cover any medical expenses incurred by private citizens, including taxpaying citizens. In a nutshell, I guess what Republicans and Rush were trying to say was this: why should the government provide health care for any individual starting from birth and ending at death, especially when these same individuals will more than likely lead poorly fit, high-cholesterol, grossly obese, cigarette-smoking, alcohol-guzzling, dope-smoking, gormandizing lifestyles, not to mention consuming all of the dangerous and malnutritious preservatives and steroids pumped into food? These are chemicals that will extend the life of foods, but at the same time shorten the lives of the people who purchase and consume those foods. Basically, we can make a Twinkie live for a 1,000 years, but we can't make people live for 70 years! Dangerous preservatives and unhealthy lifestyles have definitely taken their toll. If an individual refuses to be responsible for his or her own health, then why should the government have to pay for them? How can you expect the American people to live healthier lifestyles when they know the government, no matter what, will bail out all of their medical bills? It destroys the total concept of personal responsibility.

I have to admit that the Republicans made some valid points, and they eventually won the battle, as First Lady Hillary Clinton was forced to watch her plans of nationalized health care go down in political flames into bi-partisan hell. The Republicans and conservatives emerged victorious, while President Clinton suffered a major and crushing defeat. The ludicrous ideology of a nationalized health care system was left for dead. It appeared that it would remain that way forever—but then just

37 Rush Limbaugh, "Womb to the tomb," Bill & Hillary Parodies, (1993).

like First Lady Hillary Clinton, the idea of a nationalized health care system was resurrected in a totally new arena, with a totally different audience. With Barack Obama's election, the debate of nationalized health care has been given a second wind. During the Clinton years, the Republicans won the battle, but they did not win the war. In 2009, the Republicans prepared to do battle again over this issue of who deserves womb to tomb coverage. In 2009, the economy was in a wretched predicament, and it seemed very unlikely that the government would ever be able to afford to fund a nationalized health care system—and maybe it can't! Maybe, womb to tomb is not the answer right at this very moment, but there must be an answer and idleness is not it. How can the possibility of some people receiving womb to the tomb health care coverage create such an outrage, while the reality of others not receiving any coverage at all from the womb to the tomb is just a sad inconvenience? I guess you have to pray that you can hold on to your job and your health insurance so your trip from the womb to the tomb won't be any faster than it already is.

I will use myself as an example. I am considered to be working class, and I do have health insurance. I pay for it every week out of my paycheck. The actual amount is approximately $43 a week, and I make under $40,000 a year. The main argument I hear is in regards to the people who work for a living just like I do, but cannot afford to pay their employee-based insurance premiums. Whereas I pay $43 a week, others making less are allegedly forced to pay even more a week, to the point where they cannot afford it. I suspect these individuals are minimum wagers or those with salaries close to minimum wage, and it's my understanding that many jobs of this nature don't even offer employee insurance. This is the group the government should be focusing on, along with the uninsured, so let's deal with the lower income level workers first. Paying $43 a week is probably too stiff for the average lower income worker and it ain't no stroll in the daffodils for me either, but I manage. Fast food corporations, hotel chains, grocery chains, restaurants, retail stores, and gas stations are allegedly the worst offenders, where people work twice as hard for less money, and then can't afford to get sick or go to the doctor because many aren't offered insurance through their employer, or simply can't afford the premiums they are offered. For example, employees of Exxon Mobile, even down to the lowest level, should have a minimal health care cost. Companies such as Wal-Mart, McDonald's, Exxon Mobile, and the Hilton Hotel franchises are definitely capable of providing ample health insurance—and especially able are the companies that have been bailed out recently by taxpayer money. AIG should have the best health care coverage in the nation, just in case one of their employees gets injured at one of their bonus-laden paradise getaways. These corporations bring in billions of dollars so don't tell me they can't afford to have better coverage for their employees.

Instead of the federal government mandating a must cover policy to the employer, they should work with the employer to help cut and control the costs. Let's use my $43 a week insurance payment as the basic amount. The government could pay a portion of that $43 a week to lower the payment, helping to drop it to a more affordable amount for the lower level employees, which could be somewhere around $12 to $15 a week. It may seem small, but every little bit helps, especially to working people. The federal government could possibly even split the cost with the state government. Health care should not be free. People should pay something towards their health care, because it is their health. The goal should be to make it more affordable. It should be a leaner and meaner health care system based on the same demands the Obama administration handed down to the car companies. Reducing a weekly payment from $40 to $10 or $15 would be a definite improvement, starting out.

I have a $20 co-pay to see a regular doctor, and a $40 co-pay to see a specialist. I also have insurance help if I am admitted to the hospital for any kind of care or surgery, and I possess a prescription card that helps me buy my medicine. With that being said, even with all the coverage help I receive, there are still certain medicines and treatments that I simply cannot afford to sustain over the long haul, and I'm insured. Most of the time, after I run out of my original doctor's prescription, I am forced to go to Wal-Mart in search of a cheaper generic brand that I can more easily afford with my limited budget, because my insurance will only allow me to purchase a specific amount of medicine in a specific amount of time; no more, no less. Nevertheless, I am able to get by on my current system. The reason I say this is simple. I don't think the health care debate should necessarily be about people in my position. Employed individuals, like me, are quite capable of surviving on our own for now, barring some catastrophic health-related disaster, like terminal cancer or something of that nature. If I, like many other Americans, suddenly find myself incapacitated by a debilitating disease such as terminal cancer, only then should the government step in to help ease the cost and make sure my insurance company doesn't get economic cold feet and drop me. Governmental regulation by itself could help cut costs enormously. Womb to tomb is not really needed for people in this situation—maybe banana peel to the tomb, but not necessarily womb to the tomb. I support the government giving better tax write-offs for medical expenses and medicinal purchases, but that's about as far as it would go for me and others like me at this time. I would have to be a complete heel to go around crying about my not so perfect health care plan when there are people out here who truly have nothing to speak of and none to seek out! So, by Realacrat standards, health care assistance should be given to the uninsured first and the poorly insured next. I think this entire plan will face its toughest challenge trying to sort out what to do about the uninsured and the poorly insured, with their barren health care landscapes. Do the uninsured and the impoverished deserve to have womb to tomb coverage? If there was ever a group that did, I think this group is it, but still—do they deserve it? Does poverty entitle anyone to womb to tomb coverage—and if so, who is going to finance it? Can you say the word taxpayer? Who else is going to do it, and does anyone really deserve universal health care? As a Realacrat speaking, I say no, they don't, because I don't think anyone deserves it unless they absolutely are physically unable to take care of themselves. I don't think we should charge disabled people lying in vegetative states, but I'll charge a lazy dumpster who lies around all day in a vegetative state.

Doughnut Dana and the Dumpster

Before I address the question of whether anyone deserves womb to the tomb coverage, I will enlighten you all with a couple of true stories. What I'm about to bestow upon you, "The Dumpster/Doughnut Dana Chronicles," are two stories about some rotund, corpulent women who were professionals at milking penises and the system, usually both at the same time. Let's take Doughnut Dana, as an example; she could put away more Krispy Kreme doughnuts than Fat Albert and Jabba the Hut combined. This overweight, piggish woman was the absolute epitome of irresponsibility and gluttony, not to mention astronomical deceit, which was all charged to her insurance company and eventually charged to her fellow comrades through higher premiums and more diminutive coverage's. Doughnut Dana was a Mormon woman living in Wynne, Arkansas, who worked at a major, shipping carrier, but she spent more time at the doctor's office than she did at work. She was addicted to painkillers and prescription drugs. Despite her huge demand and consumption of this pharmaceutical plethora, her overall health was continuously plummeting. The more she charged the drugs to her insurance, the weaker and feebler she seemed to become. Her insurance quota was going up, but her actual health was spiraling down. This was the kind of person who was sick all the time. Nationalized health care would go broke just trying to accommodate this hypochondriac junkie. Doughnut Dana will personally drive up the cost of employee health care for as long as she is employed, because her condition will never improve. She'll personally see to that. This individual was off work for months on disability for some unknown, undiagnosed illness, which she could not legally prove she ever had in the first place, and this was the fourth or fifth time she had pulled this scam, and been off for numerous months each time. We're talking about two to three years of disability for a person that was never really sick. Basically, this female charlatan claimed to have some phantom muscle and nerve damage that rendered her unable to perform her laptop-related duties. That's right: all she had to do was be effective on calculators and keyboards and hand out occasional paperwork, but she refused, saying it was too painful. So, she went on disability for almost nine months, and get this: during the entire period, her doctor was never able to diagnose or treat her phantom injury, and until this very day, she is still charging her insurance company for medicines to help treat her undiagnosed injury when she was never actually hurt in the first place.

How do I know? Doughnut Dana showed up one day at the drop yard office during her disability retreat, wailing in pain over her sore upper body, her limp arm that she can hardly move an inch, two bad knees, a torn calf, possible throat cancer, a bad heart, a hint of cystic fibrosis, and a fractured pelvic bone. After she's wailed and moaned for about an hour, she uses that limp arm to open the door and walk out—but it gets even worse. About a week later, a high-ranking official decided to take a vacation at Magic Springs in Hot Springs, Arkansas, and you'll never guess who she spotted. She saw Doughnut Dana with her family riding the log ride, and flailing her arms through the air. It had only been a week since Doughnut Dana was hobbling with limited upper and lower body motion, along with her mangled appendage that she could hardly even move. The high-ranking female officer said she and her family watched as Doughnut Dana rode anything she could fit on, and as she physically moved around the entire park with ease, laughing and giggling the entire time, never once showing any signs of injury. Other employees even claimed they saw Doughnut Dana changing a flat tire on the side of the road during her time off. And right now at this very moment, Doughnut Dana has a new injury that she is using to lobby for even more months off on short-term disability. She is also shopping around for second and third opinion doctors who will refer her to a new specialist so she can get her highly anticipated knee surgery. Just the other day, she called one of her former doctors a loser, because he refused to carry on with this charlatan shuffle. He suggested that more exercise and fewer doughnuts would be more effective than new surgery, but Doughnut Dana got mad and called him a medical moron and a quack! Now, she is demanding a second opinion, which she will hopefully obtain from some new doctor/quack who is willing to do another possible surgery, while the insurance company prepares to partner up for the ride, with visions of across the board higher premiums dancing in their eyes.

Now, is this fair to me or to other members? My weekly premium has gone up and up almost every year, while I have used the bare minimum of my health care insurance; nonetheless, my coverage has just recently decreased. I haven't even been forced to meet any of my deductibles yet, but by the time I actually find myself needing any serious health care assistance, I could possibly end up paying twice as much as Doughnut Dana did for less coverage. I will, in essence, be punished for being too healthy for too long, while Doughnut Dana will have paid less for being far less healthy and far more corrupt. Doctors and insurance companies could stifle much of this, but why would they, when they stand to benefit from it? How many Doughnut Danas do you know? How many Doughnut Danas can the government afford to give womb to the tomb coverage to? To Realacrats, if Doughnut Dana is so willing to throw the universal, health care, taxpayer, money down the fast food, Krispy Kreme toilet, then some of her own money needs to take the big plunge with it.

The next con artist I met was Bertha from the trailer park. This was a fat, portly, musky, ill-bred individual; the absolute worst I'd ever seen. I nicknamed her the Dumpster, and yes, I dated her. My life was that bad. It caused me to question the existence of God and the value of my ability to breathe. This woman was a 30-year-old professional slacker. She didn't have a job, a purpose, a bar of soap, a high school diploma, or a driver's license. All she did all day was hang around out on a stump, watching the cars go by. She wouldn't even clean up her body or her room, and she ate like food was going out of style. Her ignorance was the greatest of all time. She didn't even know the significance of Washington, D.C., and she thought Memphis, Tennessee, was the capitol of the United States and Barack Obama was the mayor. All of this was undoubtedly terrible, but it didn't stop there. Apart from being a full-time slacker, she was also a professional hypochondriac. This was her excuse about why she couldn't hold a job, or even apply for one. She was always sick, and she was always at the doctor's office. Hell, she even went to two specialists. She had a slew of prescription drugs, and she had a slew of illegal drugs. How does this relate to health care you ask? Well, I didn't really think about it either until I saw her and her mother in Wal-Mart one day. They had at least two shopping carts full of supplies, and I mean full! Dumpster waddled up to the checkout line with her mother, who pulled out a food stamp card to pay for it all. Now it all made sense to me, because I had been perplexed at how this non-working slob could afford so much merchandise. So, I began to wonder: if the government is paying for her victuals, is it possible that the government is also paying for her HEALTH CARE? Later on, she informed me of her next trip to see the doctor. This time it was a specialist. She was scheduled to see the kidney doctor first and the diabetes doctor second. So I asked her point blank: "How can you afford to pay for all of these expensive specialists you see routinely?" She then proceeded to whip out a Medicaid card, and I was completely floored. I was paying for her health care. While the nation fought and bickered over universal health care, this lazy woman already had universal health care, despite having never worked a day in her life. So while unemployed workers struggle to make ends meet with no insurance at all, this rotund, buffet-plowing, fat ass sits around without a care in the world waiting to see the next specialist. I guess her economic budget never changes, because it is provided for by the government. And to make matters worse, her mother didn't work either. She was disabled by a bad foot and a bad hand, and she, too, was getting medical assistance from the government. I was paying for the mother's health care too. How many people all across this nation live this lifestyle at the expense of the taxpayers? Not only do we have to pay for our own health care, but we have to pay for someone else's health care as well. Maybe we should all be more generous when it comes to helping to shoulder the load for the less privileged, but there is a big difference between shouldering the load and carrying the entire load, which is what we Realacrats oppose. People need to pay something for their health care.

Universal Price Gouging and Profits

So on one hand, you have Doughnut Dana and the Dumpster excessively manipulating the system and running up costs, and on the other hand, you have the health care industry itself providing a counter-attack by grossly overcharging, with $25 charge for Nyquil and a $15 charge for a Bayer aspirin. When is the last time you were admitted to the hospital? Did you get a good look at the bill for a television, a private room, personal care, food, and basic hospital practices? And as far as the emergency room goes, you had better be making over $250,000 a year to afford that cost, and may the Lord be with you financially if you ever have to take a ride in an ambulance or a helicopter. The entire health care system is notorious for massively overcharging the public for any and everything possible. So who is benefiting from all of this enormous overcharging? If I was a betting man, I'd say the insurance companies, pharmaceutical companies, and the actual administers of health care, including doctors, specialists, surgeons, nurses and other operative fields that work directly under these higher-ranking professions are all profiting from it. No matter how you look at it, the facts are clear. Hospitals are like casinos. Their job is to take your money before they, in some cases, take your life. It's like a strip club. You can hardly get in without money, and you definitely won't leave with any money, because hospitals have one distinct advantage over casinos, and that is; a large number of people are born in hospitals, everyone will more than likely have to visit a hospital, and almost everyone will end their lives in some affiliation with a hospital. In other words, birth, sickness, and death pretty much affect all people. All hospitals have to do is sit back and wait like a big, Nile crocodile waiting for the annual wildebeest crossing, so they can financially gorge themselves. Just as crocodiles don't regulate their voracious appetites, the financial crocodiles choose not to regulate theirs as well—but somebody will have to attempt to regulate this industry. Otherwise, the oil-like, price gouging will only escalate. It's a tough job, but government has got to do it, and incorporated competition would be a great start. Anything to help cut cost would be a huge improvement. So no matter whom you are, you will meet the taxman and the doctor, and you will pay significantly for both.

The health care providers are directly benefiting from the corrupt pricing in the health care system. Why do you think so many people raised their daughters to go after doctors as the ideal mates? It is because the cost of health care is sky high, and they knew doctors had to be receiving their fair share of that pie? This is why doctors are frequently sued. Many of the lawsuits are frivolous, mainly because the goal is not ethical; it is financial, because doctors and nurses are all thought to be financial cash cows, whether they are or not. To help out the doctors, the government could set up a frivolous law suit committee, which would be composed of average citizens, insurance industry workers, government officials, and health care enablers to try and develop a basic model for compensation based on malpractice, with professional negligence being the harshest. If a doctor or other health care enabler is guilty of gross incompetence, they should be held accountable to the fullest capacity. It's the suing of the doctor for giving you Robitussin when you asked for Nyquil that has to be stopped.

The Sick Make Great Customers

I've heard White people complain for years about the welfare system in this country. I haven't heard many African-Americans complain about it, because the majority of us benefited in some way from the welfare system. So I never had any feelings towards welfare one way or another until I met the Dumpster. After witnessing the impoverished lifestyle of the Dumpster and her mother, it became evident to me how this was nothing less than medical welfare, prescription welfare, pacification welfare, and misdiagnosed welfare, and it was costing the country millions. From my observations of Doughnut Dana and the Dumpster, I quickly came to the conclusion that neither of them was as sick as they claimed and hoped to be. Yes, I said hoped! Here is my theory. Neither of them was actually sick; no sicker than you or me. They had learned to substitute the lack of human, sexual admiration for medical care. The sicker they could convince people they were, the more they hoped to have people feel sorry for them and pay them some attention—especially sexual attention—all at the expense of the health care system. Besides Doughnut Dana and the Dumpster, I knew at least seven other people just like them, who were always sick, always at the doctor's office, always popping multiple prescriptions, always sick enough to lay around the house, but never too sick to get laid. Both Doughnut Dana and the Dumpster, who claimed to be permanently ill, would hobble around moaning all day, until someone came along and offered them the kind of sexual healing that Marvin Gaye sang about so eloquently. Once that happened, the miraculous recovery would begin. They could lie in bed for hours at a time popping prescription pills and claiming to be sick, but when a sexual opportunity or a nutritional opportunity came along, they could go longer than the Energizer Bunny. They were too sick to work, but they were never too sick to copulate, get drunker than Ned the Wino, get higher than an astronaut, play Grand Theft Auto all day, or devour food as if they were fresh off a hunger strike. You can't tell me the doctors who serviced and enabled these mentally depressed patients could not recognize that the problems were more psychological than physiological. The doctors increase demand, and the insurance companies drive up the premiums and the prices, while the diabetic hypochondriac takes the next available trip into anesthesiology land with one suitcase full of prescription drugs, courtesy of Dr. Feel Good and another suitcase full of Big Macs, courtesy of Ronald McDonald. We spend huge amounts of money misdiagnosing or mistreating problems with no intentions of improving them, while true victims with real injuries and real health problems have to wait in line, because their health insurance is either non-existent or too cheap to provide the necessary care. You can't cure depression with stomach medications, which brings to light a very important question. How many people in this country are being routinely and purposely misdiagnosed just because they make great customers?

So, who is responsible for this pharmaceutical chaos? One thing we do know is that pharmaceutical antics have seriously helped to drive up the price of health care in this nation. Realistically, we have to hold doctors and nurses accountable, because without their assistance, none of this would be taking place. Doctors and nurses are supposed to be professionals in the medicinal landscape, but it seems to me that many of them have become nothing more than junkie enablers or FDA-approved, prescription pimps. Is it any secret that there are numerous health care workers out there that simply do not care about the patient, but instead what the patient represents, which is a golden opportunity to charge insurance companies and make money? As the old saying goes, "If you can find something wrong, doctors can find something to cut on!" After all, it all pays the same to them. Doctors and nurses know full well how piling claims onto the insurance companies will only drive up the price for everyone else, but they don't seem to care. The allure of the almighty dollar has ultimately made that decision for them, while nurses enable and abet treatment-happy doctors.

Profiting From Addiction

The second part of the hypochondriac issue is the severe addiction to treatment. With the Michael Jackson tragedy, I've heard quite a few people talking very badly about his addiction to painkillers and prescription drugs. But the question is this, how many people like you and me are in the very same addiction boat that eventually destroyed Michael Jackson? The answer to that riddle is probably hundreds of thousands, and most; if not all, have some affiliation with insurance. Whereas Michael Jackson may have had enough money to pay for his prescription drugs and personalized treatments, the average hypochondriac is piling all of their treatment on insurance. These are the types of people who cannot function without using drugs, and their numbers are in the hundreds of thousands. People like Michael Jackson, Rush Limbaugh Doughnut Dana, and the Dumpster all represent the hundreds of thousands, if not millions, of people out here who fully understand the physical risks involved with uppers, downers, muscle relaxers and addiction, but are unable to escape its grip. This nation is full of Michael Jackson's and Rush Limbaugh's. How can one ingest such huge amounts of drugs without becoming addicted? How can doctors and nurses not have any idea these patients are either already addicted or headed in that direction? Money talks, and the rest walks!

I can only imagine how much money all of this is costing. We could save millions of dollars on health care by bringing these shake downs under control, because the ones receiving all of this medical treatment are quite often the ones who really don't need it. This is nothing more than the exploitation of prescription addiction, and the cost is staggering, while the idiotic government spends all of its money on the Mitchell report, so they can investigate A-Rod's medicine cabinet. There is no way that steroids in professional sports is costing anywhere near the millions of dollars that prescriptions drug addiction is costing; not even close. Instead of tackling a real problem like the this one, the government and the media would rather establish some sort of meaningless holy ground from which to grandstand and sensationalize professional athletes who use performance-enhancing drugs; not because it is an epidemic that threatens the population, but because it is a way for politicians to act like politicians, as they normally do, by missing the bus on real issues. They are too preoccupied with chasing lame-duck issues, and the media only appears where the ratings will be the highest. Ask yourself a very simple question. Why did Congress and the media hold hearings on Capitol Hill in order to investigate Roger Clemons' alleged B-12 shots? Why don't they hold hearings to deal with the plethora of legal, drug-dealing, doctors who write out prescriptions like African-American crack dealers hand out crack? After all, when you hear about a drug dealer on the street corner, your first inclination is to classify him or her as African-American, when the problem is much bigger and much more widespread than that, and so is the other problem!

Keeping Them Honest

The cost of health care is out of control. As the Republicans say, it's time to cut spending, but as the Realacrats say, it's time to stop killing ants with an elephant gun. This brings me to the "Dumpster Rule." Under the Dumpster Rule, anyone receiving government assisted health care or disability would be subject to a thorough investigation, not only before they receive benefits, but during and after they receive benefits—long after! Anyone receiving government assisted health care or disability would be subject to random drug testing as well. Whoever failed these tests would have two choices. They could either go to rehab or be dropped from the program until they chose to go to rehab. They would also be subject to random physical examinations by independent doctors, other than their own personal physician, in order to get an accurate diagnosis of the individual's health status. If a person was found to be ill, but not ill enough to be disabled, the government would place that individual into a special job placement program, where only limited and light duties are required. It would be a job like shaking hands at Wal-Mart or passing out food at a shelter. This may seem cruel and heartless, but is it really? The reason I would have these characters do something is the same reason Republicans and others hate the welfare system. No matter how much nationalized health care we produce, a healthy, lifestyle based attitude cannot be legislated or lawfully imposed. After all, we can't have the health police going around writing tickets for unhealthy living. This is why anyone who is not disabled will have to undertake some form of responsibility, even if it's community service. The reason is a practical one. Each individual should have to pay something into their own health care plan, because it is their health, not the government's health. If the dumpsters of the world chose to disregard their doctor's health guidelines, but continue to flock at his office for check-ups and prescriptions, they should be held financially accountable. What better way to try and convince people to invest in their own well-being than by forcing them to put their own money towards it? Even that may not work, but it sure beats the hell out of the scenario we have right now.

Should We Cover Everyone?

As much as I hate to admit it, I have to agree with the Republicans on this one. I am against free, universal health care, at this moment. Universal health care is not necessarily a bad idea, but there are other contingencies, like the ones previously mentioned, that have to be addressed first, because the same corruption plaguing the current system will only continue to plague the new one, when it is finally introduced. The price tag for this nationalized health care will be astronomical at best, so we should be on a mission to contain and abolish as much fraudulent corruption as possible. As a Realacrat and an employed citizen, my suggestion is this. Only the uninsured should be the focus of the entire universal health care net. The government should not under any circumstances be forcing anyone off of their current coverage and onto any new nationalized coverage. The coverage I and many other employed people have is okay for now, and since many of us are employed and paying towards our own health care, there is no rational reason for the government to be planning out some sort of massive, coverage rearrangement on our behalf, when we can make it on our own at this point. If the government must attempt to implement its coverage plans, it should undoubtedly be on the uninsured only, which would lower the health care price tag by a ton. The way I see it is elementary! Why toss out floatation devices to the passengers who already have floatation devices, when there are people without them drowning right in front of you? The uninsured are the ones who need help the most, not employed people like me who already have decent insurance. Therefore, I don't think the government should even be promoting universal health care at this point. They should be developing and promoting a new health care plan called the "Uninsured Health Care Plan." Why don't we make an effort to deal with them first? If we can find a way to fund the coverage of at least 50 percent to 75 percent of the uninsured, I'd call that a vast improvement compared to what it is in existence right now. In fact, I'd call that an outright success story.

The Republicans have made their case about the crappy care provided by socialized medicine programs in Canada and in Europe. Americans are afraid they too will have to endure this crappy coverage if the United States produces its own version of socialized medicine. According to Republicans, Americans will be forced to wait in long lines (unlike the long-ass lines we already have to wait in now for the damn doctor), certain drugs will not be available, the frequency of prescription purchasing will be limited, the choice of doctor will be limited, the choice of hospitals will be limited, the choice of certain types of care will be limited, and the overall quality of care will be severely limited. At best, I think the government should produce a basic, health care plan to deal with the bare essentials. In reality, it probably shouldn't be an extravagant health care plan, because we Realacrats do not want to see the total elimination of the private sector from the health care business. What we want is competition, but we don't want a one-sided competition where the government dictates and monopolizes the overall health care market. We also don't want a one-sided competition, where one or two companies dictate and monopolize the overall health care market, even if it means the government creating or funding a handful of health care companies and then selling or granting them over to the private sector to ensure that a monopoly does not happen. By Realacrat standards, the profits from sales such as these belong to the people and would be distributed to them, not through tax cuts, but honest profits. The same way President Obama said he didn't want to run the car industry is the same way he should not want to run the health care industry either. The government's role would be better served as a health care safety net that, at the same time, can encourage and spur on competition within the private sector. The basic government health care plan should be good, not necessarily great—just good enough to urge coverage competition. The overall destination of the government and the people should be regular, non-governmental health care. The less the government has to get involved--the better. The government should just work to keep the private sector honest, not destroy it. If the government can make a serious dent in the corruption behemoth that wreaks havoc on the current health care system, there may not be a need for nationalized health care—at least, not as grand of a program as the one many have suggested.. To put it lightly, government's main objective should be to regulate and improve the market, not monopolize it.

The Realacrat Plan

So let's throw the notion of nationalized, mandated health care out of the proverbial window. I like some of the ideas brought forth by the Obama plan, such as non-denials for pre-existing conditions, the possibility of imported drugs from other countries, and the elimination of clientele being unwarrantedly dropped from their coverage, although I would endorse the Republican's call for interstate coverage competition. I just don't like this plan's mandate of including everyone. A Realacrat's idea of a health care system would be like this. We would offer a basic health care plan called the "Safety Net" program that would mainly focus on the millions people who don't have coverage, including underprivileged children whose parents can't afford coverage, unemployed workers whose health care benefits have ended, workers whose employment does not offer employer-based health care coverage, anyone claiming to be too disabled to work, but who are not yet receiving government assistance, and those who have insurance that covers less than a FEMA umbrella with a gaping hole in it—good job Brownie! The Realacrat plan would also keep unemployed workers covered by their employer's insurance for up to two years after they have been laid off, if they are still unemployed. Just for hypothetical purposes, let's say the going rate will be $45 a week for the health care premium. During the first year of the lay-off, the government would pay over 90 percent of the health care weekly premiums, leaving the unemployed worker to pay about $10 a week to remain insured. During the second year, the unemployed worker will be forced to pay somewhere around $35 a week to remain insured, as the government begins to ease its way out. By either the third year or the depletion of unemployment funds, the government will be completely removed, and the uninsured worker will be forced to pay the full premium. Only then can the unemployed, uninsured worker either drop or be dropped by his current employer based insurance, and apply for the government safety net plan, but unemployed workers could continue to use their employer-based insurance premium plans after their unemployment runs out by replacing it with savings account money or 401k assets, if they weren't able to be on the government safety net program. The choice would belong to them.

The basic premise of the plan would be to provide help to those unable to help themselves. The goal would be to place as many unemployed workers as possible back on employer-based, health care, even if it meant giving huge tax credits or bailout-like incentives to employers to help ease the costs. If we could at least put a dent in the millions of uninsured, I would consider it a major success for the country and a great start, because there is nothing more promising than progress, even if it means combining our plan with the Obama-care plan—but only towards the uninsured. Nevertheless, we will ensure that poor people have affordable coverage opportunities.

This basic health care plan would be just like any other government assistance program, because anyone who wanted to participate would have to apply for it. It would not be mandated. It would be optional, because Realacrats believe the government should produce an optional, health care, program that acts strictly on the basis of the safety net theory, seeing as how any of us could spontaneously arrive at the safety net at any unannounced time. The safety net program would be in place to stop me or you from hitting the ground face first, but only if we choose to utilize it. The only exceptions would be in the case of children.

Any uninsured, healthy, human being who did not feel the need to apply for this health care coverage could always choose not to. There would not be a governmental penalty for that action, and they would be held financially accountable. Whenever this uninsured individual was forced to go to the emergency room or to the doctor's office for treatment, they would be totally responsible for the footing of the bill. If they choose to be uninsured, they can pay the full amount. Enforcement of this policy will be based on the child support, collection models. The uninsured person will have a financial trail attached to them that garnishes portions of their wages and all of any income tax returns, state and federal! If the uninsured person captured a second job or a third job; they, too, would be garnished in a wage capacity and all tax returns would be also absorbed. If the uninsured person refused to work, they would be subject to the same ramifications as deadbeat parents who fail to pay child support, which would then lead to a possible trip to the county blues/jail. As long as they remained incarcerated and unable to pay their uninsured, health care debts, a serious lien will be placed on everything they own for collateral purposes, and everything they earned while incarcerated would go towards their debt. Realacrats would even go so far as to tax any governmental assistance being received by the uninsured dolt, including social security benefits and possibly even pensions. I know this may sound harsh to corporate Democrats and in-the-pocket Republicans, but any healthy individual who signed his name next to the "None for me" insurance policy would be absolutely allowed to turn it down, though the physical and financial responsibility could come back to haunt them..

The government option would not be the only one available. The safety net plan would actually seek out other health care alternatives before settling on the safety net plan, if at all possible. If the government could locate a private sector insurer, then it would at least have to offer that possibility to the individual, because the private insurer may work out better, depending on the circumstances. The more people the government can divert to the private sector, the better. This is why the government will help to develop more private insurers or universal nation-wide access to all insurers. The government would regulate activity to make sure the system remained fair to the customers and not just lucrative to the companies. The government's goal would be to remain a last resort. After all, the government is going to win regardless, because whether you choose the private program or the governmental program, all of the money finds its way back to the federal government anyway.

The Government's Role in the Realacrat Plan

The government would have no say in which doctor you could or could not see, but a second opinion would be available to detect any evidence of fraudulent favoritism by an enabling physician if the patient has a long history of applying for disability. The government would not be allowed to erroneously kick anyone off of his or her current coverage. The government would not install death panels. The government would not decide when to pull the plug on grandma. The government would not deny access due to a pre-existing condition. The government will not demand, take, or publicly distribute your private medical records. The government will not delay or negate care to save money. The government would endorse the influx of cheaper drugs from other places to spur on pharmaceutical competition, and the government would assist to make sure that poor people didn't have to pay over $90 per prescription for a couple of bottles that only last a month.

Now, I'll tell you what the government would do. There is an organization called Remote Area Medical (RAM)[38] that travels the world to supply free health care to those unable to receive proper treatment for whatever reason it may be. Some are uninsured, and some are poorly insured. RAM was originally established to service Third World countries, but it now services many right here in the United States, picking up the pieces where greedy insurance companies have either left off or totally abandoned their people. For that reason, the Realacratic health plan allows the government to step in and assist RAM in covering what the insurance companies do not. You won't even have to be on the government plan to be helped, because the ultimate goal is to diminish the number of people who are forced to resort to RAM, and increase the number of people who are completely taken care of by their private insurers. You can remain on your own personal insurance plan and still be assisted by the government plan for a small fee—or possibly even free of charge.

---

38 CBS, U.S. Health Care Gets Boost From Charity
"60 Minutes": Remote Area Medical Finds It's Needed In America To Plug Health Insurance Gap, http://www.cbsnews.com/stories/2008/02/28/60minutes/main3889496.shtml.

For example, let's take the now infamous AIG! Suppose I'm on the AIG plan, and I need a procedure that AIG won't cover. I can go online, and file my necessary health care procedure with the government, option site. The government will then contact AIG to see if they will not cover this procedure, and then the government will cover the expenses, so I can be treated. It appears that AIG, who was bailed out in 2009 by the federal government has skated again, but wait—not so fast! The government strikes back by taxing AIG at the end of the year for every thin dime of uninsured coverage it has been forced to carry in AIG's absence, and it doesn't stop there! The government will also tax any and all bonuses given out by AIG, because under the Realacrat plan, if AIG is too cheap to fully cover its customers, then it ought to be too cheap to cover any CEO, high-rolling-employee, greedy, fat cat bonuses. Republicans and corporate Democrats probably won't like this idea, but they can all kiss my country, Black, stereotypical ass!

My Medicine Is Too Expensive!

I use a certain drug to treat a breathing related illness/pre-existing condition, and this medicine is most certainly on the cutting edge. Even though I have insurance, the only time I can afford to utilize this specific, doctor-prescribed medication is when I go to a physician and receive free samples, which I exploit eagerly, happily and graciously, because I cannot afford to purchase it due to the highly expensive cost. One bottle, which lasts me for about one month, costs me about $90, and that's with my insurance and that's only one form of medication. I'd really be stressed to the maximum if the doctor gave me two or three prescriptions to buy. People earning less money than me would really be up the creek without a paddle or a toilet, and the uninsured couldn't even talk about buying medicine. Like I previously stated, I simply go to Wal-Mart and buy a cheaper generic version to help me get by until I can see my doctor again and receive more free samples.

So the Realacrats have devised a plan that once again does not require anyone to be mandated on the government option. With this new plan, even the fully insured stand to benefit from what I call the "Pharmaceutical Bailout Affordable Deductible Plan." In it, a person making under $40,000 a year would owe a medicinal deductible at the first of every year of about $150. Once this amount has been met and paid by the consumer, the government and the private sector insurance companies will work together financially to ensure that all medicinal purchases from that point on will only be $10 to $20 per prescription, and any drugs the insurance companies refused to pay for would be paid in full by the government and fully recouped through the taxation of that particular company, through bonuses or year-end profits.

Coverage Abuse Guidelines

Now anyone who decided to participate in the government safety net program would have to apply, and then be approved. Once approved, new measures would be put in place. First, anyone receiving the safety net program benefits would be subject to a random, drug testing policy. Like I said before, anyone who tested positive would face the consequences. Secondly, the parents of any children receiving these benefits would be subject to regular check-ins to monitor the health of the children and the possibility of parental neglect. Thirdly, anyone who is unemployed, claiming disability and receiving the safety net benefits would also be subject to random drug testing. They will also be checked out thoroughly and clandestinely. Anyone applying for disability that has not received it yet could enter under the safety net plan, but they had better not be caught roofing a house or doing some other strenuous activities. Anyone proven to be fraudulent would be immediately dropped from coverage and possibly prosecuted. Obviously, none of this would apply to truly disabled individuals who cannot care for themselves. This is strictly for the dumpster frauds that use a sprained wrist as an excuse to claim disability and not work. Fourthly, anyone able to go out and work would be made to do so, because they would have to pay something towards their own health care. In other words, if you weren't physically disabled, you would be working somewhere. Fifthly, all participants in this federal, safety net program would also be subject to further independent medical and psychological testing. The higher the frequency of safety net insurance usage, the more likely one would become subject to these independent, psychological, and medical probes to help break-up the buddy, doctor system, where a patient can receive a favorable, but not credible or accurate, diagnosis from their personal doctor, who would intentionally misdiagnose a condition to help that patient qualify for some form of disability, even if the patient was definitely sick, but not nearly as sick as the diagnosis.

This has to be looked at, and if at all possible--rectified, because these individuals could be prime candidates for improvement. All of these dumpster characters I've met were definitely in bad health, but they were not so far gone that they could not make a full recovery with proper doctor supervision. With proper exercise, proper diet, and psychological care, I would estimate that about 80 percent of these dumpster characters could become as healthy as any other healthy person out there. This usually does not happen, which leaves only two options for these dumpster characters. Disability would be one of them, and the other would the sometimes long and expensive road to death. Some of these individuals draw disability for years when they are absolutely healthy enough to work, until their declining health finally collapses on them, as they find themselves financially snowballing towards physical end. The allowed spiraling of patients into the health care abyss is unacceptable, and someone needs to be held accountable, and that someone should not be the taxpayers. We should not be financially responsible for enabling the epidemic corruption of health care for profit, by the patients or the doctors, through some form of universal, mandated, health care; when it is clear that over half of these cases can be corrected, which would absolutely cut costs. Optional universal health care is a decent idea, but everyone will have to contribute something to make it work.

Who Pays For This?

As I have previously stated this book, Realacrats would create new forms of revenue to help fund this health care project, and higher taxes would not be eliminated from the discussion. In fact, higher taxes would be a reality of the discussion. I hate taxes just as much as the next man, but I understand that taxes are the political DNA of our society and government. So why waste time dreaming of some far-fetched scenario where taxes don't exist? Let's be realistic. Every employee in the United States would pay an extra five dollars a week in federal taxes. Every person receiving any financial government assistance would automatically have five dollars deducted from their weekly payroll. Small businesses grossing under $200,000 a year that carry insurance on their employees would pay in ten dollars per week. Companies like Exxon Mobil who annually post multi-billion dollar profits would be taxed at the end of the year. If a company grossed $10 billion in a year, it would have to pay $1 billion in taxes, specifically to health care. If a company grossed $100 billion a year, it would have to give $11 billion in taxes to health care. All of this would have been included in the bailout stipulations. Entities such as Wall Street and AIG would have been pulled to the side before any bailout money was ever handed out to discuss the possibility of financial preparations to go towards health care coverage, so all parties involved would have an idea about exactly what was in the works for the country.

The next order of business would be to find a way to capitalize on the high number of illegal immigrants who work in this country, so they, too, will have to contribute financially to health care. I mean, there is an enormous amount of extra revenue that could be generated from such a project. All we need is a way to tap into it—and I have another Realacrat idea that just may work. It would be called the "You pay, and we look the other way" rule; meaning, all American businesses that utilize the services of illegal immigrants would be held financially responsible to document each illegal employee and then dock them five bucks a week on what Realacrats would call a guest worker fee, which would go directly to the federal government for health care. If American businesses agreed to this, they would not be hassled by the federal government to relinquish their illegal workforce—but if they did not agree to this, they would be sought out and financially investigated and taxed accordingly to the tune of $20 per illegal employee. Now, I know there are many Hispanic Americans that won't like this proposal, but charging a $5 a week guest worker fee is not as bad as it may appear, because even the illegal workers could find themselves in the emergency room at some point in the future. At least this way, some of their own money will be used to help them, and not just the revenue of the American taxpayers. Some people will be up in arms over having to pay an extra five bucks in federal taxes, but I believe five bucks is not that bad, considering the possible financial benefits. If the Realacrat plan is successful, people will make those five bucks a week back and then some, and at least this way; everyone is contributing to the cause, from the filthy rich to the filthy poor, and even those people on governmental assistance. The health care fund would be frozen for five years before it could be enacted, in order to allow as much money as possible to collect and build-up. All budget surpluses from this health care fund could only be borrowed to assist other health care programs like Medicare, because Medicaid may no longer be a factor.

Illegal Immigrants and Abortions

I'm sure the whole world has heard by now about the infamous incident of Congressman Joe Wilson of South Carolina. The words: "You lie," echoed throughout the Congress at President Obama during his address to Congress on health care. President Obama was attempting to make it totally clear that his plan would not, under any circumstances, allow free health care benefits to illegal immigrants, but Congressman Joe Wilson was unimpressed. Allow me to be perfectly clear, just as President Obama was trying to be. The Realacrat Plan will not give free, health care benefits to illegal immigrants under any circumstances. As I've stated previously, if illegal immigrants want to purchase health coverage with their own money, it is their prerogative to do so, but health care will not be distributed in the form of a free government hand out, and not one thin dime or one pathetic penny will come from the American taxpayers. In fact, speaking as a Realacrat, I believe there should be a special system set up to specifically deal with illegal immigrants. Anyone who is not a U.S. citizen would have to use this system to acquire health care, and the health care system from which we are currently trying to escape is the system I would use to insure illegal immigrants, which is basically buying it straight from the insurance companies, but the rates should be recognizably lower than previous rates. The government would not get financially involved. My Realacrat advice to illegal immigrants would be uncomplicated: if you want better health care opportunities, you will have to become a U.S. citizen or become documented.

President Obama also came under intense fire and scrutiny as charges were leveled against his plan, suggesting outright that Obama's plan would use federal money to fund abortions. This is the most phony, hoax-driven cause in the Republican brand. Nevertheless, the Realacrat plan would not be used to federally fund abortions unless the mother's life was in danger. That's right, if a doctor prognosticated a condition that could kill the mother and abortion was the only solution, it would be covered under this plan—but an abortion doctor at an abortion clinic could not make that diagnosis. It would have to be made by an emergency room physician or a family doctor. Now let's get one thing straight right here and now! Realacrats are not doing this to kiss the corrupt, self-serving asses of the Republicans, because Realacrats don't give a rat's ass about a Republican or their totally biased, genetic entitlement, religious doctrines. I care as much about being in the religious pocket of the Republicans as I do about being in the religious pocket of Osama Bin Laden. Realacrats will not succumb to religious kryptonite, whether it's from old, Christian, White men or young, Islamic hot heads! Realacrat opposition to opps abortions being covered in the new health care plans continues to follow the basic non-religious, Realacratic motto of paying for a want and only being assisted for a need. In other words, if you want an abortion just to be free of a baby, you should have to pay for it—all of it.

RAM: It Could Be You!

So let's discuss this patriotic organization called RAM, which has to be one of the greatest relief systems we have right now. Whoever is in charge of this endeavor should be given a medal of honor. In fact, Realacrats would demand legislation that forces every federal government employee to donate to RAM, which would include the president and the Congress. Realacrats would go so far as to relegate a yearly donation bailout specifically to RAM. We would also require every mayor, every governor, and every state senator to donate to RAM, because you never know when it could be you!

America is supposed to be the greatest country in the world, but now I'll tell you a story showing exactly why we continue to struggle. I was discussing the RAM program with ten bigots, ten Republican bigots, and they had never heard of it! When I told one of the bigots about the sheer number of people in Knoxville, Tennessee, and Los Angeles, California, who waited all night long, and how some were forced to sleep in their cars in 20 degree weather, the young, Republican, hot head started to crow viscously about how the poor, dumb, welfare monkeys got what they deserved, and he didn't want a penny of his Christian money going to insure any of them. So I then pulled up the

RAM footage from *60 Minutes* on my computer and showed this racist something he was not prepared to see. He looked at the RAM footage, and to his amazement and dismay, he saw the unthinkable, which were poor, uninsured White people waiting in line with the rest of the poor African-Americans, poor Hispanic-Americans and other poor minorities. The racist bastard was so flabbergasted that he dropped his head in shame and walked away. That's the problem with this country; morons living in the past! I once wrote a song called "What Yo Hood Like," where I rapped the line: "Violence is a mentality that can't be blocked off into a particular hood." Today, I just replace the word violence with poverty, because neither of them can be contained only within the poor or minority domains. Only a dunderheaded fool would believe that it could be. It's the same sentiment that fed the belief that Aids was just a gay problem. America will have to come to grips with the fact that epidemics don't discriminate, and they will eventually affect everyone. Health care is no different. It's not just an African-American problem or just an occasional, poor, White problem. It is an American problem, even if it appears like it only affects people who don't look like you! There once was a rap song called "We're all in the Same Gang."[39] How long is it going to take America to figure that one out? Health care is everybody's business, and fixing it would benefit all of us.

With that being said, I think it's about time for the uninsured to stand up and speak up. I mean, where are all of the uninsured people who can't afford to go to the doctor? Why aren't they out protesting, yelling, and screaming? All I ever see are conservative, insured, whiners throwing bigoted, temper tantrums about death panels. Where are all of the Democrats, the Pro-Obama supporters, and the moneyless disenfranchised Americans who find themselves praying for a RAM sighting in the area, so they can get treated? Why are all of these entities remaining as silent as church mice at an alley cat convention? Why is there so much reluctance to show any sign of steadfast support towards the president that the majority of these individuals voted for? Is it the fear of the erroneous, self-absorbed, God flag that Republicans gesticulate so proudly and disproportionately, or is it the proverbial nation of cowards once again being too chicken-sh*tted to own up

39 West Coast Rap All Stars, "We're All in the Same Gang," We're All in the Same Gang, http://www.youtube.com/watch?v=wXGgWf2lacM (1990).

to President Obama without some voter booth, veiled curtain to hide behind? While I see tea party/Obama protestors by the hundreds, the only thing I see from the Democratic side are politically, meek, church mice and Internet, tough guys. As Governor Schwarzenegger once put it, the Democrats, their supporters, and the uninsured should all stop being economic/political girly-men, because health care is something that can and will affect each and every one of us at some point in time. So you might as well develop an opinion, grow a set and get involved! Nevertheless, Realacrats have no intention of waiting for your courage and your conviction to kick in. Realacrats don't drink coward juice. If you are too dumb to know what all you care about and too scared to do anything about what you do know that you care about, then we Realacrats have no use for you!

POLITICS

PRESIDENT OBAMA AND THE DEMOCRATIC LEADERSHIP

So where are the Democrats on this one? I'm not even going to inquire about the Republicans, because this should be a Democratic issue. How the lame duck Democrats have allowed this one to fly under the opportunistic radar is beyond me. The Democratic Party should be all over this RAM story. The Democratic Party should be part of this RAM story. They should have aligned themselves with RAM from the very beginning, to the point where they should be going around to the media crowing about it as much as possible to hopefully begin to drown out some of the relentless, fear-based, Republican crowing. After all, the best way to fight bullsh-t is with better bullsh-t! While Republicans were tagging President Obama as the next Hitler, the Democrats should have been showcasing their newly found partnership with RAM, as they personally assisted the health care needs of those millions of uninsured people. What the hell are they waiting on—the Republicans to backdoor them out with another politically offensive maneuver, because you know they will. Where is Howard Dean? Wasn't he once in the medical field? He should go to RAM and volunteer! And for that matter, President Obama should also go to RAM to witness the situation personally. I shouldn't have to tell you this! I'm just a poor, dumb, uneducated, grammatically incorrect, socially underfunded, and ethnically challenged African-American! My ignorance and undesirability is astronomical, but even I have enough sense to realize the Democrats have both Congress and the White House, but the Republicans seem to have the one thing Democrats don't have; a pair of balls and the testicular fortitude to act! The Democratic Party is in political limbo, and the corporate Democrats are in somebody's pocket, because there is no good reason why the federal government hasn't publicly and financially stood behind RAM. According to the leader of RAM, the organization is privately funded. Well, I've got a Realacratic idea for you! If I was the federal government, I would donate money to RAM. It would be tax-free money in the form of a charitable donation. If the government can give away money to other countries around the world for a good causes, why can't it give away some of that money right here at home, to RAM?

The ferocity of this health care fiasco has caused me to re-evaluate some things, starting with President Obama! I've seen and heard some strange things during this health care, reform era. I've seen people draw pictures of President Obama with a Hitler moustache, and I've seen manufactured pictures of President Obama hanging out with Hitler. I've seen guys showing up at health care rallies with assault weapons. I was at a mini-health care rally recently where I was warned about the Obama/Nazi death tunnels. Yes, you heard it correctly! I said death tunnels! The government-run health care system would lead the old and the sick down the death tunnel into a gas chamber where they would be gassed to death to save money. I even heard that the Obama, health care, plan would close down the work of St. Jude, LeBonheur, and all other special needs hospitals around the country just to save money. Needless to say, people were furious! I had never heard such lunacy in my life. Again, the Republicans are very good at misinformation. In fact, I would call them perfectionists at it, but I think there is more to this story.

I don't think the people really believe that President Obama is going to pull the plug on grandma and then gas the old bat to hell! You know what I think, President Obama? I think these people aren't as much against health care reform as they are just totally and outright against you! As Realacrats, we are not against you, President Obama. We just feel the Democratic Party is too much like the perennially talented sports team that always collapses under pressure, too willing to be socked in the face, but not willing enough to get mad or get even. With that being said, I think that you, President Obama, should do whatever it is you planned on doing during your presidency. If I were you, I wouldn't care about how mad the Joe Plumbers and the Joe Six-Packs will probably get, because they aren't going to be satisfied with anything you do no matter what. You could provide free health care and they would still call you a socialist, or better yet; a welfare socialist, because you are damned if you do and damned if you don't! With odds like that, you might as well go for broke! They can't hate you anymore than they already do. So you should simply saddle up that political Democratic donkey, and ride it straight into the history books as the first president to sign health care reform—even if it's not the exact version that was originally proposed. Whichever Republican called this your "Waterloo" was probably right, and I have an eerie feeling that this piece of legislation could define the rest of your presidency and any ethnic executive aspirations to come—and I think the Republicans know this very well!

As a Realacrat, I believe this is much bigger than health care reform. You, President Obama, and I are both non-BCS Americans. The overwhelming majority of our people have been traditionally and automatically eliminated from contention until now, until you came along, President Obama! Your performance on health care and your performance overall will be crucial and extremely instrumental in determining whether or not your historic election is a minority spring board into orbit or a walking of the plank into the racial abyss, because, like it or not, you are the modern, international equivalent to Jackie Robinson. Your epic journey as the leader of the United States also reminds me of Sheriff Bart from the movie "Blazing Saddles."[40] In the end, Sheriff Bart was able to whip the evil Mongo and the sinister Headley Lamar, as he saved the town of Rock Ridge, and used his ability to overcome racism and win over the people of Rock Ridge! But unlike Sheriff Bart, I feel that you, President Obama, could whip the riddling Glenn Beck, the rabblerousing Rush Limbaugh and you could even find a way to upend the sabotaging Republicans, but you still may find yourself just as hated as the day you rode into town! I think people can tolerate a Sheriff Bart on their televisions much easier than they

40 Mel Brooks, Director, Blazing Saddles, 1974.

could ever accept a Sheriff Bart or President Obama in their reality! So I fully understand if you decide not to run again in 2012. After hearing all of the scandalous claims about gas chambers, Nazi, death camps; and Obama-care, government, death panels; I can see how you might say the hell with all of it. But between now and then, I'll leave you with the thoughts of another old rap song, "Ain't nothing to it, but to do it;[41] for those that can't dance then clap your hands to it!" In other words, this may be the biggest hurdle you've ever faced in your life, but it's still just a hurdle, and it should be treated as such. If you can't go over it, then go under it, and if you can't go through it; then go around it. If you, President Obama, were a White Republican doing exactly what you are doing right now, but only with Republican policies; you would be the new Ronald Reagan!

And for that suggestion, here's an idea for your health care reform, because I truly believe the momentum has swung in the direction of the Republicans, who have no legitimate interest, as a political party, in helping you become the first president in history to pass health care reform. That means you'll need a new plan of attack, because the Republicans and the Limbaugh legion have pulled a Little Bighorn on your current tender. Maybe you should take some time off from the issue and come back later on in the year or at the beginning of the next, with some new thunder and lightning. As a Realacrat, my first suggestion to you is to actually consider writing a new health care plan yourself. Personally, I never understood why you, Mr. President, didn't just write you own health care, reform plan. After all, you are a Harvard man, so I, along with the American people, expected to get a Harvard plan with a Harvard pitch—but that pitch turned out to be a wild one that has now completely gotten away from you. The decision to involve the Congressional goon squad was a mistake! Why enable a grab bag of ideas from an inept Congress that controls both houses, but cannot control both houses? We Realacrats believe that such huge initiatives should be more of a presidential/executive production than a Congressional one. You need Congress to cast the ballot, not craft the plan. As the old saying goes, "You're only as strong as your weakest link." Well, as a Realacrat, I'm saying, "A president is only as strong as his weakest Congressional member." I think we need more Harvard

41 K-9 Posse, "Ain't Nothing to It But to Do It," K-9 Posse, 1988.

and less Congress. The reason I say this is because of the repeated complaints about how no one was ever able to fully and accurately explain the health care, reform proposal—including the President—but if he had written it himself, he would be the undisputed, irrefutable, guru, pitch-man for the plan, because no one would have more insight on it than him.

The Post-Racial Society

Obama's presidency is the culmination of the Civil Rights movement! It would be totally unwise not to expect the evil empire of hatred, racism, elitism, classism, and sexism to strike back! Insecurity is at its most viscous point when it is challenged by ability! Any notion that suggests the continuation of winning should be specifically upheld by the continuation of winning is cognitive welfare, yet many believed that Obama's ascent to political power as President of the United States would be the beginnings of a mythical, post-racial society, but Realacrats weren't fooled. We knew that the post-racial society only existed in some enthralling fantasy land where Elvis, 2Pac, Bigfoot, Puff the Magic Dragon, and the most recent addition--Michael Jackson, all play bingo together on Thursday nights, because you would stand a much better chance of seeing any of these individuals than you would have of living in a post-racial society. There were glimpses of what a post-racial society just might look like, if you paid close attention to the actions of Barack Obama. The enormous multi-racial rallies of candidate Obama gave a definite glimpse into a post-racial society, but one thing stood out even more than all of that, despite the fact that it was meager, brisk, and almost sly, but not sly enough, because I, along with many others, saw it. I saw Joe Biden's wife kiss Barack Obama[42], and I saw Hillary Clinton kiss him as well[43], and they weren't the only White women to kiss him either. Both were just slight pecks, but powerful none the less. When I saw both kisses on national television, I was flabbergasted and floored!

Now you can only imagine what the bigots, the Republicans, the conservatives, and some of the NASCAR/beer-drinking boys were

42 CNN, Obama Kissing Biden's Wife on the Lips. http://www.youtube.com/watch?v=EFayZyLCLoc (August 2008).

43 Fox News, Bill Clinton Denied a Kiss From Hillary, http://www.youtube.com/watch?v=Y8ivS4N6Dak (August 2008).

thinking. An African-American man kissing a White woman still raises eyebrows today in 2009, and it's definitely not something you see on television every day. It sent a powerful message that President Obama had indeed become very successful and widely accepted by a large number of White people. I knew then that any hope of a post-racial society or a successful Obama presidency would be tested to and beyond the limit. I was listening to the Limbaugh legion back in 2008 during the presidential campaign, when the point was made about how a Black man and a White woman didn't stand a chance in this country of being accepted as a viable working couple for the highest office in the land, which meant two things. One, the country is still not ready to see Black men and White women together on a highly publicized level or any other level. And two, African-Americans still are not deemed worthy enough by certain segments of American society to be bestowed such a privilege, but the election of President Obama has literally shaken that foundational belief to its core. After all, you can't credibly tell your children that President Obama is beneath them socially when he is the President. So you have to tell them that President Obama is a Socialist, a communist, an illegal alien, an illegal immigrant, a terrorist, a Muslim, a Kenyan, a Marxist or Hitler, and hopefully it will restore and continue to reinstate the old: "If I catch you dating one, I'll disown you" motto. President or not, he's still just a Black man to some, and that is putting it nicely!

I would now like to say on behalf of all Realacrats that former President Jimmy Carter is a patriot of humanity for having the gumption to stand his ground by calling out racist bigotry for what it is. On one hand, it's great that Carter had the courage to point it out, but on the other hand, it's a deplorable and political tragedy that few other Democrats seem to possess such a fiery resolve. With Carter getting older, who will be the next Jimmy Carter or the next Bill or Hillary Clinton? Nevertheless, what Carter said is true, because there are many people in this country who feel that African-Americans are unqualified to lead this nation or anything else of serious value, but there is more to it than just a lack of confidence in African-American ability. It's not really because the bigots don't believe African-Americans are qualified. It's because the bigots don't want the African-Americans to be qualified, and it's the fact that they are qualified that has soured the political and racial grapes of many in this country. When conservatives in the Limbaugh legion said they wanted the President to fail, they meant it, and the tea bagging protestors want the same thing. There have been other presidents with questionable policies and wide-open credit cards, but you didn't have people praying for the complete collapse of a virtually new president then. Some have even prayed for him to collapse physically and die! If you can't see how that kind of hatred runs much deeper than questionable policies, then I've got a Yugoslavian, Jacuzzi, hot tub in Antarctica that I want to sell you.

This will not happen in the Realacrat Party—not on my watch! Realacrats have no intention to pursue some unfeasible, tower of Babylon, post-racial society. We will only focus on making our party a post-racial society, because we will discriminate against the behavior of a group or an individual, but never against the appearance of a group or an individual. If we can manage to achieve that goal, I'd say we've moved political mountains. But make no mistake about it, genetic entitlement plans and European, bloodline hierarchies will not be tolerated here. We will support a Hispanic American president, an Asian American president, a Native American president, a homosexual president, and even an Arab American president. We don't have to say we'd support a White president, because we've been supporting them since the beginning. Anyone who does choose to spew racist jargon can either walk out, be thrown out, or be carried out! Unlike other political parties who favor Dumbo the Elephant, we will root out racism by any means necessary! At Realacrat gatherings, all members will be required to hug, greet, and kiss (peck on the cheek or lips--the choice is yours) someone of another ethnicity, even if it's on national television, because if you refuse to accept the equality and beauty of all humans, we will hold the door open for you, and kick you in your valueless ass on your way out!

So what is it about African-American/minority success stories that cause so much fear mongering and hatred in this country? Why is it that old, conservative, White men always seem to get the benefit of the doubt, while African-Americans and other minorities just seem to get the doubt? The cowardly Democrats don't want to know, and the arrogant Republicans already have a fairly good idea, but the Realacrats want to know for sure, and we want it out in the open once and for all, because this will continue to be a problem as long as there is an African-American president. Personally, I believe it is the mere fact that Barack Obama is the president. I truly believe that if President Obama had been just another African-American basketball player/athlete, entertainer, rapper or actor he would be the next Denzel Washington or the next Michael Jordan and the immensity of the hatred would be gone. I guess the more traditional African-American roles are just easier to accept, because the sight of an African-American president holding the highest governmental position in the free world presents an intellectual fright night for the genetically entitled brood. I think it's his symbolism more than his literal status. I think President Obama is a personified glimpse into another realm, another world, another society, another time, and another frame of mind. President Obama is either a fluke of social and political evolution, or he is a precursor of what is to come, and the latter is the one that has blown the roof off of the conservative, White-male-dominated, society models, because a post-racial society would signify the end of such genetically entitled ideologies. The sheer number of insecure morons who have a vested interest in the continued cycle of overwhelming, African-American/minority failure recycling itself into future generations is a lot higher than most are willing to acknowledge. This is why race has been and continues to be, a political and social lightning rod, and it is very possible that President Obama's entire presidency could be trumped by racial turmoil no matter how much he tries to spin it away and downplay it, and as the racial grumblings keep finding a way to spring up, his racial background will remain just as, if not more, front and center than his policies. This is why there are so many bigots who are personally rooting against President Obama, and it is not inconceivable that most of these bigots are assumingly rooting for all African-Americans/minorities to fail as a whole. Unfortunately, there are those who hope and pray that President Obama and the country suffer, and there are also those who actually need him to fail. Otherwise, they will be forced acknowledge the gaping holes in their bigoted myths. To them, a post-racial society is on the level with blasphemy!

As a Realacrat, my political opinion is this. We, as a nation, are just not far enough removed from discrimination, slavery, or Jim Crow. This is no post-racial society, not today, not tomorrow, and not for a long time! Maybe in a hundred years or more, a true, post-racial society can actually exist, but ignorance, like the cockroach, can live and breed for a long-ass time, so that particular realization could remain a mystery indefinitely! President Obama may lose in the short-term regarding his policies and his political accomplishments, but his political existence and his human tenacity could have society-altering, long-term effects on the United States and the world.

Secession from the Union

I never thought that I, as an American, would be hearing debates about seceding from the union, but there are certain areas of the country that harbor such resentment for the new president that secession from the union is actually being discussed, along with the formation of a new country, which is nothing more than the revamping of an old, out-dated idea that didn't work the first time it was implemented. I've been around for some years now, and I've seen quite a few bad things happen, but I've never seen anything so hideous that it would fire up secession from the union chatter. There have been some controversial presidents and some unpopular presidents, but it's never been so bad that secession became an option. Are President Obama's policies that bad? Is the mere fact that he is the president of the United States so unbearable that some are actually considering succession? I'm not much of a betting man, but I would be willing to bet that no other president in U.S. history has ever had the threat of succession dumped in his lap six to eight months into his presidency, barring Abraham Lincoln. All of my life I've heard White men rail about how they would move to another country if a woman or a Black became president, but I didn't think they were serious. I guess President Obama is the most polarizing president in U.S. history, again, barring Abraham Lincoln. A house divided will not stand, and a people divided will not stand either—and it has now become extremely unclear as to exactly how long this house of America will continue to stand in its current recognizable state, as long as fringe elements continue to join organizations like the Tea Party and succession freaks can scare enough followers into submission. And on that note, one should always be leery of any constitution revitalization movement, because there are very few people in human existence who would actually use a document of power like the U.S. constitution to enhance the freedoms of others. These are the same so-called patriots who yell "Country First," but then threaten to leave the country when a non-traditional candidate becomes President of the United States.

So what should be done about this problem? Much like health care reform, this problem is extremely difficult to tackle, but the Realacrats have a plan—even for this! Realacrats are all about freedom. So if there are groups of people who wish to vacate this country, they should be allowed to do so, as soon as possible, because Realacrats will not deny anyone an exit or force anyone to be what they obviously have no interest in being. If there is going to be a new country or a new territory formed on American soil, the federal government will have the total authority to dictate the operation, as one final act of big government to those who use it as an excuse to distance themselves from the progressive evolution of minorities. I know this entire abridgment seems too farfetched to be legitimate, but it is definitely legitimate enough that it cannot be completely ruled out, either. It is the job of the federal government to expect the unexpected; meaning, there should be a plan just in case the unthinkable happens. I propose the extreme southern sections of New Mexico, Arizona, the southernmost part of California--excluding San Diego and the southern and western strips of land that run along the border of Texas and Mexico. Realacrats refer to this project as "Bigots on the Border!" The sparsely populated area will be jettisoned by the United States, so that all the bigots can be moved in. All Federal funding to these areas will be eliminated, American military services to these areas will be eliminated, and the Border Patrol will be reassigned further inland away from the Mexican border and deployed to the new border, which would border the United States from the new "Bigots on the Border" districts; leaving them to fend off those pesky, Mexican, drug cartels all by themselves. The next move on the Realacrat agenda would be what I call the "John Calipari Hustle," as we would then instruct the United States to go out and recruit new states to fill the void. The first country I would recruit into statehood would be Puerto Rico, then Cuba, the Dominican Republic, Haiti, the U.S. Virgin Islands, the Bahamas, Jamaica, Israel, Great Britain, Guam, Taiwan, Germany, Spain, France, Italy, Kuwait and South Korea. Hell, we've been in most of these countries for so long that they might as well be states right now anyway. Besides, some of these countries could really boost our economic means. I know this is all crazy, but it is no crazier than the talk of the crackpot loons who started this conversation. I was having this discussion with the same, old, ironing-board-shaped woman who tried to discourage me from writing this book in the first place, and she snapped angrily at me with this: "How dare you draw up such a mean-spirited plan about secession! You have no damn right to suggest such an idea—you traitor! I don't want a bunch of damn foreigners in my country!" I then replied to the old, shriveled up hag and said: "It's okay for you and your beer buddies to sit around and discuss all the possibilities about leaving the union, but it's not okay for me to draw up a plan to help you all leave! You guys are the ones considering abandoning your country, but I'm the traitor? And furthermore, if you secede from the union, then you, yourself, will be a foreigner and a prime candidate for deportation if you choose to return." I'll give you all three guesses as to which party the old prune and her beer drinking mafia belonged to, but most of you will only need one! You can't be disgusted at me for making such a revolutionary suggestion second in the form of a rebuttal without being even more disgusted at the conservative dingbats for making the suggestion first in a veiled, proclamatory threat. If you have the audacity to suggest secession from the union, then I, personally, will have the audacity to help you get the f*ck out!

Obama's Failed Bid For the 2016 Olympics

If I'm not mistaken, hosting the Olympics was always a heavily sought after honor, and other countries have showed no haste in with rolling out their best red carpet to try and woo the Olympics. The United States has hosted the Olympics before, and I never once heard any complaints about it. The United States is always a frontrunner for the Olympic Games. So why, all of a sudden, is an Olympic bid such a horrid and hideous venture? For the first time in my life, I actually heard American citizens rooting against the hosting of the Olympic Games and then cheering wildly and ecstatically when Chicago, Illinois, was not selected to be the host city, despite the fact that former President Bush, that's right; I said former President Bush, went out and stumped for Chicago to be the host city. Bush thought the Olympics would be great for the country, as it always had been, yet the very people who supported and voted for him during his presidential bids gave off a vile satisfaction and a jealous and bigoted hoorah at the denial of the United States and Chicago for the 2016 Olympics.

The image of conservative jackasses dancing in their de-facto segregated streets solidifies and personifies everything I've discussed in this book from the lack of professionalism to the inability to accept the dreams and aspirations of those who may not share their views or dance to their political and social music. Even though many conservatives and Republicans highly criticized President Obama for going to Europe to make his bid for the Olympic Games, other countries happily and eagerly sent their top world leaders and dignitaries in hopes of garnering the games for their countries. They certainly didn't seem to see it as a bad economic move. All they wanted do was consistently and vigorously chomp at the heels of President Obama's U.S. bid, just waiting for their chance to wrestle it away, and they managed to do just that! This just goes to show everyone how hatred, jealousy, and bigotry can cloud sound, rational, economic judgment. While the ethnically, insecure, conservative groups like the Limbaugh legion sit around and purposely root against the country's best interest, other nations like China, Russia, Spain, and Brazil were there waiting to pick up the pieces and tighten up the slack. This is very similar to the story I told earlier about how we used to beat ourselves up on the dance floor to show our imaginary supremacy, while the out-of-town guys sat patiently and waited for their chance to catch us in a vulnerable position, so they could step in take the girls away, which they did! Now I can plainly see why China and other countries have caught up to America! A scavenging, conservative bigot once told me that no recession or depression is worse than being forced to live and witness a second stringer, like Barack Obama, restoring the United States back into prosperity, because it would stand firm against everything that he was taught and everything he taught to his White daughters about the inabilities of African-Americans and other minorities, to be qualified for top leadership positions, high profile employment opportunities, and potential mating statuses. The more successful African-Americans and other minorities become, the more discredited the poverty stricken, mindless-violence-conducting, White-woman-raping, Black or ethnic nightmare can wreak havoc on the fragile, racially motivated imaginations of the self-appointed first stringers! In my Realacrat opinion, anyone who willingly submerges their own investments into failure just to stifle the success of people unjustly deemed as inappropriate is truly nothing more than a knuckle-dragging, foot-dragging, political and social Neanderthal. Congressman Alan Grayson may be onto to something.

The Realacrat Party strongly supported President Obama's failed bid to capture the Olympic Games of 2016, because there is no legitimate reason to be against it. Unlike the sentiments of racism cloaked in policy opposition, we have no problem with President Obama's attempts to challenge other countries for a genuine opportunity such as the Olympics. The fear of being challenged is not a myth! Until crackpot conservatives are able to thwart their fears of their fellow Americans right here in this country, they don't stand a snowball's chance in hell of staring down China, Russia or any other country clandestinely supported by either of them. I see now why Moses was forced to meander around the desert for 40 years, because it looks more and more each day like we too are going to have to meander around our economic desert until the insecure ignorance dies off. Either way, Realacrats will not be suckered in or shackled by the broken dreams and broken promises of a passive willingness to accept and execute fraudulent marching orders that were never designed to lead us to a color privileged heaven or anything that remotely resembles equality!

The Obama Effect

The election of President Obama as the first African-American in history has changed the margins of the political spectrum, and one cannot uphold the Realacrat status without complete recognition of these uncharted, political waters, because things are different now, and resistance to reality is non-progressive at best. Other political parties often appear to be confused or reluctant when faced with racial situations laced within certain criticisms of President Obama. Republicans deny the existence of racism, and Democrats protest it meekly like church mice at a starving alley cat convention, but the Realacrat ideology will now attempt to break it all down once and for all with genuine explanations that will be signed in blood to the Realacrat platform.

All of this is based on the analytical and political turmoil between the Obama administration and Fox News. Apparently, there are some within the Obama administration who feel Fox News has unfairly depicted their political intentions, while Campbell Brown of CNN attempted to find the differences between Fox News and MSNBC.[44] The Realacrat stand is reality based as usual, because Realacrats see no problem with Fox News leaning right or with MSNBC leaning left. Realacrats believe the Obama administration should fight the lies but not necessarily Fox News as a whole, because any disappointment in Fox News favoring conservatives is the epitome of political gullibility and a waste of political aggression. Realacrats do understand and recognize the one thing that neither party wants to truly address, and that would be the existence of a true conflict of interest between minorities and Fox News and the entire conservative platform. MSNBC really has no political dog in this fight despite their vast tendencies to lean left. Newsflash, the left landscape is simply more welcoming to minorities than the right. President Obama's election should prove that beyond all logic! MSNBC and the left seem as if they have both figured out where the "DON'T EVEN GO THERE LINE" is in regards to minorities, while Fox News and conservatives seem too arrogant and too willing to cross that line. Speaking as a minority/African-American first and a Realacrat second, I can look each and every one of you right between the eyes and state that my number one political enemy is the conservative movement and mediums that shoulder its political load. This is why African-American, football players did not want to play for Rush Limbaugh. I think it's time that someone finally brings this issue to light. Who better to do it than a Realacrat?

This is what I call the Obama effect, because if any other White president was in office, it would be a totally different reality, and it would not be personal! Yes, I said it! "It would not be PERSONAL!" I want everyone to take a long, hard look at the word "personal," because that is what the Obama effect has made it. It's personal, because you have every right to disagree with his policies, but you have absolutely no right to disagree with his physicality or his ability to exist in human, ethnic flesh in the highest office of the free world. For example, let's examine the Obama birth certificate controversy. There are some who believe that President Obama's birth certificate is a fake, which could possibly make him an illegal alien and not a real, authentic, genuine

44 Nicholas Graham, Campbell Brown Hits White House For Critisim of Fox News, http://www.huffingtonpost.com/2009/10/28/campbell-brown-hits-white_n_337889.html (October 2009).

American. Now what does that say about the millions of people in this country who were not necessarily born here, especially the Hispanic population? It sounds like more of that "Get back across the border where you belong" crap again. What are you going to do; deport President Obama back to Kenya? I don't blame the Hispanic populations for bailing on conservatives. When conservative, hate mongers promenade around Washington D.C. with signs proclaiming President Obama as an African witch doctor, what exactly does that say about me or other African-Americans? It's a capital insult to African-American culture and African culture. It paints a primitive, barbaric, subordinate image of all African-Americans and Africans as well. When conservative, hate mongers hold up signs telling President Obama to go back to Kenya, they might as well line up every African-American in the country, and tell them all to go back to Africa with him, because you cannot explain why President Obama should go back while the rest of the African-Americans should not, because we voted for his witch-doctor ideologies. I guess we, as minorities, should all have to go back to Africa as well, because you can't tell President Obama to go back to Africa without telling me, Bryian R., to go back to Africa too, which makes it personal! It appears that any time an African-American becomes too lucratively viable, exerts a high level of intelligence, and demonstrates a low-level of social and decisional passiveness; that long-awaited return trip to Africa always seem to re-emerge. When conservatives called candidate Barack Hussein Obama a terrorist, they might as well have lined up every Arabic person in the nation and then told them to go back to the Middle East, while accusing them of being nothing more than September 11th celebrators and contributors.

All of this became glaringly evident to me during the Arkansas State Indian name change controversy. My alma mater, Arkansas State University in Jonesboro, Arkansas, has been able to find great new success as the Red Wolves instead of the Indians, because many believed that using Native Americans as mascots was degrading to the rich, Native American culture. I never understood all of the hoopla surrounding this issue, because I'm not a Native American; therefore, it's not my problem, and it does not affect me personally—but that is not necessarily true, because it is my problem, and it does affect me personally, if I would only open my eyes as if I was a Native American. All I had to do was place myself in a blood-soiled pair of Native American shoes for a minute, and I began to see and understand all the years of corrupt disenfranchisement that has haunted the Native Americans for years in this country. I was standing at an undisclosed location in Jonesboro, Arkansas, where there was this huge drawing of a Native American mascot on a window of a business. It was being used to promote the next Arkansas State Indians home game. I sat there and took a long, hard look at the Native American image with its big, wide, rambunctious eyes; its zany, comical, buffoonish, court jester-like cartoonish smile; its huge, colossal, Brahma bull-like, flaring nostrils; its overly-big, gapped teeth; its humongous, air-inflated-like lips; and its lone pathetic feather, which looked more like a Halloween prop than anything even remotely resembling Native American culture. Every single one of my White, conservative, Republican acquaintances thought the mascot was harmless and extremely funny. And to be brutally honest, I didn't care at first either, but the more I stared into the Native American mascot's face; the more I began to see my own face within it. The more I tried to view it from the Native American point of view; the more I realized that this is exactly what Native Americans refer to as Red Sambo! It was the stereotypical, big-lipped, big-nosed features often used to describe African-Americans; only this time—it was painted red. This is why Realacrats don't show up to meet with Native Americans dressed up like a cartoonish version of a Native American slamming their hands up against their mouths doing some hideous mockery of a rain dance yelling woo woo woo woo woo woo woo woo woo. These are the kinds of jokes, pranks, and insensitive ill-judgments that create more enemies than friends, because they're not funny. Barack the magic Negro is not funny! Other people dressed up in black face or red face is not funny! In other words, all White people don't have to be cowboys and rednecks, but all Native Americans are Indians/Red Sambo, all African-Americans are Negroes/Blacks/Niggers, all Arab Americans are towel heads/camel jockeys and all Hispanics Americans are illegal aliens/taco tossers/wetbacks. None of these represent genetic choices, but they do represent genetic conditions that are irreversible and irrefutable, because ethnicity should not be subject to demeaning satire from the dominant group whose actions made the satire possible to begin with. They are all universal insults! This is why I am profusely proud of my alma mater,

Arkansas State University, for changing its name to the Red Wolves, because it was the right, realacratic thing to do.

Conservatives have been notoriously reluctant to walk a mile in any pair of non-White shoes, but they are always quick to hold up those pairs of shoes as objects of ridicule and the tail-end of cultural and racial jokes. You can't oppress people and then demoralize and poke fun of the conditions and consequences of that oppression, while at the same time; expecting these individuals to forgive and forget as they cast their ballots for your leadership, which in itself is a patronizing slap in the face of their intelligence.

This is a conservative/Republican issue and Fox News cannot be a propaganda machine for the conservative, right agenda without becoming the vehicle most identifiable with this segment and the controversy that comes along with it. Fox News has every right to exist and continue on doing what they do, and we as Realacrats have every right to challenge them—not silence them, but challenge them! The Realacrat nation does not necessarily align itself with MSNBC, nor do we currently have a problem with them, but we would, and we will; if they adopt the policies and rhetoric of those anti-minority elements of the conservative movement just previously mentioned. We'd drop MSNBC from our friendly graces in an ejaculatory minute, and that includes CNN as well!

As a Realacrat, I don't like the way President Obama appeared to be waffling on sending more troops to Afghanistan after he became president, but I don't think that he should go back to Kenya because of it. The notion of going back to Africa or Kenya has no place in the discussion whatsoever. Disagreeing with President Obama's policies DOES NOT make someone a racist, but threatening deportation based on ethnicity and jealousy is not only racist, but it is abysmally narrow-minded and cretinously unconstitutional, to say the least. Anyone who practices such ideological elimination tactics is no better than Ahmadinejad or Fidel Castro corruptly disposing of their analytical scrutinizers—no better!

The Future of Politics

There are many lessons yet to be learned by Realacrats, Democrats, liberals and all other third-party political groups in this country. It's now the fall of 2009 in early November, and the first post-Obama elections have just been held, with Republicans winning the overwhelming majority of the races in Virginia and New Jersey sporting two new Republican governors, despite heavy campaigning from President Obama. Now all sides are lining up to point the fingers of blame at President Obama. It feels more like his loss than it does for the two ousted governors, but President Obama didn't lose those elections all by himself. All parties involved are to blame, because you don't bring one gun with one bullet to face a more than formidable, well-accomplished war machine—but that is exactly what Democrats, liberals, and minorities have perennially done. They have once again failed to correctly identify the political prowess of the Republican war-wagon, which has proven, on more than one occasion, to have the Democrats' number, yet Democrats and others continue to sloppily prepare as if the war machine was actually a candy machine. The Republican/conservative, political, war machine is disciplined, monotonous, focused, united, exclusionary, and extremely persuasive, while the Democratic/liberal war machine often appears to lackadaisical, passive, mismanaged, inconsistent, directionless, event-happy, and often ethnically motivated. Realacrats need to understand the political ramifications of this landscape; a landscape in which Republicans and conservatives excel at organizing and mobilizing their political base on any given Tuesday. Republicans don't need a historical candidate, a Messiah-like candidate, or some grand, staged event to mobilize their base. Republicans tend to mobilize regardless of whatever current event just happens to be occurring at that moment, because Republicans and conservatives live and die on the premise of winning elections. Losing is not an option, as the Republican Party always displays the political tenacity to immediately begin to claw their way back into political contention. The political movement assembled by the Democrats and candidate Barack Obama during the presidential campaign of 2008 is what Republicans do every year, rendering them to be perennial threat, which keeps them in a permanent position to pick up seats in any branch of government. The Republicans are in it to win it. They obviously take it far more personally when they are the ones forced to be on the outside looking in, and they are willing to do whatever it takes, by any means necessary, to ensure that does not happen. In sports, they call this the killer instinct.

The Realacrat Party as an organization has to recognize exactly what they are up against, and so do the Democrats. The political battles both parties must wage against the Republicans cannot be viewed as what we call a "One Hitter Quitter," because super-heavyweights, also known as Republicans, have a knack for getting back up even angrier and more determined. While Democrats dance around the ring, prematurely victorious, the big elephant finds the hardiness to get back to its feet. And when the Democrat turns around, the big, red, GOP elephant hits him/her with its own one-hitter quitter—game over! The conservative movement is arguably the greatest political adversary of all time. It's the super-heavyweight of super-heavyweights, and has the political championship hardware to back it up too.

This is why Realacrats have decided to make the conservative movement political enemy number one; because I just don't see how any future elections can be successfully contentious without some plan of attack based solely on inflicting political damage on the conservative/Republican movements. This means that Realacrats and Democrats alike will have to be disciplined enough to stay the course, because the political assaults on the conservatives have to become the norm for these other parties. They will have to become the way of life in a bilaterally recognized war, and if the Democrats or the Realacrats fail to comprehend the seriousness of this attack plan, either by reluctance or ignorance; then they should both throw in the towel, because we aren't guaranteed to happen upon another Barack Obama, another Bill Clinton, or another Hillary Clinton to bail out the left every eight years. Opponents of the Republican Party and the conservative movement cannot expect to just show up whenever there is an ethnic candidate or another; "It's the first time this has ever happened candidate." While African-Americans concern themselves with riding on shiny, spinning wheels that turn backwards, Republicans concern themselves with voter turnout, and spin their wheels directly into money, power and victorious elections. In 2008, African-Americans didn't really show up in record numbers to vote for Democratic causes. They showed up in record numbers to vote for themselves vicariously through a legitimate candidate in Barack Obama, and I will not totally criticize people for that, but it cannot be allowed to just end there. The same kind of politically motivating ballot juice Dr. Willie Herenton, former Mayor of Memphis, Tennessee, used to jolt the African-American community to get out and vote for him in huge election winning numbers at every mayoral election is something the Democrats and President Obama need to find a way to bottle and manufacture immediately for future electoral contests.

African-Americans are going to have to be just as jubilant for the next Asian American candidate, just as Hispanic Americans will have to be equally as jubilant for the next Native American candidate, and as all party members will have to be jubilant for the next White American candidate. Merely showing up at the polls only when there is a candidate who looks like you is unacceptable, and that is exactly what the Republicans count on to capture political success, and unfortunately; it has worked almost to perfection on numerous occasions, because minorities have failed to see the Democrat's struggle as their potential struggle, but it is their potential struggle, whether they like it or not! Reality doesn't stop being reality, just because you don't agree with it! The plight of President of Obama is not an island! Ask yourselves a simple question! Could it be me, and the answer to that question is: yes, it could be any of you! What if the next President of the United States was a Hispanic-American who was born in this country, but with strong, undeniable, Mexican roots; a person whose family came across the Rio Grande River into the United States illegally? What if this new Hispanic president always gave his state of the union addresses in a bi-lingual fashion wearing a big sombrero? Imagine watching and hearing your next state of the union address with a personal Spanish interpreter who translated English into Spanish for the Spanish speaking world! How do you think the Tea Party would feel about that? How do you think many in the country would feel about that? What if there was an Asian-American president, who also used an interpreter, but this time the interpreter's job was to translate the president's Asian dialect into English for the people of the United States? How do you think the Tea Party would feel about that? How do you think the country would feel about that? I believe there would be hate filled riots in the streets! Anyone born in this country, which includes all minorities, has the right to seek positions in government, including the presidency. So I ask all minorities in this country to take a long, investigative look in the mirror, and ask if you could be the next President Obama. Could

President Obama be replaced by any of the minorities similar to the ones I've just described and then have the same, vile hatred and bigoted non-acceptance that President Obama has faced and continues to face? Would you, the next minority president, be the new Osama Bin Laden, the new Adolf Hitler, or the next socialist; if you were elected?

Unlike Democrats, Realacrats will not rely exclusively on star-athlete-like, political candidates to mobilize our base. Realacrats will take a page out of the Republican playbook and utilize discipline, organization, strategy, methodical tactics, cognitive suggestion, a workhorse mentality, an anti-apathetic voter driven agenda and a synergistic, motivational catalyst based plan to get out the vote of our base.

I know all of this seems mean-spirited, and it is, and it will continue to be. There is no other way to compete and survive in this arena. Politics is not for the faint at heart or anyone who likes to wear their heart on their sleeve, because there is a lot at stake in the world; always has been. The team that has best prepared itself is usually the team that wins, even if that means stepping on your mother's throat, because you can't rise up to be a champion, if you are not willing to knock someone else down into defeat. If Realacrats want power, they will have to take it, and the road to political power in this country goes through the Republicans and the conservatives, and they will not just lie down, and hand it to you. After all, political ideologies are one thing, but the winning of elections is something else. So hopefully, this book will inspire people to get permanently involved. Hopefully, it will coax people to question their fears without being defined by them, in a place where all can be free to experiment with their own ideologies. If this book can help develop the Realacrat Party into a major political party, it could prove to be a roadmap to the future, and it could also change the course of American politics and politics abroad. A man with one choice is a slave, but a man with three or four choices is a customer. Your fears will tell you there is only one choice, but it's up to your courage and rationale to tell you that there could be, and there usually are many more. The Realacrat Party is about expanding the horizon of choices and the freedoms necessary to make those choices, in an attempt to combat the mindset of what is trying to remain what was and what was trying to return to what is, with a much different perspective based on what if.

A Parting Shot at Democrats!

After finally getting their health care bill passed in the spring of 2010, one would assume that the Democrats would be riding high; coasting off of the wings of their major legislative victory, but that is not what I encompass. Once again, instead of acting like the victors, the Democrats sound more like they are tucking their political tails in defeat, while the Republicans, who lost their bid to stop the health care bill, are in full blown, attack mode appearing as if they are the ones with the winning momentum. It is this specific kind of fickle politics that caused me to rearrange my political landscape to begin with, thanks to the whimpery of the Democrats! I've been a Democrat for my entire life, and I've always voted the straight Democratic ticket until now, and this political lameness is the main reason why. Instead of steam-rolling into the elections of November 2010, the Democrats come hobbling up to the starting line engulfed in fear. It's as if they feel like they are going to lose this race before it ever even starts. Well listen up Democrats! Voters can sense your lack of confidence and so can the Republicans.

This reminds me of the 2008, NCAA, final-four, post-game interview with former, University of Memphis Tiger's guard Derrick Rose, when he told reporters how he and the rest of the team knew they were going to win and defeat the UCLA Bruins, which they had just done.[45] Reporters were bewildered by Rose's boastful claims of a pre-determined victory against a powerful, top-notch opponent, like UCLA! Reporters then pressed Rose to elaborate on how he and the rest of his teammates could be so confident. Rose then went on to explain his philosophy on competitiveness. To Rose, anyone who goes into battle with the mindset of being defeated is setting themselves up for failure, and I agree! The Democrats should take a page out of Derrick Rose's playbook, because heading into November of 2010 expecting to get led to political slaughter by the Republicans is setting up the Democratic Party for failure!

The Democrats even appear shaky about their ability to retain Senate Majority Leader Harry Reid's seat, as confidence of his re-election bid in Nevada looms uncertain. This automatic ability to accept

45 Ben Walker, AP National Writer, Derrick Rose puts on dazzling show, leads Memphis past UCLA 78-63 into title game, http://rivals.yahoo.com/ncaa/basketball/recap?gid=200804050349&prov=ap (April 5, 2008).

an oncoming defeat is definitely a Democratic flaw, because you never see Republicans slumped over ready to throw in the towel at the first sign of political turbulence. If the Democrats don't get up off of their passive asses and find a way to defend Harry Reid's seat in November, I, as a life-long Democrat, will call 2010 a failure! Almost everything that happens in Las Vegas, Reno, and most other areas of Nevada all represent the antithesis of conservatism, and Republicans have no business winning that state away from Harry Reid!

Just consider the world renowned saying of, "What happens in Vegas stays in Vegas," and that's about as liberal as it gets. The only conservative aspect of it is the hypocritical cover-up of indulging in the activities that the conservative brand staunchly opposes by many of those very same conservatives who are supposed to be in opposition of such activities. In other words, we like to participate in such activities, but we don't want anyone to know about it, which is vintage hypocritical behavior! This is why the 150 to 500 mile rule was enacted by political conservatives and religious conservatives, which states: "You are free to do as you please, as long as you travel at least 150 to 500 miles away from your home base, so no one will, hopefully, recognize you," and you wonder why religion and politics are so corrupted.

Senator Reid is not my favorite, Democratic candidate by a long shot, but he should not lose to a conservative in Vegas/Nevada! If he does, I won't consider it a failure on him, as much as I will consider it to be a failure on the Democratic Party as a whole, because Sharon Angle, the Tea Party candidate challenging Reid, sounds about as crazy as a Jonestown disciple backing up with the Kool-Aid truck! So, here is my Realacratic advice to the Democratic Party on how to save Harry Reid's seat in November of 2009. Re-assure the White vote, which Republicans plan to steal, and then go out and motivate the apathetic African-American/minority vote, which Republicans have no fear of!

If Reid loses this seat, it's not going to be good for Democrats. The Obama administration will then find two long, hard years of tough, political sledding without Reid as the wheel man of the Senate. Republicans know that they cannot beat Rep. Nancy Pelosi in her home district, but they plan on doing the next, best thing, which is winning back control of the House of Representatives; making Ms. Pelosi the ex-Speaker of the House. This Republican/Tea Party strategy will leave

President Obama without his two best political athletes to run his plays down the field of Congress. Republicans will recreate President Obama from a perception of doing too much while in office to a new perception of not doing anything at all, once they cease control of both houses of Congress and filibuster all the way to the year 2012. If they can paint President Obama as a do nothing president for the last two years of his presidency, he is almost guaranteed to suffer the incumbent jinx, as he's ushered out of the White House for, possibly, the Alaskan Queen. This is all about partisaned politics. If Harry Reid and Nancy Pelosi had this kind of congressional success under the GOP's umbrella, they would build statues of both of them. Instead, they are being politically smeared as President Obama's socialist puppets, and toothless hicks are buying it!

And as for Blanche Lincoln's re-election bid in my home state of Arkansas, the same advice would apply. Although I would not be as upset if Blanche Lincoln does not win re-election, because Arkansas is a place where the enthusiasm of bigotry is only matched by the enthusiasm of religion. The mere fact that Blanche Lincoln even acknowledged the existence of President Obama could prove to be more than enough to cost her the election in November of 2010. So Democrats need to remember this! Other would-be political entities will be watching. If you don't take care of your business, then somebody else will! No matter how corporate Blanche Lincoln may appear to be, I'd still take her over her Republican adversary any day of the week!

And to Bill Halter, who challenged Blanche Lincoln so vigorously in the 2010 May primaries, I think you should run for governor here in the state of Arkansas, because in a match-up between you and current Arkansas Governor Mike Beebe, my vote would go to you--Bill Halter. The installation of the Arkansas lottery is the most important and most impressive piece of legislation I've seen as an Arkansas resident. That makes you, Bill Halter, the front runner in my book!

Now the last order of business is the Sarah Palin/Michele Bachmann phenomenon. Why Democrats have allowed these two new jacks to hammer them at every turn is beyond me. I assume that they don't really want a man to go out and attack women, due to the savage imagery it would project, and I totally understand that, but I also know that something has to be done, and having President Obama, as an African-American man, sparring with two White women is highly treacherous with the potential to backfire at any moment! Nevertheless, the Democrats cannot politically afford to allow Bachmann and Palin to have an unrestricted, free reign of assault on the Democratic Party, because when that happens, the Democrats are defensively playing not to lose, instead of offensively playing to win! So this is my proposal to the Democratic Party as an individual who still believes in the Democratic platform.

I suggest an ideology derived from my hip hop roots called the "Roxanne Wars," which featured the rap group UTFO, Roxanne Shante, and The Real Roxanne! UTFO released a hit song called "Roxanne Roxanne,"[46] which was answered by another song called "Roxanne's Revenge"[47] by Roxanne Shante, which was answered by another song called "The Real Roxanne,"[48] by The Real Roxanne! Instead of the all guy group, UTFO, attacking a young, female artist, in Roxanne Shante, UTFO played it smart by going out and recruiting a new female Roxanne to further the attack, and it the scheme worked brilliantly! I know there are people who will say that hip hop is garbage based on the people and the culture from which it was founded, but this Roxanne episode was pure politics and strategy.

I implore the Democrats to follow in the footsteps of UTFO, by going out and recruiting their own version of a Real Roxanne; meaning, the female answers to Sarah Palin and Michele Bachmann. Why sit back while Palin and Bachmann parade all around the nation campaigning for any and every candidate they choose in hopes of influencing an election into Republican favor? One of the reasons I call my ideology Realacratic is because I have yet to see any real political bite within the Democratic plans. Is there no promising, female, Democratic contender out there? Is there no future Hillary Clinton out there? Is there no liberal, progressive, female, political motivator out there looking to make a name for herself in the realm of politics? The female candidacy is straight out of the Democratic playbook, but it is the Republicans who are having a cakewalk with it today. Democrats should be ashamed of themselves. If you can't find and recruit the next Hillary Clinton, then groom and create the next Hillary Clinton, but do not allow the

46 UTFO, "Roxanne Roxanne," UTFO, 1984.

47 Roxanne Shante, "Roxanne's Revenge," 1984.

48 The Real Roxanne, "The Real Roxanne," 1985.

Republicans to turn the female candidacy into a Republican stronghold. It's time for Democrats to finally start pressing back, and the 2010 November elections would be a good time to start! Win in 2010, or you might find a Republican hell in 2012!

The Bryian R Blog: My Untold Stories and Opinions

The Ground Zero Mosque/Community Center/Freedom of Humanity Center!

The proposed mosque near ground zero in New York has obviously caused quite a stir. The location of this proposed mosque seems to be the tipping point in the minds of many Americans who see its location as an insult to the memories of those who died in the September 11th attacks. Everyone from President Obama to Sarah Palin has chimed in on this debate. President Obama believes that the people who want the mosque have a constitutional right to build it wherever they see fit, as long as the proper procedures are met, but others, like Sarah Palin and even Senate Majority Leader Harry Reid of Nevada; who must dance a conservative jig just to try and get re-elected, consider the location to be insensitively wrong, but I agree with President Obama. I believe in freedom!

With the location of the proposed mosque being only a few blocks away from ground zero being such a major source of controversy, I think it's time we all play the distance game, since so many have suggested moving the mosque farther away from ground zero. There's an old song by The Police called "Don't Stand So Close to Me," which was remade by a rapper named Gangsta Boo. Both songs expressed strong sentiments about the close proximity of an uncomfortable object being just a little too close for comfort, with the Gangsta Boo version calling for an all-out assault of violence to deal with the uncomfortability of the threat. Now with that being said, how close is too close? How far away is far away enough? Does the constitution have a measuring stick? I know that there are city ordinances based on proximity in regard to adult entertainment establishments and the distance such businesses must remain away from residential areas, churches, and schools, but I haven't heard of any such ordinance as applied to religious structures. So again, I ask the question of exactly how far away would be far enough away, and who exactly would be authoritative enough to draw that dubious line in the political sand, and then what kind of criteria would that individual base it on?

It's very similar to the trying to determine what is obscene, and what is not obscene. Ten blocks away might be enough to satisfy some mosque opposers; but then again, others might not be satisfied until the mosque was out of the city all together! That's the problem you run into when trying to appease the public, because as the old saying goes; "You can't please everybody!" Isn't that one of the main reasons why we have laws, guidelines, and ordinances to create a legal stability to try and encourage fairness and equal opportunity? Otherwise, the decision of who builds and where would be answered by popularity contests, where the more popular and more accepted religious sects would more than likely be allowed to build more things in more places, while the lower regarded, religious sects would almost surely find less and less space to build on! To me, that looks more like a corrupt, monopolized monarchy than anything even vaguely resembling democracy or the constitution, and I can't believe the constitution toting conservatives would even have the brazen audacity to support such a measure. This is why President Obama did the right thing by supporting the right of the proposed mosque or any other religious structure to be established. If President Obama had gone in and used his executive, governmental powers to deny the establishment of the mosque for whatever reason, then he would actually and finally be living up to all of those claims of him being a Marxist Communist!

I am in favor of the proposed mosque near ground zero, because I don't believe that we should be running any faction out of the neighborhood based solely on their religious/non-religious doctrines! For example, if my neighbor had a daughter who had been raped by an African-American a few years prior to my moving in, and he decided to gather up the community to oppose my right to move into the neighborhood; quite possibly right beside him, I would fight it fervently, because you cannot blame me for something that happened that I was not a part of, and you also cannot tie me to the African-American rapist just because I, too, am an African-American. That is absolutely unconstitutional, absolutely absurd, and as un-American as it gets!

I find it fascinatingly appalling how so many of these alleged Christians who oppose the mosque are so blatantly and unjustifiably vilifying Islam in some watered-down attempt at vengeance for the September 11th attacks, while at the same time; seeking even more vengeance for the 2008 November 4th presidential attack on the status quo of the Right-Winged, GOP plans for the presidency. Their plan is to kill two political birds with one Fox News, scripted stone. The plan is simple! Tie President Obama to Islam, and then make Islam the face of all that is evil and everything that is un-American that can be mongered by the conservative, doomsday brigade.

Allah didn't attack the United States on September 11th any more than Jesus had a shootout with the FBI down in Waco, Texas at the Branch Davidian compound back in 1993. I like how alleged Christians are so quick to disassociate themselves from the Branch Davidians, the abortion, doctor killers; or the Jonestown tragedy by saying: "None of those incidents represents us as Christians or Christianity as a whole," but then they turn around and hogtie all Muslims and all of Islam to the September 11th terrorists and terrorism overall, and that by definition is the essence of a hypocrite! You can't blame the source for the misinterpretation! You can only blame the interpreter, because there is nothing more cowardice than the creation of a scapegoat to escape responsibility.

So here is my proposal. Instead of establishing a mere mosque, I propose incorporating what I call the "Freedom of Humanity Center." It would be a mosque that was much more than just a mosque. It would be a place where different religions could be showcased to try and help bring a better understanding, a sense of appreciation, and a step towards more tolerance on behalf of all religion. For once, the actuality of a unified answer between multiple religions could finally be achieved in one unanimous declaration of peace! Whether it's Islam, Christianity, Judaism, Buddhism, Hinduism or atheism, if you are opposed to violence, and you are willing and eager to denounce it, then you are welcome with open arms, because you don't need an agreement on God or childish, denominational chest-beating for everyone involved to agree on, at least, one thing: "the destruction of our planet, and the self-destruction of ourselves is unacceptable!" Differences of opinion should not equate into differences of death and destruction. If you feel that your God would disapprove of your participation in this kind of statement, then you either don't know your God as well as you'd like us to think that you do, or you obviously need to go out and find yourself another God! And while you're at it, why don't you go ahead find something else to drink besides that "Follow the leader" tea you can't seem to stop guzzling! A big jug of liberalized, freedom water should have you appreciating the truth in no time! A Christian, a Muslim, or some other religious disciple may be who many of us would like to be, but our bundle of ideas and behaviors is who we are, and that is what must ultimately be held accountable.

Dump Obama or Else!!!!

Just recently, I was asked by a multitude of people about why I like President Obama so much. One of them said: "It's obvious that you're in the tank for Obama! Almost everything that you post is pro-Obama. I bet the only reason you even like him is because he is Black like you, and that's racist! It's your racial obligation to support your own. If you didn't support him as much as you do, on places like Facebook, you would be labeled as an "Uncle Tom" or a sell-out! Where is your integrity? How can you blindly support someone just because they are the same color as you? What exactly has that similarity gotten you thus far, besides some fraudulently manufactured, ethnic unity? Instead doing what's best for the country, you, African-Americans and other minorities, did what was best for your racial identity and your racial legacy, and I think that's disgustingly wrong! And to top it all off, you people continue to blindly support this man as he literally destroys this country, all because none of you have the courage to stand up and criticize one of your own. He has put this country in the worst recession ever, and you people just sit around and say nothing! I guess no one can chastise Blacks, not even other Blacks, because you guys don't have the courage to dump him and his failed policies. I don't even want to be around people like you anymore!"

So I said to him, "If voting for President Obama because he's Black makes me a racist, then you voting for John McCain because he's not Black makes you just as racist! If my unwillingness to justly scrutinize President Obama makes me a racist, then you're willingness to unjustly scrutinize President Obama makes you just as racist again. I want you to think about this. African-Americans and other minorities have a long history of voting for and supporting people who don't look like them. Can you look into your political, ideological mirror and legitimately make that statement? Now I'm not calling you a racist, but I am suggesting that you are socially and politically unevolutionary! It's always easier to point to the lack of character, as long as that finger is not turned around and pointed back at you."

This next story is based on the summation of about five, formerly close, friends that I've lost online and off-line since the election of President Obama. Now many in the media and around this country would have you to believe that all of this is just an overblown coincidence, but I've got more than enough insight to know that there is something more dubious going on here than some random acts or some luck of the draw transactions. Don't patronize me! I've witnessed every U.S. President since Gerald Ford, and I have never had my character interrogated and picked apart until now. I've never experienced people trying to tie the entirety of my character and my patriotism to a single presidential vote until now, and I've never had friends or enemies hand me relationship ultimatums based solely on whether or not I will dump an American president until now. How did my private decision in a voting booth, which is my constitutional right to partake in, become a referendum on my entire ideological make-up?

Take this exchange for an example. I had a very special group of people that I once considered to my personal and political friends till the end. And get this, they were Democrats! Please keep that in mind. The ring leader of this alleged Democratic base that I used to be affiliated with explained his views on, then, candidate Obama by saying: "How exactly did he get into Harvard anyway? Do they have a welfare scholarship at Harvard? That must be some of that "Affirmative Action, Jesse Jackson, Al Sharpton sh*t, where they do like King did, and beg the federal government to lower collegiate standards low enough to allow Blacks and other minorities into these prestigious universities just to meet a coon quota! I don't even believe that he went to Harvard. It's probably all hype to give Blacks some hope, because you people haven't had anybody of any substance since King. Barack Obama, what in the hell kind of name is that anyway? He's a Muslim and a terrorist! The only thing separating Osama and Obama is a B and an S, and when you put them both together, you get BS! My parents were Democrats, and I am a lifelong Democrat, but I will not support this Kenyan thug! I'll quit the Democratic Party forever and join the Republicans before I'd vote for him, and if you fail to do the same, then I will quit you, too, Bryian R.!"

So I asked this great example of humanity this question, as I said to him: "So, you're willing to just throw me to the wolves if I decide to vote for Obama," and he and his stooges all looked at me and said: "Yes we are! If you support a terrorist, then we cannot support this friendship. We cannot stand for you, when you choose to stand for him. All of you guys can kiss our asses, including the liberal-loving Democrats!" I then asked this stooge brigade why they were ever Democrats in the first place, as I said, "Didn't you jackasses know what the Democratic Party stood for before joined it? If you didn't, then I'm sure, unless all of you were comatosely sleepwalking, that between Larry, Curly and Moe; one of you nincompoops could have figured it out and broken it all down into ideological baby food or moron chunks, so the other two dolts could digest it. Why would you stay in a political party that perennially gets 90% of the Black vote for all of your life, and then be shocked and appalled when this party has the political gumption to nominate someone from this 90% to lead the party? How dumb can you get? If Harvard does have a welfare scholarship, you three out-of-work rocket scientists definitely need to apply for it, because none of you would get in based on intelligence or plain, old common sense! That's for damn sure! As far as I'm concerned, the Democratic Party losing you three is the proverbial blessing in disguise, and I'm sure the overall I.Q. of the party just went up 100 points apiece. With Democrats like you three rats, the Democratic Party doesn't need any Republicans. So don't let the Democratic door hit you in your charlatan asses on the way out. I thought we had a friendship, but obviously; it was strictly conditional. Well, you all can consider my exit from this joke of a relationship to be strictly unconditional!"

This is what I'm talking about as being an abnormal, Presidential atmosphere, and don't even think about telling me that it's all because of big government and massive overspending. Like Christine O'Donnell states in her political ad "I'm you," the government is us, despite the multitude of people who swear that it is not. Yes, it is! The government suffers from the same tendencies that the general population suffers from. The overindulgence of greed will trump the discipline of savings in about 90% of the world's population on an average day and 100% of the world's population within the totality of a lifespan. I would argue that our government has grown throughout at least 95% of its existence, if not more, so this is nothing new. What is new is the ethnicity of the Commander-in-Chief, so let's be realistic. No one has ever spoliated their affiliation with me, because I have a tendency to overspend on things that I probably don't need. If you start de-friending people based on that principle, you'll find yourself friendless in a hurry. And on that note, you might as well de-friend yourself too! This is not about spending. This is about the color of the company you've been attending with your vote.

So this is my Obama statement to the world! Yes, I like President Obama, and I think he is about as fair of a person as you're going to meet in politics. No, I don't think he's the worst president ever. Yes, I think he's more genuine than President Bush. No, I don't think President Obama is a Muslim, nor do I care, because Christianity is not a prerequisite to presidential greatness, but it is a prerequisite to the traditional, status quo, comfort zones of more of the same! I wouldn't vote for President Obama because he is Black any more than I voted for those other presidents because they were all White. No, I'm not in the tank for Obama, and my political support for him or the Democratic Party is conditional at best, but that's better than my political support for conservatism, which is non-existent, especially for the Tea Party, and it's even less for Christine O'Donnell and Sarah and the Palinators.

While it's true that I don't agree with these individuals, I, under no circumstances, pompously demand that others who are associated with me agree with me on my political disagreeance of these individuals. If you want to defriend me because I will not ride on your anti-Obama, hate train, you won't have to wait until we see the next station, I'll jump off right now—hobo style! My vote is my business, so pull your indoctrinary nose out of it! Understand this! I'm going to miss those great, non-political times we had together, but as Dez Dickerson said in Prince's song called 1999, "Life is just a party, and parties weren't made to last," and neither are most relationships. After the Obama years, maybe the conservative, White male will be the re-elected and restored to political, presidential prominence, and we can be friends again.

P.S. Don't count on it!

Vick, Lassie and Chicago

If you all care as much about Michael Vick killing dogs as much as you all claim to care, then you should all be outraged at the staggering number of young people who were gunned down on the streets of Chicago, Illinois, in 2009—yet I hear little outrage about these murders or the murderers who commit them. All I see is the outrage over Michael Vick playing football again because it looks bad on the NFL. I guess dogs mean more than the youth of Chicago, because the unwarranted slaying of hundreds of innocent lives looks bad on America![49] Don Lemon and Anderson Cooper at least had the valor to venture into Chicago to help bring awareness to the issue, and they are both patriots of humanity for doing so, even if O'Reilly never gave either of them the proper credit they deserve as journalists. I speculate that the high number of poor, African-American victims has a significant correlation to the seemingly invisible outrage, minimal coverage, and the perceived lack of motivation needed to do something about it. It seems as if it's only classy to serve and protect Lassie. At least CNN understood the significance of it, I haven't heard much, if anything, from Fox News on it, and the family-value-loving Republicans seem to be preoccupied. I guess Lassie must be part of the family, while me, Vick, and the African-American

49 CNN, Taking Aim: Chicago Violence, http://edition1.cnn.com/TRANSCRIPTS/0910/03/cnr.06.html (October 2009).

youth are not. But I'll guarantee this: even without much hoopla about the 2009 Chicago murder rate on Fox News, I'll bet you that every Republican knows exactly who Michael Vick is, not because what he did is any worse than what is happening in Chicago, but because he is more of a threat to the stereotypical generalizing that goes on about African-Americans, because he beat the system, and now he will have to beat the system again, with Lassie and numerous grandstanders protesting his every move. Those trigger-happy marauders in Chicago will almost definitely end up in the system with either a number across their chest or on their tombstone. But you, Mr. Vick—you are different. You have a chance to live the American dream without the number or the tombstone, and this is why people continue to crucify you. This is not really about a dog. This is about turning you into O.J. Simpson Jr. This is about seeing you back at that construction job or incarcerated again. There is a large segment of American society that absolutely despises young athletes just like you; because of the economic opportunities you are afforded. I think they'd rather see Lassie have the wealth instead of you or anyone like you, because seeing a Michael Vick go down the same path of destruction as so many of the Chicago youth would absolutely be gratifying to many in the genetic entitlement camps. Do you remember when certain individuals openly wished for President Obama to fail? Guess who they are rooting for the failure of now. You won't get another chance, Mr. Vick. You barely got this one. I sincerely hope you know what to do with it.

Before I move on, I'd just like to share one more tidbit of information about the African-American athlete, because I feel that this information needs to be heard at all costs! In July of 2010, LeBron James, formerly of the Cleveland Cavaliers, held an hour long special to announce his big move to the Miami Heat. A clan of conservative men, some of them Tea Baggers, was discussing their disgust at some dumb, ignorant, basketball player from the ghetto receiving so much press. Now listen to me well, because this prediction was made in the form of this statement, and I quote: "I don't allow my precious, upper-echeloned, ethnically pure daughters to watch the NBA anyway, and I most certainly don't allow them to sit around gazing at people like LeBron James or anyone like his kind of people. I predict the next time we see that thug; he'll be all over television wearing handcuffs like the rest of his thuggish community!" Let that be a wake-up call to all African-American athletes and entertainers!

In light of all the violence that occurred in Chicago, Illinois, in the summer of 2009, I think that maybe I can shed some light on the fuel that seems to drive the African-American engine of self-destruction. After all, I spent the majority of my life wanting the same dreams as the Chicago youth who are dying to attain it almost every day. So why is it happening? Well, I have an idea. Do you remember the poem *Paradise Lost*[50] by John Milton? In it, Satan talked about how it was better to rule in hell than it would be to serve in heaven. I think that statement is profound, because I believe that a huge element of the African-American community has decided to rule in their own sometimes-hellish domain, where they define their Blackness, they define their culture, they define the law, they define their economy, they define their corruption, and they define their community—which they rule absolutely and quite often violently! I guess it's okay to rule with an iron fist, as long as that fist is a Black fist! Instead of assimilating into the less-respected so-called White world, it seems as if the only aspirations of many within this violent environment is to remain at home where they can be the kings, the dictators, the oppressors, the aristocrats, and the masters of their illusions, because they merely rent this highly touted domain they so proudly rule! They do not own it! They only think they do. It is an illusion of power capped by an invisible glass ceiling that everyone knows is there. When the system gets ready to reclaim those same low-income properties to build high-priced, ritzy condos, the Black-fisted rule will be over, along with all of the poverty and violence that comes along with it. You would think that we, as African-Americans, had come far enough away from the horror of the slave whip that it would not be feasible to then go back to that same slave whip and then turn it on ourselves, but it seems that many elements of our community have done just that.

African-Americans such as: D.L. Hughley, President Barack Obama, Dr. Martin Luther King Jr., Malcolm X, Steve Harvey, Bill Cosby, Michelle Obama and others soon realize the illusion of impoverished power and the glass ceiling of limitation, as they decide to try and find a way to move beyond it. This step is critical, because without it, there

50 John Milton, Paradise Lost (Samuel Simmons 1667) Book 1, line 254-5, 263.

is no defiance to American slavery, no President Obama, no Oprah Winfrey or Cosby Show, no March on Washington, no civil rights movement, no Jackie Robinson, no Bryian R., no book like the one you are reading at this moment, and no Realacratic ideology to speak of. If the box overcomes you and your limited resources, and you are forced to remain in it, it's just another causality of the sectarian system, but if you can defeat the box with those same limited resources, and then purposely decide to remain in it, it is systematic, subliminal, self-destruction by your own hands. Winners don't allow others to define or calibrate their capacity for attainment, neither do Realacrats, and nor should you. When I talk about the box, I'm not referring to a physical ghetto, but an unconscious ghetto, the same mental ghetto Malcolm X spoke about. It's that same box that destroys the credibility of and the desire to pursue a dream. It can, and has, disrupted and re-routed many of the progressions made by minorities, both historically and currently, leaving many of them in what I call evolutionary slavery. When you allow fraudulent oppressors to define you, they ultimately also define the substance of your journey, and your journey is all you truly have—so why not be the undisputed captain of it, because you cannot fully evolve as long as you believe you are everything you were ever meant to be. The creation and intent of this systematic, obstructive challenge falls on oppression, but the inability to consciously meet and ambitiously defeat this challenge falls on us as humans. No corporate Democrat or conservative/corporate Republican would ever have the guts to tell you this! Reverend Wright, Al Sharpton, Father Phleger, Bill Clinton, Michelle Obama, or President Obama could possibly have this conversation with you, but the Sarah Palin's and Mitt Romney's of the world seem more at home at Disney World than speaking out in African-American communities about such controversial subject as this. This looks like a job for another wise Latina/minority woman/man/Realacrat.

This is exactly what President Obama was talking about in his stay in school speech. It was the speech that many parents threatened to keep their kids out of school for, so they wouldn't have to hear it. What President Obama should do now is prepare a fresh, new speech strictly geared towards the underprivileged, under-served, under-educated, at-risk kids of the inner-city, the kids that really need to hear it more than any of the others, the kids that get shot at on their way to school, the kids that got shot at again on their way from school, the kids that get gunned down on the streets because no one in their family has been able to find a way to beat the system and break the cycle of poverty, ignorance, gunfire, drugs, prostitution, crime, and hopelessness—a community much like the one Barack and Michelle Obama experienced in Chicago, Illinois. In fact, President Obama should be a Realacrat and take it even further by going back to some of those old, impecunious stomping grounds of his community organizing days, where the churches and the community centers are all some kids have to keep them off of the treacherous, murderous streets. Republicans will once again be madder than hell, but President Obama should do it anyway. Now many of his critics will then accuse him of only focusing on one group of kids, despite making it more than abundantly clear that they do not want him speaking to their children, but they cannot deny President Obama the right to return and speak specifically to the old neighborhood where he once worked and lived. And for that, he should drag CNN, ABC, CBS, NBC, and especially Fox News right into the heart of Chicago's inner city. I'd pay-per-view to see Major Garrett in the old Cabrini Green, Dearborn Homes, Rockwell Gardens, K-Town hoods.

Speaking as a Realacrat, I'd also like to see him personally address the Native American communities, the Asian-American communities and other minority communities across this country; dragging the frightened media kicking, screaming and shaking behind him. The Obama's are the personification of beating the pitfalls of the corrupt system that stifles and snuffs out so many young African-American/minority minds. I was watching the movie *Menace II Society*[51] the other day for about the millionth time on BET, and there is not a scene in another movie more poignant in regards to the African-American experience than the last scene of the movie, when the killers roll up with ski-masks on, fully-loaded, semi-automatic weapons in full bloom, as the good, the bad, the ugly, the guilty and the innocent all perish together. As I watched the leading character, Caine, lie dying on the sidewalk, unable to escape his violent end, I knew in my heart that it could have just as easily been Barack Obama, Michelle Obama, Bill Cosby, Michael Vick, or me, because each of us, at some point in time during

51 Menace II Society, Allen & Albert Hughes, Menace II Society, (May 1993).

our lives, were on that same street, in the same community, facing those same problems, in close proximity with our own version of a Caine. For every young African-American shot dead in the streets, always be mindful that it could be the next Barack or Michelle Obama swallowed up by the poverty spawning; murderous, minority feeding system! It's too bad the inner city youth don't have a PETA-like organization looking out for them. Make no mistake about it; the environmental landmines of the ghetto are no excuse for failure, but you cannot deny that not having to navigate such treachery is no excuse to discount or discredit the struggle!

Conversation with a Tea Bagger

As I've often said before, I know numerous Tea Baggers. I've known them before there was a Tea Party, so the presence of Tea Baggers is nothing new to me. I'm on the road a lot, and I'm always dealing with different people, which includes conservatives and Tea Baggers. This allows me to get to know many of them on a personal level beyond the politics, and I am sharing some of those encounters here. Let's be clear! There is no hidden agenda between the Tea Baggers and me. I know they are conservative, and they know, conclusively; that I am somewhere between liberally liberal and conservatively conservative. No cases of mistaken identity occur here. Their motto is Christianity, blue-eyed Jesus, guns, a hatred of President Obama and the liberal, democratic cause; and a hatred of CNN and every other media outlet not called Fox News. The same side of the political fence will rarely ever find the Tea Party and me adjacent to each other.

Despite everything that I've told you all about my experiences with Tea Baggers and conservatives, a very intriguing event occurred recently. Hold on to your liberal, democratic hats, because I've just been propositioned, and you'll never guess by whom! Yes, you heard it right! I got propositioned by a couple of conservative Tea Baggers; some of the very same guys I've written about here previously! Normally, we are ideological, arch enemies, but this time the roles changed. Instead of political adversaries, on this occasion, I became the recruit, while the Tea Baggers took up the role of scouting! After the actual business transactions of the paper work had been completed, the two Tea Baggers asked me to sit down like we'd done so many times before to discuss the politics of the left and the right, but this was no ordinary sit down. After about 15 minutes had gone by, a guy with a couple of pizzas walks in the door and lays them down in front of us. The Tea Bagger's pay for the pizza, and then offer me as much as I want. They then explain to me how this five-meat pizza is all for me courtesy of the Tea Movement. I wanted to know why Tea Baggers would be buying me, of all people, a pizza; and it was there that it happened. The Tea Bagger's looked at me, and then one of them said, "We've got a proposition for you. We would like to know if you have ever considered attending a Tea rally or joining the movement." I then asked him if he'd been hitting the whiskey bottle, because he knows I'm not a conservative. I started looking around for the camera, because I just knew this had to be a joke, but the Tea Bagger was serious.

I will now attempt to reiterate the sales pitch/stump speech/recruitment address I was given by the Tea Bagger. All of this is based on a real statement, as he sat down beside me and said, "Come on man! Join the movement. Be a part of something real for a change. I know we've had our differences in the past, but we could use somebody like you. The Tea movement has been labeled as racist by many in the media, and that's a lie! This is where you come into the equation. We need a Black like you to help disprove such false allegations of racism. One of my friends on Facebook printed out some of your letters, and we believe that you have the talent to help our cause tremendously from a Black point of view. Ideas such as yours, coming from a person such as you would be an excellent tool for our movement to try and bring in some Blacks, which would prove to the world that we're not racist. You write pretty well, and your words could reach out to your people more than any White person could ever even think about doing. What do you say man? You could be the next Martin Luther King or the next Jessie Jackson, but this time you could lead your people in the right direction for a change. I mean, let's face it man! The liberal way of thinking has failed Blacks on a tragic level. I just can't understand why so many Blacks continue to support the liberalism of the Democratic Party, when it is painstakingly clear that they have done absolutely nothing for the Black community. All they have ever given you guys is a fraudulent puppet in Barack Obama, while your poor, mangled huts in the ghetto still look like Haiti. It's the liberalism of the Jessie Jackson's, the Reverend

Al Sharpton's, the Reverend Jeremiah Wright's, the Bill Ayers', the Al Gore's, the Barack Hussein Obama's, and the Louis Farrakhan's that have basically destroyed the Black community by teaching Blacks to use racism as an excuse to fail! These guys have convinced the Black community to find racism whenever and wherever possible, so they can blame all of their problems on the racist, White America, but it is liberalism that is to blame for selling that phony, racist, boogie man to the Blacks! Racism is more mythical than reality. Ninety percent of our society is a post-racial society, and Blacks need someone like you, Bryian R., to help them understand this. I've heard that you have a lot of White friends on your Facebook, so you know that racism is overrated and overused. Racism is not the obstacle that has devastated the Black community. That obstacle is the welfare system, which has replaced the Black father in the home and decimated the Black family! The minority based welfare system is your people's real enemy, and it was put there on purpose by the liberalism of the Democratic agenda, because it cannot survive without minority support, which cannot be sustained without minority anger aimed at America, and this is why the liberal, educational system took Black History out of the text books, so they could keep racism alive by vilifying America and the conservative way of life. The main component of liberalism is the hatred of America and the un-American ambitions to change this great country. The liberals don't care about you or your people. They just manipulate you in a pawned scheme to corrode America from the inside out. It hasn't been Jim Crow that's been holding you back for all of these years. It's been your liberal friends who've held you back to keep you angry and poor. Come join us, and help restore the Black community to prosperity by finally ridding the country of all the illegal immigrants who have been taking so many of the lower-ended jobs that are normally reserved for the Black community. That's why we, as conservatives, want all illegal immigrants gone immediately, unlike your liberal friends who only abet them, along with every other foreigner they liberally allow into this country to take our jobs away! The liberalized, federal government has made you and your people slaves all over again, by peddling drug-like, assistance programs and failing to enforce the immigration policies. You're smart enough to know better Bryian! Wise up and smell the deceit in the liberal coffee! Join us and set your people free from the lowly, liberal, democratic expectations they feel so obligated to live up to. Take some time to think about it, but ask yourself this one question. What have your liberal friends ever truly done for you Bryian?"

Wow, that was quite a statement that he made to me. He really poured it on thick. If that was not indoctrination, then I'd sure as hell like to know what it is. The Tea Bagger actually got to me. I mean, for a second, he actually got inside my head. For a fleeting moment, I actually second guessed my liberalized ideology, as I drove away asking myself this question, "Have I been duped by liberalism?" The Tea Party/conservative ideology thrives on the power of misinformation being applied to the misinformed to create a hellish element of a fear that threatens to exterminate the ways of life as you know them. I'm not saying that I'm the smartest person in the world, but what I am saying is that I am knowledgeable enough to recognize a flop-job when I'm presented with one.

Contrary to popular, overwhelmingly, conservative, beliefs, all African-Americans are not lazy, ignorant, and uneducated. A conservative, city council member once asked me this question at a local gym. He said to me: "How'd you get so smart anyway? What made you want to learn? Most of your people only learn the limited, impoverished cultures of the crime and thuggery of the Black environment."

So I said to him, "There is a public library down the street, and everyone has access to it. Even as a limited, Black kid from the hood, I had enough common sense to figure that out! I applied for a library card, and I went to the library and observed all of the information that I wanted to know about everything that I wanted to know about. Hell, they even have a library in the public school systems, and I used it too!" Barring some sort of disability, no one has to be ignorant if they don't want to be ignorant. Color is irrelevant.

With that said, it should have been transparently clear to the Tea Bagger that I, Bryian R., was not about to sell the family cow for three, conservative, magic beans in hopes of climbing some type of GOP/Tea Party bean stalk to the promised land of the good-ole-days. If I hadn't been so curious about the entire world and not just my environmental part of it, I could have very well been vulnerable to the Tea Bagger's propaganda of conservative integrity over liberal lies!

The first nail in my Tea Party/conservative coffin is any suggestion of the good-old-days. I would like to know exactly which good-ole-days are they referring to here, because I don't know that any of my African-American, good-ole-days can ever translate into the Tea Party's version of their good-ole-days. Furthermore, I would like the Tea Baggers to explain to me or show me exactly which days are supposed to be the good-ole-days for minorities? By my African-American perspective, the best days that we, as African-Americans, have experienced are occurring right now. That argument could easily be made and not just by me. I don't think it is a good idea to go around suggesting any aspirations of the good-ole-days to minorities such as African-Americans or Native Americans, because the good-ole-days for either of these groups would adamantly have to pre-date the oppressive regimes of power hungry movements eerily similar and directly related to the conservative ideology, the Tea Party, and the American expansion overall!

The second nail in my Tea Party/conservative coffin is the remodifying of racism from Jim Crow to Joe Liberal. Give me a f*cking break! The welfare system is the single most important shackle that has held African-American progress in captivity—really? You can't dupe me Mr. Tea Bagger! I've lived around African-Americans on welfare almost my entire life, and I can tell you firsthand that welfare is not the exclusive illness that plagues the African-American community. It is merely a symptom of it. What I saw growing up in my community that hurt people more than anything was what I call the limited parameters of existence. It's an old, Jim Crow echelon built to house and determine the potential of African-Americans and other minorities, similar to a glass ceiling that has been painted Black! There is no real progress and no comparable freedom with a boundary on it. The whole era of "Separate but Equal" alone was enough to place African-Americans so far behind the eight ball that fully catching up may take eons! The welfare system's inability to guarantee help to all African-Americans is definitely not perfectly constructed, but it pales in comparison to the unadulterated, unchallengeable corruption of blatant, racially distributed opportunities, which virtually guaranteed the African-American struggle and the private sector's benefit from it. Hell, sharecropping hurt African-Americans worse than welfare. You can try to polish up a Jim Crow turd all you want, but in the end; it's still a racist piece of crap!

The third nail in my Tea Party/conservative coffin was the constant ridicule of the liberal ideology of the current Democratic Party. You can't sit here and suggest to me that the same liberal electorate that voted for President Obama is the same group that conspires to keep African-Americans confused and angry at America, because nominating and electing the first African-American in U.S. history to the presidency is not a good way to keep African-Americans angry or confused! That one aspect alone has done more for African-Americans than the current conservative movement has ever done. It was the openness of the liberal ideology that dared to elect or nominate an African-American or a woman. It was the openness of the liberal ideology that helped Harriet Tubman free slaves on the Underground Railroad. It was liberalism that drove Abraham Lincoln to free slaves and allowed them to take up arms against southern Whites, and it was liberalism that pushed for civil rights and desegregation. Tea Baggers can try and say that it was the Sarah Palin's, the Rush Limbaugh's, the Ronald Reagan's, the Glenn Beck's, or the Fox News types of organizations that got out and fought to bring all of these changes to fruition, but I didn't just fall off the back of a turnip truck yesterday just to show up here today looking for leadership. Big changes made from big conservatism are a paradoxical statement in the first place, because conservatives can't stay very conservative through big changes or numerous changes. All of these accomplishments were made through liberalism and big government. That's why you didn't see Martin Luther King Jr. pleading his case to local leaders or conservatives.

The fourth and final nail in the Tea Party/conservative coffin is this disgusting accusation of African-Americans and other minorities harboring this deep, passionate hatred for America, when African-Americans have fought and died for this country in every war this country has ever been involved in. It wasn't that I didn't accept America; it just seemed that America was often reluctantly slow to accept me. The ideology of America is one of the most, if not the most, beautiful ideas ever created. I have never disputed that on any level. My only concern is that our government and our society continue to do all that it can to make the American ideology an American reality. It's not always the quantity of government that should be scrutinized. Sometimes it's the quality of government that is to blame, and it is the corrupted hand of corrupted man that regrettably connects the two, which is the same corrupt hand that held the whip of slavery. Instead of trying to give racism a sexier new make-over, why don't you Tea Partiers and conservatives focus more of your time and efforts on learning how to govern with a scalpel, as opposed to dictating with an elephant gun—the key word being elephant.

So I'm sorry Mr. Tea Bagger. I have decided NOT JOIN YOUR MOVEMENT. The only movement I plan to join is any movement that moves me to the left of you. I don't hate America. I don't hate you -Mr. Tea Bagger, and I don't hate your Tea movement. I hate the conservative ideology of trying to legislate a political time machine to reinvent time, rewrite history, pull back the present, and reframe the future into the conservatively nostalgic imagery that you alone have approved as fit! I think I'll be just fine right here where I am. I love my liberal friends too much to part with them now. They've judged me on the ideologies of my ideas and not the ethnicity of my pigmentation, and I think that's all the entire civil rights movement was ever asking for. So with this being my LeBron James moment as an Independent, free thinking, free agent which I am, I'm officially staying put with Joe Liberal and the liberalized state of mind! I'd like to personally thank you, Mr. Tea Bagger, for the five meat pizza, but I decline the glass of tea that comes along with it, as I told him the next time that I saw him. He told me that I was making a mistake, and I told him that it was my constitutional, big government right to do so!

Racial Profiling

This is the summer of 2009 in late July, and the entire nation is up in arms over the Professor Gates versus Officer Crowley controversy, during which Harvard Professor Louis Gates was arrested at his own home by a Cambridge police officer named Crowley. President Obama was asked about the situation during a press conference on health care. The president commented on how he felt the Cambridge police acted stupidly by arresting Mr. Gates even after finding out he was the owner of the home and not a burglar, which was the original reason Officer Crowley was called out to the scene. One of Gate's neighbors called 911 after seeing Gates and another man force their way into the Gates' home. Instead of focusing on why Gates was arrested at his own home on a false, burglary call, the nation focused on President Obama's decision to weigh in on the controversy. With his "acted stupidly" comment, Obama became the center of controversy and ill-will, instead of Gate's unlawful arrest. People have now used this as a ploy to fire a few holes in President Obama's popularity in hopes of stifling his new health care agenda. I can now hear the song "American Idiot" by Green Day in my mind because that is what lies ahead for as far as my eyes can see.

It is stunningly obvious to me that America does not give a damn about the unlawful arrest of a Harvard Professor at his own home, after he was unceremoniously cast as a possible intruder by a questionable, and quite possibly astronomically bigoted, neighbor. That neighbor had to know that it was Professor Gates, and not a burglar, at some point in time during this altercation, whether it was while Gates was trying to enter his house or once the police arrived on the scene. There is no way the surrounding community citizens, including the person who made the 911 call, did not know that it was Professor Gates. The person who made the call could have come out and helped diffuse the situation.

This is not a question about racism. This is not a question about President Obama. This is a question about your constitutional right to challenge the views and motives of a law enforcement officer, which we citizens have the right to do. We can question and challenge anyone's actions, even law enforcement's!

This is what happened to me. I exercise and lift weights every day, and I'm always a member of a gym somewhere. So I'm in this gym, which shall remain nameless, preparing for my daily workout, when I feel prying eyes watching me. I turned around to look, and there was a police officer and what I felt to be a plainclothes police officer staring at me in this empty locker room. Now I'd seen both of them there before and exchanged greetings on a regular basis; no big deal, but today was different. As I changed into my workout clothes, the two officers also changed into their workout gear. One of them tried to butter me up about how in shape I was. He smiled and laughed with me, trying to gain my confidence. Keep in mind; I did not know this guy from Adam. He told me how he'd seen me in the gym every day and that he liked that big, new Dodge Charger I drove. Now, I was starting to get concerned, and I tried to play it off, but it did not stop there. He then made the statement, "I hear you're pretty popular in the hood. I hear you're the man over there. I've seen you over there numerous times." Now keep in mind again that I didn't know this guy, but he obviously knew quite a bit about me—a little too much about me. By this time, I'm in full-fledged defense mode, but still; it didn't stop there. He then made another statement, "So, what makes you wanna come in here so much, why the gym? Why aren't you out doing other stuff? How do you afford to pay for this membership? Do you work?" I was furious! So allow me to school White America about something they probably don't understand, especially people like Bay Buchanan, Rush Limbaugh, and other conservative characters. The question by the officer of "Do you work" is a stereotypical, race-baiting question and a high caliber insult. When someone asks where you work, they are giving you their nod of confidence that they do believe you are gainfully employed somewhere. When someone asks, do you work? They are telling you that they believe you are not gainfully employed; possibly never have been, and more than likely never will be. What the cop was saying to me was that he believed I could be a potential drug dealer or other criminal activist. He had no right to question my employment status. This was not a traffic stop, and no laws were being broken. I didn't know if he was on or off duty. So I told him it was none of his business whether or not I had a job. I said, "I don't have to tell you that! Why in the hell are asking me 50,000 questions? I don't owe you an explanation! I don't owe you sh-t!" He then said to me, "Don't be getting all defensive with me! I just asked you a simple question, which you could not answer! Why not? Do you have something to hide?" At that very moment, I snapped! I told him; "You can get the f-ck out of my face with that bullsh-t! I ain't got nothing else to say to you man," and I did not whisper it in a nice and friendly tone either! He then said this back to me: "You don't talk to me like that, boy! I'll take your ass to jail for disorderly conduct and disturbing the peace! You'd better calm down right now, or I and my partner will be forced to restrain you, if you know what I mean!"

I thought about trying to physically confront this fool, but there were two of them, and they were probably armed with something. So I apologized to both of them for losing my temper and walked away. The last thing he said to me was, "We will be keeping an eye on you--

boy!" I'd like to be able to sit here and tell all of you how I laid into his ass, but it just did not happen. I guess you can call me a pussy because I back-pedaled. I considered everything I had to lose and decided this fight was not the one to go all out on. And even if it was, physically confronting an officer could have been a death wish. There were no witnesses, and it would have been my word against both of the officers' word. I would have lost and been made to be the villain, just like Professor Gates. Now that I look back on it, this was not necessarily racism, but it was most definitely entrapment! The cop instigated this entire exchange and came close to coaxing me into an over-budgeted fine and a free ride downtown. This is what could have happened to Professor Gates, which brings up a very important question. Do we as African-Americans have the constitutional right to protest what we deem to be oppression, even if it means protesting law enforcement? I protested the treatment I was receiving, and I refused to facilitate the requested information. The more I stood my ground, the more agitated the officer became. It was not the color of my skin that agitated him. It was my unwillingness to kiss his ass! It was my unwillingness to submit, and since most people don't really know their rights, standing down tends to be the norm. This officer would never exchange internal affairs this way. He would also never engage his superior, the mayor, a government official, a high-ranking, media mogul; the governor, the president, or any other prestigious plenipotentiary this way either. The reason the officer mistreated me is because he felt I was no threat to him, despite not knowing exactly who I was or to whom I could have been related to. I would call this dictating, submissive, class profiling or DSC, because he assumed that he could dictate his will onto me, and I was supposed to submit because my class is not supposed to be high enough to know any better. Things quickly began to spiral out of control when I bucked his system, because correctly trying to profile someone's entire class makeup is a flawed endeavor at best. This is an absolute abuse of power that goes far beyond race. Only a Realacrat could ever muster up enough courage and insight to expose this corrupt power for what it is. Democrats are too afraid, and Republicans are too uniform.

Speaking of uniforms, I am seriously perplexed at the steep number of people in this country who are just more than willing to give any cop the benefit of the righteous doubt just because they wear a uniform, as though a uniform automatically provides an aura of fairness and goodness around whoever puts one on. I find that laughable and illogical. A uniform is only as good as the person who's wearing it. A racist dogmatist is just as corrupt without the badge as he is behind the badge. You can put lipstick on a goat; only now it's a goat with shiny lips. You can also put a badge on a bigot, and what you'll then have is a badge-toting moron with the authority to enforce his personal vendettas with the usage of deadly force. Now I'll say it again. If you can't be professional, then maybe; you should find another job in a different profession, and that advice goes for everyone.

As for all of the so-called law enforcement supporters, who always use the "cops put their lives in danger everyday" argument to justify any and everything under the sun—if these people truly supported law enforcement the way they claim to support it, they would pay police officers more—a lot more! I think the fact that law enforcement is paid so poorly in this country speaks volumes about how they are actually viewed—minus the hollow, rhetorical, grandstanding support they only receive when positioned against a minority. If I was in law enforcement, I would ask to be paid more numerically and less rhetorically, because talk is cheap, but bills are not. As a Realacrat, I am in favor of law enforcement being paid more, but I am also in favor of a drastic reduction in minority-based hostilities and unjustifiable profiling aligned within the favorable possibilities of the African-American as the world's greatest criminal/drug-dealer/gang-member/pimp/rapist/violence magnet/convicted felon/automatically assumed, criminal-record-owning synopsis of a felon, and once it has been determined that I am as legal they come, I should be immediately allowed to move along. Crime can appear from any direction, but you'd never know it, if you spent all of your time looking in one specific direction, which is racial profiling if that direction just happens to be predominately minority based. I think that you have to investigate the profile, instead of just allowing the profile to become the investigation. I don't believe the sole backbone of suspicion can always be profile driven, because a profile might not always yield the pathway to the truth. In order to achieve that, some good, ole, investigative, detective work will have to be done.

For example, a law enforcement officer once told me that his basis for pulling over African-American drivers was based entirely on odds. He said to me, and I quote: "I always pull over Blacks, Mexicans, or those who appear to be beggarly, because the odds of uncovering a criminal element are so reliably good, especially for young, Black males! Here's the way I see it. Blacks represent the face of crime in this country; fairly or unfairly! So when I pull over a Black, I assume that he was either on his way to commit a crime, or he is on his way back from committing a crime, which puts the odds in my favor to uncover something incriminating when I pull the individual over. It's like shooting fish in a barrel. It's a great way to pad your stats, and it works more than it fails!"

Now don't get me wrong. I think the role of law enforcement is a very important job, and I believe it should be treated in a manner that conveys that importance, but the stat padding and fishy barrel shooting has to end, especially at my minority expense. I don't want any part of being society's homecoming, so people can have a cakewalk taking me down in front of the home crowd, because I'm proverbially easy to defeat! Homecomings are nice, but they should not make up the entire schedule. You have to play the tough games too! The idea is to serve and protect the people, not your career numbers.

Harold Ford Jr.

Harold Ford Jr. is my favorite candidate outside of Hillary Clinton. I even like Ford Jr. more than I like President Obama. At one point, I thought for certain that Ford Jr. would be the first African-American vice-president, as Hillary's running mate. My how times have changed! I still like Ford Jr., and I still believe he has the potential to do great things in his political career, but he will have to pull the well-known rabbit out-of-the-hat trick to make it happen, because his political landscape is bleak at the moment, and I have never been so disappointed in a candidate the way that I am disappointed in him right now.

Harold Ford Jr.'s father, Harold Ford Sr., represented Tennessee's ninth congressional district eleven times during his illustrious career. He retired in 1996 and personally passed the torch to Harold Ford Jr., who did quite well and began to make a name for himself. There were even rumblings of him being Hillary Clinton's possible running mate in her potential presidential campaign, but she failed to secure the Democratic nomination; eventually losing to Barack Obama in the Democratic Primaries.

The future looked bright for Harold Ford Jr., but someway somehow he was ambitiously advised to run for the U.S. Senate for the state of Tennessee in hopes of replacing retiring U.S. Senator Bill Frist, where he would ultimately lose to current U.S. Senator-Bob Corker, who is a Republican. I don't know who advised Ford Jr. to make such an over-the-top decision, but it has cost him dearly in the world of politics. He went from a rising star to political obscurity almost overnight.

What were you thinking Ford Jr.? You're from the state of Tennessee. You should know better! It's no secret how the demographics drastically change once you get outside of the Memphis/Shelby County area. Did you really believe that people from Johnson City, Tennessee, Bristol, Tennessee, Knoxville, Tennessee, Chattanooga, Tennessee or Pigeon Forge, Tennessee were actually going to vote for you? You're a light-skinned guy, but you're still too dark to be elected by that bunch! I mean, Al Gore couldn't even carry the state of Tennessee during his 2000 presidential bid, and he's also from Tennessee, and he's White! If the state of Tennessee would not accept a Democratic platform from Al Gore, what in the universe made you, Ford Jr., ever think they would accept that same platform from you? Back in 2000, there was a chance to put a fellow Tennessean in the White House as President of the United States, because if Al Gore had carried Tennessee he would have won the presidency. The state of Tennessee turned down an opportunity at a homegrown presidency and instead threw their support behind some conservative agenda; that in their minds has probably gotten them closer to the White God! Texas beat Tennessee again, as George W. Bush slipped by Al Gore, with an assist from Katherine Harris, in 2000 to become President of the United States.

Harold Ford Sr. left his ninth congressional district seat specifically for you Ford Jr., and I'm sure you could have held it for as long as you desired. You should have taken a page out of your father's book and kept your open invitation to Washington, because it's proving to be very tough for you to get back there. If you had remained in that position, I'm sure you could have been a major contributor to the health care debate in the House of Representatives. I think the Democratic Party could have definitely used your support. It's a shame that you weren't there.

I never quite understood the value of congressional districts until Ford Jr. gave up his congressional district seat in hopes of becoming a U.S. Senator. Thanks to Harold Ford Sr., I now get it! The most important political device needed for African-American success in the U.S. government regarding elected offices are the traditionally and highly African-American/minority populated congressional districts, because without such districts; the current version of the U.S. Senate would be duplicated identically by the U.S. House of Representatives-past and current. This is precisely why there are rarely any African-American/ minority U.S. Senators, but there is almost always an adequate number of African-American/minority U.S. Representatives. This has proven to be a political reality in the past, and it remains a political reality today. The Congressional Black Caucasus could not survive or exist without the demographic support of these congressional districts.

By my estimations, an African-American candidate cannot perennially win elections without a strong contingent of African-American/minority voters. Meaning, even if Harold Ford Jr. had won his senate race against Bob Corker, the odds of Ford Jr. holding on to that seat were slim to none, because some movement similar to the current Tea Party movement would finance a candidate built strictly to pillage and diminish any White voting support Ford Jr. could muster; similar to the way that Sarah Palin's handlers hope that she can reclaim White voters from President Obama. In the real world of politics, Republicans and Tea Party members aren't going out to recruit or indoctrinate African-Americans or other minorities. Republicans are only after the White vote, because they know that African-American/ minority turnout is streaky and unreliable on most occasions. Without the White vote, African-Americans/minorities can only consistently win in congressional districts like the one Harold Ford Jr. and Harold Ford Sr. won at will. Arkansas Senator Blanche Lincoln and Nevada Senator Harry Reid had better be taking notes on all of this, because their White voting support will be viscously under siege in 2010. If both can curtail a huge number of their White voting defectors over to the GOP, they will probably both be re-elected in 2010.

As for race between the current ninth congressional seat holder, Steve Cohen, and his new challenger, former Memphis Mayor, Dr. Willie Herenton, I'm in favor of Herenton, because I've always liked his political prowess. I don't believe the ninth congressional seat should be designated for African-Americans only, but I do understand that Steve Cohen, who I feel is a good politician, being elected to represent that area is, unfortunately, another missed opportunity for African-Americans to be represented in government, when African-Americans are already severely underrepresented. If I lived in Shelby County, I would vote for Herenton. If the challenging candidate was someone other than Herenton, I would have to lean towards Cohen. And for the record, I think Dr. Willie Herenton has done more the city of Memphis, Tennessee than any other Mayor in recent memory! In my book, he is the man!

As for the future of Harold Ford Jr., the only thing I can see that could potentially help him become relevant again is a spot on CNN; a possible duet venture with Roland Martin. The "Don Imus Show" is not a bad venture for Ford Jr., but it won't return him to political glory. He needs a political make-over!

CONFEDERATE HISTORY MONTH VS. BRYIAN R.

So now we have Confederate History month-how dandy. I can't think of anything more genuine than 30 days to honor the Confederacy. Now that is some time well spent! Let's get real people! I've been learning and studying the Civil War ever since I was in grade school. I would assume that most of you have also learned the same. I simply cannot see the relevance of learning the Confederacy separate from the Civil War. Why the differentiation? What exactly is it that is better learned by studying the Confederacy, either separate from the Civil War or more exclusively from a southern point of view? I personally don't think there is anything in a Confederate History Month that hasn't been thoroughly covered within the classic, Civil War, history chronicles; except for maybe sympathy for the south! Okay Mr. Confederacy, give me one reason as to why there should be a Confederate History Month that either replaces Civil War history or stands outside of Civil War history. Why not just present a Civil War History Month, if there is such a thing? And if there is not, then there certainly should be.

Now why would anyone feel the need to establish a Confederate History Month separate from the Civil War history? Do they feel as if the historians have painted an unfair portrait of the Confederacy? I would bet they probably do! Are they using this as a subconsciously, suggestive message used as a declaration of their remaining and continuing ideological succession from the Union? I would argue yes again, and it is here that the answers become more visible. The Civil War defeat has always been a source of bitterness and dissent for the south! I think it's safe to say that the term sore loser is an understatement when applied here. The southern disdain at the proverbial, carpetbagging Yankee/northerner is as real as it gets. Now, I know Bubba and Jim Bob, from the pick-up truck with a 30 pack in it, will accuse me of fabricating my ideologies to stir racism, but I'm from the south, and I live in the south.

I'm here to tell you that there is a definite disconnect and a definite dislike for the following: liberals/Democrats/Reconstruction/the Union Army/the north/the federal government/Abraham Lincoln/ John F. Kennedy/the acknowledgement, acceptance, and ownership of American slavery/ the acknowledgement, acceptance, and ownership of the dire decimation of Native Americans and the plundering of their land/any microscopic inkling at American slavery reparations/Roots or any movie dealing with racial tensions showing the oppression of African-Americans by White oppressors/the Ted Kennedy ideology of liberalism/Hollywood/legal immigration/illegal immigration/the public option/the minority based welfare system/interracial relationships, especially Blacks and Whites/middle-class minorities/Arabs of any kind/ turbans/foreign accents or anyone who speaks in their native tongue/ Jesus as a Middle-Easterner/Black Jesus/ethnic Jesus/any non-European Jesus/The Martin Luther King Jr. Holiday/Black History Month/the success of the Civil Rights Era/Charles Darwin/Evolution/Global Warming/Al Gore/Nancy Pelosi/San Francisco/Chicago/New York/ California/Oregon/Illinois/Hawaii/Science as a whole/any technology or science that threatens the religious status quo/any educational premise that threatens the religious status quo/any inkling of a possibility of extraterrestrial life/Harvard, because Obama went there/Roe vs. Wade/

foreign cars/too many rich, Black athletes/the NBA and all of its thugs/ hip hop and all of its thugs/affirmative action/the NAACP/ the Native American's unwillingness to be mascots/the race mixing indoctrinations of CNN and MSNBC/gay marriage/Islam/Communist China, because they kick our ass industrially/learning Spanish or any other foreign language/John Kerry's African wife and her Heinz Ketchup/the evil, dark inner-cities/Tiger Woods' Black half, which made him cheat/ Michelle Obama/Reverend Wright/Al Sharpton/Jessie Jackson Sr./the success of the race mixing Clintons, and most of all, the Black president! All of these abominations (Obamanations) all represent this so-called "New America!" This is the place where the Tea Partiers intend to take their country back from! In under a week, I can hear passionate disdain spewed at over 95% of everything in that list. And then the next week, I'll be forced to hear it all again! After absorbing all of these ideological piñata beatings, it has now become ingrained in my psyche, so I decided to write about it.

To Confederacy sympathizers, all of this represents new America, and it was all made possible by the Civil War defeat. You know, there's an old saying down here that was turned into a song called "If the South Would 'a Won, We'd a Had It Made," People still sing it, and people still believe in it. The south still has not gotten over the ramifications of the Civil War. This Confederate History Month is a way of saying I still hate the federal government for freeing the slaves and paying them undercover reparations in the form of welfare, which comes out of my hard earned tax dollars! If you're a Democrat, and you've often wondered why your party is so despised, now you know why, because even though Abraham Lincoln was a Republican, the modern day Democratic Party just happens to be the last man standing; similar to the way Dr. Conrad Murray just happened to the doctor holding the I.V. at that specific time when Michael Jackson died. Again, Joe and Bob, from the land of denial, will not believe me, but I know! As I've said before, people are blatant about their racist views in the south! Just yesterday, I saw a pick-up truck with the words, "Obama and Osama are terrorist brothers here to destroy America! Let's get them first!" People have either come up to me and told me these things personally, or they have held conversations stating these beliefs right in front of me. Now you have to wonder why sane people would be so brazen in front of someone like me, when they can clearly see that I'm an African-American. Maybe they think I'm too dumb to pick it all up and too uneducated to know what to do with it, even if I did experience a serendipitous brain fart, but you'd be amazed at what you can learn just listening and observing people. Arrogant anger and arrogant ignorance will often show their hand quickly and proudly regardless of whom they are showing it to, because there are many who equate my cognitive ability to that of a convicted felon or an ethnic, royal fool. Some have even accused me of hiring a White ghostwriter to impress my friends on Facebook, and if you believe that; I've got some condos and golf courses in Antarctica I'd like to sell you!

Why don't we all dress up like Nazis and have Nazi History Month, where we celebrate the herding of innocent people into cyanide showers? Let's see how the Jewish Community feels about that! Why don't we all dress up like the U.S. Calvary and have U.S. Calvary Month, where we celebrate the ethnic, genocidal plundering of Native Americans? Let's see how the Native Americans would feel about that. So Virginia Governor Bob McDonnell wants to acknowledge Confederate History Month! I'm sure he does, and I'm not surprised by it! Why don't you ask the former U.S. Mississippi Senator Trent Lott about hoisting up Confederate ideologies? McDonnell's omission of slavery falls right in line with an ideology I'm already familiar with. There is a strong sentiment that operates on the notion that slavery was overrated; nothing more than trumped up, grossly, exaggerated charges of oppression and racism. There are some who have even suggested that slavery was good, and it actually resembled something along the lines of indentured servantry, which means the Confederacy was not fighting to uphold the horrors of true slavery, but merely fighting for the sanctity of their homelands like the true patriots they were. This is undeniable proof that you can almost justify anything!

Basically, tales of slave horror are nothing more than a liberal/ Democratic plot to vilify the Confederacy and indoctrinate minorities into the Democratic Party to horde their votes. I have even been told that there were White slaves who got out in the fields and worked side by side with Black slaves in some sort of plantational co-op. Let me just say this. If you were White back in the 1700s or 1800s, and you were relegated to slavery, you must have done something so bad that it must have fallen just underneath a hanging offense, for you to be forced into slavery!

I also had some idiotic, young person tell me that her mother told her that slavery wasn't that bad. It was just a little hard work-that's all! So I posed this question to her. I asked the dolt, "Well, if that's the case, why don't you, your mother, and your other siblings, especially your female siblings, come on over and be my slaves! It won't be that bad. It will just be a little hard work-that's all!" She then became vehemently and visibly bad-tempered and ill-mannered, as she yelled to me, "I'll never be an f'n slave! I'll kill myself first! You'll never own me! You Black monkey!" I then said to her, as she stormed away, "I thought you said it wasn't that bad! I didn't even tell you what I wanted you to do yet!" She power walked herself away in a fury giving me a parting shot by saying, "F*ck you! You tar baby looking nigger!" I think I'd rather be a tar baby, instead of a pseudo-religious, pseudo-entitled, pseudo-educated, pseudo-humanistic jackass!

As President Obama would say, let me be perfectly clear! Anyone who is monumentally and colossally ignorant enough to ill-advisedly use the phrase "It's not that bad" as a descriptor for slavery should be dragged kicking and screaming through the streets eerily reminiscent to the dragging of the Saddam Hussein statue by the U.S. military in Baghdad, to a dungeon-like pit about 30 feet down below a jail, where they would have a can of spam and a bottle of warm water dropped in on them three times a day. Whether it's a White slave, a Mexican slave, a Jewish slave, a Native American slave, an Asian American slave, an Arab American slave, an African-American slave, or an extraterrestrial slave, it is unequivocally wrong, unequivocally indefensible, and unequivocally unjustifiable!

There is nothing wrong with studying the Civil War. I think not learning about the totality of the Civil War is academically and humanly unacceptable. If you want to learn about the Confederacy's abundance of highly-qualified, military generals like Robert E. Lee and Stonewall Jackson, that's one thing! If you want to learn about the Confederacy's audacious fortitude to succeed from the federal government, and then confront the federal government militarily, that's one thing! If you want to learn about the Confederacy's bravery in facing a much more physically stronger opponent with limited supplies and an outnumbered fighting capacity, that's one thing! If you want to learn about how the Confederacy made a huge mistake by allowing 90% of the war to be fought on southern soil, which gave the Union an advantageous opportunity at sabotaging and cutting southern supply lines, that's one thing! If you want to learn about the loyalties of the Confederacy to fight for their local neighbors and not against their local neighbors, that's one thing! If you want to learn about how the influx of Black Union soldiers put the death nail in the Confederacy's chances of winning the Civil War, that's one thing, but if you intend to learn about the Confederacy's ethical treatment of slavery or a complete omission of slavery all together in some half-assed attempt sweep the slave picked cotton underneath the plantational rug, that's bullsh*t! You can't just close your eyes and make the truth go away. You can always rewrite your version of history, but you cannot change history's version of history.

No matter how you dissect it, the Confederacy fought to uphold the rights of the southern states, who just happened to be slave states, to defy the federal government and make their own rules, and the first rule made would be the continuation of free, slave labor for the sake of unadulterated profit absent of a labor induced payroll! The Confederacy was nothing more than pre-Wall St.; pre-corporate; pre- big oil; pre-insurance company; pre-fat cat executive, golden parachute clutching greed mongers!

NIGGER, NIGGA, NIGGAH, THE N-WORD!

One could certainly make the argument that there has never been a more polarizing controversial word than the n-word. If you want to get a fight started, then start tossing that word around. Just recently, here on a previous thread, someone made a comment about a house niggah, and people went berserk! The conversation had to do with the aspect of whether or not President Obama is a house nigga, due to his perceived lack of accomplishments in the field of African-American issues! The person who made this comment was White, and that didn't help the situation in the least bit. People began to question the merits of this individual, and then some even began to question my merits, even suggesting that I was a house niggah myself for even being affiliated with this individual, as only a bonafied house niggah would befriend a White person who would so willingly use the n-word in any formation, because it is strictly off limits to everyone except African-Americans. I guess there were some who were expecting me to enforce this unwritten rule of ethnic behavior, even to the point where a couple of them have decided to vacant my friendship because of it.

I am not a racial babysitter, and I'm not here to teach you or anyone else racial ethics! I can only tell you what I do. I do everything within my power not to address other African-Americans as nigger or nigga. I just have no desire to walk up to another African-American and say, "Hey nigga! Come here nigga!" Now I used to engage in such behavior when I was much younger, but part of being youthful is to be careless, shortsighted, and foolish! At this stage in my life and even as far back as my mid 20's, the terminology of nigga just became ignorant to me. The statement: "Hey nigga! Come here nigga" just sounds very unintelligent to me, but that's me. It may not be you. In my opinion, for me to address another African-American as a nigga, it would be a grand, disrespectful insult to that individual and to me. It exemplifies my ignorance by calling someone a nigga when it is clearly apparent that not everyone wants to be addressed that way. By doing this, I have imposed the arrogance of my ignorance on someone else who obviously does not deserve it; making me a fool of grand proportions! This is why I don't do it, but I can only speak for me. It has nothing to do with my illusionary ownership of the word, because none of us can truly own a word; but we can make a conscious effort to either own or live up to the societal baggage that comes along with a word or a label, or we can make that same conscious effort to disown and not live up to the societal baggage that anchors a word or a label in the murkiness or clarity of its perceptions.

The n-word is not really just a word. It's a perception, an opinion, a judgment, and a label. The word nigger or nigga means absolutely nothing, without the baggage that comes drudging along with it. The n-word implies a second classed citizenship of nationality and of humanity, depending on how it's used. For example, if a White person says, "You stupid nigger or stupid, Black nigger," the meaning behind the word comes across as an accusation of genetic inferiority; meaning, "I'm better than you, because I'm White! I'm also better than you because, most of all, I'm not Black!" Like the symbolisms behind such words as: blackballed, Black Monday, Black Death, Black Plague, Black cat, or blackmail, the full weight of all that is negative has been placed on the color Black, which just happens to be your skin color, if you are an African-American. The perpetrator didn't actually say that you, as an African-American, were all of these negative aspects, but they certainly implied strongly that you, as an African-American, seem to harbor more reasons that you should be on that Black list than reasons to say that you should not.

For example, when another African-American walks up and says, "Hey Nigga!" It's still only highly controversial at best. When I say to my African-American friend Tyrone, "You're a dumb ass nigga," I'm essentially implying that same negative sentiment about blackness that I spoke about previously when emanating from a White person. The only difference is, by me saying it; Tyrone can take some racial comfort in knowing beyond a shadow of a doubt that I am just as Black, just as stereotyped, and just as limited as he is, which disallows me to truly look down on him like other ethnicities can often attempt to do.

Now here is the flipped side! I represent what is referred to as a typical, medium, brown-skinned brother. I once dated this extremely light-skinned, African-American woman. It was here that I discovered a disturbing trend of racially, charged colorism. Whenever she and I would get into any kind of disagreement, insults would fly around like the stones that shatter glass houses! That part is normal behavior, but whenever she was really angry with me; she would take it down a notch to really try and hurt me by, that's right; you guessed it, insulting the color of my skin! For example, if the argument got vicious enough, she would say something to the effect of; "You no good, Black, burned up, nigga! You're nothing but an oily, Black "Creature from the Black Lagoon," with your ugly, Black, nigga ass!" The verbal assaults I suffered from her were actually astronomically more frequent and astronomically more vicious than any of the racial shots that I took from White people! So, why did she do it, and she wasn't the only light-skinned woman to do it either? In fact, I cannot recall a single time during my life that a dark-skinned, African-American woman ever said anything even remotely close to that.

Here is why. It all goes back to that infamous "House Niggah" statement that I spoke about at the beginning that started this entire discussion. The typical imagery of the house nigger of the American, slavery era was that of a lighter-skinned slave who was allowed to work in the house serving the master, without having to be out in the blistering, punishing heat of the cotton fields. The darker a slave was; the more likely that slave would be given a life-time membership into the fields. This created a riff between light-skinned African-Americans and dark-skinned African-Americans that still exist till this very day.

There is a very infamous scene from the movie *New Jack City,* where the dark-skinned character Nino Brown, who is played by Wesley Snipes, confronts one of his light-skinned workers, who is played by Christopher Williams. In a scene that has resonated throughout the African-American community, Wesley Snipes stabs Christopher Williams in the hand, and then verbally elaborates his disdain at the proverbial prettiness of the light-skinned Christopher Williams after he has stabbed him! Now to the ethnically untrained eye, that probably appeared to be nothing more than a ruthless act of a violent punishment, but to African-Americans; it was the quintessential shot fired around the African-American communities of dark, Black men finally getting a chance to strike back at their in-home, arch nemesis, as Mr. Snipes struck a blow for dark men all over the planet! And think about this, I have never lost a woman to a darker-skinned, African-American man, but when a light-skinned man, African-American or other, decided that he wanted my woman, he got her!

Basically, what you have is the Obama Black vs. the Wesley Snipes Black, with the Obama Black being the preferred choice among African-Americans, Whites, and most of the other ethnic groups. This is specifically why so many light-skinned, African-American women felt they had the privilege to look down on and talk down to the darkness of my skin color, and I'm not the only with this experience! I've also witnessed light-skinned, African-American men say the same things to dark-skinned, African-American women! Gender is not the issue here, although there are many who would probably like to turn it into that. The fact that my light-skinned, African-American girlfriend was light-skinned gave her a false sense of entitlement over me and my dark-skinned appearance. I was luckier to have her light beauty than she was to have my dark handicap, and she treated me like it; and I graciously accepted it! We could be having a fight about the remote control, bathroom tissue, or a rusty bolt, but somehow someway the subject would always find its way back to calling me a black gorilla! I'd approximate that about 99.9% of the insults hurled at me with the strong intentions of hurting my feelings were all based on my dark skin, and that's no coincidence! In her mind, and quite possibly in mine too, she was a cut above me on the scale of humanity, which she took great pride in! It's very similar to the White, goodness motto which says, "I'm better than you because I'm not Black like you!" This is a false sense of entitlement to an extent. There is no doubt that light-skinned, African-Americans usually get the better breaks in life, but no matter how successful any African-American may become due to skin color or ability; they are all one incident away from being demoted back down to plain, old nigger again by the hatred and fear that still exist.

The underlying theme to all of this is something that is not really all that underlying at all, which is Black is ugly, Black is nasty, Black is the lowest of the low, with the word nigger meaning Black. And just like with those previously mentioned words such as: blackmail, blackball, or Black Plague; our society has also engineered the opposite effect by attaching certain qualities to all that is good, with the word nigger not a part of that equation. For instance, in the African-American community the term "Pretty Boy" means an African-American or somebody who is not White, but they are light-skinned or close to White. Someone like a: Smokey Robinson, a Ginuwine, or an El Debarge type of individual would be the perfect replicas. Many of these individuals often have what's known as "Good Hair," which means unkinked, straight, curly straight hair that is very similar to White, Caucasian hair. The last thing these individuals sometimes have is an exotic, natural, eye color like: blue, green, blue-green, hazel or anything greyish. This is what's known as having "Good Eyes" or "Pretty Eyes," because such eye colors are thought of as being something you would see in Whites more than you would ever see in Blacks. In other words, the closer you are to White; the closer you are to what's right, to the point where you're, at least, not as much of a nigger, but the closer you are to Black, the pendulum of goodness swings hard back in the other direction! Either purposely or inadvertently, whenever you hoist up the characteristics most closely resembling Whiteness, you are also culturally decimating and aimlessly throwing those other opposite characteristics that least resembles Whiteness under the throw-away bus!

It's to the point now, where some African-Americans have taken to genetic engineering; meaning, many have made it mandatory to seek out more White/light-skinned characteristics to incorporate into their children. I'm sure it has always gone on, but now we're at the point that people are blatantly admitting to engaging in this behavior. I've had at least 5 to 10 African-Americans privately admit to genetically engineering their children's DNA structure to make it less dark and more lightened, and not a one of them was of a lighter-skinned complexion! These were all darker individuals. I'll never forget when this special person said to me: "I don't want no dark-skinned kids. I know what's it's like to be dark-skinned, and it ain't pretty, but my kids will be different. I've seen to that. I purposely fathered my children with a White woman, so they won't have to endure the full brunt of niggerism like I did. My kids will be able to date Whites and Blacks, because of the way they look, and they won't have to be racially ridiculed as if they were some Black, tar-baby niggers who completely disappear when the lights go out! You hear White people say how much they disapprove of mixed kids more than you hear it from Blacks, and that's pure jealousy! They say that mixed, bi-racial kids will grow up confused, but that's not their real concern. White people understand that mixed kids will have a much better chance at attracting their White children as potential mates, because mix kids are further removed from the stigma of nigger Black than a person like me could ever hope to be. I've given my kids the pigmentation needed to win, by simply not being Black/dark-skinned."

Now I was stunned to hear such an admission, but I think I understand the point of it all. This person's mixed kids were Black ideologically, but they were not Black figuratively, which means that the world may not be as judgmental of their pigmentation; giving them an advantage over those that are darker. Honestly, I don't know if there is another word or if there has ever been another word that carries more extra, circular negativity; has so many different meanings, and is colored in such extraordinarily shades of dark grey than the word nigger! It is arguably the most complex word that many of us may ever use, because it is so circumstantial!

With that being said, now would be a great time to explain the terminology of nigger vs. the terminology of nigga! The negativity behind the word nigger is derived from the American slavery/Jim Crow days. Whether it was the slave master, law enforcement or anyone White, the word nigger was used as a marker to designate and castigate Blacks into their rightful places underneath the bottom of the barrel, which in all likelihood, was the precursor to the modern day version of the have's and the have not's!

Some African-Americans such as 2Pac Shakur and others have tried to fight back against the powerlessness of the nigger baggage that all African-Americans must carry, by trying to change and rearrange the spelling, meaning, ownership, and power of the word nigger by re-branding it nigga with an A instead of an ER. I think 2Pac Shakur personally redefined the nigger baggage into something less diminutive towards African-Americans, by defining it as such: "N.I.G.G.A., Never Ignorant Getting Goals Accomplished!" This is a way for African-Americans to try and restructure the power base of the n-word/nigger/nigga terminology, imagery, and symbolism. In my opinion, this was just the newer version of the old "Black Is Beautiful" campaigns, which you just don't seem to hear about as much during this current era. Again, in my opinion, when it comes to the "Black Is Beautiful" saying, it appears that there are far more people who say it than there are those who truly believe in it, mean it, or live it. The idea of restructuring the word nigger to nigga is a valiant effort, and it is also well-intended, but I just don't know how effective it can actually be. Since African-Americans independently defined the word nigga, they feel like the word, and the usage of that word belongs to them only, which ideologically it might; but realistically it does not, which cracks the door open for the word nigger to always be just a turned door knob away.

When you look at everything that's going on right now with Dr. Laura Schlessinger's recent n-word comments, you can see just how controversial the usage of this word truly is, whether you spell it with an A or an ER. Dr. Laura, similarly to Axl Rose back in the late 80's and early 90's, feels that since other African-Americans are allowed to use the word, then she; along with other White people, should be allowed to use it as well. She points to the many Black comics and Black rappers who use the nigga version of the word as a term of endearment. I've even heard other White people call themselves niggas! The argument I used to always make was based on common sense. How can you expect

White people to buy Black music or participate in Black culture that has nigga terminology all throughout it without someway being influenced by it, at least to the point where they'd sing along to it?

I remember when I was riding down the street with some of my White friends, and we were listening to a rap group called "The Geto Boys!" All of my White friends would sing along to the words of the song until the nigga parts came up. Every time that happened; they would try to censor themselves as not to offend me. The line in the song went something like: "I'll blow your f*cking head off nigga! I ain't afraid to pop a cap in a nigga!" Now I could listen to that all day long and not be offended, but if the White guy sitting beside me, who was actually playing this music, incidentally said the word nigga as he sang along, I'm supposed to get irate and go off on him! This entire thing is childish. Instead of getting offended by a song which represents, perpetuates, and glorifies a culture of Black on Black crime and Black on Black communal destruction, I, along with many other African-Americans, would rather spend my time waiting on some White person to just say the word nigga, even if it was inadvertently; so we can lash out at him for everything racism has put us through!

Whether it's nigger or nigga, I'll tell you what I have chosen to do. I don't care how many comics I hear or how many songs I play. I don't go up to Hispanics or Hispanic Americans using derogatory definers like: wetbacks, greasy Mexicans, or border jumpers! I don't go up to Jewish people and refer to them as: Jesus killers, corporate slobs, or Holocaust wannabes! I don't go up to Asian Americans and refer to them as: slant eyed chinks, sushi lovers, or gooks! And last but not least; I don't go up to African-Americans and using destructive terminology like: welfare checker, coon, porch monkey, watermelon, nigger, or nigga! I don't care how many of these groupings use such terminology amongst themselves. I'm not going to address people that way. Life is filled with choices. We should never be afraid to make a few, and you don't have to choose to disrespect people because some entertainer or some hot head engages in it. As my version of the old saying goes, "Monkey sees! Monkey do, but you don't have to allow that monkey to be you."

The last story I'm going to tell you all is about a White friend of mine who asked me a very perplexing question about a year ago. He asked me point blank: "Why can't I call you the n-word? It should be my first amendment right to say whatever I want to say, even to you!" So I asked him a question. I asked him to think about it, and then tell me what he would consider to be the worst insult that someone could say about him, not his family or friends--just him. He thought about it and said; "I guess the worse thing anyone could say about me would be to call me a fag or an n-word lover!" So I said to him, "What does that say about our society as a whole, most of it claiming to be Christian, when the worst thing that can be said about you is based completely on your loose affiliation with me or others just like or similar to me; not a Hispanic lover, not an Asian lover, but only a fag lover or an n-word lover! Since you are supposed to be my friend, maybe I'll ask you that same question. You tell me. After thinking about what you just said, why would you want to call me the n-word, and if you did; why would I want to continue calling you a friend?"

In the end, this all comes down to respect vs. disrespect, and there is nothing in your DNA or mine that gives any of us a "Manifest Destiny Right" to try and permanently engrave disrespect into any of the different woods of our great forest of humanity! You don't have to be a rocket scientist to be intelligent enough to know how to treat people the way you want to be treated in return. Whether it's nigger, nigga, or the n-word, if you have to think about whether or not it's a good idea to say something, then that in itself is a pretty, good indicator that it probably is not! You can change the spelling of a word all you want, but it means very little without changing the intent behind it, and once you change the intent behind it; you'll probably have enough courtesy to pick another word all together!

One more thing; contrary to popular beliefs, I am pro-Black in my views! I am just as sick as any other African-American who is tirelessly committed to defy the shackles of containment with Jim Crow written on them. I want to see African-Americans succeed with the rest of them and the best of them. Yes, I am pro-Black, but life is complex, and so am I! Not only am I pro-Black, I'm pro-human! I don't like seeing any group of people being unjustly oppressed by corruption and greed. I guess that makes me pro-underdog too! If the participants of the human race could ever learn how to run together, I would be satisfied! For that matter, I would almost be satisfied if we could at least get all of the participants out onto the track, because I believe the competition of life should be entered by all.

And furthermore, the usage of the word nigga, niggah, or nigger, however you want to spell it, is highly controversial and rarely ever produces a positive result; just something to consider before tossing that word around to the public. Some hate it. Others love it, but you will destroy just as much as you attempt to build with the n-word tool as your hammer.

AMERICA

If I had to pick the one thing I like least about America, it would have to be its superstitious fears of being challenged domestically on its long-standing social model of the haves and have not's based on the corrupt predetermination of who deserves to win and who deserves to fail. The seismic shifting of these social and economic mores should be celebrated-not interrogated. Those who consciously choose to govern through biased superstition are the ones who fail themselves and this country!

If I had to pick the one thing I like most about America, it would have to be its triumphant ability to overcome its superstitious fears of being challenged based on those same previously mentioned long-standing social and economic models on an international level. America has perennially led the way in the relief and restructuring of the global models of those who have, and those who have not. The worldly beacon of hope hoisted up by the United States has constantly sought to limit the number of those who fail and increase possibilities of success, and there aren't many countries in existence that can't vouch for that one, because the United States has helped a number of countries, and that's putting it lightly! So, to answer the age, old question regarding my love for my country, I love the ideology of my country, but I loathe the situational, environmental, circumstantial, frequently half-assed executions of that ideology in a domestic capacity.

With the recent events that have unfolded in Haiti in 2010, it is overwhelmingly clear that the United States can be, and still is, a global phenomenon for good. I don't know if this makes America the greatest nation on earth, and I don't particularly care, because this is not some global, beauty pageant! I ask all of the nations around the world, especially the citizens of the Middle East, to stop and take a long, hard look at what the United States has done to try and help the people of Haiti, which is a very poor country that deserves an opportunity to become a U.S. Commonwealth, just like Puerto Rico. The United States did not go in to recruit Haitians into Western culture or to recruit them into the folds of Christianity, and it is no big secret that many of the Haitians are not traditional Christians; some even practice voodoo, but then again, so do many others right here in the United States. I'm sure that if we all looked into our own closets, we could all find items that not everyone on the planet will agree with, but that is no reason to let people die! The United States went to Haiti to try and help save lives. America is a reasonable country that is willing to work with almost anyone.

I don't think you could say the same thing for all of the Osama Bin Laden's of the world, because they give out ultimatums, not humanitarian assistance. Maybe, just maybe, people around the world and in the Middle East should sit down and reconsider their views on the United States and its ill-conceived, evil, political agenda. America has almost always been a country that is unafraid to compromise or negotiate, so I certainly hope that other nations, including Middle Eastern areas, will take this as an opportunity to come to the table and at least talk open-mindedly about the potential of potential instead of the possibility of not having a possibility, because if there is one image the tragedy in Haiti has shown the entire world, it's the rarely seen glimpse of a pro-human society, where the saving of lives outweighs the manipulation and destruction of lives in a mindset where people don't have to wait until they get to heaven or paradise to engage the ideologies of God. As the great Bob Marley said in the song "Get Up Stand Up"[52]: "But if you know what life is worth, you will look for yours on earth." Instead of waiting to die into paradise, why not do everything within our power to bring some of that paradise to each other right here-right now! I just don't believe that God, Allah, Muhammad, Jesus Christ, Buddha or Yahweh would ever say the best, or only, way to enter heaven or paradise is to absorb and participate in as much destruction and corruption as humanly possible in my name, while lifting one finger to help makes you weak and diminishes your quest for salvation. I don't

52

believe it, and neither should you! If that's what heaven is about, I'll take my chances in hell!

As far as I am concerned, America must find a way to become equally as good domestically as it is internationally. There should be more efforts like the one in Haiti and fewer efforts like what happened during Hurricane Katrina. Americans should focus on just being the greatest based on actions, and not propaganda, even if it means reaching out for something new at the cost of leaving behind something old. In the sentiment of the philosophical Ollie Caradine, America must not be afraid to prosper, even if it means diversity prospers with it. Isn't that supposed to be the American dream? I completely understand how I did not get to be where I am today or who I am today, without help, and neither did America. Like all of us, America was, and still is, a team effort; a team which includes all Americans. The most important thing America can lose is its unwillingness to accept that undisputable fact. Also, true greatness is not narcissistic, because there is nothing so great about you that it forces you to have to tell anyone willing to listen what is so great about you, and what ever happened to personal responsibility? There are many who are quick to harp on personal responsibility, but a huge part of that is the willingness to acknowledge and own up to your mistakes and misgivings, which also means being able to man-up and apologize for them. The fool that is too arrogant to acknowledge his mistakes is that same fool that is arrogant enough to keep on making them. The rules that allow for the acceptance and reveling in one's greatness are the same rules that also enforce the reluctant ownership of one's transgressions—just ask Tiger Woods about that! In closing, I leave all Realacrats of the world with this saying: "To strive for perfection is honorable, but to be perfection is impossible. Govern by the first one."

The Bryian R. Doctrine

The Right to Do!

I'm reminded of a song by Jesus Jones called "Right here, Right Now," because it specifically represents the frame of mind I'm in right here right now! As John Calipari looked at his University of Memphis basketball team in the elite eight of the 2008 NCAA tournament and tried to convey his message of how it was their time and their moment to write their page in history, and I couldn't I agree more. This is my time to write my page in my history! This is why I have decided to go all out for this project. To quote my father's sentiments on life, "You might as well go out with both guns blazing!" If you're about to be annihilated, and you have a weapon of mass destruction in your back pocket, why not fire it as one last act of an independent, defiant, declaration, because you most certainly cannot take it with you. This book is my weapon of mass destruction, and I intend to ignite every inch of it! There is an old saying that goes, "Why put off tomorrow what you could do today?" Again, I couldn't agree more.

The reason I say this is due to some of the questions that I've been asked regarding my ideology. I have been asked repeatedly why I have decided to write so much material in this book. The advice given to me was to make it as short as possible, so I wouldn't be forcing people to read a long book. I don't know about you, but no one ever forced me to read anything that I didn't want to read. If people don't want to read it, then I'm sure they won't, and I have no problem with that. In my opinion, each intellectual refrigerator should be in charge of its intake capacity. I'm just here to supply the optional, scholarly food for thought! But like Michael Jackson said, "This Is It!" I consider this to be my "Freebird," my "Purple Rain" moment, my legacy, my signature on my life and life abroad, and most definitely my cognitive opus. I consider this to be my Neverland; a metaphor of my often misunderstood identity. I apologize to all of the political junkies who may appear categorically clouded by these doctrines, but has it ever occurred to you that just maybe these passages were written for me far more than they could ever be written for you, even though I am not the reader. To you, it may seem like a simple book on politics, but to me; it is my grandest attempt to place an ideological Band-Aid on my deepest most devastatingly bruised wound, in spite of my lack of gullibility in firmly knowing that an ideological Band-Aid is ideologically incapable of a cure, yet I have spent most of my life trying to do just that, and these doctrines are just a continuation of it. I do understand that any attempt to recapture, rekindle, or reinvent my Neverland is innately flawed to begin with, but the desire to undo the flaw is like the subconscious call of a drug, where the closer I get to my mirage, the farther it slides away from me. It is impossible to try and turn the utopia of your memory lane into a reality, but it is also impossible to not try and turn the utopia of your memory lane into a reality. I have unsuccessfully tried everything that is humanly comprehensible to deprogram my sensors away from the void that I cannot seem to fill. In the end, I think our Band-Aids are just our way of trying to minimize the painful reality of a journey and a destination that lies just beyond our control. By my judgment, the only thing I really have left to lose is time, as I seek to re-identify myself, in all likelihood, for the last time. Ironically, the same gift/curse that empowers my ability to vividly describe and communicate my tragically, flawed passions is the same curse gift that permanently enslaves me within them!

The second concern I've been confronted with is trying to do too much! The concern voiced to me centered on the possibility of my huge plate of knowledgeable tidbits overwhelming my audience's ability to decipher them all. A person asked me this question, "Why don't you eliminate half of it, and try to come back next year or somewhere further down the line, which is the worst advice anyone can give to another human being. All of my life, people have been trying to convince me to put it off till next year, put it off till next week, or just put it off indefinitely. They've always said to me, "You'll get other chances. There will be other opportunities out there. Good things come to those who wait! This is not the time for you! This is not the place for you. This is not the person for you. This is not the success for you. If you miss it this time, life will re-run it for you a second time, and you can capture it then." It is this kind of lunacy that pinpoints the fear of being challenged, not necessarily your fear to go out and meet the challenge, but the fear of others who are afraid of the possible changing dynamics of their relationship with you, if by some chance you are victorious against the challenge. They project their fears onto you, because it only takes one seed of doubt to sprout a forest of defeat, and it has bludgeoned me for the strong majority of my life, and it is the predominant reason why I don't have a life! I fully understand my exasperated plight and my deteriorating situation! I fully understand how the best aspects of life have passed me by, and I fully understand how the act of salvaging is now my only option. So right here right now, I have decided to leave nothing in the cupboards! As a good friend of mine named Rod "Dodje" McDaniel once said to me, "You only have one of two options! You can either put it all out there, or you can take it to the grave with you!" Originally, I had chosen to take it to the grave, but at this point in my haggardly life; I have no desire for ideological company on the other side!

When I looked at great individual talents like: Sir Iaasc Newton, Geoffrey Chaucer, Nicolaus Copernicus, Rene Descartes, Aristotle, Plato, Albert Einstein, James Baldwin; George Washington, Sojourner Truth, Saint Joan of Arc, Lucretia Mott, Emmeline Pankhurst, Mary Wollstonecraft, Thomas Jefferson, James Monroe, James Madison, Dr. Martin Luther King Jr., Malcolm X, Socrates, Confucius, Immanuel Kant, Sun Tzu, B.F. Skinner, Sigmund Freud, Ivan Pavlov, and my personal favorite—Charles Darwin, it became evidently apparent to me that I had a chance to do exactly what they did! There was nothing preventing me from making observations, studying, critiquing, and analyzing those observations, and most importantly; writing them down and documenting them! There are many who may consider my ideologies to be garbage when compared to all of those previously mentioned great talents, but once I gather the information about the world I live in based on the way I see it, and then have it published in a document and made available for the world to examine; I will officially be in the league!

Here's an example of one of my observations. Charles Darwin derived the concept of "Survival of the fittest" based on animalistic patterns of wildlife behavior, migratory rites of passage, seasonal migratory routes, and the inner-workings of the predator vs. prey food chain. Darwin was great, but I'm sure the Native Americans and other so-called primitive groups also had knowledge that was very similar, if not identical, to all of these facets of the wild. Darwin gets the credit, because Darwin documented it for the world to see. Darwin's documentation allows for his ideology to be used as a springboard for further research. Unfortunately for many of the Native Americans, Eskimos, and even older hunting groups, they were largely overlooked, undervalued, intellectually and conceptually passed over, due to social, economic, and disadvantageous, time-period limitations; and were forced to take what little they had left to the grave with them! Earlier groups of hunters and wildlife experts like the Native Americans didn't have the necessary resources to share their observatory wealth, but we do. There is nothing standing in our way except for air and opportunity. My words are the air, and this book represents my opportunity! It also represents yours!

My next order of business has to do with my right to enhance my point of view. From the moment I started this endeavor, I've encountered an immense amount of skepticism surrounding my right to opine. It's as if some people are actually offended by the declarations of my visions of individuality. Some have even asked me outright, "Who are you? Who do you think you are? What gives you the right to express such views? What gives you the right to own such views? What gives you the right to share such views in a published document? What are your credentials? Are you rich? You're not very tall! You're not White! You're not famous! You are a nobody, and you have proven absolutely nothing! Why should anyone listen to you?"

My reply to such elitist, judgmental rhetoric is a basic human rights allegation. The fact that I am alive, and the fact that I think therefore I am gives me the only credentials I'll ever need to command my own voice, and elaborate my own thoughts in any direction and in any medium I see fit! Every great philosopher, psychologist, politician and so on were all once just like me; marred in the criticisms of non-accomplishments and social obscurity. This does not mean that I am a great anything, but it does mean that I, like those great thinkers, have exercised my plans to be in a class of doers, instead of a class of talkers, because doers produce results. Talkers are only exclusive in producing resultless carbon dioxide. I have just as much of a right to report my information, as any would-be camera/video phone carrier who comes across an accident, records it, and then sends it in to the news media. To me, it looks like the only credentials needed are the media mechanisms that allow it to happen.

Freedom is the most beautiful thing ever created, and I find it ironic how it frightens so many, but it does not frighten me! In fact, I consider freedom to be the oxygen of the mind and the soul. I think the price of freedom is never too high, and I think the desire for freedom can never be nullified. I think everyone should have the right be free, which includes all of us, our offspring, and our choices. For those who want to be a Democrat, be what you want to be. For those who want to be a Republican, be what you want to be. For those who follow academics, choose what you want to be. For those who want to be athletes, chose what you want to be. For those who embrace religion, believe in what you want to believe in. For those who aspire to be as rich as possible, dream and achieve all that is possible. For those who fall in love with someone of a different ethnicity, love and cherish who you want to love and cherish. For those who are gay, you should be who you feel you are meant to be. For those who chose to be in the working-class/middle-class, you should be what you want to be! And for those who are happy with unemployment, government assistance, self-doubt, meager resources, and limited dreams, don't allow the fear of being challenged to define you, because winning is not guaranteed to anyone, but neither is losing. Think about it!

The Right to Question

When I first learned about the horrors of Jonestown as a kid, I could never understand how so many people could allow themselves to be manipulated by what appeared to be a bonafied fraud in my book! I asked my mother why people would agree to such a thing. I asked her why they couldn't see the lies and deceit for what they really were. I told my mother that there was no reasonable way to justify why over 900-hundred people would all willingly surrender their common senses to a mere man, who claimed to know all of the answers and have all of the questions! My mother simply told me that sheep were made to be led. Nevertheless, it puzzled me as to how the Jonestown mentality could become so appealing, but I now see exactly how it can not only become appealing, but also overpowering as well. I guess there are people who truly lack the confidence to believe in themselves, so they aspire to believe in somebody, and there will always be "a somebody" who's more than willing to take advantage. It reminds me of the song called "Sweet Dreams(Are Made of This) by the Eurythmics, because that is precisely what the world will sell you; sweet dreams of anticipative perception that quickly morph into the nightmares of a morbid reality! As Annie Lennox said, "Some of them want to use you. Some of them want to get used by you. Some of them want to abuse you. Some of them want to be abused." When you allow your insecurities to delineate the road you travel, the potholes of despair and the dead-ends to nowhere will always be a step away, and you can't blame that on anyone else but you!

When I was a kid I used to believe in Santa Clause. Every Christmas Eve I would be filled with gleeful anticipation of finally getting to stay up late enough to catch Santa in the act, but that day never came! Despite my family continuing to insist that there was a Santa Clause, I was growing more skeptical every year. And like most of us, I was forced into the realization that my family was only telling me what they wanted me to hear, not because it was true, but because it was necessary at that time, in order to sustain the inflation of my imaginary atmosphere, where money grew on trees, you could eat all the candy you wanted, everything was going to be alright, and most of all; you never had to grow up. You could play in Neverland forever, where cupboards never go bare, and the well never runs dry in the innocence of our uncontrived, naïve fantasy land!

That innocence is part of our childhood, and one could make the argument that it represents the best days of our lives! I would also argue that it represents a very important turning point in our lives, when we are forced to shed our skins of blamelessness to be left in the naked confusion of the real world, where everything that we thought we knew is now everything that we now know we don't know. It's a feeling of helplessness and vulnerability that none of us like to experience, but all of us will experience. One of the most humbling aspects of life is the realization of our pseudo-control over our world and the sheer vastness of certainties that now lie beyond the realm of our cognitive grasps! When life punches you in the intellectual gut, it completely minimizes the dynamics of your existence, and it forces you to relinquish the nostalgia of the old and approach fearfully into the new, and most people want no part of this scenario, despite the fact that this is what we are born to endure as humans. At our best, we boldly confront and patiently defeat the hurdles of the new the same way we once defeated the hurdles of the old, but at our worst; we boldly deny and reluctantly engage the hurdles of the new and cling irrationally and diminutively as the horizon disappears on the old; reaffirming our mortality and the fears of being challenged that accompany it!

For example, when I finally came to the realization that there was no Santa Clause, it signified the ending of an era. When my mother finally broke down and admitted to me that my suspicions were correct, because there was no Santa Clause. She was Santa Clause! I was overjoyed with satisfaction that I'd managed to solve the riddle, but Christmas was never the same for me again. I soon realized that I could never go back there. That bubble had burst! Hearing my mother tell me that she was Santa Clause hit me in the face like a sack of bricks! Although I continued to receive about the same amount of gifts for Christmas as I'd always received, I now knew that there were economic limits and consequences that had nothing to do with the naughty and nice list that affected everything in our lives. All of a sudden, perspective had been shoved in my face for ideological consumption, and I didn't like it either, but I was powerless to change it, or stop it! No matter how dissatisfied I felt at the time, the truth had come in and torn my playhouse down, and it was down for good! Believing that Santa Clause had a fountain of youth filled with unlimited toys is a child's world, but understanding that your parents may be forced to work two or three jobs just to give you a Christmas is an adult's world, so I did the only thing that I could. I said goodbye to my childhood and began re-adjusting my wants and needs based on the family economy, like most sane people do. I knew then that everything in life was created to be questioned, because our inquisitiveness is what allows us to pass by an era, but the indoctrination of that inquisitiveness is what allows an era to pass by us. Since no one will ever have all of the answers, there will never be a time to not question. The world will never give you all of the answers you seek. If you want the answers behind the answers, you'll have to question what's given, and search for what's not!

People will say this has nothing to do with real life, but it has everything to do with real life. It does not have to be Santa Clause. I simply used St. Nick to make a point, because in my estimations, Santa Clause, the president, religion, governments, and political parties, such as Democrats and Republicans, are all very similar. They all have astounding high hopes, lucrative demands, and great expectations placed upon them, and they all fail, at some point, to live up those magical dreams of the improbable, because the truth is rarely in the highest of the highs or in the lowest of the lows, but quite often somewhere in the center! In my opinion, it's better to find the truth, instead of allowing the truth to find you. When we find the truth, we can prepare ourselves in the hopes that we might decorate it accordingly, but when we allow ourselves to be blindsided in the middle-of-the-night with no warning whatsoever, the ramifications of the truth punishes us, and it usually is not a pretty sight! Whether it's a political movement, a family scheme, Rudolph the Red Nose Reindeer, a relationship setting, or the Great Pumpkin; the willing allowance of a suspended, intellectual, inquisitive, independent compass is exceedingly detrimental to our abilities to process the common sense approaches to life. The day we stop questioning is the day we nail freedom to the cross.

If you ever encounter an ideology that coddles obedience, uniformity, cerebral boundaries, individual dormancy, group assimilation, overall limitations, or a containment of knowledge, but at the same time; frowns on, denounces, forbids, discourages, and displays a blatant resistance to the cognitive freedom to challenge all that the world encompasses, run away as far and as fast as you humanly can, because there is nothing in this world with your best interest in mind that aspires to shackle you. True authenticity does not fear the challenge! It welcomes it. True authenticity will always embrace the competitive instead of the scripted, because competitiveness produces possibility, while the scripted only produces manufactured slavery! The best things in life arise from the unlimited, and they are all destroyed by the death of such a freedom. I choose to pursue the unlimited, while my limitations choose to pursue me! It's that simple! You define what you believe in, or what you believe in will ultimately define you. Trust me! There is a difference.

We have to question our world! We have to question ourselves! We have to question our beliefs, and sometimes, we even have to question our questions, but the essence of the question is the soil of our cognitive growth. Whenever we decide to allow our assumptions to dictate our consumption, we are no longer the true navigators of our destinies. If something sounds fishy, then it probably is, and I'd rather find out through investigation as opposed to realization. I don't hate the existence of the Tea Partiers, but I do hate the filtered deductions of the Tea Partiers. There is no gold standard of leadership. Anyone can be deceptive! The credentials of a leader have to be far more than "Hey, I'm a Republican! I'm a Democrat! I'm rich! I'm sexy! I'm a maverick! I'm a Christian! I'm a Muslim! I'm a hockey mom! I'm a leader—you leader, follow me!" Spare me the knob polishing rhetoric! Don't waste my time trying to convince me of what you are, while clandestinely trying to distract me from who you are! In my judgment, it may not be your job to divulge your true identity to me, but it is always my job to question and remain skeptical until I can acquire enough of your identity to better understand the portrait of your persona.

Anyone can claim to be anything at any time! You can always tell me a story, but you can't always sell me a story. A picture is worth a thousand words, and an ideology is worth a thousand pictures. So when you hear stories of how the census is an anti-Christ ploy to count and collect souls for the devil, and President Obama is a terrorist or Nazi. You have to question these allegations, and then you have to question the source of these allegations, and then you have to question the motives of the sources behind these allegations! If you can't trust Obama, then there is a very good possibility that you can't trust the information that says you can't trust Obama either, because everyone in the political business is a politician first, a business person second, and everything else last! Politics is politics, and a politician is a politician; good or bad or corrupt or clean. I think the only difference between the two is the point of view and the perception of it. We hope to vote for a person with at least a hint of a conscience, but we are often tricked into voting for a person with a well-hidden ton of self-absorption, and that is why it is up to us to find out as much as we can about all that is possible! Sometimes we have to question the heights of power sanctity find the truths we seek, even if that machine represents certain aspects of our lives we hold dearly—that's life. It doesn't matter if it's your vote or your marriage. The human existence is flawed and so is the journey. If we're lucky, we can find the flaws that aspire, instead of the flaws with no desire. So the next time some cretinous idiot runs up to tell you that the sky is falling, maybe it will occur to your intellect to take a couple of seconds to, at least, look up! It's not that I don't trust the scriptures. I just don't always trust the hand that writes them!

I, Too, Have a Dream! Shouldn't We All?

I, too, have a dream, because the ability to dream is a tool shared by all who are bold enough to aspire to be more tomorrow than they are today! The ability to dream is the motivational epitome of faith, desire, hope and the directional progress of leadership in the face of morally corrupt resistance! Dreamers are leaders, and leaders are dreamers, because it takes vision to acknowledge and understand the entire journey, and it takes an extraordinary courageousness to embark upon it, but that's what dreamers are built to do. They don't just dig in behind the safety of the current transitory herd, because true dreamers often lead a numberless herd until they are somehow able to convince a few to dare and become many! A dream with only one follower is merely an idea, but a dream with a following is a movement, and it is that movement that will be utilized to garner the social momentum needed to sustain and change the landscape of humanity! A world without dreams is a dark, abysmal place where no one is distinguished, and all are marginalized. It is a place where expression is suppressed, and individuality is destroyed. It is a place where assimilation is dictated, and the capacity for success is diminutive. It's a place where the canvas remains artless, songs remain unsung, visions remain unseen, roads remain untraveled, ideas remain undeveloped and potentials remain unfulfilled. A world without dreams would be more like an ideological prison where the mind itself is behind bars, which would be the metaphorical equivalent to death itself!

In light of everything that has gone on since the election of President Obama, with the recent, religious intolerances; and this attempt by the arrogance of right to reclaim the civil rights movement, the need for dreams is now stronger than ever, because dreams are the silver bullets that pierce through the corrupt hearts of fear! America itself was a dream. The Declaration of Independence and The United States Constitution were both dreams. The desire of Moses to free God's people from the pharaoh was a dream. The mirage of freedom in the eyes of African slaves, here in the United States and abroad, was a dream. The entire civil rights movement was a dream. The opportunistic existence of a President Obama was a dream. Hitler's quest for world domination and a master race was also a dream, and on August 28th 2010, Glenn Beck revealed to the world his dream. I'm not comparing Glenn Beck to Hitler the way that many of his supporters have done to President Obama on numerous occasions! I am only pointing out the fact that the ability to dream is not as unique as one might think.

Realistically, the best dreams, the friendliest dreams, and the most unifying dreams of peace and prosperity don't always become reality. The dreams that do become reality are the most pushed dreams. Like an idea, a dream is the wallpaper that decorates the mind, but the will to create that dream is the steam that powers the human engine. The same element that decides who will become a winner or a loser is the same element that will decide which dream remains a dream, and which dream will be forged into life. In my opinion, you have to dream it first, and then enact it secondly, because the true dream is not simply to stop at the vision of it! The goal of a dream is to infect as many people as it possibly can, and the goal of the dreamer is to make sure that it happens, and the only way that I know how to accomplish such a feat is to live it each day. Not only do I have a dream, but I am the dream, and so are you, if you choose to be, because just having the ability to have and make a choice is the spirit of the Dr. King dream.

Unlike dreams of a holocaust or some form of oppression, I've made a personal choice to dream beyond the limitations that I often place upon myself, and the limitations we often place upon each other! Within the freedoms of my assessments, I would say that there is nothing that possesses more freedom than a dream; a personal, utopian vision of images we wished we could do over, and new challenges we plan to succeed against--limited only by depths of our subconsciousness. I think that if you are afraid to dream freely; then you are afraid to live freely, because the shackles and fears that bound your dreams are the shackles and fears that bound you.

I want my dreams to stretch as far as my mental eye can see and as vividly as my thoughts may visualize them. I construct my dreams to be the post-departure glimpses of the energy that ignited the breath into my soul. This is why my dreams will strive to be inclusive and not exclusive, tolerant and not intolerant, open and never closed, humanly and never elitist, possible, but not impossible; colorized, but never Black and White; ideological, but not indoctrinary; universally free, and not segmented; a unifying belief of love, but not the unifying anger of hatred; and the opportunity to build something up, without the obligated ignorance to tear everything down!

My first dream is for the continuation of the dream, because true greatness grows from the soil of aspiration! So I implore everyone to embrace whatever dreams they may have and dream even harder to, hopefully, turn them into reality. Never be ashamed to dream, because dreaming does not make one naïve. Dreaming makes one cognitively conscious about the possibilities of the future, because to dream of the past is fruitless, if the dreams of the future are not regeneratively seasoned from it. True failure is not the failed fruition of a dream, but the successful abandonment of one.

My second dream is for us, as humans, to finally develop the evolutionary maturity needed to accept all of its moving parts equally, so that it can one day look into the mirror of life, and see all of the many faces that it presents and represents. I often dream of a world where people who would accept your money or your liver would somehow someway learn to accept "You the Person," in a world where the human race can actually start to live up to that terminology and that responsibility of one world one people! It should take much more than large bodies of water to separate us from our larger body of global humanity, which we should all share ever so proudly, because unity is power. Division is just the manipulation used to try and take it away.

My third dream is for the freedom of religious expression, whether that expression is pro-religion, anti-religion, or just politically religious to make a point. This should be a place where everyone has the right to form and govern their own personal, belief systems and religious relationships with whomever they see fit, because you're God is ultimately your business! Whatever stairway to heaven you choose will only have room for one climber, so I suggest you buy the one that will be most comfortable for you and not necessarily someone else. I dream that religion, as a whole, will allow its followers to come to it, instead of unjustly oppressing those who choose to go elsewhere. The bitterness and precursors to violence displayed at one's right to choose another brand of worship is detrimental to all religion, because it is fundamentally wrong to lay the misinterpreted sins of the follower on the credibility of the ideology, as interpreted by the flawed perfection of people!

My fourth dream is for a renewed fight and a renewed focus on equality and the lack thereof, because there is nothing more sacred to the ingredients of America and the human existence than equality. I am adamantly opposed to any notion of built-in advantages being deployed to the chosen few to help ensure a positively desired result for that chosen few, with a less-than-stellar result for all others. I dream of a time when those who have much more than what they need will not be bestowed the title of well-deserved any more than those who have very little will find themselves subjected to that same title, because that is not for you or me to decide. When the honesty of equality becomes a lightning rod for resentment and hatred, the hope of the American Dream, along with the essence of our humanity, will cease to exist! I dream that the evolutionary integrity of hearts and minds can keep pace with the evolutionary breakthroughs of our technology.

My fifth dream is that we, as a people, find the courage to teach our children the realities of what is, as opposed to the propaganda of what we want it to be, where "Do as I say! Don't do as I do" is passed off as a rite of passage, where "Manifest Destiny" is decorated in Democratic paint, and where the plight of the poor is unilaterally clothed in the misconceptions of self-inflicted wounds. My dream is that all will learn that what you believe, and what you will learn is usually going to be two totally different things, so deal with it! I would also like to see the younger generations being taught to respect, understand, and acknowledge the enormity of the global perspective as it relates to them, not just a slanted view of the ballooning superiority and the foolishly, exaggerated patriotism of a propped up image of a superpower that still believes it is the only thing super and the only one with true power.

My sixth dream is that we restore the honor of courage, while diminishing the societal vandalism of fear, whether it's the fear of diverse ideologies or the fear of being challenged by them! None of us can ever own an ideology, even if we are its originator. Once we put that idea out into the world, we can no longer dictate its ideological parameters, and I dream that all of us will one day learn not to fear that, because everything is open to interpretation; and the addition of one's personalized, religious faith does not bring it any closer to the omniscient truth than it ever was without it! In other words, I hope to see the day when one's faith in God will no longer be used as an excuse to become non-investigative when confusion abounds, because God has become the antidote for a fear that is usually derived from a lack of communicative information. The only thing we have to fear is the ignorance that seeks to limit us with that fear.

My seventh dream is for the continued opposition of limitations. Protest whatever it is you believe to be wrong. Protest it with your words, and protest it with the actions of your life, because rhetoric is still cheap no matter how eloquently priced the words may appear. My protest against the bowels of social conservatism has given me a declaration to my identity, and I hope and dream that even more of you will come to such an epiphany based on the aspects of your lives that you may find opposition to. The status of the status quo does not have to be the anointed status of you. The glass ceiling of our lives should be cracked wide up whenever possible, so I implore you all to pick up a stone or a sledgehammer! Never be afraid to step on oppositional toes on your way to your right to clear a space where you can stand free of that opposition.

My eighth dream is for a new appreciation for the strength of who we are, instead of the popularity of who we often try to be, for the appeasement of others. The diminutive numbers of individuality should not be discredited based on the proliferated numbers of assimilation. It requires more strength to be an individual than it does to join a group, because in a group; you can always pass-the-buck of defeat, and you can always fraudulently take credit for victory! When you stand as an individual, you can only pass that buck to yourself. There is no straw man, and you become you're excuse. Not everyone who hoists up a trophy is a winner, and not everyone who doesn't is a loser. In my dream, the integrity of the individual will be the deciding factor of a win, not the color of the uniform or the affiliations attached to it. A true champion knows the difference between "Who they are, and who others expect and often demand them to be!" I'd rather walk alone with the truth, as oppose to leading the crowds with a lie!

My ninth dream is for the unconditionality of unconditional love! Let no negativity put asunder what the truthfulness of your love has lifted up. Whether it's love for the human race, love of friends, love of family, love of faith, or the love of a mate; regardless of sexual orientation, embrace the connection of the human heart, and reject the disconnect of irrational, human fears. My dream consists of an ideological openness, where everyone will be guaranteed the opportunity to love anyone! While some look to preserve the sanctity of marriage between a man and a woman, I look to preserve the sanctity of love without persecution. The ones who can routinely find ways to hate unconditionally are usually the ones who routinely fail to find ways to love unconditionally. Since we all have the right to access life, death, God/faith/nothing; however you want to put it, then we should all have the right to access each other as well. If we all begin at the same origin, and end at the same destination, then why should it matter who we choose to accompany us during our brief stay in the middle? Hopefully, the time will come when it won't!

My tenth and final dream is for the dismantling of hypocrisy, because I believe that what a person says, and what a person does should always be close enough to the point where they can at least wave at each other. I dream of a place where people are encouraged not to write a rhetorical check that their truthfulness cannot cash in a place where the content of character is what will be suggested, but the passing on pigmentation is what will be enacted! Don't go around quoting such sayings as, "All men are created equal," when your behavior only promotes the equal distribution of others beneath the arrogance of your entitlements. Whatever it is you claim to be, you have to try to live up to it. I sincerely dream of a day when charlatans in their ideological costumes will not be allowed to pose as the standard bearers of the truth.

And as far as Glenn Beck's big day at the steps of the Lincoln Memorial goes, you can stand where a person stood, but that does not mean that you can be what that person was. You can speak what a person has spoken, but that does not mean that you can personify or deliver that same message. You can claim to fight what others have fought, but that does not mean that you are now on the same team. You can march where others have marched, but that does not mean that you now march in that same direction, and you can dream what others have dreamed, but that does not mean that it is the same aspiration! Imitation is the highest form of flattery, but it is also the lowest form of creativity, but true dreamers create far more than they imitate.

So I'll leave with this tidbit of Revonerism—Mr. Glenn Beck. While it is impressive to see a conservative, civil rights novice attempt to emulate Dr. Martin Luther King Jr., it is utterly preposterous to expect the real followers of Dr. King and the real followers and institutors of the civil rights movement to find anything that you say as credible! ~Bryian "The Revoner" R.~

ACKNOWLEDGEMENTS

To my family members who have helped me; some more than others, Vernell Revoner, Willie "Bo" Revoner, Erdell Revoner, Eugene Revoner, Alma Scott, Dora Beck, Alma Stegall, Marsha Barlow, Essie Barlow, Eva Hopson, Debby Lynn Thomas, Sherry Ann Gathright, Liza Hopson, Ernestine Barlow Peters, Inez Hopson, Alan Barlow, Michael Stegall, Clevon Meabon Sr., all of the other Stegall's, the Hopson's, the Barlow's, and the Revoner's.

To a few of my friends—online and off, Patrick Jones, Chase Gardner, Joy Shepard, Beverly Bassham, Julie Kindle Driscoll, Terri L. Beaudin Willmott, Angel Wings, Cindy Payton, Gayla Nelson, Cheryl Gilberg, Patricia Mangan, Nancy Snowden Dupree Parker, David Stanley, Sam and Mandy Wilson, Yuritzi Alejandra Santillan Aranda, Pattie Rae, Pd Lietz, Angela Ayers, Larry Swearingen, Terry Harlan, Janet Reyes, Patsy Clarke, Rita Bryant, Charlotta C. Cummings, Jeannie Bruno, Lateshia Revoner, Shanna Revoner, Justin Peters, Brandy Barlow, Brandi Hopson, Zoe Dickey, Cheryl Jenkins Jackson, Rose Budd, David W. Moore, Deborah Covington, Terry Callen, Eric "The Real Deal" Hill, Ann R. Doll, April Hunter Hightower, Dorothy Willse, Dana Hughey, Tanya Cribbs, Alitha Smith, Kim Wilson Lawrence, Kristi Belknap Soto, Renee Campbell, Lee Hostettler, Matt Yeazel, Marisol Conde, Angie Bumgarner, Terry Vossman Bitzel, Gale Abernathy, Controversial Betty, Linda Dillworth, JenniferBaggerplease Woodroff, DoctorJohn Raymond Baker, Joy Erasmus, Christa Van Vuuren, Roshonda Moore, Carolyn Youra, Ronald Dene Larson, Melissa Singleton Hartman,

Sandy Essley, Alan D. Kardoff, Nancy Wilson, Susan Kelly-Roatche, Karen Caoilfhionn, Heather Mash, Angie Bumgarner, Fran Strombotne, Cheryl F. Batoon, Kristin Jones, Susan Kenyon Pitts, Mary Fooshee, Tresa Lovern, Judi Zimmer, Virginia Bossett, Kathryn Visser, Anthony P. Johnson, Stephanie DeGuzman, Jatavia Irby Rhodes, Diane Gandee Sorbi, Patricia Pereira, Kimberly Galanti, Maure Briggs-Carrington, Kia Shakur, Eslem Kasraoui, Roy Greene, Peggy Pendleton, Windy Bradley Coburn, Hope Grable, Pamela Thum, Amy Spinelli-Coronado, Tammy Blair, Rhonda Adams, Kristi Diggs, Tammy Marie Rose, Peggy Ruch, Julie Stonecipher, Beth Hayes Strohmeyer, Ann McElroy Lavigne, Henery Ahlf, Jayla Smith, Shannon Equality Kern, Nancy Ann Kiser-Ceballos, Jeff Reynolds, Hazel Lee, Kelley Gardner, Judy Kolbaba, Lynda Walker, Terra Chappell Shahan, Tim Wozny, Dorothy Dotson, Karen Lynette Gore, Linda M. TheBerge, Linda Saloff, Barbara Zimmerman, Jennapher Frankie Lawson, Shanda Butt, Jo Anne Moore, and everyone else that I can't remember right now. Thanks to all of you for reading my boring stories.

Now, I would like to acknowledge the educators and educational systems that helped me get to this point. I thank the Wynne School System as a whole, East Arkansas Community College, and Arkansas State University. I thank my teachers and administrators: Mrs. Dobson, Mrs. Brown, both of my counselors; Mr. Shaw and Mr. White, Mrs. Davis, Mrs. Potter, Mrs. Ross, Mrs. Bradshaw, Mrs. Brawner, Mrs. Kennedy, Mrs. Draper, Coach Westbrook, Coach Dallas, Mr. Carl Easley, Mr. Charles Cobbs, Mr. Duval, Mrs. Washington, Dr. Mott, Mrs. Sisk, Mrs. Macallom, Mr. Sprat, Mr. Hill, my special reading teacher, Mrs. Clark, my remedial reading and remedial writing teacher; Mrs. Simpson, Dr. Reginald Martin; my literary mentor from the University of Memphis, Mr. Clyde Rogers, Mr. Mike Hill, Mr. Jim McCinturf, and Gamma Beta Phi, of which I was once a member. I would have to say about 90 percent of my teachers were White, and about 90 percent of them, including the few African-American and other minority teachers, always encouraged me to achieve, and that is the way it should be. Leave your personal crap at home!

As for my inspirational entertainers, celebrities, and politicians, they would be: Dr. Martin Luther King Jr., the best ever; Malcolm X, the best ever, Frederick Douglas; the best ever, Harriet Tubman; the best ever; John Brown, the dazzling Jessie Jackson Jr., the inspirational Jesse Jackson Sr., the outstanding Harold Ford Jr., the phenomenal Dr. Willie Herenton, the phenomenal Gwen Ifill, Steve Harvey, Russell Simmons, Tom Joyner, the outstanding Reverend Al Sharpton, the wholesome Dalai Lama, the brilliant Mahatma Gandhi, the powerful Oprah Winfrey, Denzel Washington, James Earl Jones, the most underrated man in Hollywood; Regina King and Clarence Williams III, the most underrated, most overlooked, most unappreciated actress and actor of all time; D.L. Hughley, Morgan Freeman, Wesley Snipes, The Hughes Brothers, John Singleton, F. Gary Gray, Johnny Depp, Christian Bale, Dave Chappelle, Heath Ledger, the intellectual Bill O'Reilly, the knowledge-laden Dennis Miller, Lou Dobbs, Larry King, Juan Williams, Shepard Smith, Geraldo Rivera, the entertaining Glenn Beck, Alan Combs, the outstanding Bill Maher, the smartest person in the nation; Colin Powell, the phenomenal Condoleezza Rice, Van Jones, the politically savvy Roland Martin, honest Anderson Cooper, the courageous President Obama and his courageous wife Michelle Obama, the phrenic David Gergen, the phenomenal Soledad O'Brien, Jessie Ventura, the other smartest person in the nation; the exceptional Hillary Clinton, who is my favorite politician ever; Bill Clinton, Mike Huckabee, the smartest Republican in the nation; Ronald Reagan, Rodney Slater, Ron Brown, Ron Paul, Bernie Sanders, Newt Gingrich, Rush Limbaugh, who could be the most influential radio personality of all time; Father Phleger, Reverend Jeremiah Wright, Earvin "Magic" Johnson, Vince McMahon, the furious Steven A. Smith, the enlightening Michael Ware, the creative Michael Moore, the savvy Whoopi Goldberg, the great Rudy Ray Moore, Rachel Maddow and Donald Trump.

These are all of the musical artist I listened to while writing this book: Al Green, Michael Jackson, the best ever; Prince & The Revolution, the best band ever; Gangsta Pat, the founding father of Memphis rap; Public Enemy, the best ever; The Geto Boys, N.W.A., Dr. Dre, Ice Cube, Eazy-E, Curtis "50 Cent" Jackson, Ice T, Black Eyed Peas, Eminem, who is arguably the best songwriter of the modern era; Three Six Mafia, LL Cool J, the best ever; Nirvana and the introspective writings of Kurt Cobain, Rage Against the Machine, one of the best bands ever; Soundgarden, the Red Hot Chili Peppers, Alice in Chains, the underrated INXS, the great Johnny Taylor, Bobby Blue Bland, the amazingly talented Eddie Van Halen, Van Halen, the outstandingly talented Jeff Beck, Jimi Hendrix, greatest of all time; the outstanding Duran Duran, Coldplay, the Beatles, who's musical and lyrical abilities were astronomically beyond extraordinary; John Lennon as a solo artist, George Harrison as a solo artist, Paul McCartney as solo artist, the underrated John Mellencamp, the phenomenal politics and music of U2, the Dead Milkmen, Dead Prez, Paris the Black Panther and lyrical assassin, the phenomenal Gang Starr, the phenomenal Boogie Down Productions, Eric B. & Rakim, the magnanimous Run-DMC, Rihanna & T.I., Linkin Park, Culture Club, featuring the very talented Boy George; Wu-Tang-Clan, Rush, the Doors, Billy Squire, Green Day, the music and politics of Eddie Vedder and Pearl Jam, the gutsy Dixie Chicks, the unparalleled Temptations, the wondrous, most influential rap artist of the modern era; 2Pac Shakur, the great Notorious B.I.G., the great Jay-Z, Bone Thugs-n-Harmony, Bob Marley, the best ever; the outstanding New Edition, the outstanding Eric Clapton, the outstanding Alicia Keys, the great Bruce Springsteen, Bon Jovi, one of the best bands ever; the great Phil Collins, the PowerStation, Above the Law, Pete Rock & CL Smooth, Heavy D. & the Boyz, and most definitely Epitaph, which would include my lyrical partner in rhyme, Reggie "Skanlz" Watson, the business minded Mardell "D-Roc" Davis of the phenomenal "Flat Town" productions crew featuring the philosophical Ollie Caradine, James Davis, cool Dirk and Tony Squalls, the multi-talented Jimmy "F-Troop" Martin Jr., the visionary Alvin "Double-A" Brown, the lyrical juggernaut, Jeremy "Macrophonic Mc" Martin, and the underrated Koreon Prunty. You can hear them at www.cdbaby.com/cd/chauceriin or just Google the word "Chauceriin." Other musical collaborators involved: Carl "Guitar" Holden, Bret "Guitar" Walzer, William "Glass Master" Glass, Aaron "Fink Dog" Baker, Nature Boy I.P., the fabulous Mark L. Williams, Rod "Dodje" McDaniel, and the original rap group "Delta Rock," featuring Donte Wright, Don "Playboy Rock" Smith, Ray Long, James Starks, Orlando Scott, Tomeko Settles and cool Tred. Delta Rock was the most important rap group ever assembled in Wynne, Arkansas—period! Task Force was just a spin-off of Delta Rock; know your history! My life would have been completely void, empty and unmotivated without all of these individuals, because a life without the communicative beauty of art is death.

I studied and learned from the following writers: Mark Twain, Nikki Giovanni, Richard Wright, T. S. Elliot, William Wordsworth, Walt Whitman, William Shakespeare, Henry David Thoreau, Emily Dickinson, Alfred Lord Tennyson, Elizabeth Barrett Browning, Langston Hughes, Alfred Edward Housman, James Baldwin, Dr. Michael Eric Dyson, Dr. Cornel West, and Frederick Douglass—but the most powerful writer to influence me was Geoffrey Chaucer, whom I named myself after.

And last but not least, I sincerely thank all of my Facebook friends who have encouraged and supported me. I can honestly say that Facebook has changed my life forever. It increased communication by removing the obstacles of geography, and that has allowed the world to become accessible to all at any time. Instead of relying on foreign policy gurus to help connect the differences of the world, thanks to Facebook, we can literally become our foreign policy for a change, and that could be the spark that changes the world eventually! I know it's changed me, so there is hope.

You're the love that loves me back. You give me support in places I lack. Your ideas awaken my brain. You are the peace that eases my pain. You're the tribe that I feel honored to fight with. You're the slice of humanity I've longed to unite with. You're the men with whom I talk about life, and you're the women that I admire as much as I like. You're the friend I've never had. You are my Facebook Nation! ~Bryian R.